Basic Appraisal Procedures

3rd Edition

Timothy Detty
Certified General Appraiser
AQB-Certified USPAP Instructor

HONDROS
LEARNING™

HONDROS LEARNING™

4140 Executive Parkway

Westerville, Ohio 43081

www.hondroslearning.com

© 2014 by Hondros Learning™. All rights reserved

Published 2014. Printed in the United States of America

18 17 16 15 14   1 2 3 4 5

978-1-59844-240-3

For more information on, or to purchase, our products, please call 1-866-84LEARN or visit www.hondroslearning.com

TABLE OF CONTENTS

SUGGESTED SYLLABUS

BASIC APPRAISAL PROCEDURES

COURSE DESCRIPTION: This basic appraisal course provides an overview of real property valuation procedures, the approaches to value, and residential applications, This course also explores real property analysis and description, including land and site description, improvement construction, and property inspection. Finally, the course provides an overview of appraisal reporting, including appraisal reporting forms most commonly used by residential appraisers. Through theory, case studies, and examples, the course offers practical application of appraisal procedures. A calculator is recommended.

COURSE OBJECTIVES:

1. Demonstrate a basic knowledge of real property concepts and appraisal procedures
2. Demonstrate a basic understanding of developing the approaches to value
3. Gain working knowledge of residential appraisal applications
4. Gain a general understanding of residential construction and property description
5. Identify significant appraisal reporting obligations for residential appraisal reporting

COURSE TEXTBOOK: *Basic Appraisal Procedures*, 3rd edition, Hondros Learning™, Copyright 2014

COURSE CREDIT HOURS: Pre-licensing: 30 credit hours. Attendance is mandatory to receive course credit.

INSTRUCTION METHOD: Lecture and group exercises

COURSE OUTLINE with Suggested Time Increments:

DAY 1   (total classroom hours 7.5)
        Introduction and Overview
         Chapter 1: Appraisal Development and Reporting
         Lunch
         Chapter 2: Property Analysis and Description—Land

DAY 2   (total classroom hours 7.5)
         Chapter 3: Property Analysis and Description—Improvements
         Lunch
         Chapter 4: Overview of the Sales Comparison Approach

DAY 3   (total classroom hours 7.5)
         Chapter 5: Overview of the Income Approach
         Lunch
         Chapter 6: Overview of the Cost Approach & Final Reconciliation
         Chapter 7: Overview of Land and Site Valuation

DAY 4   (total classroom hours 7.5)
         Chapter 8: Real World Residential Appraisal Applications
         Lunch
         Chapter 9: Overview of Reporting Forms
         Final Examination and Student Surveys

PREFACE

Hondros Learning™ is proud to present the third edition of *Basic Appraisal Procedures,* part of the market-leading textbook series for appraisal qualifying education. Written specifically to correspond to the Appraisal Qualifications Board's educational requirements, *Basic Appraisal Procedures* features **clear writing**, **real-world examples** and **case studies**, useful **illustrations**, numerous **practice questions**, and an extensive **glossary**, making this text the most up-to-date tool available for achieving appraisal mastery and exam success! As well as launching a successful program of study, this text will continue to bring value as a reference tool throughout your appraisal career.

This basic appraisal course provides an overview of real property valuation procedures, the approaches to value, and residential applications, This course also explores real property analysis and description, including land and site description, improvement construction, and property inspection. Finally, the course provides an overview of appraisal reporting, including appraisal reporting forms most commonly used by residential appraisers. Through theory, case studies, and examples, the course offers practical application of appraisal procedures. A calculator is recommended.

COURSE OBJECTIVES

1. Demonstrate a basic knowledge of real property concepts and appraisal procedures

2. Demonstrate a basic understanding of developing the approaches to value

3. Gain working knowledge of residential appraisal applications

4. Gain a general understanding of residential construction and property description

5. Identify significant appraisal reporting obligations for residential appraisal reporting

EXAM PREP

Additional appraisal products available from Hondros Learning to help students prepare for the licensing exam include the *Appraisal Review Crammer*™—a valuable self-study or classroom exam preparation guide and *CompuCram*™ *Appraisal Exam Prep Software.*

ABOUT THE AUTHOR

Revising author, Timothy Detty, has taught thousands of real estate and appraisal students over the course of his teaching career at Hondros College. A practicing Certified General Appraiser, he has also written numerous real estate and appraisal courses and served as both author and expert reviewer for several real estate and appraisal textbooks. In addition to being certified by the Appraiser Qualifications Board of The Appraisal Foundation as a USPAP instructor, Tim is a frequent guest lecturer and contributor to various real estate and appraisal publications.

Chapter 1
Appraisal Development and Reporting

For those unfamiliar with appraisal, the consensus might be that an appraiser gathers data about the property being appraised and then goes to work crunching numbers. Some may even be under the impression that an appraiser inspects a property and then instantly forms an opinion about the property's value—the "crystal ball" misconception. Beginning appraisers are often amazed how often they encounter this thinking. This chapter introduces the fundamental concepts, terminology, and processes involved in performing an appraisal.

Assumption That which is taken to be true.*

Effective Date The context for the appraiser's opinions and conclusions. Effective dates can be current, retrospective, or prospective.

Exposure Time Estimated length of time a property interest being appraised would have been offered on the market prior to the hypothetical consummation of a sale at market value on the effective date of the appraisal.*

Extraordinary Assumption An assumption, directly related to a specific assignment, as of the effective date of the assignment results, which, if found to be false, could alter the appraiser's opinions or conclusions.*

General Data Information that covers the forces that affect property values, but are not directly related to a particular piece of property. General data covers economic, governmental, social, and physical factors, and can be local or national.

Hypothetical Condition A condition, related to a specific assignment, which is contrary to what is known by the appraiser to exist on the effective date of the assignment results, but is used for the purpose of analysis.*

Intended Use The use or uses of an appraiser's reported appraisal or appraisal review assignment opinions and conclusions, as identified by the appraiser based on communication with the client at the time of the assignment.

* *Definitions*: USPAP 2014-15

(continued on page 3)

The Appraisal Process

Appraisals are valuable tools that clients and intended users can rely upon as credible resources when making decisions. Appraisal opinions are developed *objectively*. There is no place in the world of professional appraisal practice for unsupported or "off the top of the head" subjectivity. Therefore, USPAP (Uniform Standards of Professional Appraisal Practice) provides a specific appraisal process that is to be followed when performing an appraisal.

The appraisal process of USPAP defines two separate and defined actions by an appraiser—**development** and **reporting**. The steps in the appraisal process serve as a pathway for developing and reporting an opinion of value. The process can be applied to tangible and intangible assets and can be used to solve all types of valuation problems. The first five steps in the process relate to the development of a value opinion while the last step in the process addresses the performance obligations of reporting.

The steps in the appraisal process are shown in the following flow chart.

STEP 1	PROBLEM IDENTIFICATION						
Identify client and intended users	Identify the intended use	Identify the purpose of the assignment (type of value)	Identify the effective date of the opinion	Identify the relevant characteristics of the property	Assignment Conditions*		
					Extraordinary assumptions	Hypothetical conditions

STEP 2

Scope of Work

STEP 3	Applicable Data Collection and Analysis	
Market Area Data	Subject Property Data	Comparable Property Data
Market Analysis		Highest and Best Use Analysis

STEP 4	Application of the Approaches to Value	
Cost	Sales Comparison	Income Capitalization

STEP 5	Reconciliation and Final Opinion of Value

STEP 6	Report of Defined Value

* Assignment conditions also include assumptions, limiting conditions, jurisdictional exceptions, laws and regulations, and other conditions that affect the Scope of Work.

Appraisal Development

Development of an appraiser's opinions and conclusions encompasses the first five steps in the appraisal process. This process entails:

1. Identifying certain elements of information regarding the appraisal assignment and the property being appraised.

2. Determining the type and extent of research and analysis to be applied in the assignment.

3. Gathering and analyzing data to be used in forming conclusions.

4. Application of recognized valuation methods and techniques.

5. Reconciliation of the various indications produced through analysis, leading to the appraiser's opinions and conclusions.

For real property appraisals, this process is comprised as a checklist through the Standards Rules 1-2 through 1-6 of USPAP STANDARD 1. But, before these Standards Rules and how they apply to the appraisal process are discussed; the introduction to STANDARD 1 and Standards Rule 1-1 should be overviewed.

The introduction to STANDARD 1 sets forth the basic obligations of the standard and reminds appraisers that when developing a real property appraisal, the appraiser must:

- Identify the problem to be solved.

- Determine the scope of work necessary to solve the problem.

- Correctly complete research and analyses necessary to produce a credible appraisal.

The Comment integral to the introduction reminds us that the standard acts as a checklist for developing a real property appraisal that can be used by appraisers as well as users of appraisal services.

Key Terms

Intended User The client and any other party as identified, by name or type, as users of the appraisal or appraisal review report by the appraiser on the basis of communication with the client at the time of the assignment.

Jurisdictional Exception An assignment condition established by applicable law or regulation, which precludes an appraiser from complying with a part of USPAP.

Limiting Conditions Statements intended to protect the appraiser and inform the client and other intended users of the appraisal report of the limitations placed by the appraiser.

Multiple Listing Service MLS® A listing service whereby local member brokers agree to share listings and commissions on properties sold jointly.

Partial Interest Any interest in real estate one may have other than the full bundle of rights.

Reconciliation Analyzing the values derived from the different appraisal approaches to arrive at a final opinion of value.

Scope of Work The type and extent of research and analyses in an appraisal or appraisal review assignment.

Specific Data Information that is relevant to the subject property. Two types of specific data are subject property data and comparative purpose data.

- **Subject property data** is data that includes information on the subject property site and improvements.

- **Comparative purpose data** is specific data that includes information about comparable sale properties, as well as income and cost information.

Uniform Standards of Professional Appraisal Practice (USPAP) Professional appraisal standards promulgated by The Appraisal Foundation, and widely recognized throughout the United States as accepted standards of appraisal practice.

Workfile The documentation necessary to support the appraiser's analyses, opinions, and conclusions.

Definitions: USPAP 2014-15

Standards Rule 1-1 elaborates on requirements found in the COMPETENCY RULE and places obligation on the appraiser to:

- Be aware of, understand, and correctly employ recognized methods and techniques necessary to produce credible results.

- Not commit a substantial error of omission or commission that significantly affects an appraisal.

- Not render appraisal services in a careless or negligent manner.

Appraisal Development Step 1 – Identify the Problem

Identifying the problem consists of *identifying information the appraiser uses to determine the scope of work in an assignment.* This step is also referred to as *problem identification* or *defining the problem.* The compliance obligations for problem identification can be found in USPAP Standards Rule 1-2(a)-(g). Here the appraiser identifies several elements:

- Client and other intended users

- Intended use

- Type and definition of value

- Date of value opinion

- Relevant property characteristics

- Other assignment conditions (includes extraordinary assumptions, hypothetical conditions, jurisdictional exceptions, assumptions, limiting conditions, and other conditions that affect the scope of work)

These items are referred to as elements of problem identification and should be carefully considered by an appraiser in order to appropriately decide the scope of work to be used in the assignment. It should also be remembered USPAP acknowledges that communication with the client is necessary to obtain most of this information.

Identify the Client and Other Intended Users

The **client** is the *party who engages the appraiser in an appraisal assignment, and with whom the appraiser has an appraiser-client relationship.* An **intended user** is a party *identified by the client* at the time of the assignment. The *client is always an intended user* in an assignment.

Additional intended users may be specified by the client when the appraiser is engaged. An additional intended user may or may not have the same need or use as the client. Therefore, additional intended users in an appraisal assignment might require additional steps or a different process for the appraiser than if the client was the only intended user.

Identifying the client and other intended users assists the appraiser in determining the expectations and requirements of the parties relying on the appraisal report. Simply, what the appraiser does from here out in the appraisal assignment should *meet the needs of the client and other intended users.*

> *IMPORTANT POINTS...*
> - *Simply paying an appraiser does not make one the client or an intended user.*
> - *Unless engaged by the property owner, he or she is not the client or an intended user.*
> - *A party receiving a copy of a report does not become an intended user.*
> - *Once determined at the time of the assignment, the client and intended user(s) cannot change.*
> - *Appraisal reports cannot be transferred, readdressed, or reassigned after completion of the assignment—the original client's and other intended users' needs and requirements played a primary role in what the appraiser performed and how the conclusions were reported.*

Identify the Intended Use of the Appraisal

An appraisal is the basis for a decision regarding real property. What that decision will be, or the **intended use of the appraisal**, is a *key determinant* of the research and analysis performed during the appraisal's development. Similar to intended users, different intended *uses* might require different research and/or analysis, or at different levels.

To name just a few, there could be numerous intended uses of an appraisal:

- Financing
- Litigation
- Accounting
- Marketing

Even within one of these general categories, the specific intended use may signal a lesser or greater level of analysis in the assignment. For example, if the property is being used as collateral in a loan transaction to secure a small line of credit in a low risk situation for the lender, the level of research and analysis in the assignment (scope of work) might be less than if the intended use of the appraisal was to secure a large low down payment mortgage loan for purchasing the property with a higher degree of risk.

IMPORTANT POINTS...

- *The appraiser determines the intended use by communicating with the client.*
- *To properly identify the intended use, the appraiser must identify the client and the client's requirements.*
- *The intended use may have different development and reporting requirements for one or more intended users.*
- *The scope of work decision is heavily dependent upon the intended use of the appraiser's opinions and conclusions.*

Developing opinions and conclusions for some intended uses could possibly require a special level of competency. The COMPETENCY RULE of USPAP specifies intended use as one of the specific areas for which an appraiser must consider his or her competency.

Identify the Type and Definition of Value

The **type and definition of value** are sometimes referred to as *purpose of the appraisal*. Care must be taken not to confuse *purpose of the appraisal* with *intended use*. Appraisers do not use the term "value" without further defining the term. The **purpose of an appraisal** is always to *develop a value opinion for a **defined type** of value*.

Market value is the value conclusion *most frequently specified* in an appraisal. However, other types of value can be derived, based on the intended use and the intended users. The type and definition of value should always be appropriate for its intended use. A common example is when the client specifies the appraisal's intended use for settlement of a legal matter, with the appraisal's purpose being to determine the value of a property for a "quick sale." The term "quick sale" most likely infers *liquidation value* as the type of value desired in the assignment. Of course, before coming to this conclusion, the appraiser should confirm the client is suggesting the property must be sold in a less-than-typical marketing period, with less-than-typical market exposure. Many of the various types of value and their applications are discussed in *Basic Appraisal Principles*.

Standards Rule 1-2(c), which presents the obligation to identify the type and definition of value, in part, also obligates the appraiser, in a market value assignment, to **ascertain whether the value is to be the most probable price in terms of cash, in terms of financial arrangements equivalent to cash, or in other precisely defined terms.** The Standards Rule continues, stating that **if the opinion of value is to be based on non-market financing or financing with unusual conditions or incentives, the terms of such** *financing must be clearly identified and the appraiser's opinion of their contributions to or negative influence on value must be developed by analysis of relevant market data.*

Determining the type and definition of value is also important for determining whether other analysis must take place in the appraisal process. USPAP Standards Rule 1-3 requires that when the type of value is *market value*, the *appraiser must analyze the effect on use and value of public and private restrictions and regulations, and whether it would be probable to modify them.* If so, how would value be impacted? Standards Rule 1-3 further requires the appraiser, when the opinion of value in the assignment is *market value*, to *analyze supply and demand characteristics of the subject market, the physical adaptability of the subject, and market trends.* Probably, one of the most notable obligations of Standards Rule 1-3 is the requirement, when the type of value is *market value*, for the appraiser to *analyze highest and best use.*

Standards Rule 1-5 requires, when the value opinion developed is *market value, analysis of any agreement of sale, listing, or options for the subject and all sales of the property occurring within three years prior to the effective date of the appraisal.*

None of these steps is required by USPAP for other types of value, as they often ignore these factors, or the analyses are not applicable for that value type. For example, *value in use* ignores highest and best use, current restrictions and regulations (assuming the use can continue), potential modifications of current restrictions and regulations, physical adaptability, etc.

The <u>Comment</u> to Standard Rule 1-2(c) obligates the appraiser to develop an opinion of reasonable exposure time linked to the value opinion, when exposure time is a component of the definition for the value being developed. *Market value* is generally considered to be one of the instances where developing an opinion of reasonable exposure time would be required. The appraiser must be very careful not to confuse *exposure time* with *marketing time.* They can be the same in some circumstances, but in others, the two periods of time are very different. *Exposure time* occurs *before* the effective date of the appraisal; *marketing time* occurs *after.*

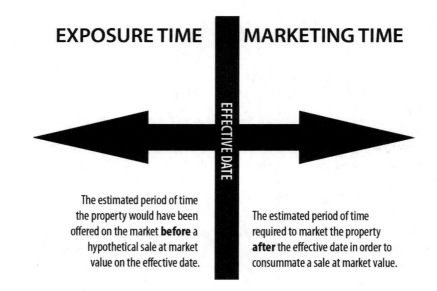

EXPOSURE TIME / **MARKETING TIME**

EFFECTIVE DATE

The estimated period of time the property would have been offered on the market **before** a hypothetical sale at market value on the effective date.

The estimated period of time required to market the property **after** the effective date in order to consummate a sale at market value.

In other words, **exposure time** expresses "*for the property to have sold for market value on the effective date, the property would have had to have been on the market for (a particular period of time)."* *Exposure time* looks at historic market conditions preceding the effective date. In stating *marketing time*, the appraiser looks to the future and forecasts that "for the property to sell for *market value* determined on the effective date, the property **will need to be on the market** for (a particular period of time)," considering historic trends analytically forecasted into the future after the effective date. Corresponding requirements are also integral to STANDARD 2, requiring the reporting of exposure time when it has been developed in an assignment.

For Example

Let's use an area with defined busy and slow marketing seasons, coinciding with the seasons of the year. In the winter months, sales are slow, but as spring approaches, sales activity increases. Using an effective date of April 1, looking back to determine *exposure time,* the appraiser considers the colder and slower marketing months of the year. Looking forward from April 1, however, the appraiser observes some of the best and most active real estate sales months of the year. In this case, *exposure time* would be much longer than *marketing time.* Using this same scenario but with an effective date of July 1, *exposure time* and *marketing time* might be very similar, as market *activity* would most likely be similar.

Work Problem 1.1: Fill in the Blank

1. *If an investor orders an appraisal for his accountant to use for tax purposes, the accountant would be an _____ of the appraisal report.*

2. *A lender orders an appraisal from an appraiser. The appraiser collects the fee at the door from the property owner. The client is the _____.*

Work Problem 1.2: On the Street

An appraiser completed an appraisal two weeks ago. The client, the owner of the property being appraised, needed to know the market value, as he was considering selling the property. After receiving the appraisal report, the client/owner decided against selling, opting to refinance instead. The appraiser has now been contacted by a local lender asking the appraiser to readdress the appraisal report to the lender for its use in facilitating the mortgage refinance transaction.

What can the appraiser do?

_____

_____

_____

_____

_____

_____

_____

_____

_____

Identify the Effective Date of the Value Opinion

Two dates are required in every appraisal report—the *effective date* and the *date of the report.* Statement 3 of USPAP defines the **effective date** as *establishing the context for the value opinion;* and **date of the report** as *an indication of the perspective from which the appraiser is examining the market.*

Because real estate markets are in constant change, the *effective date* of the value opinion must be identified during problem identification and clearly stated in the appraisal report. Once again, intended use often dictates the date of relevance to a value opinion. The *effective date* can be a *current date, a retrospective date,* or a *prospective date.* Not specifically addressed by USPAP, but usually included in most appraisal reports, is the signature date or date of a transmittal (cover) letter.

Usually, appraisals are performed with a *current effective date.* In such a case, the *effective date* and the *date of the report* are *contemporaneous.* In other words, the appraiser is considering the property value as of the conditions present on the effective date. A *retrospective appraisal* uses an *effective date in the past,* or an *effective date prior* to the date of the report. In a **retrospective appraisal**, the appraiser considers *the value opinion on the date of the report in the* **context of prior conditions**.

Retrospective appraisals are performed for a variety of intended uses when a prior value opinion is needed, including estates, insurance claims, litigation, tax matters, etc. An intended use calling for a *prospective* value opinion is usually a rare instance in residential appraising. In a **prospective appraisal,** the appraiser is *determining an opinion of a property's value on the date of the report as of a date in the future* (effective date) utilizing anticipated market conditions. The *effective date* occurs *after* the date of the report in a *prospective appraisal.*

IMPORTANT POINTS...

- *The effective date doesn't necessarily have a relationship to the date of the inspection.*
- *The date of the report isn't always the date the report or letter of transmittal is signed.*
- *A retrospective appraisal can consider data that occurred after the effective date to confirm trends.*

Identify the Relevant Characteristics of the Property

Here, the appraiser is identifying the *characteristics of the property that are relevant to the type and definition of value and the intended use of the appraisal.* Relevant property characteristics have significant influence on the extent to which the property is identified and/or inspected, data that will be researched and analyzed, valuation methods employed, and the final reconciliation of value.

The characteristics of the property identified at this point in the appraisal process are broad and could include an extensive list of property characteristics. Standards Rule 1-2(e) summarizes various inclusions in this category by specifically obligating an appraiser to identify:

- *The property's location and* **physical**, **legal**, *and* **economic** *attributes*
- *The real* **property interest** *to be valued*
- *Any* **personal property, trade fixtures, or intangible items** *that are not real property but are included in the appraisal*
- *Any known* **easements, restrictions, encumbrances, leases, reservations, covenants, contracts, declarations, special assessments, ordinances**, *or other items of a similar nature*
- *Whether the subject property is a* **fractional interest, physical segment, or partial holding**
  *Bold added for emphasis

Often, this is the point in problem identification that most necessitates the appraiser to consider competency.

- Does the appraiser have experience in this particular geographic area or market segment?
- Has the appraiser ever dealt with a property or property interest of this type and use?
- Is a specific analytical method required to develop a credible value opinion with which the appraiser is not experienced?
- Does the appraiser possess the competency to value non-real property assets?

The <u>Comment</u> to Standards Rule 1-2(e) is quite lengthy, but contains important guidance regarding the obligations of identifying the property characteristics and is particularly relevant to this discussion.

- *The information used by an appraiser to identify the property characteristics must be from sources the appraiser reasonably believes are reliable.*

- *An appraiser may use any combination of a property inspection and documents, such as a physical legal description, address, map reference, copy of a survey or map, property sketch, or photographs, to identify the relevant characteristics of the subject property.*

- *When appraising proposed improvements, an appraiser must examine and have available for future examination, plans, specifications, or other documentation sufficient to identify the extent and character of the proposed improvements.*

- *Identification of the real property interest appraised can be based on a review of copies or summaries of title descriptions or other documents that set forth any known encumbrances.*

- *An appraiser is not required to value the whole when the subject of the appraisal is a fractional interest, a physical segment, or a partial holding.*

An appraiser will likely approach an assignment of a single-family residential property and a residential apartment complex quite differently. An appraisal which includes proposed improvements will require a different analysis than an existing structure. Identification of proposed improvements requires extensive analysis of construction documents, whereas an existing structure usually entails a completely different identification process. A drive-by inspection may not be sufficient if the property being appraised is not visible from the road. Appraising a fractional interest in real property is technically different, depending on type and definition of value and the property's characteristics. More will be discussed regarding the various data collection and analysis processes in different types of assignments later in this course.

Properties can be *specific* or *general* in use. Sometimes the property design determines its use. In other matters, zoning and deed restrictions play a key role, as these relate directly to the property's locational characteristics. A single-family home, limited by regulation to a single residential use, is specific in use. But when regulations allow for, say, residential *or* commercial use, the diligence imposed on the appraiser becomes greater and the residential property's use could become general. Another example is a retail building in a mixed retail/office location.

Another *relevant property characteristic* inherent to location relates to economic considerations. One example is a property that lacks demand due to a depressed economy. Consider a developable parcel of land situated between two recently completed residential subdivisions. Most of the new home residents in the adjoining subdivisions work at a local primary industry, or one of the secondary employers whose business depends on the primary industry. The parcel has great utility to accommodate future residential development and, considering conformity, this use seems most logical. However, the primary industry has eliminated one entire shift in the factory, and laid off one-half of its workforce. Economically, the physical characteristics of the land parcel are challenged, especially if regulations limit its use to residential development.

Another circumstance related to economics and physical characteristics is *supply and demand*. The physical characteristics of the property limit the use, and the market segment for that use is out of balance, with a far greater supply of that particular property type in relation to demand. When these situations are recognized in problem identification, or at some time later in the development process, they indicate the research and analysis steps necessary to address them.

In most cases, an appraisal is performed for an opinion of value for the *fee simple interest,* or entire physical property, including the bundle of rights. However, a **partial interest**, *including a lease or life estate, fractional interest, or even a physical segment of the property*, is frequently the subject of an appraisal. Additionally, the appraiser must identify any personal property being considered in the assignment.

For many residential appraisers, when a partial interest, a portion of a property, or just one co-owner's interest is being appraised, the appraisal would be defined as *complex*. In these cases, special methodology is usually required to conclude on a value opinion, and the appraiser's competency needs to be considered when taking on such an assignment. Nevertheless, based on these characteristics defined during problem identification, the appraisal process, going forward, is developed.

Identify Other Assignment Conditions

Other assignment conditions include other elements applicable in an appraisal assignment. They include:

- Assumptions
- Limiting conditions
- Extraordinary assumptions
- Hypothetical conditions
- Jurisdictional exceptions
- Laws and regulations applicable to the assignment
- Other assignment conditions that affect the scope of work

These elements are usually identified by the appraiser during problem identification, but one or more may be revealed later in the appraisal process. Let's take a look at how USPAP defines some of these terms, and how they are handled in the appraisal assignment.

Assumptions

USPAP defines an **assumption** as "*that which is taken to be true.*" *Because there are limitations to an appraiser's scope of knowledge or expertise,* most appraisal reports will contain a certain amount of general *assumptions.* Assumptions *inform the client and intended users of the issues taken for granted.* Common examples might be:

- There are no unobservable adverse conditions.
- An income-producing property is, and will continue to be, adequately managed.
- The property has good title.
- There are no environmental concerns.
- There are no zoning violations.

In other words, the appraiser has no reason to believe the opposite of any of these *assumptions* exists. In many of these circumstances, making a determination regarding these issues would be outside of the appraiser's professional scope, such as legal determinations that could be interpreted as practicing law or making judgments regarding issues requiring an engineering background. Of course, if the appraiser has been made aware, or could be aware, of any of these elements in the normal course of business, the information should be clearly stated and considered in the value opinion.

Limiting Conditions

USPAP does **not** define **limiting conditions**. Limiting conditions statements are intended to *protect the appraiser and inform the client and other intended users of the appraisal report of the limitations placed by the appraiser.* We'll talk more about limiting conditions later, but here are a few that are customarily seen in most appraisals.

"The appraiser is not required to give testimony in court in connection with this appraisal. If the appraiser is subpoenaed pursuant to a court order, the client agrees to pay the appraiser the regular per diem rate plus expenses."

"Information, estimates, and opinions are verified where possible, but cannot be guaranteed."

"This appraisal is to be used only for the purpose stated herein. While distribution of this appraisal in its entirety is at the discretion of the client, individual sections shall not be distributed. This report is intended to be used in whole and not in part."

"No part of this appraisal, its value estimates, or the identity of the firm or the appraiser(s) may be communicated to the public through advertising, public relations, media sales, or other media."

Extraordinary Assumptions

An **extraordinary assumption**, per USPAP, is "*an assumption, directly related to a specific assignment, as of the effective date of the assignment results, which, if found to be false, could alter the appraiser's opinions* *or conclusions.*" The appraiser may use an *extraordinary assumption* when credible assignment results can still be obtained with its use. The appraisal report must clearly state that if the *extraordinary assumption is found to be false, the value opinion may be affected.* An excellent and common example is in the case of a drive-by appraisal.

The appraiser makes the *extraordinary assumption* that the interior condition/quality of the property is consistent with that of the exterior.

Hypothetical Conditions

A **hypothetical condition** is "*a condition, related to a specific assignment, which is contrary to what is known by the appraiser to exist on the effective date of the assignment results, but is used for the purpose of analysis,*" per USPAP definition. *Hypothetical conditions* are "What if?" situations, when the value opinion is **subject to** a specified action or event.

An appraisal for the purpose of new construction with a current effective date typically contains the *hypothetical condition* that presumes the construction were completed per plans and specifications presented to the appraiser on the effective date. Like extraordinary assumptions, the report must clearly state that the use of a hypothetical condition might have affected the assignment results.

Jurisdictional Exception

Sometimes, USPAP can conflict with some form of law or public policy. USPAP defines a **jurisdictional exception** as "*an assignment condition established by applicable law or regulation, which precludes an appraiser from complying with a part of USPAP.*" In other words, *jurisdictional exception* is something that *takes away* from the purpose of USPAP. *Jurisdictional exception* can be invoked by a federal or state constitution; legislative and court-made law; or federal, state, and local administrative rules, regulations, and ordinances. *Jurisdictional exception* is not a common element in most everyday appraisal. For example, a probate court has an established rule that all estate appraisals must be performed with an anonymous client, and that the workfile indicates the client is anonymous.

Laws and Regulations Applicable in the Assignment

The Scope of Work Rule in USPAP requires the appraiser to properly identify the problem to be solved, including determining if there are assignment conditions that include laws, regulations, and other conditions that affect the scope of work in an assignment. The appraiser must be competent and knowledgeable of the laws and regulations to be applied in an assignment as well as recognizing other conditions of the assignment, and is ethically obligated to observe and apply them properly. The intended use and the intended user drive the assignment conditions.

Assignment conditions most often *add something* to the general development (and reporting) requirements imposed by USPAP, rather than take away from the requirements of USPAP, as jurisdictional exception does. Entities such as HUD, the FHA, and the VA have certain property identification (inspection), analysis, and reporting requirements. Government-sponsored enterprises such as Fannie Mae, Freddie Mac, Ginnie Mae, etc., each have their own regulations. A state regulatory agency (such as a state appraiser board) is an example of an entity that establishes public policy, with laws and regulations concerning the general behavior and performance of an appraiser varying from one jurisdiction to another. It is fairly safe to say that, in all appraisals performed for secondary market or federally related transactions, there will be certain regulations the appraiser will need to comply with in one form or another. Here are examples of just a few that are common:

1. The FHA requires the appraiser to view the crawl space and attic, and observe the operation of mechanical systems of the subject property (as applicable).

2. Fannie Mae does *not* allow for the appraisal of a physical segment (or part) of a property.

3. Fannie Mae (and others) requires the use of the standardized residential reporting forms.

4. Fannie Mae (and others) requires that the interior of a manufactured dwelling be inspected, as well as the exterior.

5. Fannie Mae (and others) requires a *minimum of three* comparable sales when developing the sales comparison approach.

The importance of recognizing laws and regulations applicable in an assignment during problem identification, especially in many appraisal assignments for use in residential lending, is that if the laws and regulations apply, the appraiser cannot disregard them. This obligation is embedded in the COMPTENCY RULE. *Thus, it is the responsibility of the appraiser to be aware of, or have access to, the laws and regulations applying to the assignment of a particular lender.*

Other Assignment Conditions Which Affect the Scope of Work

It is important to remember that USPAP presents the *minimum* requirements for appraisers and appraisals. Clients and other intended users can *always* request additional diligence in appraisal development and reporting. When the additional request results in research and analysis beyond what would typically be necessary for credible assignment results by an appraiser (scope of work), the appraiser must comply with that request. Of course, this is provided the request would not violate professional standards or cause the assignment results or appraisal report to be misleading.

One of the more frequently observed examples is when the client requests that a certain valuation approach be developed, when development of that approach would not have been deemed necessary by the appraiser otherwise. This is such a common question, a USPAP FAQ has been issued by the Appraisal Standards Board (ASB) to address the issue and is appropriate to be presented here:

DEVELOPING AN UNNECESSARY VALUATION APPROACH

Question: I have a client requesting that the cost approach be included in every appraisal assignment, including those where I feel the cost approach may not yield meaningful results. I am concerned that by complying with the client's request, I may be providing a misleading appraisal report. How can I comply with USPAP and satisfy the client at the same time?

Response: Performing a cost approach that may not yield a meaningful indication of value does not result in a misleading appraisal report if the appraiser properly addresses the applicability and suitability of the approach in the report. Many appraisers address this in the reconciliation by including statements such as, "The cost approach was included solely at the request of the client; it has been given no weight in arriving at the final opinion of value because ...." (FAQ #290, USPAP 2014-2015 Edition)

Appraisers must be very cautious regarding client requests. The request(s) should not result in the client dictating an unacceptable scope of work. It is the responsibility of the appraiser to determine if the request(s) is appropriate.

Work Problem 1.3: Test Your Knowledge

List the primary elements of Problem Identification.

1. _____
2. _____
3. _____
4. _____
5. _____
6. _____

Work Problem 1.4: On the Street

Appraiser Carla Long has accepted an appraisal assignment from property owner, Joe Owens. Joe and his lawyer need to know the value of a single-family dwelling Joe owns. Joe's parents gave him the property 1½ years ago as a gift. A legal question has now surfaced regarding possible gift taxes Joe might owe, based on the property's market value at that time. The property is located in Shyville, a small rural village. Appraiser Long is aware that Shyville has no published flood information or detailed zoning. It appears unlikely that the property is in a flood plain, but the appraiser has no professional experience in this area. The appraisal will be based on an exterior and interior inspection.

1. *Who is the client in this scenario?* _____

2. *Are there any other intended users of the appraisal?* _____

3. *What is the intended use of the appraisal?* _____

4. *What is the purpose of the appraisal?* _____

5. *What is the effective date of the opinion?* _____

6. *What are the property characteristics?* _____

7. *Are there an assumptions or limiting conditions?* _____

8. *Any extraordinary assumptions?* _____

9. *Any hypothetical conditions?* _____

Appraisal Development Step 2 – Scope of Work Decision

The *scope of work* decision is driven by the information learned while defining the problem. The SCOPE OF WORK RULE states that to correctly decide the appropriate scope of work for an assignment, the appraiser must properly identify the problem—considering all information obtained during problem identification and deciding on the necessary and appropriate development elements for the remainder of the assignment. Although all elements of problem identification are important to the scope of work decision, the elements that are primary drivers of the scope of work are the *intended users, intended use,* and *relevant property characteristics.* At this point, the appraiser must look at the whole picture and consider competency—does the appraiser possess, or is he or she willing and/or able to acquire—the knowledge and experience necessary to complete the assignment? *If not, the appraiser must decline or withdraw from the assignment.*

It may be helpful to think of **scope of work** as *an appraisal plan—an outline identifying the work needed to complete the appraisal.* The "plan" can be used as a guide for all who will participate in the appraisal, as well as a basis for the appraiser to establish an appropriate fee for the assignment.

Appraisals are not "one size fits all." The *scope of work* determines the steps going forward including, but certainly not limited to:

- Extent to which the property is identified
- Extent to which the property is inspected
- Type and extent of data researched
- Type and extent of analysis applied

The decisions made here must lead to credible assignment results. In other words, the *scope of work* determination must be logical and reliable for the intended user in the context of the intended use, and will depend greatly on the relevant property characteristics.

Extent to Which the Property is Identified

The extent to which the property is identified could greatly vary, especially depending upon the intended use and intended users of the appraisal. Consider that an appraiser is asked to appraise a physical segment of a property, in this case, a 5-acre portion of a 20-acre vacant parcel. USPAP allows for this, given there are no laws, regulations, or assignment conditions to the contrary. *By what method will the five acres be identified?* The answer depends on *who is relying on the value opinion* and *for what purpose.*

Suppose the client in the appraisal is the property owner who just wants "a general idea" of what the five acres are worth, because he may give the proposed parcel as a gift to one of his children. His primary concern is that the value of the five acres is about the same as other 5-acre parcels he has given his other children. (And he doesn't want a family uprising!) No survey has been performed yet. An appraiser *might* conclude that a hand-drawn map supplied by the farmer and the use of one or more extraordinary assumptions is sufficient to provide the farmer with "a general idea."

For this use and user, credible assignment results would likely be achieved. However, if the client is a lender whose use for the appraisal was to transact a new-construction loan for the farmer's child to build a new house on the yet-to-be-surveyed parcel, the extent to which the property is identified would be much more complex. In this case, the appraiser would most likely insist on examining a proposed survey and legal description, as well as supporting documentation stating the proposed survey has been approved by jurisdictional authorities to be divided or "split" legally.

Extent to Which the Property is Inspected

Interior and exterior, drive-by, prior inspection, photographs, blueprints...what does the assignment call for? USPAP allows for any one, or a combination, of these inspection methods. The answer, again, depends on intended users, intended use, relevant property characteristics, and of course, any laws, regulations, or assignment conditions being applicable in the assignment.

Unfortunately, there is no textbook answer for what extent of property inspection fits a particular property in a particular assignment. The appraiser must rely on experience as a compass for determining the level of inspection appropriate for achieving credible assignment results. Obviously, the appraiser will have the most confidence in data relied on if it is gathered through a complete personal inspection of both the interior and exterior of a structure, as well as a full observation of the subject site. Keep in mind, though, this level of inspection may not be necessary, or even possible, in every assignment.

Type and Extent of Data Researched

It's impractical to think the same data research is applicable when the subject of an appraisal is an income-producing property or a proposed, owner-occupied new construction; or in an assignment with the type of value being market value versus going concern value; or a fee simple interest as opposed to a partial interest. Each case requires collection and analysis of various and differing types of data. The elements determined in problem identification are critical to determining this. The physical characteristics of the property and the type and definition of value, in context with the intended use of the appraisal, lend great insight to the type and extent of data that needs to be researched. And of course, the research being considered here includes both general and specific data. We'll discuss data research later in this chapter.

IMPORTANT POINTS...

- *The scope of work determined by the appraiser is considered appropriate when it **meets or exceeds the expectations** of those who are regularly intended users, and what the appraiser's peers actions would be in the same or similar situation.*
- *Determining the appropriate scope of work is an **ongoing process** and can change during the assignment based on information and conditions learned by the appraiser, which can lead to reconsidering the scope of work.*
- *The scope of work an appraiser performs should **not** be limited by the client or intended use, to the extent that credible results cannot be obtained or results are biased.*

Type and Extent of Analysis Applied

Here, the appraiser must consider what and how much analysis is necessary for credible assignment results. Decisions made here will affect the preliminary analysis, valuation methods applied, and reconciliation. A 20-year-old, 2-unit, income-producing dwelling being appraised for market value in a mortgage transaction would likely signal the need for income and expense analysis, zoning analysis, lease analysis, etc. However, a cost analysis may pale in relevancy in such an assignment, so many appraisers would not apply this development step in the process.

A single-family dwelling limited to that use by zoning and deed restrictions would not likely require an analysis of probable use modifications, unless some drastic change is forthcoming. For most assignments of single-family, owner-occupied dwellings, the income approach would not typically be used. More discussion of the type and extent of analysis will be presented a little later.

As a final thought, the SCOPE OF WORK RULE provides broad latitude to an appraiser in forming the scope of work decision. However, it is also the appraiser's responsibility to determine that the scope of work performed was appropriate and will lead to credible assignment results. An appraiser must be able to support the scope of work decision.

The scope of work must include the research and analysis necessary for credible assignment results. Credible assignment results require *support from appropriate evidence and logic*, based on the intended use of the appraisal.

Appraisal Development Step 3 – Applicable Data Collection and Analysis

Recognition of appropriate and relevant data to be collected and analyzed in an appraisal assignment is part of the scope of work decision. Thus, at this point, it should be recognized by an appraiser what data is needed and from where it will be obtained. The data collected is relative to describing the property, and later for analysis purposes.

Data Collection

An appraiser has numerous sources of data to consult on a regular basis: The Internet, personal data files, notebooks, and databases built into appraisal software or other informational technology. The proliferation of online information and databases as a means of accessing and verifying information has significantly increased efficiency. Most sources are available online. In addition, most courthouse records and other public information can be obtained online, and still more information on building costs, economic trends, and real estate, in general, can be found on the Internet. And, of course, there are multiple listing services (MLS°) available online in most areas. As tasks become more automated and information can be more easily accessed through evolving technology, it is more important now than ever for an appraiser to take steps to *verify the accuracy* of the information used.

All data collected should first be verified by a party familiar with the transaction for relevancy, accuracy, and reliability. Appraisers must also consider the timeliness of data. It's important for the appraiser to ensure that all data and facts relied on in performing the appraisal are the most current and complete available.

Remember, ideal *sales comparison data* should be that which is most similar. *Cost approach data* should be from the most recent costing sources. *Income and expense data* should be from the most recent reporting period for the property. The data to be collected and analyzed is divided into the categories of *general data* and *specific data*.

General Data

General data is used to form conclusions regarding the status of market elements and any change that is or has occurred, as well as any change anticipated. This most generally reflects the status of the *broad forces that affect value*: PEGS—physical, economic, governmental, and social.

Appraisers should have ready access to typical general data information required for an appraisal, since most appraisers work within a given region or area. Appraisers must be current on interest rate trends and business conditions affecting the economic base of an area. Changes in federal laws are as important as changes in local laws—particularly for zoning. Demographic changes, population shifts, and buyer tastes on a national and local level are all important. Physical and environmental changes and trends can be very important to consider.

General data sources are *typically government records, public records and filings, magazines, newsletters, trade publications,* and *other sources* the appraiser relies on because of their timeliness and accuracy. Professional appraisers keep files with information on economic trends in an area, as well as changes in laws and other aspects affecting real estate markets. This stored data includes social trends and neighborhood physical characteristics, and information relevant to business and the housing markets nationally and locally, like economic trends, interest rates, and government policies.

GENERAL DATA RESOURCES

Government Respositories	Professional Repositories	Other Resources
government census data	trade publications or newsletters	magazines, newspapers
government publications	professional magazines, journals	maps and reports
government records	REALTOR® boards, publicatons	lenders, mortgage co.
courthouse and registrars	multiple listing services	property mgrs, rental co.
public records and filings	computer databases & Internet	moving & storage co.
US Dept of Commerce or local chamber of commerce	home builder associations and other professional assn.	employment agencies or labor groups
planning, highway, county commissioner's offices	accountants, lawyers, engineers, business people	builders, contractors, architects
FHA or other government agencies	specialized research co.	colleagues and contacts

Note: These lists are not all inclusive. Other data sources may also be used Much of this information is available online from various Websites on the Internet.

Specific Data

Specific data covers *all relevant information unique to the subject property* and the *comparable data.*

Specific data about the subject property includes information on the *subject's site and improvements.* The site's legal description is often found in title work or public records. Description of improvements can be by personal observation or data obtained from another source, consistent with the scope of work.

Specific data for comparable properties is *obtained for each of the applicable appraisal methods.* Comparable sale information for the sales comparison approach is obtained from buyers, sellers, real estate agents, multiple listing services, other third-party sources, and public records. For cost information, appraisers use cost services that detail building and construction costs in a given area and information obtained from the local building market. Finally, information for income, expenses, lease terms, etc., used in the income approach is obtained from sellers, investors, accountants, and others in the marketplace.

SPECIFIC DATA RESOURCES		
PROPERTY SPECIFIC		
personal inspection	county records: deeds, mort., tax	multiple listing services
buyer, seller, broker, agent	computer databases & Internet	published recorded info
COMPARATIVE DATA		

Sales Comparison Data	Cost Approach Data	Income/Expense Data
personal inspection (condition)	personal inspection (depreciation)	personal inspect. (vacancy)
buyer, seller, broker, agent	cost manuals (books, elec., online)	seller, broker, agent
county records: deeds, mort., tax	supply houses, labor pools	property mgrs, rental co.
multiple listing services	architects, contractors, engineers	accountants, other prof.
computer databases	computer databases & Internet	financial statements
published recorded info	professional journals, org.	professional journals, org.

Note: These lists are not all inclusive. Other data sources may also be used Much of this information is available online from various Websites on the Internet.

Property Description

The extent to which property is described is determined in the scope of work and consistent with the intended use and intended user of the appraisal, as well as the manner in which the appraisal will be reported. When describing property, the appraiser must ensure the information is concise and accurate so it is meaningful and understandable. Much more will be discussed regarding *property description*, including specific examples, in Chapter 3.

Data Analysis

In this step of the appraisal process, the appraiser takes the information collected and begins to interpret and understand what it means. This is a critical step, as the indications found here directly influence other elements of the valuation process. Data analysis consists of two primary functions:

1. Market analysis
2. Highest and best use analysis

Market Analysis

In market analysis, the appraiser determines the conditions for a particular type of property. Here, the appraiser *first studies the broad market* without the subject or any other specific property in mind. As a second step, the appraiser looks at that *market in the context of the subject property* and where it competes. The key elements of analysis are:

- National and regional trends
- Economic base
- Local area and neighborhood trends
- Subject site and improvements

This information is analyzed to conclude how the subject property would compete in relationship to the supply and demand conditions in its particular market. Usually, in most residential appraisal assignments, the market analysis is not a lengthy process, given the property is not unusual or complex, and the subject's market is one in which the appraiser actively practices. But in some assignments, the market analysis can be vast and involved. The topic will be more fully explored and demonstrated later in this text and in other appraisal courses.

Highest and Best Use Analysis

Highest and best use is the *most profitable, legally permitted, financially feasible, and physically possible use* of a property. This is one of the most important analyses an appraiser considers in developing opinions of value. A number of factors contribute to an appraiser's highest and best use conclusions. When the type of value in an appraisal assignment is market value, highest and best use is *always* considered, although in some assignments, the analysis is more extensive than other assignments. For example, with most houses in zoned and/or deed restricted residential neighborhoods, the opinion of highest and best use is most often limited to the current use, provided the improvements conform and no significant deterioration or obsolescence is present.

Developing an opinion of highest and best use becomes a more complex consideration, though, when examining vacant land or land with a zoning change since the original structure was built. The objective is to decide whether the property is being used for its most profitable permitted use. To make this decision, the appraiser follows a systematic order of analysis, which must be fully analyzed before he forms his conclusions:

1. Value the property as though vacant
2. Value the property as it is improved (when improved)
3. Determine highest and best use

To competently perform a highest and best use analysis, the appraiser must be aware of all public and private limitations on a parcel of land. Plus, the appraiser must also know the characteristics of that land. If the ground is too soft to support a large building, for example, this must be considered in determining the highest and best use for that land. Also, it's possible that a parcel of land would be more valuable if the current structure was torn down and replaced with a new type of building (e.g., an old house on land that is now zoned commercial). This type of situation must also be examined carefully.

Highest and best use is an area of analysis covered in some detail in Chapter 3, and is explored thoroughly in other real estate courses devoted to this topic. It is, however, important to understand the basic concept at this point. If a house sits on a widened street surrounded by commercial buildings, it is very likely the land would be more valuable if also put to a commercial use, provided that zoning laws permit the use and the proposed structure is physically be able to be built on the land.

> *IMPORTANT POINTS...*
> - *The highest and best use represents the greatest economic advantage to the owner.*
> - *The opinion of highest and best use is critical to the selection of appropriate valuation methods and comparable data used in the sales comparison approach.*
> - *An important decision made in forming opinions regarding highest and best use of improved properties is whether the improvements should remain as they are, be converted to another use, or razed.*

Appraisal Development Step 4 – Application of the Approaches to Value

As can be seen so far, there are many steps leading to the development and application of the approaches to value. Three development methods may be used by the appraiser to determine a value opinion:

1. Sales comparison approach
2. Cost approach
3. Income approach

There are also various accepted techniques that may be used for development of each approach, with some being more extensive than others. The appraiser's choices in the development and application of the approaches to value is a major component of the scope of work decision - the appraiser could elect to use one approach, more than one, or all three approaches as a result of that decision. As well, the extent of that development and the techniques to be used are also part of the scope of work decision. The primary problem identification elements considered when making the scope of work decision are:

- Intended use
- Intended user
- Type and definition of value
- Relevant property characteristics

Assignment conditions imposed by the client or an intended user may specify the particular approach to be used in the appraiser's development and even the technique and extent of the analysis. Those conditions could also specify that a particular approach to value is not necessary to be developed. It is very important to remember that the appraiser is responsible for determining if the conditions are appropriate and will lead to credible assignment results. An appraiser must not accept an assignment that includes unacceptable assignment conditions.

When an appraiser considers the approaches to value to be developed in an assignment, an important consideration is the amount and quality of data available to process a particular approach. As data becomes scarce or dissimilar, the difficulty of arriving at a meaningful and supported conclusion becomes more of a real issue.

Frequent dilemmas include, but are not limited to:

- *How can the sales comparison approach be developed if there are not enough (or any) recent comparable sales in the area for an uncommon building being sold, such as a school, church, or library?*
- *How can the cost approach be applied to develop an credible value through costing methods for a unique building, such as a historic structure?*
- *How useful is the income approach for residential properties in an area almost exclusively owner-occupied and with little or no data on rent or income data for residential properties there?*

All three methods, when properly developed, can be reliable for producing value indications. Each approach, when applicable, can also be a check against the others. Or, a particular approach or approaches, can serve as support for another approach that the appraiser has deemed most reliable. For example, in many residential appraisals of existing owner-occupied homes, the cost approach is used as support for the conclusions of the sales comparison approach.

An overview of each approach to value is presented here, while other parts of this course provide a more detailed explanation of each method and the various techniques for its application.

> ***IMPORTANT POINTS...***
> - *Each approach to value deemed applicable in an assignment and identified in the scope of work should be developed by the appraiser.*
> - *Regulations of lending participants (assignment conditions), such as Fannie Mae, FHA, VA, etc., may dictate the approach or approaches to value that must be developed and reported, and the extent to which the appraiser should rely on the approach in the final value conclusion. However, the appraiser is responsible for determining the appropriateness of the assignment condition.*

Sales Comparison Approach

Generally, the **sales comparison approach** is the most frequently developed approach of the three approaches to value in a market value assignment for residential properties when there are sufficient sales (e.g., often for houses). For most residential assignments, reliable data with which to develop the approach is usually available. Of course, for some properties and in some assignments, there may be an absence or scarcity of reliable comparable data.

Cost Approach

In residential assignments, the **cost approach** is often most applicable for unique properties or for properties for which there is a deficiency of data to develop of the sales comparison approach. The cost approach is also excellent for newly constructed improvements and when the type of value in the assignment is insurance value. The cost approach relies heavily on many variables, including local cost differences for labor and materials. It becomes less reliable for older buildings when estimation of site value, cost new, and/or depreciation is complex. However, properly developed, the cost approach is a reliable and acceptable methodology for developing value conclusions.

Income Approach

The **income approach** is typically most applicable for properties of an income-producing nature and for which income and expense figures are readily available. Furthermore, the income approach offers a method of analyzing the value of a future income stream. But caution must be exercised since income and expense figures reflect a property's past performance and will not necessarily reflect future projections.

Appraisal Development Step 5 – Reconciliation and Final Opinion of Value

Appraisers can undertake the most thorough and comprehensive analysis, meeting or exceeding the obligations of professional standards and the expectations of clients and intended users. However, unless there is a process to make sense of the analysis and bring the analysis conclusions together properly into a final opinion of value, the appraiser's diligence may fall flat and the resulting opinions and conclusions may be less than credible. This is why the process of reconciliation is so very important and its value to the appraisal process must not be discounted.

USPAP Standards Rule 1-6 provides that the process of reconciliation, once the analysis has concluded, and the necessary approaches to value have been developed, consist of two steps.

In developing a real property appraisal, an appraiser must:

(a) reconcile the quality and quantity of data available and analyzed within the approaches used; and

(b) reconcile the applicability and relevance of the approaches, methods and techniques used to arrive at the value conclusion(s).

Given within this obligation is that an appraiser first look at each approach to value that was developed, determine the strength and weaknesses of each analysis, and make decisions as to the reliability of those conclusions. Second, the appraiser looks at the conclusions of the approaches and determines which is to be given the most weight in the final value opinion – often referenced as the final reconciliation.

Final Reconciliation

As was mentioned earlier, reconciliation is actually ongoing throughout the appraisal development process. An appraiser is constantly forming conclusions regarding the indications produced by the various analyses; *recognizing the strengths and weaknesses of the data and data analysis*—what shows strong support and credible indications and what does not. Thus, in the final reconciliation the appraiser brings together all the data collected, verified, and analyzed during the appraisal process so it relates to the final opinion of value. As part of the reconciliation, the appraiser must determine the strengths and weaknesses of each appraisal approach used. Judgment, logic, and relying on skill and experience play a key role as the appraiser completes the reconciliation process.

Conclusions derived from the valuation approaches are reconciled to arrive at the final opinion of value. The value conclusions are rarely equal when developing an opinion using more than one approach. This is why the appraiser's knowledge and experience are invaluable, as judgment must often be applied. Reconciliation involves giving each method an appropriate weight, depending on the type of property being analyzed, and the amount and quality of data available.

For example, if the appraisal is for a single-family residence, the appraiser would usually give the most weight to the sales comparison approach. This is because it uses data derived directly from the market and represents the actions of buyers and sellers and, therefore, the approach typically provides the most reliable indicator of a property's market value. If the appraisal were for an income-producing property for which there was sufficient market income and expense data, the appraiser would typically give the most weight to the income approach and so on.

The indications from each of the approaches developed in the assignment are *never simply mathematically averaged*. This is where the appraiser's experience aids in deciding the importance of the results and conclusions produced through the development process. It is important to remember that, even with all of the appraiser's knowledge and experience, and the extensive research and analysis that go into an appraisal, the appraiser is *only develops opinions of value*—he does not determine the value of a property. For market value appraisal assignments, *only the marketplace can truly speak to the value of a property through the price the market is willing to pay*. The reconciliation process will be dicussed further in Chapter 6.

IMPORTANT POINTS…

- *The data analyzed in each of the valuation approaches developed are given consideration by the appraiser, who then decides the reliability of the indications produced by that particular approach.*
- *The appraiser then must decide which valuation approach or approaches is the most relevant and applicable in indicating a credible final value opinion for the subject property.*
- *Reconciliation and forming conclusions of the final opinion of value require competency in applying logic and judgment to the process.*

Final Opinion of Value

Although not always, there is often one single value concluded on in an appraisal. Alternatively, the appraiser may conclude on a value range; for example, between $100,000–$110,000. Or the value opinion might be a relationship to a numeric benchmark. For instance, the appraiser might form a range of value and determine the property value is toward the "mid-part" of the range, without stating a specific number. The range is the benchmark, and the mid-part is the relationship to it. That is an expression of a value opinion, which is an appraisal. Or the opinion could be expressed as a relationship to a former value opinion, such as "current value is more than the value found in a previous appraisal".

In the instance of the single number value conclusion, if only one approach to value has been developed, the *final opinion of value* most often will coincide with the result from the one approach developed. If two or three approaches have been developed, the appraiser can use the range of those conclusions, concluding the final value estimate with the method lending the strongest support. For owner-occupied single-family properties, this is often the sales comparison approach. Numerous possible conclusions could be cited here. The process requires logical and rational thought combined with experience.

Fill in the Blank 1.5

1. A _____ condition assumes something is present that is known to be false.

2. _____ data includes demographics, economic data, and interest rates.

3. A _____ decision is formed by the conclusions formed in defining the problem.

4. The final analysis in the valuation process is _____.

5. Joan is performing an exterior inspection for an appraisal. She will probably use an _____ in the final opinion of value.

6. An example of a _____ interest might be a life estate, a lease, or subsurface rights.

7. For an estate, a value as of the owner's date of death might be required, which would be in _____.

Appraisal Reporting

The final step in the appraisal process, Step 6, is the Report of Defined Value, or *appraisal report*. USPAP allows an appraisal report to be *oral or written*. Oral reports are rare for most appraisals, and have special USPAP requirements. In most cases, the appraisal report will be written. The appraisal report is the primary means of communicating the appraisal results to the client. The appraiser's obligations for real property appraisal reporting are recited in USPAP STANDARD 2.

Reporting Step 6 - Report of Defined Value

The appraisal report not only reports a final opinion of a defined value for the subject property, but also explains the appraiser's reasoning to the client and intended users. The appraisal report should lead the reader through the rationale and process used in developing the appraisal and the conclusions. With this in mind, the report should be clear and concise, logical and consistent, and supported and documented with market evidence in defense of the conclusions reached. The appraiser's opinions must be supported by evidence and logic. USPAP contains Rules, Standards, Standards Rules, and other obligations that appraisers must follow in appraisal reporting.

USPAP defines a Report as:

> *any communication, written or oral, of an appraisal or appraisal review that is transmitted to the client upon completion of an assignment*

The PREAMBLE of USPAP references (in part) appraisal reporting through a general caveat:

> *It is essential that appraisers develop and communicate their analyses, opinions, and conclusions to intended users of their services in a manner that is meaningful and not misleading.*

Standards Rule 2-1 of USPAP references three fundamental requirements for all appraisal reports, written or oral:

1. The appraisal report must be *clear, accurate, and not misleading.*
2. The report must *contain sufficient information to be understood properly by the intended users.*
3. The appraisal report must *disclose any extraordinary assumptions, hypothetical conditions, or other assignment conditions* that directly affect the appraisal, and in the case of extraordinary assumptions and hypothetical conditions, indicate that their use could have affected the value opinion.

STANDARD 2 sets forth the **minimum requirements** for the level and content for each report type. An appraiser must supplement a report form, if necessary, with other information, addenda, exhibits, etc., so that intended users are not misled and the report complies with the content requirements.

Receiving a copy of a report, regardless of the reporting option, **does not make that party an intended user** unless that party has been identified by the appraiser as an intended user at the time of the assignment.

Reporting Options

For written real property appraisal reports, STANDARD 2 of USPAP allows for two reporting options:

1. Appraisal Report
2. Restricted Appraisal Report

The essential *difference* of these options is the *content and level of information* provided. As a simple way for the appraiser to distinguish each of these reporting options, USPAP uses the terms **summarize** and **state**.

- *Summarize:* Denotes a more *concise presentation* of information. Appraisal Reports *summarize* information.
- *State:* Denotes the *minimal presentation* of information. In a Restricted Appraisal Report, information is *stated*.

Don't confuse the reporting options with *formats* of presentation. USPAP does *not* dictate the style or format of an appraisal report. The format of any of these reports could be some type of **narrative** style or fill-in-the-blank **forms**. A narrative format is somewhat like a thesis, which leads the reader through the information and process used for the conclusion, at the required level. There are numerous forms from many sources that are used. For residential mortgage purposes, most appraisals are reported on forms developed by Fannie Mae/Freddie Mac.

Appraisal reporting software is available for both narrative and form reporting. USPAP Standards Rule 2-2 contains two checklists, one for each of the reporting options, Appraisal Report and Restricted Appraisal Report.

Appraisal Report

An **Appraisal Report** *summarizes the information and analyses performed in the appraisal.* Some of the detailed information and data used in the development process might be contained in the appraiser's workfile, with the report summarizing the data and conclusions. The report might reference the amount and type of data contained in the workfile. Many narrative appraisal reports and the most common fill-in-the-blank appraisal forms used today are considered Appraisal Reports. Appraisal Reports are often a requirement of secondary market participants (such as Fannie Mae), government entities (such as FHA), and other residential lenders. Fill-in-the-blank forms, though simple and concise, must still be supported by strong evidence and data to support the value conclusions. The reports often contain photos and other documentation.

Restricted Appraisal Report

A **Restricted Appraisal Report** can be *brief and to the point* when compared to an Appraisal Report. The Restricted Appraisal Report *states the facts and conclusions* of the appraisal. A minimum level of these reporting elements must be included, as prescribed by USPAP. *Restricted,* in this case, refers to the *restrictive nature of the user* of the report. In a restricted report, there is **one intended user—the client**. And because the reported elements may be so minimally reported, USPAP reporting standards require a prominent statement in the report, which warns that the opinions and conclusions found in a Restricted Appraisal Report may not be understood properly without additional information in the appraiser's workfile. This workfile must contain all of the data, analysis, and documentation used in the appraisal sufficient to produce an Appraisal Report.

Choosing the Reporting Option and Format

What determines which reporting option and format is appropriate for an appraisal assignment? Decisions regarding the reporting option and format chosen by an appraiser in an assignment are NOT a function of the scope of work decision. Scope of work addresses only the level and extent of the development process. The method of reporting an appraisal chosen by an appraiser must be appropriate to the *intended use* and the *intended user* of the report, and, as mentioned earlier, some lending regulations may impose specific reporting requirements.

IMPORTANT POINTS...

- *Regardless of the reporting option and format chosen, the value opinions expressed in each should be equally credible.*
- *The reporting option and format should be consistent with the intended user and intended use of the appraisal.*

Report Disclosure Requirements

When applicable, USPAP contains certain disclosure requirements. Some of the disclosures must be included in specific sections of an appraisal report, such as any letter of transmittal in which conclusions are stated, or the report certification (discussed later in this chapter). Other disclosures must be simply contained within the report.

The Conduct section of the ETHICS RULE requires disclosure by an appraiser in an appraisal report of:

- Any current or prospective interest in a subject property or the parties involved in the assignment.
- Any services as an appraiser, or in any other capacity, regarding the subject property performed within a three-year period prior immediately proceeding acceptance of the assignment.

In addition to the disclosure made prior to accepting the assignment or one made if discovered any time during an assignment, **disclosure must be made in the certification** of the report. Disclosing this information is important to preserving public trust, and it gives the client an opportunity to evaluate the information before engaging the appraiser.

The disclosure regarding prior services cannot be made if the appraiser has agreed with the client in a prior assignment not to disclose the prior service. In USPAP, the Comment to this portion of the Conduct section of the ETHICS RULE provides specific advice regarding how these requirements interact with the appraiser's obligation of confidentiality:

> *Comment: Disclosing the fact that the appraiser has previously appraised the property is permitted except in the case when an appraiser has agreed with the client to keep the mere occurrence of a prior assignment confidential. If an appraiser has agreed with a client not to disclose that he or she has appraised a property, the appraiser must decline all subsequent assignments that fall within the three year period.*

The Management section of the ETHICS RULE requires that fees, commissions, or things of value relating to the procurement of an assignment **must be disclosed**.

> *An appraiser must disclose that he or she paid a fee or commission, or gave a thing of value in connection with the procurement of an assignment.*

> *Comment: The disclosure must appear in the certification and in any transmittal letter in which conclusions are stated; however, disclosure of the amount paid is not required. In groups or organizations engaged in appraisal practice, intra-company payments to employees for business development do not require disclosure.*

> *The required disclosure:*

- Refers to payments being made **by the appraiser**, not to the appraiser.
- Is specific to a particular assignment and does not reference gifts or other things of value provided to a client as a "thank you" or other appreciation for business in general.
- Does not need to state the amount (or value) of the payment, only that a payment was made.

The COMPETENCY RULE of USPAP sets forth steps an appraiser must take during the development process to address a lack of competency in a particular assignment as well as certain disclosure mechanisms that must take place in the reporting process regarding the lack of initial competency and the steps that were taken to complete the assignment competently.

From a reporting perspective, whether the lack of competency was initially recognized or was discovered at some point during the assignment, an appraiser must:

> *describe, in the report, the lack of knowledge and/or experience and the steps taken to complete the assignment competently*

The SCOPE OF WORK RULE of USPAP specifies three fundamental duties that must be performed by appraisers in an assignment. The first two duties are related to the development process – identification of the problem to be solved and determining the appropriate scope of work. The third duty is to *disclose the scope of work in the report*.

The disclosure obligations of the SCOPE OF WORK RULE provide the following requirement:

> *The report must contain sufficient information to allow intended users to understand the scope of work performed.*

> *Comment: Proper disclosure is required because clients and other intended users rely on the assignment results. Sufficient information includes disclosure of research and analyses performed and might also include disclosure of research and analyses not performed.*

USPAP Advisory Opinion 28 (Scope of Work Decision, Performance, and Disclosure) offers additional guidance regarding disclosure of the scope of work through these excerpts:

- *An appraiser must disclose research and analyses not performed when such disclosure is necessary for intended users to understand the report properly and not be misled.*

- *These disclosure requirements apply to the scope of work performed, rather than the scope of work initially planned by the appraiser.*

- *The appraiser must disclose the type and extent of research and analyses that were actually completed in the development process.*

- *Additionally, the information required to allow intended users to understand the scope of work may include disclosure of research and analyses not performed.*

- *There is no requirement for the scope of work description to be in a particular or separate section of the report.*

Finally, the JURISDICTIONAL EXCEPTION RULE of USPAP specifies certain disclosure requirements when there is an exception to USPAP due to applicable law or regulation. The reporting compliance requirements of the rule consist of two distinct reporting steps in an assignment involving jurisdictional exception – *an appraiser must:*

- *clearly and conspicuously disclose in the report the part of USPAP that is voided by that law or regulation; and*

- *cite in the report the law or regulation requiring this exception to USPAP compliance.*

Signed Report Certification

Within STANDARD 2, Standards Rule 2-3 addresses the obligations for the signed report certification. All written real property appraisal reports (for **BOTH** reporting options) must contain a signed certification containing language similar to the following:

I certify that, to the best of my knowledge and belief:

— *the statements of fact contained in this report are true and correct.*

— *the reported analyses, opinions, and conclusions are limited only by the reported assumptions and limiting conditions and are my personal, impartial, and unbiased professional analyses, opinions, and conclusions.*

— *I have no (or the specified) present or prospective interest in the property that is the subject of this report and no (or the specified) personal interest with respect to the parties involved.*

— *I have performed no (or the specified) services, as an appraiser or in any other capacity, regarding the property that is the subject of this report within the three-year period immediately preceding acceptance of this assignment.*

— *I have no bias with respect to the property that is the subject of this report or to the parties involved with this assignment.*

— *my engagement in this assignment was not contingent upon developing or reporting predetermined results.*

— *my compensation for completing this assignment is not contingent upon the development or reporting of a predetermined value or direction in value that favors the cause of the client, the amount of the value opinion, the attainment of a stipulated result, or the occurrence of a subsequent event directly related to the intended use of this appraisal.*

— *my analyses, opinions, and conclusions were developed, and this report has been prepared, in conformity with the Uniform Standards of Professional Appraisal Practice.*

— *I have (or have not) made a personal inspection of the property that is the subject of this report. (If more than one person signs this certification, the certification must clearly specify which individuals did and which individuals did not make a personal inspection of the appraised property.)*

— *no one provided significant real property appraisal assistance to the person signing this certification. (If there are exceptions, the name of each individual providing significant real property appraisal assistance must be stated.)*

The <u>Comment</u> to Standards Rule 2-3 addresses, among other items, the obligations of the appraiser regarding the certification signature. It states, in part:

> *A signed certification is an integral part of the appraisal report. An appraiser who signs any part of the appraisal report, including a letter of transmittal must also sign the certification.*
>
> *In an assignment that includes only assignment results developed by the real property appraiser(s), any appraiser(s) who signs a certification accepts full responsibility for all elements of the certification, for the assignment results, and for the contents of the appraisal report...*

Other portions of the <u>Comment</u> to Standards Rule 2-3 addresses acknowledgement of significant appraisal assistance in the assignment by individuals not signing the certification. The names of those providing significant assistance in an assignment **must be stated in the certification**. However, a description of what those individuals actually did that was significant to the conclusions found in the report is not specifically required to be in the certification but, depending on the reporting option, **must** be summarized or stated **in the report**.

√ **Note:** As all written appraisal reports must include a signed and dated certification, an oral report must have a certification contained in the workfile.

Workfile Requirements

A workfile must be in existence prior to a written or oral report being issued. **The workfile must include:**

- The name of the client and the identity, by name or type, of any other intended users
- True copies (which may be a photocopy or electronic copy) of any written reports
- Summaries of any oral reports or testimony, including a signed and dated certification
- All other data and documentation necessary to support the appraiser's opinions and conclusions and to show compliance with USPAP

√ **Note:** A written summary of an oral report must be added to the workfile within a reasonable time after issuing the oral report.

A **workfile** *preserves evidence of the appraiser's observance of USPAP and other information as required to support the appraiser's findings and conclusions.* An appraiser must retain the workfile for *five (5) years after completion* of the appraisal and report, or *two (2) years after the final conclusion of any judicial proceedings in which the appraiser provided testimony*, whichever comes last. The appraiser is responsible for retention or retrieval arrangements of the workfile. Workfiles are to be made available to state enforcement agencies, such as a state appraisal board conducting an investigation, or by due process of law (e.g., a subpoena).

True or False 1.6

1. *Determining the appropriate reporting option and format is a scope of work decision.* T F

2. *A Restricted Appraisal Report is less credible than an Appraisal Report.* T F

3. *An original signed appraisal report must be contained in the appraiser's workfile.* T F

4. *Workfiles must be maintained for a maximum of five years.* T F

5. *In relation to the depth of reporting, an Appraisal Report "summarizes."* T F

Summary

1.   The appraisal process of USPAP defines two separate and defined actions by an appraiser—**development** and **reporting**. The steps in the appraisal process serve as a pathway for developing and reporting an opinion of value.

2.   There are six steps in the appraisal process. The first five steps in the process relate to the *development* of a value opinion, while the last (sixth) step in the process addresses the performance obligations of *reporting*.

3.   During problem identification, the appraiser must identify certain assignment elements, which are critical to the scope of work decision. The appraiser identifies the *client and other intended users; intended use; type and definition of value; date of value opinion; relevant property characteristics;* and *other assignment conditions*.

4.   An **intended user** is a party *identified by the client* at the time of the assignment. The *client is always an intended user* in an assignment. Additional intended users may be specified by the client when the appraiser is engaged.

5.   The **intended use of the appraisal** is a *key determinant* of the research and analysis performed during the appraisal's development.

6.   Two dates are required in every appraisal report—the *effective date* and the *date of the report*. Statement 3 of USPAP defines the **effective date** as *establishing the context for the value opinion* and **date of the report** as *an indication of the perspective from which the appraiser is examining the market*. The **effective date of the value opinion** may be current, retrospective, or prospective.

7.   **Identifying the relevant characteristics of the property** includes the physical, legal, and economic characteristics.

8.   **Assignment conditions** included in an appraisal assignment include *assumptions, limiting conditions, extraordinary assumptions, hypothetical conditions, jurisdictional exceptions, laws and regulations applicable to the assignment,* and *other conditions that affect the scope of work*.

9.   An **extraordinary assumption** is something *assumed in the assignment, which, if found to be false, could alter the appraiser's opinions and conclusions*. **Hypothetical conditions** *are contrary to what the appraiser knows to exist*, but are supposed for the purpose of analysis.

10.   A **jurisdictional exception** is something that *takes away* from the purpose of USPAP. *Jurisdictional exception* can be invoked by a federal or state constitution; legislative and court-made law; or federal, state, and local administrative rules, regulations, and ordinances.

11.   The **highest and best use analysis** allows the appraiser to analyze the highest and best use for which the final opinion of value will be concluded. An opinion of highest and best use is developed by valuing the land as vacant and valuing the property as improved, and then forming conclusions.

12.   USPAP presents the *minimum* requirements for appraisers and appraisals. Clients and other intended users can *always* request additional diligence in appraisal development and reporting.

13.   The *scope of work* decision includes, but is not limited to, the extent to which the property is identified, extent to which the property is inspected, type and extent of data researched, and type and extent of analysis applied.

14.   The scope of work must include the research and analysis necessary for credible assignment results. Credible assignment results require *support from appropriate evidence and logic*, based on the intended use of the appraisal.

15. **General data** is used to form conclusions regarding the status of market elements and any change that is or has occurred, as well as any change anticipated. **Specific data** includes *all relevant information unique to the subject property* and the *comparable data*.

16. Three development methods may be used by the appraiser to determine a value opinion: The sales comparison approach, the cost approach, and the income approach. There are also various accepted techniques that may be used for development of each approach, with some being more extensive than others. The appraiser's choices in the development and application of the approaches to value is a major component of the scope of work decision.

17. USPAP Standards Rule 1-6 provides that the process of reconciliation, once the analysis has concluded, and the necessary approaches to value have been developed, consist of two steps.

18. The opinion of value in an assignment may be expressed as a single value, a range of value, or a relationship to a numeric benchmark or previous value opinion.

19. An appraisal report must be *clear, accurate, and not misleading; and contain sufficient information to be understood properly by the intended users.*

20. For written real property appraisal reports, STANDARD 2 of USPAP allows for two reporting options: An Appraisal Report or a Restricted Appraisal Report. The essential *difference* of these options is the *content and level of information* provided. As a simple way for the appraiser to distinguish each of these reporting options, USPAP uses the terms **summarize** and **state**.

21. Decisions regarding the reporting option and format chosen by an appraiser in an assignment are NOT a function of the scope of work decision. The method of reporting an appraisal chosen by an appraiser must be appropriate to the *intended use* and the *intended user* of the report.

22. USPAP contains certain disclosure requirements. Some of the disclosures must be included in specific sections of an appraisal report, such as any letter of transmittal in which conclusions are stated, or the report certification. Other disclosures may be made anywhere within an appraisal report.

23. All written real property appraisal reports must contain a signed certification containing minimum level specified certification statements. Oral reports must have a certification contained in the workfile.

24. A workfile must be in existence prior to a written or oral report being issued. **The workfile must include** the name of the client and the identity, by name or type, of any other intended users; true copies (which may be a photocopy or electronic copy) of any written reports; summaries of any oral reports or testimony, including a signed and dated certification; all other data and documentation necessary to support the appraiser's opinions and conclusions and to show compliance with USPAP.

Quiz

1. *General data does NOT include*
   a. employment rates.
   b. local employment statistics.
   c. regional economic indicators.
   d. the subject's site dimensions.

2. *All are acceptable methods for stating the final opinion of value EXCEPT a*
   a. mathematical average of the approaches used in the assignment.
   b. range of value.
   c. relationship to a benchmark.
   d. single dollar amount.

3. *An extraordinary assumption is something*
   a. known to be false, but is being supposed as true.
   b. supposed to be true but, if found to be false, could lead to different results.
   c. the appraiser can't find out and that won't affect value anyway.
   d. used in appraisal of new construction.

4. *Which is NOT a hypothetical condition?*
   a. A proposed survey is put on record.
   b. Proposed improvements are complete.
   c. A mechanical component, which appears to be in good condition, actually operates.
   d. The new construction is completed as described on a current effective date.

5. *The purpose of the appraisal should always be*
   a. an assumption of the appraisal.
   b. highest and best use of the property on the date viewed.
   c. to determine market value.
   d. to develop an opinion of value appropriate to the intended use of the appraisal.

6. *One function of the highest and best use analysis is to*
   a. decide whether improvements should be left as is, changed, or razed.
   b. indicate the value of the land now, and at a future date.
   c. see what the property would be worth if zoning were changed.
   d. suggest to the appraiser which appraisal form to use.

7. *What primarily determines the date of the value opinion?*
   a. highest and best use
   b. intended use
   c. intended user
   d. type and definition of value

8. *An appraisal report*
   a. always has some hypothetical conditions.
   b. can be written or oral.
   c. is available for use by anyone to whom it is given.
   d. must be in writing.

9. *Defining the problem primarily assists the appraiser with*
   a. defining highest and best use.
   b. the final opinion of value.
   c. quoting the appraisal fee.
   d. a scope of work decision.

10. *The decision of which approach(es) to use in an assignment is primarily driven by*
    a. age of the property.
    b. highest and best use.
    c. quality of the sales comparison data.
    d. scope of work.

11. *An Appraisal Report _____ certain information and analyses performed in an appraisal assignment.*
    a. abbreviates
    b. interprets
    c. states
    d. summarizes

12. *The value opinions expressed in an Appraisal Report and a Restricted Appraisal Report for the same property, by the same appraiser, and on the same effective date*
    a. are always expressed as a single number.
    b. must be stated in the certification of the report.
    c. should be equally credible.
    d. will be developed using a different scope of work.

13. *When jurisdictional exception is an assignment condition, the report must include a(n)*

a. appropriate disclosure of the exception in the certification.

b. citation of the law or regulation requiring the exception.

c. disclosure that USPAP does not apply in the assignment.

d. extraordinary assumption regarding its use.

14. *When an appraiser has paid a fee or given a thing of value in connection with the procurement of an appraisal assignment, the report must include a statement that*

a. discloses payment of the fee or that an item was given.

b. hypothetical conditions are present in the assignment.

c. jurisdiction exception is taking precedence in the assignment.

d. sets forth the amount of the fee or value of the item given.

15. *When significant appraisal assistance has been provided to the appraiser in an assignment, the extent of that assistance must be _____ or _____ in the report, and the name(s) of those individual providing the assistance must be _____ in the certification.*

a. described/summarized/disclosed

b. discussed/narrated/summarized

c. summarized/detailed/stated

d. summarized/stated/stated

Chapter 2

Property Analysis and Description – Land

Analyzing and describing the land in an appraisal assignment is a development step that must be thoughtfully performed. Appraisers must be equipped to recognize all of the elements of the property from a legal, economic, and physical standpoint. To adequately perform the analysis and appropriately describe the property, an appraiser must be able to analyze the market as well as the marketability of the particular property.

In this chapter, legal descriptions, analysis and description of the market area and neighborhood, and geographic and geologic characteristics and their analysis will be discussed.

Appurtenant Easement An easement that burdens one piece of land for the benefit of another.

Area Variance An exception that allows a property owner to legally deviate from certain building codes or setback requirements.

Balance 1. A condition that exists in the real estate market when there are slightly more homes available than buyers. 2. The right mix of **c**apital, **e**ntrepreneurship/management, **l**abor, and **l**and that results in best return on investment from land (remember: CELL). This determines land's highest and best use.

Building Density A limit on the number of buildings that may be constructed within a given space.

Business Cycles General swings in business, resulting in expanding and -contracting activity during different phases of the cycle.

CC&Rs A declaration of Covenants, Conditions, and Restrictions; usually recorded by a developer to create a general plan of private restrictions for a subdivision.

Conditional A land use that does not comply with the general zoning rules for the zone in which it is located, but is permitted because it benefits the public—i.e., a hospital in a residential neighborhood. Also called **Special Exception**.

Covenant 1. A contract. 2. A promise. 3. A guarantee (express or implied) in a document such as a deed or lease. 4. A restrictive covenant.

Dominant Tenant A person who has easement rights on another's property; either the owner of a dominant tenement or someone who has an easement in gross.

Key Terms

(Continued on page 32)

Legal Descriptions For Land

Before an appraiser begins to accumulate data for use in the land analysis valuation, he or she needs to be sure that data is collected on the correct parcel of land. Sometimes the address is not enough, particularly when dealing with vacant land. Identifying the correct parcel involves obtaining and verifying the legal description of the land. The test of a valid description of property is the ability to identify and distinguish that property from any and all other parcels of land.

There are three primary types of legal descriptions:

1.   Government survey system
2.   Lot and block system
3.   Metes and bounds system.

There are several important measures that must be remembered that relate to many legal descriptions.

Important measurements to know:

- Each **township** is six miles by six miles or 36 square miles.
- Each **township** is divided into 36 one-mile by one-mile township sections.
- Each **township section** contains 640 acres or six square miles.
- Each **acre** contains 43,560 square feet.
- Each **mile** is 5,280 feet.
- A **rod** or **pole** each consists of 16.5 feet or 5.5 yards.
- A **chain** consists of 66 feet, or four rods.

Government Survey System

The **government survey system** (also called **government rectangular survey** or **rectangular survey system;** some parts of the country also use the similar Virginia Military Survey System) is a *type of legal description for land referencing principal meridians and base lines designated throughout much of the country.* With the government survey system, a parcel of land is identified by directions and coordinates that use these lines as reference points.

Key Terms

Dominant Tenement A property that benefits from an easement.

Easement A right to use some part of another person's real property for a particular purpose. An easement is irrevocable and creates an interest in the property.

Easement in Gross An easement that benefits a person instead of a piece of land; there is a dominant tenant but no dominant tenement.

Frontage The dimension across the access side of a parcel of land (usually along the road). When a lot size is stated, the first number is the lot frontage.

Government Survey System A legal description for land, referencing principal meridians and base lines designated throughout the country. Also called **Government Rectangular Survey** or **Rectangular Survey System**.

Grandfathered A pre-existing condition allowed to continue under old laws, even though laws have since changed.

Inlot A middle or inside lot.

Life Cycles A general pattern of four phases (growth, stability, decline, and revitalization), which neighborhoods, districts, and other market areas typically (but not universally) go through.

Location Exact position of real estate.

Metes and Bounds System A legal description that starts at an easily identifiable point of beginning (POB), then describes the property's boundaries in terms of courses (compass directions) and distances, ultimately returning to the POB.

Neighborhood Any constant, contiguous area that may be identified by similar characteristics of physical boundaries. Also referred to as **Market Area**.

Nonconforming Use Property use that does not conform to current zoning laws, but is allowed because the property was being used that way before the new zoning law was passed.- Also called grandfathered use. *See:* **Grandfathered**.

Additional *north-south lines*, called **ranges** or range lines, run parallel to principal meridians at six-mile intervals; and additional *east-west lines,* called **township lines**, run parallel to base lines at six-mile intervals. *This process divides land into six mile by six mile squares* called **townships**.

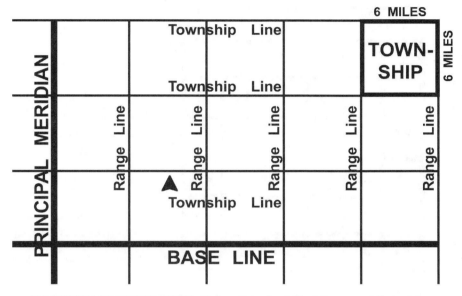

TOWNSHIP IDENTIFICATION: Using Principal Meridians and Base Lines
(Each Principal Meridian and Base Line has a unique name or number.)

Pass-through Zoning Zones set up in a hierarchical fashion, such that all uses above the current zoning are permitted. Pass-through zoning goes in only one direction.

Plat Map A detailed survey map of a subdivision or other grouped lots of land, recorded in the county where the land is located. Subdivided property is often called **Platted Property**.

Progression A principle that says the value of a home is positively affected by the other homes in an area. Usually said about the "worst" home in the "best" area.

Regression A principle that says the value of a home is negatively affected by the other homes in an area. Usually said about the "best" home in the "worst" area.

Restrictive Covenant 1. A limitation on real property use, imposed by a former owner. 2. A promise to do or not do an act relating to real property, usually the owner's promise to not use property in a particular way. Cannot cause forfeiture of title.

Servient Tenant The owner of a servient tenement is someone whose property is burdened by an easement.

Servient Tenement A property that is burdened by an easement.

Setback Requirements Provisions in a zoning ordinance that do not allow structures to be built within a certain distance of property lines.

Side Yard The area between a building and one side boundary of the lot on which it is located.

Use Variance An exception that permits a property owner to use land in a way that is not allowed in that zone, such as a commercial use in a residential zone.

Variance A permit obtained from the local zoning authority allowing the holder to use property or build a structure in a way that violates the zoning ordinance. *Compare*: **Conditional Use**; **Nonconforming Use**.

Zoning Laws Local ordinances dividing a city, county, etc., into zones, specifying different types of land use in different areas. This is a type of government restriction via police power.

Key Terms

The 36 square miles of a township are subdivided into 36 sections of one square mile (640 acres) each. Each section in a township is numbered sequentially, so that the land parcel can be located by referring to the section number and subsequent references to half and quarter sections with compass points. Any portion of land that cannot be divided into equal fractional lots is designated as a **government lot**.

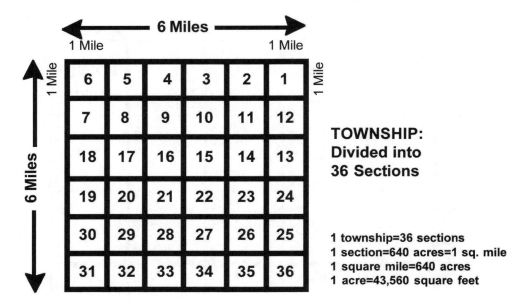

TOWNSHIP: Divided into 36 Sections

1 township=36 sections
1 section=640 acres=1 sq. mile
1 square mile=640 acres
1 acre=43,560 square feet

A typical parcel of land is located within a section. A legal description from this method would use directions and quadrants. Look at the following diagram.

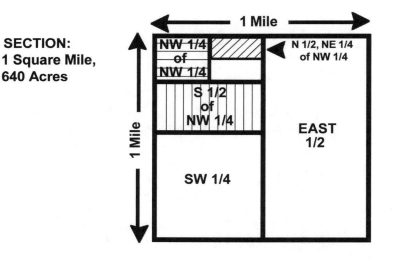

SECTION: 1 Square Mile, 640 Acres

A legal description might read: N 1/2, NE 1/4 of NW 1/4. Always start from the end of the description and work backwards. First find the NW 1/4, then at the upper left corner of the section, then determine which part of the NW 1/4 is being referenced. Here are some examples.

Example 1: The S 1/2 of NW 1/4 is shaded like this:

Example 2: The NW 1/4 of NW 1/4 is shaded like this:

Example 3: The N 1/2, NE 1/4 of NW 1/4 is shaded like this:

With the government survey system, calculating acreage is rather easy. Again, start from the end of the legal description and work backward from right to left. An entire section of land in the government survey system always equal to 640 acres, therefore take 640 and divide by the denominators (bottom number) for each fractional part.

Example 1: For the S 1/2 of NW 1/4, take 640 ÷ 4 ÷ 2 = 80 acres.

Example 2: For the NE 1/4 of NW 1/4, take 640 ÷ 4 ÷ 4 = 40 acres.

Example 3: For the N 1/2, NE 1/4 of NW 1/4, take 640 ÷ 4 ÷ 4 ÷ 2 = 20 acres.

Lot and Block System

The **lot and block system** is *a type of legal description used for platted property.* Platted property is *any property that has been subdivided from a large tract into smaller lots.* These lots are numbered, first with a block number for the area, then individually with each lot receiving its own number. The lot and block description states only the property's lot number and block number in the subdivision, so to find the exact location of the parcel of land, the appraiser must consult a **plat map.**

Plat Map

A plat map is *a detailed survey map of a subdivision (or other grouped lots of land), recorded in the county where the land is located.* Different jurisdictions have different rules about when land must be platted and a plat map recorded.

Example

In some jurisdictions, dividing land into five or more lots of less than five acres each may constitute that the land is being developed as a subdivision, which would require filing of a proposed plat map and other documentation with local authorities for special approval.

Plat maps are generally found in public records. A plat book covering the land's location would contain the specific plat map, allowing someone to find the exact location of the lot using the lot and block number. In addition to the lot and block numbers, the plat map usually will also give details, such as streets and public easements. Other information may include zoning, elevations, and flood plains.

Example

In the following diagram, the legal description of the shaded area is Lot 19, Block 17 of Golden Valley Estate.

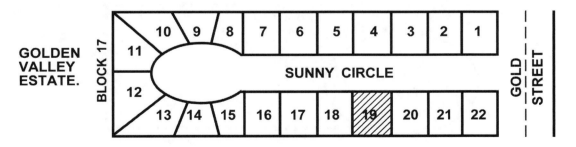

Sample Subdivision Plat Map: Golden Valley Estate, Block 17, Lots 1-22

Metes and Bounds System

The **metes and bounds system** is *a type of legal description that starts at an easily identifiable point of beginning (P.O.B.), then describes the property's boundaries in terms of courses (compass directions) and* *distances, ultimately returning to the point of beginning.* A legal description may also refer to monuments, which are fixed physical objects used as reference points.

√ **Note:** The point of beginning might also be referred to as the point of origin. Monuments are also called markers.

This type of legal description gets its name from the way land is described. From the P.O.B., a line is extended in a specified direction (metes). The line changes direction at specific points (bounds). The bounds are often permanent physical objects (e.g., monuments or markers). Care must be taken when selecting monuments to make sure that they are more or less permanent. A tree that is chosen as a monument may be cut down at a future date. A lake that is chosen as a marker may have the shore recede. Often the safest marker is a **pin**. A pin is *simply a rod that is driven into the ground.* This may be done by the original owner, a subsequent owner, or a surveyor.

The final important thing to remember about metes and bounds descriptions is that they must always return to the P.O.B. or the point of origin. Descriptions that do not return to the point of beginning are considered inadequate and inaccurate. They must be corrected if such an error exists, or if any markers or monuments have been moved or destroyed.

Example

A legal description of the land in the following diagram might read:

Beginning at a pin in the center of Miller Road, go SE 300 feet at an angle til the edge of the road meets another pin, then go due south 250 feet til you hit a pin at the adjoining property's fence, then go due west 350 feet to a pin at the edge of Miller's Pond, go due north 200 feet to another pin, then go due west 100 feet to a pin near the base of an old oak tree, then go due north til you hit the road, then NE at an angle to the point of beginning at the pin in the center of Miller Road.

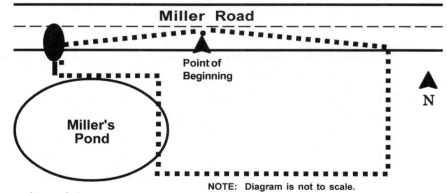

Sample Metes and Bounds Survey

General Property Description

After the site has been identified, the appraiser can begin collecting and analyzing the appropriate data for other land characteristics. In addition to analyzing *general data* regarding the physical, economic, governmental, and social forces, an appraiser will also focus on the *specific data* factors, which are important to the land analysis.

It is important that an appraiser be thorough in the data collection process, recognizing all of the elements relevant for analysis in the scope of work. Property description, in general, encompasses not only the subject property, but also how everything surrounding the property affects it. Therefore, the information gathered for the property description consists of data that is either general or specific in nature. Much of this information is later funneled down to help recognize the market appeal factors that may affect the appraiser's opinions and conclusions. Intended users in the assignment also need to understand the appraiser's process and rationale for their diligence and conclusions. Thus, consistent with the specific reporting option, the data collected and analyzed should be reported in a manner that allows intended users to clearly understand the characteristics of the property being appraised.

If the subject property is located in an area for which the appraiser is familiar and experienced, **general data** may be already stored in the appraiser's *data files* or *databases*, and may only require verification and testing for the data's current relevance and applicability. However, **specific data** is *gathered for the subject property in each assignment*. In some cases, if the appraiser has the data on the subject property from a previous assignment, that information may only need to be verified and be updated as necessary.

We will step through some of the most common information needed and the sources used by appraisers for describing property, along with how the information is described and illustrated in appraisal reports. Keep in mind though, this information is general. To meet some client and regulatory requirements, additional, specific commentary or documentation must be provided by the appraiser in the appraisal report.

> ***IMPORTANT POINTS…***
>
> - *The property description concerns not just the subject property, but everything around it.*
> - *Collected and analyzed data should be fully explained, and conclusions reported in a manner easily understood by the intended users.*
> - *Data collected and analyzed is **general** (in regard to the subject's surroundings) and **specific** (in regard to the subject itself).*

Basic Subject Information

Some of the subject information gathered for an appraisal is straightforward, such as the address, legal description, tax information, etc. Much of this data can be gathered from public records: Legal description, assessor's parcel number, taxes, current owner, etc. Flood information, map reference, and census tract may take a little more research, but are easily attainable. Census data or other data on age, occupation, income level, etc., should be gathered and compared as part of this final step. (A good resource for information is www.census.gov.) "Neighborhood" information could be simply the name of a subdivision or other easily identifiable moniker, such as a recognizable and common reference to an area of a town or city, or perhaps a specific suburban or rural reference. An important point to keep in mind is that the information must be clear and understandable to intended users. Locally, the "Nicholas Heights" area of a large city might be commonly known, but for an intended user with no local knowledge, the reference probably means little unless further explanation is provided. Typically, more detailed neighborhood information is given in the appraisal report in order to assist intended users in understanding the setting of the property being analyzed.

In some cases, the client may furnish some primary information such as the property address, terms of a pending transaction, the property occupant, etc. Other information, such as parcel number and real estate taxes, often may not be known by the client, and must be researched by the appraiser. Fortunately, much of this information is available online in most areas.

Elements of Subject's Description

Property Address	• Street address. city, state, county/parish, and zip code • If there is no street address or number (such as a vacant lot or land parcel, or some rural areas), identify the property in relation to the nearest intersection. • USPAP requires that the property in an appraisal assignment be identified.
Owner of Record	• The name exactly as stated on public records.
Legal Description	• The legal description is usually a lot and block, metes and bounds, or government survey. Some localities use the geodetic survey system. • Often, especially for metes and bounds descriptions, a copy of the subject's legal description is included as addenda in the appraisal report. • Deed reference information, such as the volume and page where the deed is recorded in county records, is usually also noted and reported, *but is not in itself a legal description.* • A property address is **not** a legal description.
Auditor/Assessor's Parcel or Tax Information Number	• This number is usually found on the auditor or assessor's tax records and corresponds with tax or county/city record maps.
Real Estate Taxes and Assessments	• Tax information is collected from public records. • Do the taxes appear to be typical for the market? • Have all improvements been assessed? • Are the taxes anticipated to increase due to a sizable tax levy or recent improvements to the property? • The appraiser should note any tax reduction programs common in some areas (e.g., for senior citizens, handicapped, some agricultural properties). • The appraiser should note any special assessments for the property for street lighting, sewer and water projects, etc.; the appraiser should also note how long the assessment is for, if the assessment is common for the area, and any affect on the marketability of the property.
Census Tract	• This information is found on the U.S. Census Bureau's Website— www.census.gov.
Occupant	• The appraiser should indicate if the property is occupied by the owner, a tenant, or if the property is vacant.
Property Rights Being Appraised	• This determination is made during *problem identification.* • In most cases, the appraiser will be valuing the fee simple interest of the property. • The subject of an appraisal could be a partial interest.

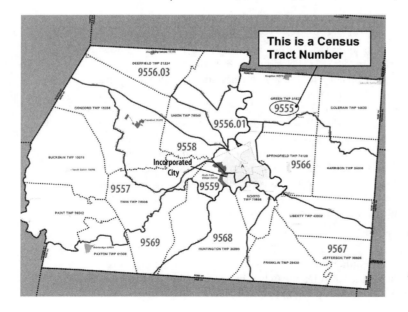

Census Tract Map

The numbers represent census tracts. The darker lines represent each census tract's boundaries.

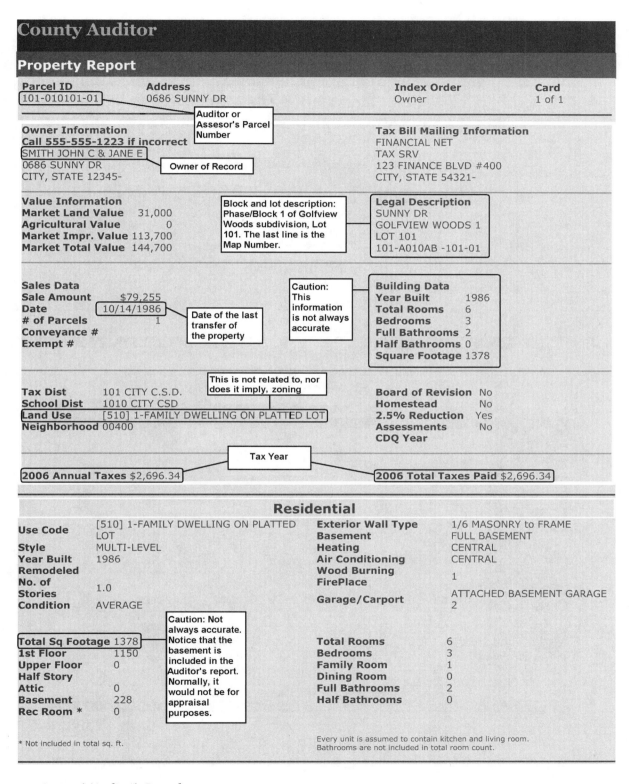

County Auditor

Property Report

Parcel ID	Address	Index Order	Card
101-010101-01	0686 SUNNY DR	Owner	1 of 1

Auditor or Assesor's Parcel Number

Owner Information
Call 555-555-1223 if incorrect
SMITH JOHN C & JANE E
0686 SUNNY DR
CITY, STATE 12345-

Owner of Record

Tax Bill Mailing Information
FINANCIAL NET
TAX SRV
123 FINANCE BLVD #400
CITY, STATE 54321-

Value Information
Market Land Value   31,000
Agricultural Value   0
Market Impr. Value 113,700
Market Total Value 144,700

Block and lot description: Phase/Block 1 of Golfview Woods subdivision, Lot 101. The last line is the Map Number.

Legal Description
SUNNY DR
GOLFVIEW WOODS 1
LOT 101
101-A010AB -101-01

Sales Data
Sale Amount $79,255
Date   10/14/1986
# of Parcels   1
Conveyance #
Exempt #

Date of the last transfer of the property

Caution: This information is not always accurate

Building Data
Year Built   1986
Total Rooms   6
Bedrooms   3
Full Bathrooms   2
Half Bathrooms   0
Square Footage 1378

This is not related to, nor does it imply, zoning

Tax Dist   101 CITY C.S.D.
School Dist   1010 CITY CSD
Land Use   [510] 1-FAMILY DWELLING ON PLATTED LOT
Neighborhood 00400

Board of Revision No
Homestead   No
2.5% Reduction Yes
Assessments   No
CDQ Year

Tax Year

2006 Annual Taxes $2,696.34

2006 Total Taxes Paid $2,696.34

Residential

Use Code	[510] 1-FAMILY DWELLING ON PLATTED LOT	**Exterior Wall Type**	1/6 MASONRY to FRAME
		Basement	FULL BASEMENT
Style	MULTI-LEVEL	**Heating**	CENTRAL
Year Built	1986	**Air Conditioning**	CENTRAL
Remodeled		**Wood Burning FirePlace**	1
No. of Stories	1.0		
Condition	AVERAGE	**Garage/Carport**	ATTACHED BASEMENT GARAGE 2

Caution: Not always accurate. Notice that the basement is included in the Auditor's report. Normally, it would not be for appraisal purposes.

Total Sq Footage	1378		
1st Floor	1150	**Total Rooms**	6
Upper Floor	0	**Bedrooms**	3
Half Story		**Family Room**	1
Attic	0	**Dining Room**	0
Basement	228	**Full Bathrooms**	2
Rec Room *	0	**Half Bathrooms**	0

* Not included in total sq. ft.

Every unit is assumed to contain kitchen and living room. Bathrooms are not included in total room count.

Assessor's/Auditor's Record

The Assessor's or Auditor's property (or tax) record contains myriad data and information an appraiser uses in an appraisal. While property or tax records may look and be organized differently in various jurisdictions, this illustration highlights several information points that are commonly found in most records. (continued on following pages)

Improvements

Type	Improvement	Dimensions	Measurements	Year Built

No Records Found

Sketch/Photo

Transfer

Transfer Date	Conveyance	Owner	# Parcels	Sale Price
10/14/1986		SMITH JOHN C & JANE E	0001	$79,255

Tax Information
Current Year Tax Detail

	Prior	Prior-Adj	1ST Half	1ST Adj	2ND Half	2ND Adj
Orig Tax	$0.00	$0.00	$2,557.07	$0.00	$2,557.07	$0.00
Reduction		$1,016.30		$0.00	$1,016.30	$0.00
Subtotal	$0.00		$1,540.77		$1,540.77	
10% RB			$154.08	$0.00	$154.08	$0.00
2.5% RB			$38.52	$0.00	$38.52	$0.00
Homestead CR			$0.00	$0.00	$0.00	$0.00
Net Total	$0.00		$1,348.17		$1,348.17	
Penalty / Int	$0.00	$0.00	$0.00	$0.00	$0.00	$0.00
RE Chrg	$0.00		$1,348.17		$1,348.17	
RE Paid	$0.00		$1,348.17		$1,348.17	
SA Chrg	$0.00		$0.00		$0.00	
SA Paid	$0.00		$0.00		$0.00	
Total Owed	$0.00		$1,348.17		$1,348.17	
Total Paid	$0.00		$1,348.17		$1,348.17	$2,696.34
Balance Due	$0.00		$0.00		$0.00	
Future Charge			$0.00		$0.00	$0.00
Future Paid			$0.00		$0.00	$0.00

Detail of Special Assessment

	Prior	Prior-Adj	1ST Half	1ST Adj	2ND Half	2ND Adj

No Records Found

Payment Information

Date	Half	Proj	Prior	1ST Half	2ND Half	Surplus
06/14/07	2-06		$0.00	$0.00	$1,348.17	$0.00
01/19/07	1-06		$0.00	$1,348.17	$0.00	$0.00
06/16/06	2-05		$0.00	$0.00	$1,253.38	$0.00
01/18/06	1-05		$0.00	$1,253.38	$0.00	$0.00
06/16/05	2-04		$0.00	$0.00	$1,189.86	$0.00
01/14/05	1-04		$0.00	$1,189.86	$0.00	$0.00

Levy Info

Proposed Levies for August 7, 2007 election	Mills	Current Monthly Tax	Estimated Monthly Tax	Note

Levies Passed or Commencing in Tax Year 2007	Mills	Current Monthly Tax	Estimated Monthly Tax	Note

Tax Distribution

Current Owner (s)	SMITH JOHN C & JANE E	Tax District	101 - CITY C.S.D.
		School District	1010 - CITY CSD

County			
	General Fund		$65.13
	Children's Services		$160.66
	Alcohol, Drug & Mental Health Services		$97.30
	MRDD		$202.01
	Metro Parks		$18.44
	County Zoo		$28.30
	Senior Options		$28.02
School Dist	CITY		$1,866.45
Township			
Vocational School	CENTRAL STATE		$57.61
City / Village	CITY		$139.16
Library / Other			$33.26
Total			$2,696.34

Tax Year 2006
The above distribution was updated on 5/8/2007

Analyzing and Describing the Neighborhood and Market

Once the information needed for the subject property has been gathered and identified, the appraiser can begin **collecting** and **analyzing** neighborhood and market data. First, some key definitions should be reviewed.

Market Area: A market area is the broadest of all terms identifying the boundaries of a particular area. When describing a market area, the appraiser is providing an account of the land uses and characteristics of typical market participants within the defined area.

Neighborhood: When describing a neighborhood, which is *a compilation or a group of complimentary uses*, the appraiser is looking at all of the uses, though varied, which create the overall environment. The complementary uses could be a mix of residential, commercial, service, as well as other amenities.

District: The term district is the narrowest of definitions of a market area. A district is *an area consisting of one particular land use,* such as multi-family residential, commercial, and industrial, etc.

When an appraiser analyzes and describes a market area, there could be more than one neighborhood or district included in the process.

Market analysis is one of the steps in the valuation process discussed in Chapter 1. In order for the market analysis to be performed, however, certain neighborhood and market characteristics must be recognized. Here, the appraiser will look at two forms of data—*economic* and *physical*. Once the market has been analyzed, that data is then considered primary information for performing the highest and best use analysis, which will be discussed later. For this, as well as all data used to describe the property, the source of that information should be cited in the appraisal report, appropriate to the reporting option chosen.

Neighborhood Characteristics

Location of a particular property, within the context of geographic characteristics, will be discussed in the next section of this chapter. But, before that analysis takes place, an appraiser must consider the property's location within a community. The appraiser often must communicate the neighborhood characteristics thoroughly since often the client or other users of the appraisal may not be familiar with the area. For example, the distinction between "urban" and "suburban" is fairly obvious in large cities, but could be more problematic in less populated areas.

Neighborhood Boundaries

A neighborhood is a group of houses or properties that share a common or complimentary characteristic(s). Properties might share physical characteristics (e.g., similar style or age) or physical boundaries (e.g., natural boundaries such as a river, or artificial boundaries such as a highway). Neighborhoods can also be defined by other characteristics, such as zoning, demographics, or income levels. In fact, almost anything can define a neighborhood, **except** *for race, religion, national origin, ancestry, familial status, disability, or any other protected classes.* A neighborhood is simply a small part of a larger community.

When defining a neighborhood, an appraiser often starts with natural and artificial geographic boundaries of an area. Natural boundaries include the obvious rivers and lakes, but also the less-obvious parks, mountains, or valleys. Artificial boundaries include manmade things like streets, highways, and railroads, and may also be drawn along school, zoning, or political districts. Next, the appraiser performs a personal inspection of the area, looking for similarity of land usage and types of improvements, as well as consistency of building style, landscaping, and even maintenance or upkeep. Finally, the appraiser confirms neighborhood boundaries by comparing the social and economic characteristics of the area.

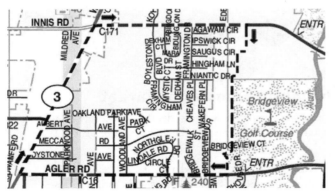

Neighborhood Boundary Map

The neighborhood boundary map serves to illustrate what the appraiser has defined as the subject's immediate neighborhood. The description for the map above would be Innis Road to the north, Bridgeview Golf Course to the east, Agler Road to the south, and Route 3 to the west.

IMPORTANT POINTS...

- *Data regarding the neighborhood and its characteristics are necessary to perform a market analysis, which is, in turn, necessary to perform the highest and best use analysis.*
- *A **neighborhood** is defined by its common or complimentary characteristics (e.g., similar architectural style, zoning, or occupant income level) or physical boundaries—either natural or artificial (e.g., a natural river or a manmade road).*
- *A neighborhood may **not** be defined by race, religion, or any other protected class.*
- *The characteristics of the neighborhood create market appeal or resistance.*

Elements of a Neighborhood Description	
Neighborhood Name	• The appraiser may identify the neighborhood by a subdivision name, or a common reference to an area.
Neighborhood Boundaries	• The appraiser must describe the boundaries of the defined neighborhood to create an understanding of neighborhood composition. • The neighborhood boundary description may include any physical boundaries by streets, city or jurisdictional area, manmade barriers, rivers, etc.
Neighborhood Description	• Here, the appraiser describes the factors that would create market appeal or resistance: - Level of maintenance - Housing styles, ages, sizes, etc. - Surrounding land uses - Presence of employment, services and shopping, including the time distance relationship, or *linkages*, to employment and amenities - Stability and variety of employment - Overall appeal of the neighborhood compared to competitive neighborhoods in the same market - Schools and their proximity, as well as the availability of transportation • If the neighborhood is a smaller market within a larger market, the relationship and characteristics of the larger market should be described.

Neighborhood Market Conditions

Gathering and evaluating neighborhood data is an important part of the appraisal process. Much emphasis is placed on this analysis because so much of a property's value is dictated by the neighborhood in which the property is located. For this analysis, information must be gathered that is *both* general and specific. The analysis entails looking at all of the conditions and trends within the determined market area and neighborhood of the subject property.

Part of the market analysis is focused upon observing:

- Changes in property use in the area.
- Overall changes to maintenance levels in the area.
- The number of available properties being marketed in the area.

Change taking place in an area can be short-term or long-term in nature. An appraiser must also recognize when change is taking place, or is about to take place, in a neighboring or nearby area that could impact, positively or negatively, the defined subject market.

The four forces that influence the value of all aspects of the real estate market—**p**hysical, **e**conomic, **g**overnmental, and **s**ocial forces (P-E-G-S)—also influence neighborhoods. The effects can be positive or negative. These factors can serve to make a particular neighborhood more or less desirable and hence, grow or decline based on the characteristics of properties in the neighborhood.

Physical Forces

There are many factors to consider when examining land or site, including the dimensions and shape of the usable area. The appraiser can use various sources from which to obtain this data.

Configuration of the parcel of land is important as well as how the land is situated in relation to the road and other parcels of land. Generally, a large parcel is more valuable than a smaller one—but not always; a commercial parcel with significant road frontage is often more valuable than one with limited frontage and visibility.

Other physical factors specific to the property include topography of the land (flat or hilly), drainage, soil type, and view. Environmental issues are also an important point of recognition. In addition, the presence or absence of utilities or other site improvements should be noted. The location of the lot within a neighborhood, position of the lot (corner, cul-de-sac, etc.), and access to the lot are other factors taken into consideration. This data can be obtained through a personal inspection by the appraiser and from public records.

Economic Forces

There are numerous conditions within the market that are recognized as economic forces. Business cycles can create swings of activity affecting available supply and demand. For instance, if a new factory is located in a particular market area, and an undersupply of existing houses is available, it would be a necessity to develop lots on which to build new houses. This economic factor would positively affect the value of land and is directly tied to employment. However, an oversupply of available building sites would occur if land developers developed more sites than the current demand could absorb in a reasonable period. The cost of money, or interest rates, impacts land values when the interest rate of a construction loan is perceived as unfavorable and discourages new construction.

Governmental Forces

In most cases, the most recognizable governmental force is zoning. Most land would be worth more if it can be legally used for commercial purposes instead of for residential homes, but the government uses zoning laws to limit the uses of property. Government restrictions on land use also include public easements for roads or sewer, and building codes that restrict building size or placement. Some non-government restrictions can also affect value in the same way, namely private easements and deed restrictions.

Other governmental forces that affect value are taxes and public services. A heavy tax burden can lower the value of a site, whereas tax abatements can make a site more attractive. Public services that are nearby, such as police and fire, can make a site more desirable than one with services perceived as too far away to provide adequate service and protection. This data can be obtained from public records or by verification with the appropriate authority.

Social Forces

Many of the social aspects regarding **demographics, buyer's tastes, and social trends** have had dramatic impact on what and where people want to build, the size of the site they desire, and location. Some of the data for the analysis of social forces can be obtained from market observation and interviews with market participants. Certain data is also collected by the U.S. Census Bureau and is helpful in the appraiser's analysis.

U.S. Census Bureau

American FactFinder

Fact Sheet

Anytown, USA

2000 2005 data not available for this geography

Reference Map

View a Fact Sheet for a race, ethnic, or ancestry group

Census 2000 Demographic Profile Highlights:

General Characteristics - show more

>>	Number	Percent	U.S.
Total population	26,705		
Male	12,688	47.5	49.1%
Female	14,017	52.5	50.9%
Median age (years)	34.0	(X)	35.3
Under 5 years	2,076	7.8	6.8%
18 years and over	19,782	74.1	74.3%
65 years and over	4,140	15.5	12.4%
One race	26,051	97.6	97.6%
White	23,801	89.1	75.1%
Black or African American	1,321	4.9	12.3%
American Indian and Alaska Native	144	0.5	0.9%
Asian	309	1.2	3.6%
Native Hawaiian and Other Pacific Islander	30	0.1	0.1%
Some other race	446	1.7	5.5%
Two or more races	654	2.4	2.4%
Hispanic or Latino (of any race)	960	3.6	12.5%
Household population	25,608	95.9	97.2%
Group quarters population	1,097	4.1	2.8%
Average household size	2.32	(X)	2.59
Average family size	2.99	(X)	3.14
Total housing units	12,450		
Occupied housing units	11,036	88.6	91.0%
Owner-occupied housing units	4,740	43.0	66.2%

Census Data

Information on demographics, housing, and area economics is available from the U.S. Census Bureau at www.census.gov.

State of the Market

Another observation by the appraiser regarding change of a neighborhood or market area is for evidence of whether the neighborhood is experiencing change related to its life cycle, or if transition is taking place in the area. **Transition** is when *the land use is changing*. Transition is a complete change of land use, such as from residential to commercial. Transition is typically long-term. However, neighborhoods could go through up to four stages in its life cycle.

Four phases neighborhoods go through in their life cycles are:

1. Growth
2. Stability/equilibrium
3. Decline
4. Revitalization

Growth

Growth is *the first stage a neighborhood goes through, when property values tend to rise as development activity begins and continues.* Buyers fuel this growth by continuing to purchase property in the area. This demand equals acceptance of the area and the prices being charged for housing, and causes the area to grow into maturity.

Stability

Stability, or sometimes called a form of **equilibrium**, is *the second stage a neighborhood goes through, when the area is built up to the point there is little, if any, vacant property.* Demand typically remains high, as buyers continue to prefer this neighborhood as it enters a mature stage. Prices rarely drop during this period. Stability and maturity are characteristics of the equilibrium stage in a neighborhood's life cycle.

It is important to note that neighborhoods could remain stable indefinitely.

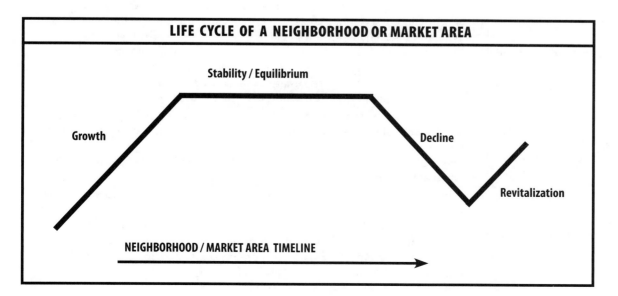

LIFE CYCLE OF A NEIGHBORHOOD OR MARKET AREA

Stability / Equilibrium

Growth

Decline

Revitalization

NEIGHBORHOOD / MARKET AREA TIMELINE

Decline

Decline is when *property values begin to fall as demand falls—possibly due to some type of change that has, or is, occurring.* Decline in a neighborhood is typically observable through decay or deterioration. This, in turn, leads to the area becoming even less desirable and the cycle feeds on itself. A less desirable area in which properties exhibit deferred maintenance means lower prices, and lower prices mean lower-income residents with less money to spend on repairs will be attracted to the properties. As values decline, the problem is compounded by conversion of some properties to rental units (where upkeep is often not as meticulous as by owner-occupants), or to commercial uses. This can accelerate the decline.

Revitalization

Revitalization is *the final stage a neighborhood goes through, when property values begin to rise again as demand increases, resulting in increased renovation and rehabilitation.* After a complete revitalization stage, the neighborhood can return to a stability/equilibrium stage and the cycle will begin again. Revitalization occurs when properties are again seen as attractive for their location, architectural features, or even price. Whatever the reason, people begin to spend money to fix up these homes and they become desirable again. Revitalization is typically the result of some form of public effort, such as urban renewal in which properties are revitalized and current residents are often displaced.

Related to the process of rapid revitalization is the concept of gentrification. **Gentrification** is a form of revitalization with displacement of current residents that takes place in a more natural fashion and is not driven by any public movement.

Elements for Describing Neighborhood Market Conditions	
Economic Climate	• The appraiser should consider and detail the economic conditions of the neighborhood that affect the marketability and values of properties in that neighborhood, including, but not limited to: - Interest rates - Employment - Per capita income and wealth - Business trends - Seasonal trends - National and regional trends and events
Supply and Demand	• The appraiser should analyze local inventories of existing properties, new construction, and planned construction, reflecting the results of that analysis with economic data regarding anticipated demand of buyers in the market. • Historic, current, and projected data are used to determine demand. • Sources for observing supply and demand include data published or furnished by local government officials, real estate professionals, business professionals, and others that typically monitor business and real estate trends.
Property Value Trends	• One of the best methods for determining property value trends is to analyze the arm's length sale of the same property, in the same condition, over (preferably) a period of time. • The appraiser should analyze and describe the cause of change in value trends and whether the trend is expected to continue.
Predominant Value and Age	• Here, the appraiser describes the most common age and value typically seen in the market. • The appraiser will observe the neighborhood, noting the high and low extremes. • The appraiser's description should include how the subject property is positioned in this range and whether *regression* or *progression* of the subject property is occurring, if *conformity* or *nonconformity* of the subject property is affecting its value, and possibly highest and best use.

46

Elements for Describing Neighborhood Market Conditions (continued)	
Predominant Occupancy	• Who primarily occupies properties in the neighborhood? • If a neighborhood is predominantly tenant-occupied, is this trend recent? - A trend of tenant-occupied properties may be a concern for some lenders, a consideration in the highest and best use analysis, and also an indicator for use of the income approach in the valuation analysis.

Land Use	• A key indicator of highest and best use, the present land use is usually stated as the use of all properties in the market, including vacant land.
	• The appraiser will typically describe the land use by breaking it down into percentages, for example:
	  - Single-family
	  - 2- to 4-family
	  - Multi-family
	  - Commercial
	  - Industrial
	  - Vacant land
	  - Institutional (such as churches and schools)
	  - Other uses
	• Observation of land use trends helps the appraiser in the highest and best use analysis and also in determining conformity of the subject property.

Growth Rate and Built-Up	• Observing the growth and built-up rate of a neighborhood or the subject development lends insight as to market acceptance and success in the area. • The growth rate is most often described as *rapid*, *stable*, or *slow*. • The built-up rate is usually stated as a *percentage*. • Clients and other intended users of appraisals depend on the appraiser's description of growth and built-up rate as a means to assess risk of the property value.
Typical Marketing Time	• Analysis and description of marketing times are usually made using the conclusions from the study of economic conditions and the resulting supply and demand analysis. • Marketing time is the *expected time* (looking at future conditions) the property will stay on the market before a sale transaction will take place. • Typical marketing time is most often stated as a range of days or months, such as 30-90 days.
Other Market Changes	• Other market changes might be caused by special conditions in the subject neighborhood, such as offering special financing terms, typically offered concessions, or down payment assistance programs typically taken advantage of in the market (often observed in new subdivisions with builder incentives and neighborhoods attracting first-time homebuyers).

Geographic and Geologic Land Characteristics

There are numerous land characteristics that are important to recognize and consider in land analysis. A preliminary discussion of the topic should be the distinction between the terms **land** and **site**. **Land** *refers to the surface of the earth—actual dirt on the ground, part of a waterway that is owned, or even a swampy marsh.* From a legal standpoint, land also refers to everything under the ground to the center of the earth, and everything over the land into the air (within limits to allow for air traffic). **Site** *refers to the land with enhancements that make it ready for a building or structure.* These enhancements typically refer to preparations made to ready the land parcel to make it usable.

Geographic and geologic land characteristics include all of the positive and negative factors of land or site that make the parcel desirable or undesirable. In more broad terms, these factors address location and utility (usefulness) of the parcel. However, there are specific points of analysis within each category.

Geographic Characteristics of Land & Site

Geographic characteristics of the land or site contain more details than just size and location. Certainly, these are important, but there are other considerations. With residential properties, wooded lots may be more desirable than non-wooded lots, and waterfront property may be more desirable than property that does not border the water. These geographic characteristics must be considered in each neighborhood to determine whether they contribute significantly to the value of the site. The most common method of analysis is through paired data. Paired data analysis for land will be discussed in Chapter 7.

For example, if data analysis suggests that buyers will pay $10,000 more for a waterfront lot than one across the street, this difference needs to be addressed with an adjustment in the appraisal. On the other hand, if buyers are paying the same price for a cul-de-sac lot as they are for a corner lot of the same size, this difference would not warrant an adjustment. Typical items considered for adjustments include, but are not limited to, *geographic characteristics* of the lot, lot *size*, *restrictions* on the lot, and *location*.

Beyond the simple characteristics of a land parcel or a site that are either present or absent, there are more detailed analyses that may be done with regard to size and location. For example, an appraiser might need to consider not only the total gross size of the site, but also what percentage of the site can be built on. Furthermore, sometimes size in one direction (e.g., across the front) is worth more than size in another direction (e.g., depth).

When looking at the location of a site, neighborhoods are only one aspect of the value as values can sometimes be markedly different depending on the position of the sites within the same neighborhood. For example, a corner lot may be more beneficial for commercial properties than for residential properties.

Site Size

There are two basic considerations with regard to size. The physical size of the site is more than just the total area or acreage of the site; the *shape and dimensions* of the site determine the usable area, as do *zoning regulations*. For example, a one-acre site with flat topography may be worth more than a two-acre lot with a steep ravine that takes up the back two-thirds of the lot. There are numerous other natural (and manmade) features that may take up a portion of the site. Some of these features may be desirable and add value, while others may not be desirable in that marketplace and may detract from the value.

Frontage

It is important to understand that some land may be more valuable than other land. This is especially true for commercial property, which is usually compared by the front foot. A commercial site with greater **frontage** (*dimension across the access side*) is usually more valuable than a deeper lot that has the same total area. So, even if two commercial lots have the same total area, a 200' x 100' lot is often more valuable than a 100' x 200' lot. (Note that the *first number* in a lot size is its frontage.) Commercial properties usually value front footage more because it is more useful for business purposes. On the other hand, the marketplace generally does not make that same distinction for residential properties, where site value is based more on the total size and utility of the lot. With residential sites, an increase in lot size (whether frontage or depth) generally contributes about the same amount of extra value. In fact, in some residential markets, additional frontage may, in some cases, be detrimental to value since it may require higher assessments and taxes for things like sidewalks. Of course, these are issues that must be analyzed within each market and neighborhood.

Public Controls - Zoning

Zoning laws are *local ordinances dividing a city, county, etc., into zones, allowing different types of land use in different areas.* This may limit development and affect property values. In addition to regulating the type of building or activity permitted on a property, zoning laws also regulate how and where the building may be constructed on the property. Each type of zone generally has its own minimum lot size and building height limits. There are usually **setback** and **side yard** rules, *requiring buildings to be at least a specified distance from the front, rear, and side property lines.* There may also be a limit on how much of a lot can be covered by a building, **building density**—*how many buildings may be constructed within a given space,* requirements for parking lots, or other similar types of restrictions that limit the size of the usable site area. These regulations are sometimes referred to as **bulk area requirements**.

Zoning Map

This zoning map example demonstrates several zoning classifications. An appraiser can locate the subject property in one of the zones, then find the zoning regulations for that particular area.

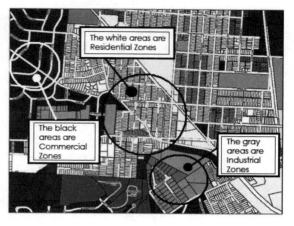

The white areas are Residential Zones

The black areas are Commercial Zones

The gray areas are Industrial Zones

Early zoning laws usually established four land use categories:

1. Residential

2. Commercial

3. Industrial

4. Agricultural/rural

Modern zoning laws tend to be very specific and can be somewhat complicated. In addition to the four basic categories, numerous subcategories are used. For example, even a small city might have three types of residential zones: In zones designated R-1, only detached single-family houses are allowed; in R-2 zones, row houses and duplexes (as well as detached houses) are permitted; R-3 zones also allow multi-family housing. In addition, there are likely to be separate zones for light industrial and heavy industrial uses, light commercial and heavy commercial, etc.

Zoning laws regulate many development aspects in addition to type of use, building size, and placement. For instance, a zoning ordinance is likely to include requirements for off-street parking, landscaping, outdoor lighting, and other details that a local government may feel are necessary.

Sometimes, zones are set up in a hierarchical fashion, such that all uses *above* the current zoning are permitted. This is sometimes referred to as *pass-through zoning*. **Pass-through zoning** *goes only in one direction.* So, in industrial zoned areas, you could build another type of commercial-use building, but in a commercial zone, you would not be permitted to have industrial-use buildings.

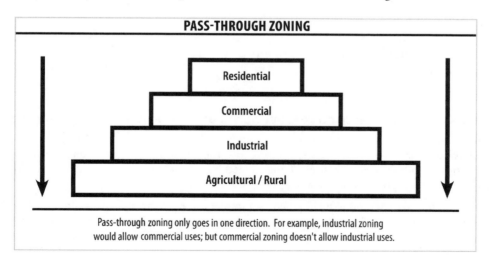

PASS-THROUGH ZONING

Residential

Commercial

Industrial

Agricultural / Rural

Pass-through zoning only goes in one direction. For example, industrial zoning would allow commercial uses; but commercial zoning doesn't allow industrial uses.

Exceptions to zoning laws are possible, but often not easily obtained. When a particular property use does not conform to current zoning, that use could be permitted using as one of the exceptions to zoning – non-conforming use, permission through a granted variance, or as a conditional use.

Nonconforming Use

Nonconforming uses occur *when land use doesn't conform to current zoning laws, but is allowed because the land use was established before the new laws were enacted or the property has been granted a variance.* This is also referred to as **legal grandfathered nonconforming use.** These landowners are permitted to continue using their land the same way they always have as a grandfathered use. Permission to continue nonconforming uses are not always tied to a particular owner. If the property is sold, the new owner may be allowed to continue with the nonconforming use if it is **grandfathered** under the old or pre-zoning laws, usually provided the property is not altered and the use has not ceased for a specified period.

Variance

Variances occur *when permission is granted by the zoning authority to allow some deviation from strict zoning laws.* Variances permit a building or property usage that is not otherwise allowed. Specifically, a **use variance** permits a property owner to *use land in a way that's not allowed in that zone*—such as a commercial use in a residential zone. **Area variances** *legally permit a change in the rules* regarding building size, height limits, setbacks, side yards, and other similar requirements. When a zoning board denies or grants a variance, the applicant or neighbors may appeal the decision to the courts.

Conditional Use

Conditional uses occur *when land usage does not comply with the general zoning rules for its location, but the use is permitted because it benefits the public good* (sometimes called **special exceptions**). Most zoning laws permit uses that are inconsistent with a neighborhood's zoning designation, but are necessary or beneficial to the community, such as schools, hospitals, and churches.

IMPORTANT POINTS...

- Early zoning laws had only four classifications:
  1. Residential, 2. Commercial, 3. Industrial, and 4. Agricultural/rural. Modern zoning laws still use the basic four, but each individual classification may have numerous subcategories within it.
- **Pass-through zoning** refers to a hierarchical organization of zoning. It travels in only one direction. Those zone classifications above the current one are permitted (e.g., a commercial zone may contain a residential property, but a residential zone may not contain a commercial property).
- There are exceptions to zoning laws, which include: Nonconforming uses, granted variances, and conditional uses.

Private Controls – Restrictive Covenants and Subdivision Regulations

Covenant is another term for contract—*a binding promise to do or not do something.* A **restrictive covenant** is *a binding promise concerning the use of real property.* These binding promises require or prohibit the property owner to do, or abstain from doing, something. Restrictive covenants diminish a property owner's right to use a property in any way he desires.

Most often, restrictive conditions are imposed by a former owner of the property—often by the original developer. In many cases, restrictive covenants place requirements or prohibitions greater than those specified by zoning or other land use regulations. Covenants can be enforced; however, an action contrary to the covenant does not jeopardize title.

In most cases, the restrictive covenant "runs with the land." In other words, when the property transfers to a new owner, the new owner is also bound by the restrictive covenant. While most restrictive covenants are imposed upon transfer of a property in a deed, an express agreement can create a restrictive covenant between the two parties. Common examples of restrictive covenants include deed restrictions setting a minimum size of house that must be built on the land or prohibitions against certain types of fences.

Today, subdivision (or condominium) developers impose most private restrictions by recording a declaration of covenants, conditions, and restrictions, known as **CC&Rs.** The purpose of CC&Rs is to keep the subdivision attractive and protect the market value of properties. It is important to check these thoroughly as they can restrict a buyer's enjoyment of the property. For example, a subdivision's CC&Rs may forbid installing fencing, painting the exterior a particular color, or the size and number of pets a property owner may keep.

Developers use CC&Rs to establish a general plan of restrictions for the whole subdivision by clearly stating in the subdivision's recorded plat, or in the deed to the first buyer of each lot, that CC&Rs are binding on all homeowners. Although any homeowner can enforce CC&Rs, usually a homeowners association or the developer enforces CC&Rs.

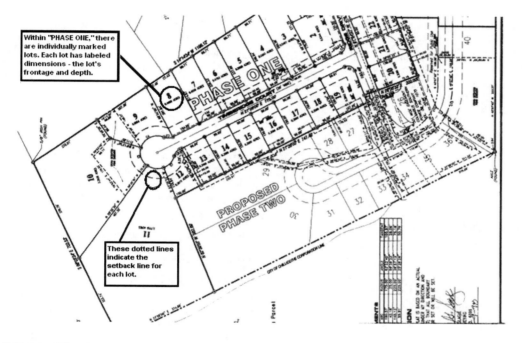

Subdivision Plat Map

Illustrated is a typical subdivision plat that is put on record when the subdivision is dedicated. This particular map represents one phase in a subdivision. Notice that the dimensions of each numbered lot are on the plat, as are the building set-back boundaries, utility easements, etc. For a lot and block description, the appraiser may need to refer to a subdivision plat map.

Easements

An **easement** is *a right to use another's real property for a particular purpose.* Easements are normally for an indefinite period of time and are created by written agreement or by action of law. An easement is classified either as an **appurtenant easement** or **easement in gross**.

Appurtenant Easements

Appurtenant easements *burden one parcel of land for the benefit of another parcel of land.* An appurtenant easement *runs with the land*—hence the term appurtenant. (This may also be referred to as an easement appurtenant.) No matter who owns the land, an appurtenant easement benefits and burdens the same two properties.

SUBDIVISION COVENANTS AND RESTRICTIONS

1. APPROVAL

No building shall be erected, placed, or altered until the building plans, specifications, and elevations have been approved by the developer in writing.

Quality of materials, workmanship, and harmony of exterior design with existing structures must also be approved by the developer in writing.

2. USE

Each and every lot will be used for residential purposes only.

Each lot must be improved with a residential structure not to exceed two and one-half stories and must have an attached garage of not less than two cars and not more than four cars.

No temporary structure, trailer, basement, tent, shack, garage, barn, or other outbuilding shall be used at any time as a residence either temporarily or permanently.

No lot may be split to create another building lot.

No animals, livestock, or poultry of any kind shall be raised, bred, or kept on any lot, except that dogs, cats, or other household pets may be kept provided they are not bred or maintained for commercial purposes.

No noxious or offensive activity shall be carried on upon any lot, nor shall anything be done thereon which may become an annoyance of nuisance to the neighborhood.

No commercial vehicles, recreational vehicles, boats, trailers, construction equipment, or trucks over ¾ ton capacity shall be on any lot or street, except if in a garage; completely enclosed.

3. BUILDING REQUIREMENTS

The ground floor of any dwelling shall have a minimum living area of:

> one-story – 1,400 square feet
>
> one and one-half story - 1,200 square feet
>
> two story – 900 square feet
>
> split - level and tri – level – 1,100 square feet on the upper floor
>
> bi-level – 1,300 square feet on the upper floor

All dwellings must be constructed of brick, stone, or cedar siding with the color approved by the developer in writing.

No building materials may be on-site for more than 60 days prior to construction or 15 days after completion, and construction must be completed within 6 months after commencement.

No outside sheds shall be erected.

4. LANDSCAPING

All lots shall be kept mowed and free from obnoxious weeds and grasses.

Shrubs, trees, bushes, and plantings of any kind shall be kept well maintained and free of unsightly material.

Initial landscaping design must be approved by the developer.

5. MAINTENANCE

No lot, building, or other improvement shall be permitted to become overgrown, unsightly, or fall into disrepair. All improvements shall be kept in good condition at all times.

6. SWIMMING POOLS

Above-ground pools are prohibited.

7. FENCES

No fence, wall, or barrier of any kind (including shrubbery or hedges) may be erected, except underground dog fences, which are subject to the approval of the developer.

8. ANTENNA

No antenna or dish for transmission or reception of television signals, radio signals shall be erected on any lot.

9. FUEL TANKS

No above-ground fuel tanks shall be permitted.

10. SIGNS

No sign of any kind shall be displayed to the public view on any lot, except one sign of not more than 6 square feet to advertise the sale of the property.

11. LIGHTING

No house may be erected on any lot unless there is an outdoor post yard light of either gas or electric power. The owner shall keep said light in good working order and properly maintained.

12. MAILBOXES

To insure conformity with the subdivision, all mail boxes shall be of a construction compatible with the subdivision, and is subject to the approval of the developer.

13. LIMIT OF RESTRICTIONS

These covenants are to run with the land and shall be binding for a period of thirty days from the date of these covenants, and shall be extended for successive periods of 10 years unless the majority of the owners of the lots file an instrument with the recorder agreeing to change the covenants in whole or in part.

14. ENFORCEMENT

In the event of a violation of any of the covenants or restrictions, it shall be lawful for any owner of any of the lots to prosecute any proceedings of law or in equity against the person or persons violating or attempting to violate any of these covenants or restrictions and either prevent such violations or recover damages for such violations.

Subdivision Regulations

The subdivision regulations are placed on record at a subdivision's dedication along with the subdivision plat. Here, we see typical restrictive covenants in this sample subdivision covenants and restrictions.

The land benefited by an appurtenant easement is called the **dominant tenement**. "Tenement" is an old legal term that refers to the land and all the rights that accompany it. *The land burdened by that easement* is the **servient tenement**. The owner of the dominant tenement and thus, *the person who benefits from the easement*, is referred to as the **dominant tenant**. The owner of the servient tenement and thus, *the person whose land is burdened by the easement*, is referred to as the **servient tenant.**

If the dominant tenement is transferred (sold, willed, or given away), the easement is also transferred. Whoever now owns the dominant tenement also now benefits from the easement. If the servient tenement is transferred, the new owner takes title subject to the burden of the easement.

Easements in Gross

An **easement in gross** *benefits a person or entity only and not a parcel of land.* Therefore, there is a dominant tenant (person benefiting from the easement) but no dominant tenement (because there is no land benefiting from the easement). And since an easement in gross, like all easements, is a right that burdens another's land, there is still both a servient tenement (land burdened by the easement in gross) and a servient tenant (person owning the land burdened by the easement). Although there are exceptions, most easements in gross belong to commercial enterprises rather than individuals.

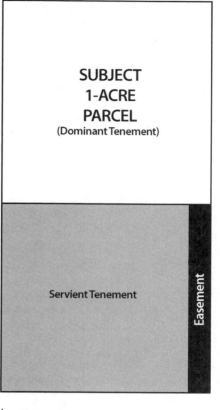

However, easements in gross do not particularly "run with the land" as with an appurtenant easement and must be assigned or they will terminate. An easement in gross can be assigned by the dominant tenant. On the other hand, if the owner of the private property transfers the servient property, the easement that is in place which burdens the servient property is binding upon the next owner.

It is important to understand that easements are typically not, themselves, valued, but rather, the effect in dollars, of the easement on either the property it encumbers or the property benefiting from it. Take for example an **access easement** for the purpose of ingress and egress. The property burdened may or may not be experiencing some downward effect on value, while the property being served likely enjoys an increase in value due to the easement. The dollar effect won't necessarily be equal. When analyzing an easement for either a dominant or serviant tenement, the most common method used for analysis is the sales comparison approach using paired data in a "before" and "after" scenario.

Location

Location is the *positioning of a building lot or land parcel.* Location can be discussed with respect to a given neighborhood, and even within the neighborhood itself. It is easy to understand that houses in a growing, popular, and prosperous neighborhood are more highly desired and valued than those in declining neighborhoods. It's also important to recognize, though, that each individual house's location within that neighborhood affects its value. Here, there are two factors to consider: *Location of the site in relation to other desirable or undesirable properties* when considering the theories of progression and regression, and the *exact location of the property within its geographic area.*

Linkages: Linkages refer to the time-distance relationship to services between properties and services that people in the market rely on, such as schools, employment, shopping, etc. Also considered is transportation available and how affordable the transportation is. The concept could also relate to the efficiency of how products might be transported as well.

Progression and Regression

The theories of progression and regression go with the concept of location. **Progression** holds that the *value of a property is positively influenced by the other properties in an area.* The theory is that the value of the "worst" property in a given area is increased by the other properties in the area. The value of a "rundown" property can benefit from being in a good area among other properties that are well kept. The value of this theoretical "worst" property can only go so low because the desirability of the other properties in the neighborhood will keep it from falling too far. People will pay more for this rundown property, anticipating they can recoup their investment by fixing it up, because of its desirable location.

Regression, on the other hand, maintains that the *value of a property is negatively impacted by other properties in an area*. The theory says the value of the "best" property in a given area is held down by the other properties in the area. The value of an expensive structure in an average area can be hurt by the fact that people may not want to pay too much for a property that is not surrounded by similar, comparable properties with perhaps a lower resale value. The value of this theoretical "best" property can only go so high because people who can afford this "best" property will be attracted to other neighborhoods with like-property values.

A common saying in relationship to real estate is that the three most important aspects of land or a site are *location, location, location*. A house next to the park would most likely have a higher value than a house next to a railroad track, but only through appropriate analysis can the appraiser determine the impact upon the market that can be attributed to this geographic characteristic.

The location of the lot within a neighborhood, the position of the lot (corner, cul-de-sac, etc.), and access to the lot are other factors taken into consideration when determining value. For commercial properties, a corner lot is usually more valuable than an **inlot** (*inside or middle lot*), but for residential lots, the corner influence may or may not be beneficial (and, it may be a detriment if assessments or taxes are high, or the corner lot is exposed to high traffic and noise.) An analysis must be done to determine whether one type of lot is more valuable in a given residential market.

IMPORTANT POINTS...

- Both the shape and dimensions of a site and its zoning regulations are critical to the usable area and resulting value.
- **Progression** holds that the value of the "worst" property in the "best" area will increase due to the higher value of the properties around it.
- **Regression** holds that the value of the "best" property in the "worst" area will decrease due to the lower value of the properties around it.

Geologic Characteristics of the Land/Site

Geologic characteristics of the land or site include features that influence the use of land and its value when compared to land or sites in other areas. Most properties in the same area share the same geologic influences, but questions of value differences may arise when one site has a specific geologic characteristic and a similar site in another area does not. Any appraisal or analysis must also consider the additional expenditures to rectify a specific geologic characteristic or problem before a site can be developed.

Some common geologic considerations include *bedrock*, *soil composition*, and *topography*. Bedrock is important to a site because the underlying rock may be too hard to permit construction of a basement at a reasonable cost. In fact, basements are not found in many areas for this very reason. The soil may be too permeable and porous for a basement to be a viable construction option, since it would likely not stay dry. Similarly, the soil composition may provide insufficient support for certain tall or heavy structures. Topography may limit the buildable area of the site and restrict the types of structures on the land, but is also important for controlling the flow of surface and subsurface water. All of these geologic aspects also influence wells, septic systems, and storm water management.

Subdivision development is a good example of effective geologic management. Land must be cleared, leveled, and graded in a way that allows adequate drainage of the land. Typically, a plan is submitted to the county planning commission that establishes conservation and management strategies for all aspects of the site. For example, for a large parcel of land to be developed, the owner may have to allocate some land area for creation of on-site drainage facilities (such as a retention pond). Everything from clearing to landscaping to retention ponds is designed to maximize land use while minimizing potential dangerous situations from storm drainage and other hazards. Experts in hydrogeologic engineering can offer invaluable advice in these areas.

Other geologic considerations may be present when developing a site in certain parts of the country. These include concerns over mudslides, rock slides, earthquakes, and floods.

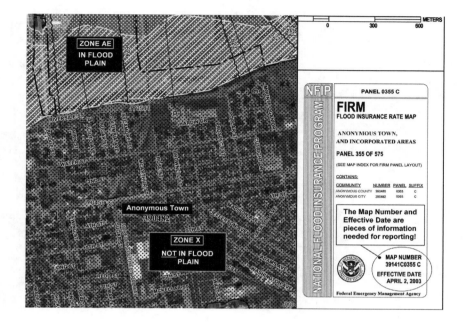

FEMA Flood Map

The FEMA flood panel (map) is available from www.fema.gov. The appraiser can use it to locate the subject property and recognize a flood hazard area. Flood hazard areas on the Flood Insurance Rate Map (FIRM) are identified as a Special Flood Hazard Area (SFHA). SFHA is defined as the area that will be inundated by the flood event having a 1% chance of being equaled or exceeded in any given year. This is also referred to as the base flood or 100-year flood.

SFHAs are labeled Zone A, Zone AO, Zone AH, Zones A1-A30, Zone AE, Zone A99, Zone AR, Zone AR/AE, Zone AR/AO, Zone AR/A1-A30, Zone AR/A, Zone V, Zone VE, and Zones V1-V30. Moderate flood hazard areas, labeled Zone B or Zone X (shaded) are also shown on the FIRM, and are the areas between the limits of the base flood and the 0.2% annual-chance (or 500-year) flood. The areas of minimal flood hazard, which are the areas outside the SFHA and higher than the elevation of the 0.2% annual-chance flood, are labeled Zone C or Zone X (unshaded).

The flood panel number and date of FEMA's flood determination should also be included in the appraisal report.

IMPORTANT POINTS...

- *Bedrock, soil composition,* and *topography* are common geologic considerations.
- *Geologic characteristics influence the types of building to be constructed, the buildable area of the site, flow of surface and subsurface water, wells, septic systems, and storm water management.*
- *There are geologic concerns specific to regions: Mudslides, rock slides, earthquakes, and floods.*

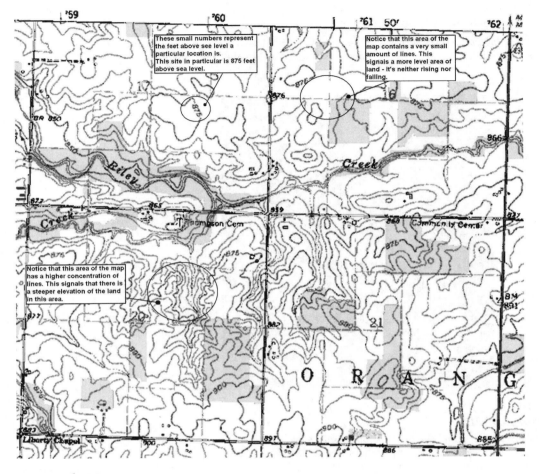

Topography Map

This map is available from local and national sources. The topography map details the contour of the land. Notice that as the topography lines are closer together (or more dense), the steeper the elevation is at that point. More space between the topography lines indicates a level, or gentle slope. Periodically throughout the map, the topography lines will indicate the number of feet above sea level. Local information is available to assist with determining how many feet above flood plain the land parcel must be so as not be in a flood plain.

Final Elements of Land and Site Description

The site information needed for most appraisals is a combination of researched facts and personal observations. When considering what data to gather for the site portion of the appraisal analysis, the legal description, zoning information, maps, and other necessary data should be included.

Zoning information is important for determining highest and best use. For many residential properties, due to zoning and any private limitations, determining highest and best use may be simple. For other types of property, especially commercial properties where zoning may be broader, this could be a complex process.

The plat maps found in public records illustrate the position, boundaries, easements, and other details of a site. The appraiser is *not* required to do a survey to determine boundaries or encroachments (a separate person or company may need to do that), but the appraiser must still use judgment in determining if the site has any adverse restrictions, encroachments, or easements. The appraiser's initial research or personal observations may necessitate more research in this area.

Often times, an appraiser will make a simple site sketch for inclusion with the site data form, and keep it in the property's file. In this sketch, the appraiser will note shape and dimensions, as well as any encroachments, easements, or physical features that prevent a portion of the site from being built on. This sketch may or may not be included with the appraisal, depending on any points of significance present. At the very least, the appraiser must alert a client to any points that seem special or unusual and may impact the value of the property. A street map showing the exact location of the property and the comparable sales used for the sales comparison approach is also usually included as part of the appraisal report.

Most other site data items that are part of the appraisal report are personal observations made by the appraiser as he or she inspects the site. The presence of public utilities and off-site improvements can affect the value of a site. The appraiser must also note the topography, drainage, landscaping, and even the view of the site. All may or may not be important, depending on the particular site. For example, topography usually only affects the value of a site if it prevents construction of certain building types, or precludes building in certain areas of the property. Drainage and landscaping are usually considerations only when they are not adequate. The view can add or subtract value from a site if it is at one extreme or the other—breathtaking mountains or an unsightly landfill.

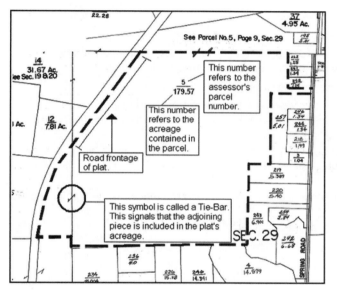

Plat Map

This is an assessor's, or tax, map and is available from local authorities. Its appearance can vary from area to area. It is used by the appraiser to obtain various elements of data, some of which is labeled.

Site Sketch

This site sketch indicates the primary dwelling, the barn, the pond, and the driveway. Notice that it also illustrates the location of the driveway easement running through this property to access the property next door.

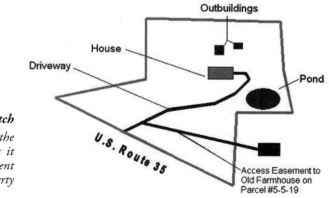

Elements for Describing the Subject Site

Location	• Several locational characteristics of the subject site are described by the appraiser. Some are broad characteristics, such as whether the location is considered urban, suburban, or rural; other characteristics focus on more specific information and could become as detailed as to which side of the street the subject site is located on, if it is a corner lot, or what is next to the site.
Dimensions	• Describe the width and depth of the site by feet, with the frontage dimension stated first. • For larger parcels, the frontage is sometimes described as fractional portions of a mile (state exams have been known to use this method). • A mile contains 5,280 feet.
Area	• Site area is described using square feet and/or acres. • An acre contains 43,560 square feet.

Shape	• The shape of the site or land parcel should be described using common references, such as:
	  - Rectangular
	  - Square
	  - Triangular
	  - Pie-shaped
	  - Trapezoidal
	  - Pan handle
	• It is good practice to illustrate the shape description with plat or survey maps of the site, especially when the shape is so irregular or different that it is difficult to describe.

Topography	• The topography description elaborates on the site or parcel's contour or shape.

View	• The appraiser should describe the specific view of the property from all sides.
	• It is important to describe both the positive and negative factors of the view that could affect the marketability or value of the subject property.
	• The appraiser should carefully describe, in detail, the use of the property being viewed, as well as what element of that use the subject is exposed to (such as a parking lot of a commercial business).
	• Depending on the geographic area, some examples of common references to the type of view might be:
	  - Residential housing (single-family, multi-family, etc.)
	  - Commercial
	  - Industrial
	  - Institutional
	  - Agricultural
	  - Rural
	  - Wooded
	  - Water or oceanfront
	  - Golf course
	  - Panorama

Zoning	• The appraiser should note and describe the specific zoning classification as designated by the local jurisdiction. • A general description of what the zoning classification means as well as the permitted uses should be included. • Whether or not the subject is in compliance with the zoning regulations should be discussed, and if not, the affects on highest and best use and value should also be described. • The zoning status could be legal, legal (grandfathered) nonconforming, or illegal. • If there is no zoning, the appraiser should describe how typical the lack of zoning is for the market and if its absence will affect marketability and value.

Elements for Describing the Subject Site

Private Restrictions	• Ideally, the appraiser should have copies of any restrictive covenants and conditions, or deed restrictions to fully analyze them. • Unusual or atypical limitations or requirements should be analyzed and described along with their influence on marketability and value.
Utilities	• The appraiser should describe the utilities on site and whether they are public or private. • If a particular utility is available to the site, but not on site (such as public sewer service), that too should be described.
Off-site Improvements	• Off-site improvements include such items as streets and roads, alleys, sidewalks, street lights, etc. • The appraiser should further describe the surfaces of streets, roads, alleys, and sidewalks. • The description should also include whether the improvements are considered public or private and who is responsible for maintenance.
Easements	• Easements across, or used for access to, the subject property should be described along with how the easement affects the value of the subject property. • Illustrations are often helpful to describe the location and impact of the easement. • The appraiser should also describe whether the easement is considered typical, such as a utility easement, for the neighborhood.
Flood Hazards	• The Federal Emergency Management Agency (FEMA) publishes flood data maps for most areas, illustrating what areas are or are not located within a designated flood hazard zone. • The appraiser's description of flood hazard information should include the map reference number and date of the flood hazard determination. • In most cases, a copy of the FEMA flood map panel is included in the appraisal report as a descriptive illustration.
Other Zoning and Regulations	• Some localities have other zoning types and regulations, such as airport zoning, coastal zoning and regulations, National Register of Historic Places regulations, etc. • The appraiser should analyze and fully describe, in a fashion similar to the zoning discussion preceding, the zoning or regulations and how they affect the property. • Market competence is necessary to recognize and describe these elements.

Adverse Site Conditions	• Conditions that could be hazardous to the safety and welfare of people and/or could be detrimental to the property or its ownership should be described.
	• Certainly not all inclusive, examples might be:
	  - Environmental concerns
	  - Swampy areas
	  - Ponding areas
	  - Cliffs
	  - Burial sites
	  - Landslide areas
	  - Electric transmission towers
	  - Gas wells

Externalities	• Nuisances outside the property boundaries should be fully described by the appraiser. • The appraiser should determine and explain in his or her description, whether the externality results in external obsolescence.
Natural Site Characteristics	• The natural site characteristics could be positive or negative features of a property—enhancing or detracting the appeal and value. • Wooded sites, ravines, ponds, etc., should be described along with their affect on the property's potential use or uses.

Chapter 2 Math Practice

Lot and Land Measurements

Appraisers encounter assignments and properties that require the use of different types of measurements relating to building lots and land parcels. There are four measurements that are important to remember:

1. Front feet (frontage)
2. Square feet
3. Acreage
4. Mile

Front Feet *Also known as **frontage**, the linear dimension across the access side of a parcel of land.* In a measurement, front feet is always the *first* number. This measures the portion of the lot facing the street. There are usually no corner lots on the state exam, unless the test problem says otherwise.

Example

If a lot measures 250' x 200', what is the amount of frontage?

Since the first number is 250', that is the amount of frontage.

Square Feet *The area of a parcel, calculated as **length x width**.*

This is a very simple calculation for squares or rectangles. You are not likely to see irregularly shaped lots on the exam. If you do, simply break the parcel into smaller squares, rectangles, or triangles and add them together.

Examples

#1: If a lot measures 250' x 200', what is the area of the land?

250' x 200' = 50,000 square feet

#2: What is total area of these two lots combined?

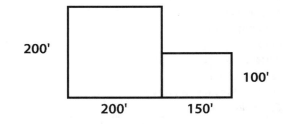

Calculate the area of each rectangle separately, then add them together.

200' x 200' = 40,000'   150' x 100' = 15,000'

40,000' + 15,000' = 55,000 square feet total for the combined parcels

Acreage *There are 43,560 square feet in an acre.*

To calculate acreage, first calculate the square feet of the lot, then divide that number by 43,560.

Example

If a lot measures 220′ x 396′, what is the amount of acreage?

First, determine the area of the lot by multiplying 220′ x 396′ = 87,120′.

Next, divide that result by 43,560: 87,120′ ÷ 43,560′ = 2 acres.

A lot that measures 220′ x 100′ is being sold for $88,000. Calculate the cost per front foot, cost per square foot, and cost per acre.

Step #1: Calculate cost per front foot by dividing cost by frontage.

$88,000 ÷ 220 = $400 per front foot

Step #2: Calculate the cost per square foot by first calculating the area of the lot (length x width), then divide cost by lot size.

220′ x 100′ = 22,000 square feet of lot area

$88,000 ÷ 22,000 = $4 per square foot

Step #3: Calculate cost per acre by dividing the area of the lot by 43,560, then dividing cost by lot acreage.

Cost per acre: 220 x 100 = 22,000 square feet of lot area

22,000 ÷ 43,560 = 0.505050 acres

$88,000 ÷ 0.505050 = $174,240.17 per acre

In this last calculation, note the cost per acre is *greater* than the price of the lot because the lot is smaller than one acre.

Mile *There are 5,280 feet in a mile.*

Very often, the road frontage of a parcel might be stated as a percent or fraction of a mile.

Example

If a parcel of land is 1/8 of a mile by 250′, how many acres are in the parcel?

Step #1: Find the frontage of the parcel in feet.

5,280′ ÷ 8 = 660′

Step #2: Calculate the total square feet of the parcel.

660′ x 250′ = 165,000 square feet

Step #3: Determine the acres in the parcel.

165,000 ÷ 43,560 = 3.7879 acres

Work Problems 2.1

1. A commercial lot is priced at $1,800 per front foot. If the lot measures 170′ x 550′, what is the price of the lot?

2. If the same lot is priced at $2.75 per square foot, calculate the price of the lot.

3. What is the price of a parcel of land selling for $9,000 per acre and that is a quarter mile squared?

Calculating Sections

The **government survey system** is a *type of legal description for land that references principal meridians and base lines designated throughout much of the country.* This is also called the **rectangular survey system** or **military survey** system. This system divides land into six-mile-square townships, which are further divided into sections. A particular parcel of land is identified by directions and coordinates within these sections.

There are two types of math problems you may encounter with these. In the first, you will be given a description and asked to calculate the number of acres in that particular area. It is important to remember that there are **640 acres in a section**.

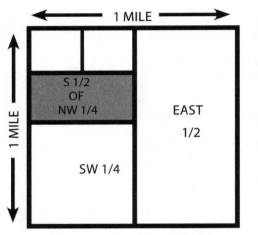

Example

Find the amount of acreage in the S 1/2 of the NW 1/4 of a section.

Since an entire section of land always contains 640 acres, start with 640 and divide by the denominators (bottom number) of each fractional part in the description, starting with the last number.

640 ÷ 4 ÷ 2 = 80 acres in the S 1/2 of the NW 1/4 of the section

In the second type of problem, you may be shown a diagram of a land parcel and asked to write the description. Whether locating a parcel or writing a description of it, start from the end and work backward.

Example

Locate the S 1/2 of the NW 1/4 of a section.

Since the indicated area is located in the NW 1/4, look at the upper left corner of the section, then read the next part of the description to determine which part of the NW 1/4 is indicated. Finally, find the S 1/2 of that part. This is the shaded area in the diagram at right.

A. Calculate the number of acres in the parcel of ground described as the N 1/2, NE 1/4, NE 1/4 of the section.

Since we know that the total number of acres in a section is 640, we simply calculate the following:

640 ÷ 4 ÷ 4 ÷ 2 = 20 acres;
therefore, there are 20 acres in the N 1/2, NE 1/4, NE 1/4 of the section.

B. Write a description for the diagram to the right:

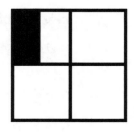

A description for the dark area would read W 1/2, NW 1/4 of the section.

Work Problems 2.2

1. Write a description for the diagram at right:

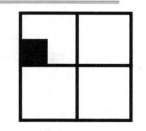

2. Calculate the number of acres in the parcels described as the SW 1/4, SW 1/4 of Section 17 and the NW 1/4, NW 1/4, NW 1/4 of Section 20.

Summary

1. Identifying the correct parcel involves obtaining and verifying the legal description of the land. The test of a valid description of property is the ability to identify and distinguish that property from any and all other parcels of land. There are three primary types of legal descriptions: Government survey system, lot and block system, and metes and bounds system.

2. Collecting and analyzing site data involves **general data factors** and **property-specific factors**. Property-specific factors are the same four great forces that affect all real estate: **P**hysical, **e**conomic, **g**overnmental, and **s**ocial (P E G S). *Physical*: Size, configuration, topography, drainage, soil type, view, utilities, location, access. *Governmental*: Zoning, public easements, taxes, services. *Economic*: Supply and demand, employment, and availability of money. *Social*: Demographic changes, migrations of the population.

3. **Geographic characteristics** of the land or site are more than size and location. Other geographic characteristics must be analyzed in each neighborhood to determine whether they contribute significantly to the value of the site. Paired data analysis can be useful to determine value impact for geographic characteristics of the lot, size of the lot, restrictions on the lot, and location of the lot.

4. Physical size of the site is more than its total area or acreage. *Shape and dimensions* determine usable area of a site, as do *zoning laws*. **Zoning laws** are local ordinances dividing a city, county, etc., into zones, allowing different types of land use in different areas. This may limit development by restricting how and where a building may be constructed on the property. A commercial site with greater frontage (dimension across the access side) is usually more valuable than a deeper lot that has the same total area. With residential sites, an increase in lot size (frontage or depth) usually contributes about the same amount of extra value to a residential lot.

5. An **easement** is *a right to use another's real property for a particular purpose.* Easements are normally for an indefinite period of time and are created by written agreement or by action of law. An easement is classified either as an **appurtenant easement** or **easement in gross**.

6. **Site location** must be considered in relation to other desirable or undesirable properties, and the exact location of land in its geographic area. **Progression** occurs when the value of a property is positively influenced by other properties in an area. **Regression** occurs when the value of a property is negatively influenced by other properties in an area. Lot location within a

neighborhood, position of the lot (corner, cul-de-sac, etc.), and access to the lot are other factors that influence value. Commercial sites often prefer corner lots; in comparison, corner influence may or may not be beneficial to residential sites. An analysis must be performed to determine if one type of lot is more valuable in a given market.

7. Neighborhoods could go through up to four stages in its life cycle. Four phases neighborhoods go through in their life cycles are: 1. **Growth,** 2. **Stability/equilibrium,** 3. **Decline,** and 4. **Revitalization**.

8. **Geologic characteristics** of the land or site are features that influence the use of land. Some common considerations include bedrock, soil composition, and topography. Bedrock may limit basements. Soil may limit tall or heavy structures. Topography may limit buildable area and structures, and restrict water flow. All of these geologic aspects influence wells, septic systems, and storm water management. Subdivision development requires a plan for such things as storm drainage. Other geologic considerations are mudslides, rockslides, earthquakes, and floods.

9. **Zoning laws** divide different types of land use into different areas. Early zoning laws often had four land use categories: Residential, commercial, industrial, and agricultural/rural. Modern zoning laws tend to be very specific and somewhat complex with numerous subcategories. Zoning also regulates lot size, building height, building setbacks, parking, and more. Zones set up in a hierarchy are referred to as **pass-through zoning**.

10. *Exceptions to zoning laws*: Nonconforming uses, variances, conditional uses. **Nonconforming** uses are established uses that violate new zoning laws, but are allowed to continue, usually provided the property is not altered. **Variances** allow an owner to build a structure or use property in a way that violates zoning laws. Area variances bend the rules regarding building size, height limits, setbacks, side yards, and other aspects. Use variances permit owners to use land in a way typically not allowed in that zone. **Conditional uses** allow land to be used in a way that does not comply with zoning laws, many times because it benefits the public.

Quiz

1. **A mile consists of _____ linear feet.**
   a. 640
   b. 2,360
   c. 5,280
   d. 43,560

2. **A cost for an improvement that is divided among several property owners on a street and billed by a jurisdiction would be an example of a(n)**
   a. escheat.
   b. improvement burden.
   c. special assessment.
   d. special tax bill.

3. **A land area divided into 36 parts is known as a**
   a. district.
   b. plat.
   c. section.
   d. township.

4. **What is an area consisting of one particular land use known as?**
   a. district
   b. dominant tenement
   c. market
   d. neighborhood

5. **Which is NOT one of the recognized forces that influence property value?**
   a. economic
   b. governmental
   c. social
   d. stability

6. **A very nice house in a rundown neighborhood**
   a. benefits from the principle of progression.
   b. benefits from the principle of regression.
   c. suffers by the principle of progression.
   d. suffers by the principle of regression.

7. **What data may an appraiser NOT use to describe a neighborhood?**
   a. demographic information
   b. ethnicity of residents
   c. government zoning
   d. upkeep and maintenance

8. **An example of an often permitted use with pass-through zoning is a(n)**
   a. agricultural use of residential land.
   b. house in a commercial district.
   c. industrial plant in a commercially zoned area.
   d. office building in a residential neighborhood.

9. **What type of zoning exception would be needed if a new office building was to be built on a commercial lot that did not have enough space for parking?**
   a. area variance
   b. conditional use
   c. grandfathered use
   d. use variance

10. **Which phase of a neighborhood is denoted by an area being refurbished with displacement of tenants?**
    a. decline
    b. equilibrium
    c. gentrification
    d growth

11. **Which is a characteristic of a restrictive covenant?**
    a. can only be used when there is no zoning
    b. diminish owner's right of use
    c. do not run with the land
    d. never are imposed by a developer

12. **Which is NOT a component of an easement in gross?**
    a. dominant tenant
    b. dominant tenement
    c. servient tenant
    d. servient tenement

13. **What is the road frontage along the west boundary of the NE ¼, NW ¼, SE ¼?**
    a. 2,640 feet
    b. 1,320 feet
    c. 660 feet
    d. 330 feet

14. **If a land parcel is 230' x 477' and is priced at $9,750 per acre, what is the price of the parcel (rounded to the nearest one hundred dollars)?**
    a. $19,300
    b. $24,600
    c. $31,200
    d. $36,800

Chapter 3

Property Analysis and Description - Improvements

3

A proper improvement analysis and description requires a general level of building construction knowledge on the part of the appraiser. The analysis portion of an appraisal assignment typically consists of an appraiser's on-site property inspection and analysis of the property's improvements from a market perspective. Appraisers must be able to recognize quality and condition factors of improvements.

The opinions and conclusions formed through the improvement analysis, coupled with the opinions and conclusions formed in the appraiser's site analysis (discussed in Chapter 2) provide the basis for the opinion of highest and best use, as well as the description of the improvements in an appraisal report at the appropriate level.

BTU (British Thermal Unit) Amount of heat needed to raise the temperature of one pound of water by one degree Fahrenheit. (Measure of furnace, A/C -capacity.)

Building Code A means of setting construction standards, requiring builders to use particular methods and materials. Building codes are adopted by authorities under their exercise of police power for building codes to be enforceable.

Concrete Footers Base that a foundation sits on. Must be poured on solid ground, below frost depth, and wider at the bottom than the structure to be supported.

Foundation Basic structure on which the rest of the house will rest. Can be concrete slab, pier and beams, crawl space, or basement.

Framing Basic load-bearing skeleton of the house to which interior walls, exterior walls, and roof are attached. Can be platform, post and beam, or balloon.

Gross Living Area (GLA) Residential space that is finished, livable, and above grade. Garages, finished basements, and storage areas usually do not count as GLA.

Interim Use Temporary use of a property while it awaits conversion to its highest and best use (e.g., waiting for a zoning change, accumulation of investment dollars).

Manufactured Housing Any dwelling unit built on a permanent chassis and attached to a permanent foundation system is a manufactured home for purposes of Fannie Mae's guidelines.

Key Terms

(continued on page 69)

Basic Residential Construction

From a general point of view, appraisers need to be able to recognize the quality of building materials and construction. Although the appraiser is not acting as a home inspector, recognizing construction deficiencies is important so disclosure can be made in the appraisal report and further investigation by a trained construction professional recommended. Today, more than ever, appraisers are being held to a higher degree of accountability. Fannie Mae, for instance, no longer allows the appraiser to "assume" that an adverse condition is *not* present in a property. Appraisers who perform appraisals for FHA and VA are bound to recognize minimum construction and condition standards that conform to the agency's criteria. If the cost approach has been deemed applicable and necessary, the appraiser must be able to recognize the quality and types of materials used in the structure for the purpose of estimating the cost new.

For proposed construction, the appraiser is often involved in the construction process, from the point of the initial plans and specifications to the final completion of the construction project. An important initial step in the assignment of a proposed new construction is examining and analyzing the building plans and construction specifications. From that point, the appraiser will analyze the proposed materials and labor costs of the improvements for the purpose of the cost approach.

Sometimes this process may reveal proposed costs that are actually higher than typical for the market, or proposed elements that have diminished contribution. This could result in the client being at risk due to the costs substantially exceeding what the house could bring in a resale market. A proposed construction estimate may also be lower than that typically found in an area. This situation could be especially troubling to a lender as this might be an indication that construction funds could be exhausted before the house is completed.

As the construction project progresses, the appraiser is often asked to observe the stages of completion for the purpose of draw reports that the lender can rely on for the release of payments to those providing work and materials. For these reasons, it is important for an appraiser to understand and recognize what the typical building process is.

IMPORTANT POINTS...

- *Although an appraiser is not acting as a home inspector, recognizing structural deficiencies and being familiar with the construction process are important aspects of the job.*
- *Lenders rely on appraisers to verify that standards are met with regard to the loan approval and payments during the construction process.*

Residential Construction Process

There are various steps that are typically taken during the process of constructing a new house. The complexity of these steps will vary depending on each individual project. However; typically, there are 10 basic steps, which begin with the early **research and planning** phase and end with the final **completion** of the construction project. Appraisers must be familiar with the construction process for application in assignments which include new construction, for developing the cost approach, and for general construction knowledge.

Research and Planning

Although it is not thought by most to be an actual phase of the construction process, careful research and planning is an essential first step for any new construction project. Good research and planning should result in a financially sound decision that meets the goals of the homeowner's lifestyle and satisfies their desires. Without good forethought, the construction project can be clouded with problems and pitfalls from the beginning. Choosing a style of house that is faddish, not conforming to an area, opting for a poor location, using materials that are not consistent with the market segment, or simply not considering the individual's requirements and future needs are examples of poor research and planning.

At this point it should already be concluded that the prospective new homeowners have already eliminated existing houses as a choice and that only a new house will meet their needs and desires. Once this decision is made, several other factors should be considered by the new homeowner:

- What type of house does the homeowner want?
- How much should the homeowner spend?
- What features are important to the homeowner?
- How long will the homeowner live there?
- Are there changes in the future needs foreseeable in the homeowner's life or lifestyle?
- What location best fits the homeowner's needs as well as the type of house to build?
- How involved will the homeowner be in the construction process?

The depth of research and planning will depend on the individual's knowledge and experience in undertaking a new construction project and the market. Sometimes appraisers are engaged by the homeowner to assist and advise in the research and planning phase of new construction. An appraiser can assist an individual in making sound decisions regarding options and choices prior to proceeding with a new construction project.

> *IMPORTANT POINTS...*
>
> - *Construction of a new home typically has 10 steps, the first of which is "research and planning."*
> - *Financial concerns should be considered, but so should present and future needs and requirements—these are areas in which an appraiser can sometimes assist.*

Pre-Construction

Once some of the primary decisions are made, it's time to move on to some other very important choices. Probably one of the most critical choices, unless the prospective new homeowner already has a building site, is the *acquisition of the lot or parcel* to construct on. The unique characteristics of the lot or parcel are critical to the positioning and design of the proposed house. For instance, a site that slopes toward the rear may be ideal for a walk-out lower level. A site with abundant frontage and a shallow depth would probably accommodate a side-load garage, with the doors on the end rather than on the street side. The considerations of the physical aspects of the site and what is around it are very important to the design and features chosen in a house plan. Construction options are discussed later, but if the homeowner has chosen to site-build (sometimes referred to as stick-built), a house plan should be chosen, keeping in mind the site characteristics. Possibly, the homeowner will opt for a custom design. In that case, an architect will be engaged. This choice will incur additional costs to the project.

Once these options have been explored, it is time to obtain working building plans or **blueprints** that can be used for obtaining quotes from prospective builders. The individual must then make decisions for the finish materials and components for the entire project. Do they want hardwood floors or carpet over a sub-floor? What type and brand of cabinetry will be used? What type of interior trim? As can be seen, this can be a taxing, but often exciting, point in the process. These choices will be detailed in a materials list. After all, a builder cannot bid on a project, nor can an appraiser perform a new construction appraisal assignment, if the quality, type, and quantity of the materials have not been decided.

Permits Official government documents that acknowledge the proposed work meets the department's standards and grants permission for it to be performed.

Pitch The rise of a roof as stated in vertical inches per horizontal foot.

Principle of Consistent Use Implies that land cannot be valued for one use while the improvements are valued for another use.

Rough-ins Any type of interior work to a house or building that is not part of the finish work, (i.e., plumbing, HVAC, electrical).

Key Terms

Another important part of pre-construction is getting the working building plans or **blueprints** approved by the local building authorities. A **plot plan** also may need to be prepared and submitted, *showing the proposed layout of the property site, including the house position.* This starts the sometimes-tedious process of obtaining **building permits**. **Building permits** are *official government documents that acknowledge that proposed work meets the department's standards and grants permission for it to be performed.* Permits acknowledge that the proposed project is in compliance with building codes and regulations in every aspect or stage of a project. This will be discussed further in the section on building codes and inspections.

> *IMPORTANT POINTS...*
> - *The second step in constructing a new house is "pre-construction."*
> - ***Blueprints** are working building plans that can be used for obtaining quotes from prospective builders and need to be approved by local building authorities.*
> - *Blueprints (and sometimes a plot plan) are needed to obtain **building permits**—government documents that actually grant permission for the construction to be performed.*
> - *A "materials list" contains all finish materials choices and details.*

Site Work

The next important step is to perform the **site preparation** work. If the lot is part of a subdivision, some or all of the site work may already be complete. If the anticipated location is raw land, though, it will be necessary to tap into the public water or sewer lines or drill a well for water, and/or install an on-site septic system. In the latter case, it will be necessary to obtain approval from the jurisdiction's health department. Health departments issue on-site septic system permits based on soil type (for capability of percolation) and site characteristics (for placement of a leaching system). There are various types of on-site septic systems that are common today and are used in specific circumstances.

Other site work will depend on the house plan chosen—its style, features, and position. Trees may need to be cleared, a basement may need to be excavated, or a rough driveway may need to be put in place. Of course, the first consideration should be the setback requirements, easements, or other restrictions on the lot. Are there deed restrictions that dictate the style, size, or even the exterior building materials of the house that must be complied with? Are there easements that cannot be built on? How far back from the street and how far away from neighboring houses does zoning regulation require the house to be constructed?

In addition to restrictions and local zoning ordinances, the positioning of the house on the lot should take into account aesthetics, such as a view, and the individual characteristics of the design chosen.

> *IMPORTANT POINTS...*
> - *The third step in construction of a new home is "site work."*
> - *This is the stage in which the plot is connected to water and sewer—either by tapping into the public lines, or installing an on-site well and septic system.*
> - *Restrictions and local zoning ordinances need to be considered in regard to laying out the plot of land at this point.*

Foundation

After site work is finished, the next step is the foundation. The **foundation** is the *basic structure on which the rest of the house will be built.* The foundation will hold up the rest of the house, so it is important for it to be strong and dry. Usually, a foundation will have **concrete footers**. **Concrete footers** are *the base that a foundation sits on.* A trench is dug so concrete may be poured onto solid ground, such that the footer is wider at the bottom—and wider than the structure it will support. Local building codes dictate how the footers must be built (their size and placement), based on the characteristics of the ground being built on, the type of foundation to be used, and the frost depth common in the area (footers go below the freeze line—the deepest depth that the ground freezes in winter). Typical residential foundation types found in many areas of the country are **concrete slabs**, **piers and beams**, **crawl spaces,** and **basements**.

Concrete Slabs

A **concrete slab** is a *foundation made from a layer of poured concrete reinforced with steel rods* (called **rebar**). This type of foundation lies directly on the ground, called a floating slab, or is constructed on a footer. The slab is then poured over a sand or gravel base with a vapor barrier. In some parts of the country, the concrete slab is common, due to the underlying soil or preference. In other markets, the concrete slab may be thought of as inferior.

Piers and Beams

Often seen as a primary method of housing construction along a waterfront for being able to elevate living areas above flood level, this type of foundation method can also be found in other construction applications. A **pier and beam** *foundation has columns of concrete, wood, or steel* (the **piers**) *resting on footers or another type of reinforced base, with supports of wood or steel* (the **beams**) *that span the columns to provide support for the floors, roof, etc.* The lower beams that span the piers are called the **floor joists**. The floor and framing support for the walls and ceiling are nailed to the floor joists. Sometimes, building codes will limit the height of the piers to discourage using this as a way to build a house onto the side of a hill.

Crawl Spaces

A **crawl space** is the *unfinished space below the first floor of a house or other structure, but less than a full story in height.* A crawl space can be a foundation in and of itself. In that case, the weight of the structure is actually borne on the foundation walls. The crawl space is accessed most times from an exterior scuttle so that the structure can be serviced from beneath. In other cases, a crawl space is the result of a pier and beam foundation with the piers sticking out of the ground less than a full story in height and supporting the weight of the structure. An example of this would be a manufactured dwelling. Typically these are placed atop concrete block piers. A non-weight-bearing "skirt" of various types of materials is then placed around the perimeter of the manufactured dwelling structure.

Basements

A **basement** is *part of a house or building that is partially or entirely below grade (ground level), and used to support the weight of the structure.* Basements are typically at least one full story in height. A basement is formed as a result of space that is first excavated before a house or building is erected. The walls of the basement can be from many different materials. The most common is either poured concrete walls or concrete block. However, it is not unusual to find brick and stone, especially in older dwellings. Though not common, even treated timbers are found in some locations. In any case, the basement walls sit on concrete footers, and the basement walls serve as the foundation for the house. The floor joists sit on the ledges or sills of the basement walls around the perimeter of the house. The floor joists are usually supported in the middle of the house and sit on some type of support column or beam that rests on the support column. Support columns may be concrete, wood, metal, or block piers. These piers, in turn, sit on a slab or footer.

> ### *IMPORTANT POINTS...*
> * *The fourth step in the construction of a new house is the "foundation."*
> * *Typical foundation types include **concrete slabs**, **piers and beams**, **crawl spaces**, and **basements**.*
> * *"Below grade" is synonymous with "ground level."*

Framing

The **framing** is the *basic load-bearing skeleton of the house to which the interior walls, exterior walls, and roof system are attached.* Framing also includes the solid support structure surrounding window and door openings. When interior framing is complete, one can actually walk around the floor plan of the home, experiencing the layout.

Other than wood, other types of framing include concrete block, metal, and poured wall. Metal studs that in the past were typically used for commercial buildings are also becoming popular with residential construction. The three basic frame construction types are *platform*, *post and beam*, and *balloon* frame.

Platform Framing

Platform framing is *a type of framing by which the house or building is constructed one story at a time, with each story serving as a platform for the next.* Studs are cut to the height of each story, with horizontal flooring and support across the top of the studs. The studs for the next story are then cut and attached to the flooring. This is a very common type of framing.

Post and Beam Framing

Post and beam framing is *a type of framing with the floor for higher stories (and the roof) supported by beams that sit on top of posts and the outside wall perimeter.* This is similar to the way a post and beam foundation is constructed. With post supports, not as many interior walls are needed, allowing for larger and more open rooms. Posts, beams, and frame members are heavier than with other types of framing and, in the case of wood, may often be left exposed for decorative purposes.

Balloon Framing

Balloon framing is a type of framing with long studs going up the entire length of the house, from the foundation to the roof. Horizontal studs (called **ledger boards**) are nailed to these tall studs to provide support for the floor and roof joists. Although this was common in older multi-story brick buildings, it is rarely used today, or illegal, because of its poor fire-resistant design and the high cost of long studs.

> *IMPORTANT POINTS...*
> - *The fifth step in the construction of a new home is "framing."*
> - *Typical frame construction types include **platform**, **post and beam**, and **balloon**.*
> - *Once framing is complete, one can walk around the floor plan of the home, experiencing the layout.*

Roofing

The roof of a house is part of the last step in framing. *There are several styles of exterior roof design* that can be used. Roof style can influence the choice of roof frame. Three roof frame types are **truss roofing**, **joist and rafters**, and **sloped joist**.

Truss Roofing

Truss roofing is a type of roof frame that consists of several pieces attached together into a triangular structure that creates a beam of support to hold up the roof covering. Trusses are held together by nails, bolts, or metal plates (called **gusset plates**). A truss must be used when the span or weight of the roof would be too great for a single beam. Pre-formed trusses are often used because they are less expensive than longer pieces of wood, can be engineered to be stronger than beams, and come to the job site pre-assembled.

Joist and Rafters

Joist and rafters roofing is a type of roof frame with joists supported by the outer load bearing walls and a central load-bearing wall (that acts as the beams do for floor joists). The ceiling joists run horizontally, parallel to the floor. The ceiling rafters begin on the outer load bearing walls, but rise as they come to the center peak of a roof. This rise is referred to as a roof's **pitch**—*the rise of a roof as stated in vertical inches per horizontal foot.* Where the rafters meet at the peak, there is only a ridge board between the two sets of rafters. The rafters are supported by opposing pressure, which each side places on the other.

Sloped Joist

Sloped joist roofing is a type of roof frame with joists going from the outer load-bearing walls to a central load-bearing wall that is higher than the outer walls. Instead of the joists being parallel to the floor, they slope up with the pitch of the roof. There are no rafters because the joists essentially take that position. This type of roof framing allows for **vaulted and cathedral ceilings**. These types of ceilings rise as they follow the roofline, on one or both sides, extending up into the roof peak. They are not flat across the top and do not run parallel to the floor, creating a feeling of openness, and are ideal for skylights.

> ### IMPORTANT POINTS...
> - The sixth step in the construction of a new house is "roofing."
> - Three roof frame types are **truss roofing, joist and rafters**, and **sloped joists.**
> - The roof of a house is also part of the last step in framing.

Rough-Ins

After the frame is complete, the next step is to perform rough-ins. Essentially, these items are not seen because they will be hidden later by the finished walls, but they are vital to the operation of the house. **Rough-ins** *include electrical wiring, plumbing, heating, air-conditioning, and so on.* In some cases, permits might need to be acquired for each type of work performed. Nevertheless, thorough inspections will follow, usually after each type of work has been completed to ensure it complies with all building codes and safety regulations.

> ### IMPORTANT POINTS...
> - The seventh step in the construction of a new home is "rough-ins."
> - Rough-ins are typically not visible after construction as they are hidden by the finished walls.
> - Typically, inspection of each individual rough-in will occur after its completion to ensure compliance with codes and regulations.

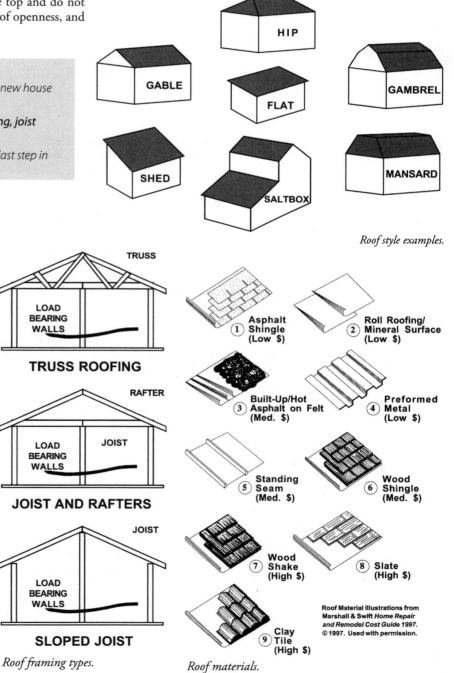

Roof style examples.

Roof framing types.

Roof materials.

Interior Finish Work

Once the rough-in work is completed and inspections have been performed, the interior finish work can commence. This is a long and detailed process of covering everything that is exposed. Ceilings and walls of studs will be covered with drywall or other material. Painting, wall coverings, or other similar surface finish is the next step. Floors will be covered. Today, there are numerous floor-covering materials, which include wood, carpet, laminate, vinyl, and ceramic tile. Light fixtures, electrical switches and outlets, plumbing fixtures, and cabinetry will also be installed. If there are built-in items such as kitchen equipment or media components, these are installed at this point, as well. Finally, all interior trim is installed along with other special finish items.

> *IMPORTANT POINTS...*
> * *The eighth step in the construction of a new home is "interior finish work."*
> * *Because interior finish work is a process of "covering up," this step can only commence when all rough-ins inspections have been performed.*

Exterior Finish Work

Exterior finish work, ideally, is completed as soon as final framing is finished to protect the exposed surfaces from the elements. The specific steps taken in finishing the exterior will depend on the exterior finish chosen. In most cases, the stud framing is usually covered with some type of composition sheet goods. Today, it is common for the entire exterior to be wrapped in a thin layer of house-wrap. In the past, felt paper was used. While it appears to be a minimal step, the wrap is a significant improvement in construction and is designed to prevent air permeation through the exterior side of the wall.

Many types of exterior finishes are available today. It is most common for brick construction to first have veneer laid up over the wrapped framing. Vinyl and wood siding products are similarly applied. Concrete composition siding has the appearance of wood and is installed and finished in a similar manner. However, it has an advantage over wood products in that it is unlikely to suffer from deterioration. In recent years, several synthetic stucco materials have been introduced to the market. Early types of this exterior surface material were riddled with problems due to water permeation. These problems were addressed and the result is considered to be a high quality, versatile product. In applying these synthetic stucco finishes, a foam board underlay is used with a mesh product immediately following. The synthetic product is then applied over this prepared surface. The product is extremely versatile, as it allows easy creation of architectural detail using shaped and patterned foam forms.

The final exterior finish will include the finish of soffits, installing window and door trim, and other decorative trim as specified in the building plans. Exterior finish also includes the completion of porches, decks, and other exterior components.

> *IMPORTANT POINTS...*
> * *The ninth step in the construction of a new home is "exterior finish work."*
> * *Exterior finish work takes place once all framing is complete to protect exposed surfaces from the elements.*
> * *This step usually involves covering the framing with some type of composition sheet goods, or wrap, to significantly improve construction and insulate.*
> * *A type of exterior finish is then applied and all exterior details and decorations are also completed.*

Completion

Technically, from an appraiser's point of view, the construction project is complete when the house is in a 100% marketable state. In other words, a typical purchaser would consider the property to be acceptable and in move-in condition. In most cases, the appraiser may be asked by the lender/client who is financing the project to certify that the construction is complete. Usually, if any item or process is incomplete that would have an adverse effect on the value of the property, the lender will not be willing to release the funds from the new construction loan or convert the loan to a permanent type.

At this final point in the construction process, the site should have received its final grade with seed and straw applied (or sod installed). The contractors have removed their tools and materials. Cleanup will have taken place and all debris and discarded materials have been removed.

Ideally, as a true judgment of final completion, completion has taken place when the building authorities have approved the structure for final occupancy. In some cases, a Final Occupancy Permit will be issued as part of the permit process.

IMPORTANT POINTS...

- The tenth and final step of construction of a new home is "completion."
- Completion has occurred when the house is in a 100% marketable state—it is move-in ready and, in some cases, a Final Occupancy Permit will be issued as part of the permit process.
- The plot is no longer a construction site—final grade seed, straw, or sod has been installed and the site will be generally cleared of all construction remnants.

Build Your Knowledge 3.1

Number the processes for the construction of a new home in order from 1–10.

_____ a. Site Work	_____ f. Exterior Finish Work
_____ b. Foundation	_____ g. Completion
_____ c. Pre-Construction	_____ h. Rough-ins
_____ d. Research and Planning	_____ i. Interior Finish Work
_____ e. Framing	_____ j. Roofing

Work Problems 3.2: Customer Satisfaction

Appraisers may be involved in the construction of a new home as early on as the research and planning stage. Practice your knowledge of construction options and preferences by determining what is needed to achieve the buyer's goals.

1. *The client wants vaulted ceilings. What type of roofing should be considered when working on the blueprints?*

_____

2. *The clients love the look of wood siding, but fear pricey repairs in the future due to its tendency to deteriorate over time. What would your suggestion be for a substitute?*

_____

3. *The clients love the look of exposed wooden beams. What framing method would you suggest in order to create this effect?*

_____

4. *The clients have obtained a great plot along the lake with great views but they are also concerned about the possibility of flooding from living so close to a big body of water. What type of foundation would you suggest during the blueprint stage to take advantage of the views and still protect from flooding?*

_____

Building Codes, Permits, and Inspections

There are numerous building codes that can prevail when performing any type of construction work. This is true for new construction as well as for remodeling existing buildings. Application of these standards might be broad, depending on the geographic area and location, and could vary by type of work being done and/or what type of building structure is involved. Here, the emphasis is mainly on residential construction. And although building codes were established first, followed by a permit system to enforce building codes, and then an inspection system to ensure compliance with the codes and permits, they will be discussed here in reverse order.

Building Inspections

Building inspection is the *process whereby government authorities, usually state or local, are charged with the duty of ensuring compliance with prevailing building codes.* Since building codes are written to ensure that buildings are safe, enforcement of those codes through inspection is in the best interests of the community. Building inspections, though, differ from home inspections in that building inspectors do not inform a prospective buyer of any potential future problems with a house, but only ensure compliance with current building standards.

Building inspections cover all aspects of a new construction project, from the initial plans to the final completion of the structure. Building inspections are also performed for lesser projects that only deal with altering specific aspects of an existing home. The contractor or homeowner usually must call for an inspection when work is completed, based on a permit obtained prior to beginning the work. For existing houses, the inspection is very specific to the particular work or repair being done. For a new build, though, the inspection process is a sequence of inspections that roughly follows the new house building process outlined in the previous section.

Sequence of Inspections

The Uniform Building Code details basic inspections that are common for new construction houses. The sequence of inspections for a new house can vary depending on the city or locale, and sometimes there is overlap between the inspection phases listed here, so always check with the local government building compliance office.

1. **Preliminary Preparation.** During this first inspection, much of the focus is on the building plans and blueprints to ensure they are accurate, viable, and in accordance with all local regulations. During this inspection phase, it also may be necessary to have temporary power and temporary sanitation facilities approved.

2. **Site Foundation.** This inspection is done after trenches and holes are dug for footers, after concrete forms have been erected, and after reinforcing steel is in place, but **before** concrete is poured. (An additional inspection may be required or performed after the footers and/or basement walls are poured.) Other site inspections that are likely to be performed during this phase are underground conduits, gas lines, water lines, sewer lines, and the slope or grade of the lot. Compliance with setback requirements is also checked. From this point forward, it is important for all plans and permits to be kept at the job site, prominently displayed, and available for inspection on request.

3. **Underfloor.** Underfloor inspections cover foundation walls and floor joists, as well as any rough plumbing (water pipes, drains, and sewer), heating (ducts, returns, and vents), gas lines, electrical, or other mechanical items that are to be installed under the floors. This inspection takes place before subflooring or insulation is installed.

4. **Close-in Inspection.** This inspection is made after the framing, exterior sheathing, and roof are complete. Other items inspected include windows, doors, stairs, etc., as well as fire blocking and bracing. Sometimes, final rough inspections are included in this phase.

5. **Rough Inspection.** Additional rough inspections are performed, as necessary, during this inspection phase, including completed plumbing, heating, electric, and mechanicals. These completed systems likely will be load tested if this was not already done as part of the close-in phase. Basically, this inspection phase covers all items that will be covered by insulation and drywall in the next construction phases.

6. **Insulation.** After final approval during other inspection phases, the "okay" is given for the installation of insulation in the house. Once insulation has been installed throughout the house, it must be inspected before being covered up.

7. **Dry Wall/Wall Cover.** After approval is received on the insulation, then the dry wall, gypsum board, or other wall covering can be installed. Once the initial boards are installed, though, they may need to be inspected again and approved before they can be taped, seamed, plastered, or painted. Again, local ordinances will dictate exactly when and how dry wall is inspected.

8. **Final Inspection.** The final inspection takes place after all other inspections have been performed and passed. Typically, the final inspector will look down an inspection card to verify the signatures for all prior inspections, then retest the mechanicals of the house before giving final approval. This final inspection must be performed before the building can be occupied and, in some areas, a Certificate of Occupancy based on the final inspection is issued.

Remember, these inspections often vary in different areas. Check with your local building compliance authority. Also, the inspections outlined here are for newly built houses, and may also apply to major home additions, but may not be applicable to smaller remodeling projects.

IMPORTANT POINTS...

- *Building inspections differ from home inspections in that **building inspectors do not inform prospective buyers of future problems**; they only check and ensure that current building standards are complied with.*

- *The sequence of inspections consists of eight parts: 1. Preliminary, 2. Site foundation, 3. Underfloor, 4. Close-in inspection, 5. Rough inspection, 6. Insulation, 7. Dry wall/wall cover, and 8. Final inspection.*

- *As of the second step of inspections (site foundation), all plans and permits need to be kept at the job site, prominently displayed and available for inspection on request.*

- *These eight steps apply specifically to newly built houses but may not be applicable to smaller remodeling projects. It is always important to check with your local building compliance authority.*

Build Your Knowledge 3.3

Number the steps of inspection below in order from 1–8.

3 a. Underfloor   7 e. Dry Wall/Wall Cover

2 b. Site Foundation   6 f. Insulation

1 c. Preliminary Preparation   8 g. Final Inspection

4 d. Close-in Inspection   5 h. Rough Inspection

Work Problems 3.4: Construction Inspection

As an appraiser, a lender may ask for your verification that construction is going according to plan before it will make the payments. For this reason, basic knowledge of the construction process is necessary. Test your knowledge by determining which stage of the inspection sequence each act is performed.

1. *From this stage on, all permits and plans need to be kept on site, prominently displayed, and available for inspection upon request.*

   _____

2. *Dry wall/wall cover can only begin AFTER the inspection and approval of*

   _____

3. *Before subflooring or insulation can be installed, the _____ needs to be inspected and approved.*

   _____

4. *During which phase should temporary power and temporary sanitation facilities be approved?*

   _____

5. *What inspection needs to take place before the house can be occupied?*

   _____

Permits

Permits are *official government documents obtained from the locale's appropriate government authority that acknowledge that proposed work meets the department's standards, and grants permission for it to be performe*d. Permits also prompt the government authority to monitor projects and follow-up with appropriate inspections. In some areas, one building permit may cover the entire new construction, building addition, or renovation project. In other areas, however, separate permits may be needed for the building, electric, and plumbing. In those cases, different inspectors may be utilized.

> **IMPORTANT POINTS...**
> - Permits prompt the government authority to monitor projects and follow up with appropriate inspections.
> - Permits may cover an entire new construction, or separate permits may be needed for different steps (e.g., building, electric, plumbing).

Building Codes

Building codes *set construction standards, requiring builders to use particular methods and materials.* A local government usually has many building codes: A fire code, plumbing code, electrical code, etc. States have minimum building standards, but a local government could be more strict. Although there is not a single national building code, there are several model building codes that are widely adopted. Example model building codes include the Uniform Building Code, the National Electric Code, and the Uniform Plumbing Code.

In an effort to bring national standardization to building codes, the International Code Council (ICC) is working on a series of codes. ICC was founded by three major regional building code councils—Building

Officials and Code Administrators (BOCA), International Conference of Building Officials (ICBO), and Southern Building Code Congress International (SBCCI). ICC is melding the building codes of these three organizations into one standard national building code. Remember, though, that building codes must be adopted by governments under their exercise of police power for the building codes to be enforceable.

Most local jurisdictions adopt some form of model building code and make regional modifications based on local conditions for weather, soil composition, etc. Without seeing a complete building code, it may be difficult to understand just how detailed these codes can be. For example, in addition to regulating plumbing and electric, which are obvious safety issues, a building code may also dictate an exhaust fan is needed in a bathroom without a window, the minimum height for ceilings, the placement of lights and outlets in a room, landings that may be required at the bottom of a doorway, and the minimum and maximum rise for a flight of stairs. Generally, there are solid reasons for these requirements, even though the building code may appear to be needlessly meticulous and demanding.

An important fact to know about building codes that are adopted and enforced by local jurisdictions is that they generally allow older work to stay in place in residential properties, as long as the work was up to code at the time it was installed, and presently is in safe condition. Often, though, if remodeling or improvements are performed, all conditions must reflect the current code (so check your jurisdiction).

But with commercial buildings, every structure must comply with certain building codes, not just new or remodeled ones. Depending on the use of a commercial structure, there might be routine fire and health inspections for some buildings. Another area of required compliance is accessibility under the **Americans with Disabilities Act** (**ADA**). And when new, stricter standards are imposed, property owners may have to bring old buildings to code. Experts and specialists can be consulted to ensure that buildings comply with different regulations, including fire, health, and ADA requirements. Fines and injunctions can be used to enforce these laws and codes.

Although appraisers typically do not have the necessary knowledge and experience to specifically recognize building code compliance issues, it is wise for appraisers to be able to recognize conditions and potential signals for which a further professional inspection should be performed.

Typical Building Code Deficiencies - Electrical

To obtain a comfort level that no major problems exist with the electrical service in a house, a buyer or homeowner should call a home inspector or electrical contractor. In a typical residential appraisal, appraisers may reference the electric service if it was upgraded and any influence it might have to the property value. Likewise, if the service appears to be inadequate for the house, that would be noted and considered, and a professional inspection probably should be recommended. Otherwise, specific observations about a house's electric service will most likely be left to a home inspector. Some common ways that residential electric service can fall short of modern building codes should be discussed.

1. **Inadequate Electric Service.** Most newer homes now have 200-amp electric service. Where problems can occur is with older electrical services because many of them only have 100 or even occasionally a 60-amp service. The electric requirements of appliance systems today could deem this type of system inadequate.

2. **Not Enough Circuits or Outlets, Not Enough Grounded Outlets.** Older homes often had too few outlets in each room. Current building codes, for example, might require that outlets be placed every six to eight feet on each wall, lessening the need for extension cords (and permanent extension cords), which can contribute to overloaded circuits. Some building codes might also require each room to be on a separate circuit. Additional outlets might be required in the kitchen to handle appliances, and many of these should be on separate circuits, as well.

   Many older homes also lack grounded wiring. One reason for grounded wiring is to ensure that cords are not plugged in backwards. Older outlets have one slot bigger than the other, but all electrical cords do not have this type of plug. The main reason, though, for grounded wiring is that the ground prevents major damage in the event of an electrical fault in the device or appliance. The ground serves to draw dangerous electrical current away from the device—and the individual. Some electrical devices need to be grounded to operate properly and safely.

Most building codes also require kitchens and bathrooms to have specially grounded outlets, called **ground fault interrupters (GFI)**. This specially grounded outlet turns off power at the outlet instantly if the device or appliance that is plugged into it gets wet, shorts out, or malfunctions. These types of outlets are usually required next to sinks and other potentially wet and/or hazardous areas.

3. **Undersized or Worn Wiring.** High-wattage items draw large electrical current. If the wiring is too thin, the wire may get hot as the device attempts to pull more power. This not only hurts the device, but can also cause wires to get hot and possibly catch fire. Many devices state how much current they need. Overloading wires is very dangerous. Overloading can be caused by one item drawing too much current or many small items together using too much current, more than the wiring was designed to handle. A sign of overloading is when lights dim or flicker as other electrical items are used.

   To use high-wattage items, it may be necessary to install at least some new wiring. Often times in older houses without updated electrical services, the existing wiring cannot handle microwave ovens, air conditioners, and other high-drain power items that are so common today. Worn or frayed wiring can also significantly reduce the wire's load capacity and increase the risk of fire. When this is the case, the best solution is to replace the wiring.

Typical Building Code Deficiencies - Plumbing

Just as with electrical service, plumbing should be inspected by a home inspector or plumbing contractor to ensure there are no major problems. Again, an appraiser is not a home inspector and, as such, generally may not have the expertise to identify any plumbing code deficiencies. In a typical appraisal, the appraiser may reference the fact that plumbing has been replaced, or a new kitchen or bath installed, if it warrants an adjustment in value for the subject property. An appraiser should note the presence of lead pipes, if recognized. Otherwise, specific observations about a house's plumbing service will most likely be left to a home inspector. Here are some common instances where existing residential plumbing components and methods can be deficient with building codes:

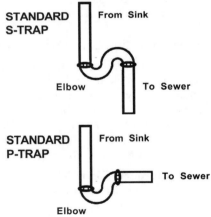

1. **Drain Traps.** Older-style S-traps have been replaced in most building codes with P-traps. The purpose of a trap is to keep some water in the elbow so fumes or gases from the sewer are not allowed to escape back up into the drain.

   P-traps have been determined to be better at stopping the back-flow of gases and fumes. In an S-trap, the water seal can be broken more easily. When the water in the S-trap emits a gurgling sound, this is a sign that the water seal has been broken and has allowed a small amount of sewer gas to escape back up through the drain opening of the sink.

2. **Outdated Pipe Materials.** Most jurisdictions allow for several types of piping materials, including copper and plastic components such as PVC, CPVC, and PB. Copper is an ideal material for water lines and generally considered to be superior. Some flexible piping systems have also been recently introduced. Plastic may be easier to work with than copper because it can be glued rather than soldered. However, not all jurisdictions allow plastic piping to be used for drinking water supply. Older houses may have water lines made from iron, steel, or other galvanized materials, and even lead. Lead pipes are extremely hazardous to health since they can contaminate drinking water, and should be replaced immediately. Other types of metal pipes, other than copper, are susceptible to corrosion, mineral deposits, and deterioration. Although not an immediate threat, they can lead to low water pressure, leaks, and breaks.

Other Common Building Code Deficiencies

There are numerous other types of building code deficiencies that may be found in houses, particularly older ones. Only electrical and plumbing deficiencies have been discussed because these (along with heating) are the most important systems in the house, and often the most urgently in need of repair and attention. But as long as the systems are functioning properly and meet the code of their day, building inspectors and other officials will rarely require replacement or repairs unless there is an immediate health risk or threat.

Houses are rarely inspected by building officials to determine their code compliance. Therefore, it becomes necessary for homeowners or buyers to take steps to protect themselves. An appraiser should always disclose and consider obsolescence, inadequacies, and defects if they can reasonably be recognized. Even in a newly constructed house, unsatisfactory conditions can be found. An appraiser would typically defer questionable conditions to the opinion of a professional. Consumers would be wise to rely on a professional home inspection.

> ### IMPORTANT POINTS...
>
> - *States have minimum building standards but local governments' may be stricter.*
> - *The International Code Council (ICC) is working to bring national standardization to building codes.*
> - *Commercial buildings are required to comply with requirements of accessibility under the Americans with Disabilities Act (ADA).*
> - *An appraiser should always disclose and consider inadequacies or defects if they can be reasonably recognized, but should defer questionable conditions to the opinion of a professional.*

Styles, Parts, and Systems of Houses

Different styles of roofs and different points about plumbing and electrical systems have been introduced, but there are many more areas covered by a home inspection. As an appraiser, it is important to be familiar with some of the other major components of a house. Being familiar with these components, as well as different styles and types of houses, is important for good communication. It is also helpful to have knowledge of some of the major mechanical systems of a house, what their purposes are, and how they function.

Styles of Houses

There are two basic ways to define a house—by the *exterior style* or by the *functional layout* of the house. When discussing the exterior style of a house, there are several basic architectural styles that are popular. They include American Colonial, English Tudor, French Provincial, Spanish Villa, Cape Cod, Traditional Ranch, and Modern Contemporary. There are innumerable variations of these basic designs, as well as more traditional, plainer, and more modern styles.

SPANISH VILLA

CAPE COD

ENGLISH TUDOR

MODERN CONTEMPORARY

TRADITIONAL RANCH

Images from Clipart Collection, © 1994, Explore the World of Software Inc.

AMERICAN COLONIAL

Home style examples.

In addition to these basic architectural styles, there are functional layouts that also serve to describe a home. Generally, this functional definition is thought of in terms of the number of stories or levels that a house has. These include a one-story house, which can include the Traditional Ranch style as well as many other variations. One-and-one-half-story styles include the Cape Cod, New England Saltbox, and Craftsman style. The American Colonial is usually a two-story house. Other common layouts are split-level, bi-level, and raised ranch. Again, there are myriad combinations of architectural styles and functional layouts.

> *IMPORTANT POINTS...*
> - *Houses can be defined two ways: By the **exterior style** or the **functional layout**.*
> - *There are innumerable variations to the basic architectural styles and functional layouts.*

One-Story

One-story residences have one level of living area. The roof structure has a medium slope. The attic space is limited and is not intended for living area.

One-and-One-Half Story

One-and-one-half story residences have two levels of living area. Characterized by a steep roof slope and dormers, the area of the upper level, whether finished or unfinished, usually equals 40% to 60% of the lower level.

Two-Story

Two-story residences have two levels of finished living area. The area of each floor is approximately the same. The roof structure has a medium slope. The attic space is limited and not designed for usable living area.

HOUSE LAYOUT EXAMPLES

Illustrations from Marshall & Swift *Home Repair & Remodel Cost Guide 1997.* ©1997.   Used with permission.

Two-and-One-Half Story

Two-and-one-half-story residences have three levels of living area. Having a steep roof slope with dormers, the area of the third floor, whether finished or unfinished, usually equals 40% to 60% of the second floor.

Two-Story Bi-Level

Two-story bi-level residences have two levels of living area. Unlike a conventional two-story, the lower level, which may be partially below grade, is partially unfinished. A distinguishing characteristic is its split-foyer entry.

Split-Level

Split-level residences have three levels of finished living area—lower level, intermediate level, and upper level. The lower level is immediately below the upper level, as in a two-story. The intermediate level, adjacent to the other levels, is built on a grade approximately four feet higher than that of the lower level.

Manufactured, Site-Built, and Factory-Built Houses

It is especially important for appraisers to recognize the distinction between manufactured, factory-built, and site-built houses (sometimes called stick-built). There are many different mindsets regarding their definitions. Over the years, the industry has referred to manufactured homes as trailers, mobile homes, modular, etc. Just about any type of construction that was *not* site-built has been labeled "manufactured" by many. The difference between these structures is not always in the outward appearance. As the technology to build them is refined, the physical characteristics become more difficult to distinguish.

Technically, there have always been distinctions to define these various construction types. The problem has been that these definitions were not broadly known throughout the real estate industry, nor was the issue a major problem due to the small number of these properties being bought, sold, and financed. However, types of construction other than site-built are growing rapidly. Due to many trends, the popularity of non-site-built houses is increasing every year. Therefore, it is important to review the most common types of construction in this category.

Site-Built Houses

Site-built construction probably does not need a lot of discussion. Predominantly the most common, the building materials are transported to the site with all assembly taking place there. Often considered to be the highest quality, especially with custom-built houses, site-built houses take longer to build and the pace of construction is dependent on the elements.

The **pre-fabricated and panelized** type of construction could arguably be termed site-built, although some would advocate that it is not. Pre-fabricated and panelized houses go back many decades and were even sold by major mail order companies. After World War II, as soldiers returned from the war and needed housing, the pre-fabricated house gained popularity. Some were even constructed completely of metal! Pre-fabricated and panelized homes continued to be built through the decades following the war, as the baby boomer generation required more and more houses. They are still constructed today, but the popularity has diminished somewhat due to more efficient construction methods.

Factory-Built Houses

Rising strongly in popularity, the factory-built house (sometimes called factory engineered) is becoming a major factor in housing throughout the country. What was often referred to as a modular or sectional house, the factory-built house has become harder and harder to distinguish from site-built houses. These houses are, for the most part, fully constructed in a factory in two or more sections. The construction materials, like site-built, can range from the most economical to the extravagant. Once constructed, the sections are loaded onto trailers and transported to the site where they are "rolled off" onto a conventionally built foundation. The advantage to this type of construction is that it can be quicker, has not been exposed to the elements, and can be very cost competitive with site-built houses. Many states have enacted laws that prohibit exclusion of this type of housing within zoning and restrictions. As time has passed, the acceptability of the factory-built house, within most markets, has increased.

Manufactured Houses

Until this point, nothing that has been discussed would be termed a manufactured house, at least by major mortgage entities such as Fannie Mae. In a 2003 communication regarding manufactured housing, Fannie Mae offered the following definition of a **manufactured house**:

> *"Any dwelling unit built on a permanent chassis and attached to a permanent foundation system is a 'manufactured home' for purposes of Fannie Mae's guidelines. Other factory-built housing (not built on a permanent chassis), such as modular, pre-fabricated, panelized, or sectional housing, is not considered manufactured housing and continues to be eligible (for financing) under the guidelines stated in the Selling Guide."*

It is important for appraisers to recognize this definition, as appraisal guidelines for Fannie Mae (and some others) require additional analysis, research, and reporting. For Fannie Mae, appraisals of manufactured houses are reported on the URAR form with an addendum know as the 1004C. To qualify for secondary market financing through Fannie Mae, the property must meet the following criteria (FHA has similar guidelines):

- The manufactured home must be built in compliance with the Federal Manufactured Home Construction and Safety Standards established June 15, 1976 (as amended and in force at the time the home is manufactured) and that appear in HUD regulations at 24 CFR Part 3280. Compliance with these standards will be evidenced by the presence of a HUD Data Plate that is affixed in a permanent manner near the main electrical panel or in another readily accessible and visible location.

- The manufactured home must be a one-family dwelling that is legally classified as real property. The towing hitch, wheels, and axles must be removed and the dwelling must assume the characteristics of site-built housing. The land on which the manufactured home is situated must be owned by the borrower in fee simple, unless the manufactured home is located in a cooperative or condominium project. Mortgages secured by manufactured homes located on leasehold estates are not eligible. Multi-width manufactured homes may be located either on an individual lot or in a project development (i.e., cooperative, condominium, PUD, subdivision).

Mortgages secured by single-width manufactured homes are eligible for delivery to Fannie Mae only if the manufactured home is located in a cooperative, condominium, or PUD project.

- Project acceptance is required for multi-width and single-width manufactured homes if the project development is a cooperative or condominium. Project acceptance is also required if the property is a single-width manufactured home and the project is a PUD. In the case of cooperatives, both the land and dwelling must be owned by the cooperative.

- In the case of condominiums, both the land and dwelling must be subject to the condominium regime.

- The manufactured home must be at least 12 feet wide and have a minimum of 600 square feet of gross living area. Further, the manufactured home must have sufficient square footage and room dimensions to be acceptable to typical purchasers in the market area. They do not specify other minimum requirements for size, roof pitch, or any other specific construction details.

- The manufactured home must be attached to a permanent foundation system in accordance with the manufacturer's requirements for anchoring, support, stability, and maintenance. The foundation system must be appropriate for the soil conditions of the site and meet local and state codes.

- If the property is not situated on a publicly dedicated and maintained street, it must be situated on a street that is community owned and maintained ,or privately owned and maintained. There must be adequate vehicular access and there must be an adequate and legally enforceable agreement for vehicular access and maintenance.

- The manufactured home must be permanently connected to a septic tank or sewage system and to other utilities in accordance with local and state requirements.

IMPORTANT POINTS...

- *Appraisers need to know the difference between factory-built, manufactured, and site-built homes.*
- *Fannie Mae does not accept mortgage loans for manufactured homes unless they meet certain criteria, similar to FHA guidelines.*

Parts of Houses

All parts of a house are important. Other than the interior decor, each serves a useful function. The exterior is important to a home's strength, insulation, and the level of maintenance required. Windows provide a means of letting light in and keeping cold air out. Doors provide a means of security, entry, and insulation on the outside, and privacy inside.

APPENDIX 2: EXPLODED HOUSE DIAGRAM

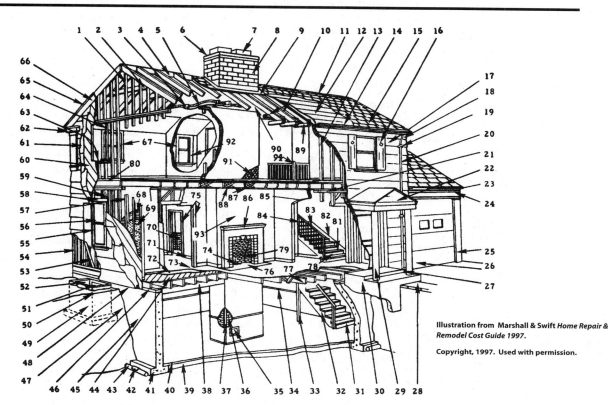

Illustration from Marshall & Swift *Home Repair & Remodel Cost Guide 1997*.

Copyright, 1997. Used with permission.

1. Gable Stud	25. Door Jamb	49. Areaway Wall	73. Finish Floor
2. Collar Beam	26. Garage Door	50. Grade Line	74. Ash Dump
3. Ceiling Joist	27. Downspout Shoe	51. Basement Sash	75. Door Trim
4. Ridgeboard	28. Sidewalk	52. Areaway	76. Fireplace Hearth
5. Insulation	29. Entrance Post	53. Corner Brace	77. Floor Joists
6. Chimney Cap	30. Entrance Platform	54. Corner Studs	78. Stair Riser
7. Chimney Pot	31. Stair Riser (Bsmt)	55. Window Frame	79. Fire Brick
8. Chimney	32. Stair Stringer	56. Window Light	80. Sole Plate
9. Chimney Flashing	33. Girder Post	57. Wall Studs	81. Stair Tread
10. Rafters	34. Chair Rail	58. Header	82. Finish Stringer
11. Ridge	35. Cleanout Door	59. Window Cripple	83. Stair Rail
12. Roof Boards	36. Furring Strip	60. Wall Sheathing	84. Balusters
13. Stud	37. Corner Stud	61. Building Paper	85. Plaster Arch
14. Eave Trough/Gutter	38. Girder	62. Frieze Board	86. Mantel
15. Roofing	39. Cinder, Gravel Fill	63. Rough Header	87. Floor Joist
16. Blind/Shutter	40. Concrete Floor	64. Cripple Stud	88. Bridging
17. Bevel Siding	41. Footing	65. Cornice Molding	89. Lookout
18. Downspout Neck	42. Tarpaper Strip	66. Fascia Board	90. Attic Space
19. Downspout Strap	43. Drain Tile	67. Window Casing	91. Metal Lath
20. Downspout	44. Diag. Subflooring	68. Lath	92. Window Sash
21. Double Plate	45. Foundation Wall	69. Insulation	93. Chimney Breast
22. Entrance Canopy	46. Mudsill	70. Wainscoting	94. Newel Post
23. Garage Cornice	47. Backfill	71. Baseboard	
24. Frieze	48. Termite Shield	72. Building Paper	

ALUMINUM OR VINYL SIDING

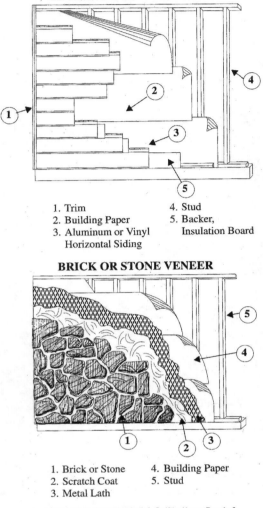

1. Trim
2. Building Paper
3. Aluminum or Vinyl Horizontal Siding
4. Stud
5. Backer, Insulation Board

BRICK OR STONE VENEER

1. Brick or Stone
2. Scratch Coat
3. Metal Lath
4. Building Paper
5. Stud

Illustrations from Marshall & Swift's *Home Repair & Remodel Cost Guide 1997,* © 1997. Used with permission.

Typical exterior wall systems.

Previously, some of the different types and styles of roofs that will commonly be seen on houses was discussed. That discussion is expanded here by identifying other parts of a house with the correct terminology, starting with exteriors, then looking at common types of windows and doors.

House Exteriors

House exterior materials can contribute greatly to the appeal and value of a home. Materials are chosen for their ability to stand up to the elements, to protect the house, and keep it looking good with minimum maintenance.

Vinyl siding is a very common type of siding. It is popular because it is relatively inexpensive and easy to maintain. Vinyl siding typically needs some type of backing or insulation board before it can be installed over stud walls. Vinyl can also be installed over existing house siding. Vinyl does not dent like aluminum siding can, and the finish and color are molded into the material so there is no need to worry about the finish wearing off. It can fade in the sun, though. Vinyl can also crack from severe cold weather or a hard thrown baseball but, typically, vinyl siding can last 25 years or more.

Aluminum siding is a common type of siding on older homes, but seldom used today. Aluminum siding typically needs some type of backing or insulation board before it can be installed. In addition to being relatively inexpensive, aluminum is easy to maintain. The main drawback to aluminum is that it dents easily and needs to be painted after the factory finish deteriorates.

Wood siding was the common exterior finish for houses in years past. New homes may also use wood siding, often cedar. It is more expensive than vinyl or aluminum, and will last longer, but needs regular maintenance and painting or staining. Common varieties of wood siding include wood lap, board and batten, T-111, and wood shakes and shingles.

Stucco was a popular material used on the exterior of houses several decades ago. The older type of stucco was durable because it had no seams to let water or moisture in, but it could crack from repeated freeze and thaw cycles. Newer forms of synthetic stucco have been developed that have accelerated its use in recent years. It can be found in all types of construction. Stucco can be applied over masonry block walls or over hardboard siding with wire mesh.

Brick and stone veneer sidings are costly, yet popular, types of siding. They are considered by many to be the most attractive and the most durable. Brick and stone are easy to maintain—cleaning is not even necessary. Older brick and stone exteriors may show signs of deterioration from the weather and water. If older brick has missing or crumbling mortar joints, they must be replaced with new mortar by a process called **tuckpointing**. Brick can be painted, if desired, but then must be repainted when the paint starts to peel. New brick or stone walls need some type of backing and wire lath before being installed over stud walls or concrete block walls.

Windows

Windows provide beauty, let light in, and keep cold out. There are several types of windows. **Single-hung windows** have only one sash that moves vertically; **double-hung windows** have both sashes that move vertically; **casement windows** swing out right or left.

Common window materials are wood, vinyl, and aluminum. Wood is the best insulator, but needs upkeep. Vinyl clad windows are an alternative. **Low-E glass (low-emissivity glass)** coated windows block summer heat wavelengths and trap winter sunlight. **Gas-filled** windows have gas between panes to act as an insulator. The window type, material, features, and manufacturer may be noted in an appraisal.

Doors

Doors provide entry, security, and privacy. In addition to standard exterior doors, there are sliding glass doors, storm doors, and screen doors. Interior doors are passage doors between rooms, and passage, bi-fold, or bypass doors for closets.

Exterior doors can be solid wood, hollow wood (with insulating material inside), or metal (exterior metal sheets with supports and insulation inside). Interior doors can be solid wood, hollow core (wood), or formed particleboard (hollow, imitating wood designs). Many new doors can be bought **pre-hung**—the door is already mounted on the hinges in the door frame.

> ***IMPORTANT POINTS…***
> - *Exterior finish materials include: Vinyl siding, aluminum siding, wood siding, stucco, and brick and stone veneers. Each exterior finish material has its own benefits and setbacks and can affect the appeal and value of a home.*
> - *Windows come in different styles and levels of insulation.*
> - *Both interior and exterior doors need to be considered, as well as their style and the materials they are composed of.*

Mechanical Systems of Houses

There are three basic mechanical systems in a house—the **electrical system**, **plumbing system**, and the **heating and cooling system** (HVAC).

Electrical System. The electrical system is comprised of several elements, which include the wiring, distribution box, circuit breaker box, circuit breakers, fuses, lights and lighting fixtures, light switches, and wall outlets. Standard electric service in the U.S. calls for a minimum of 100 amps and 110 volts for normal usage. Both of these can be higher, and for some types of appliances or equipment, they must be higher. For example, many clothes dryers require a special line carrying 220 volts of electricity. Actually, most homes have 220 volts running to the home, but it is split in half at the distribution box to provide multiple 110-volt lines. By combining these lines, 220-volt service is achieved when needed.

As an appraiser, it is good practice to at least open the distribution box or circuit breaker box to check for obvious signs of trouble. Some of these warning signs are patched wiring in the box, sparks or light flashes, sounds coming from any part of the electrical system, and any part of the electrical system (including a cord) that is warm or hot to the touch. Additional warning signs are installed fuses that are rated higher than the amp capacity of a circuit, and lights that flicker when additional lights or devices are turned on.

Plumbing System. The plumbing system of a house is comprised of several elements, which include the piping, drains, clean outs, vents, valves, faucets, sinks, toilets, tubs, showers, and hot water tank (gas or electric). The piping includes all supply lines (cold water), hot water lines, and waste water lines (sewer lines). Often times, gas lines are also included as part of the plumbing system. It's important to understand that supply lines carry water under pressure from the source. Water heaters are specially designed to retain this pressure when delivering hot water. Waste water lines, on the other hand, rely on gravity to move waste into the sewer. That's why vents are so important—not only do they let sewer gases escape from the house, they also allow atmospheric pressure to come in and drive wastewater down the pipes. (Sewer pipes must be sloped according to code.)

Although washing machines and dishwashers are connected to the plumbing, they are generally not included as part of the "plumbing system." Their valves, connections, and drains may be checked for leaks, but these machines are not routinely inspected except as "other mechanicals" or "other systems." Garbage disposals may or may not be included, as well.

WINDOW TYPES

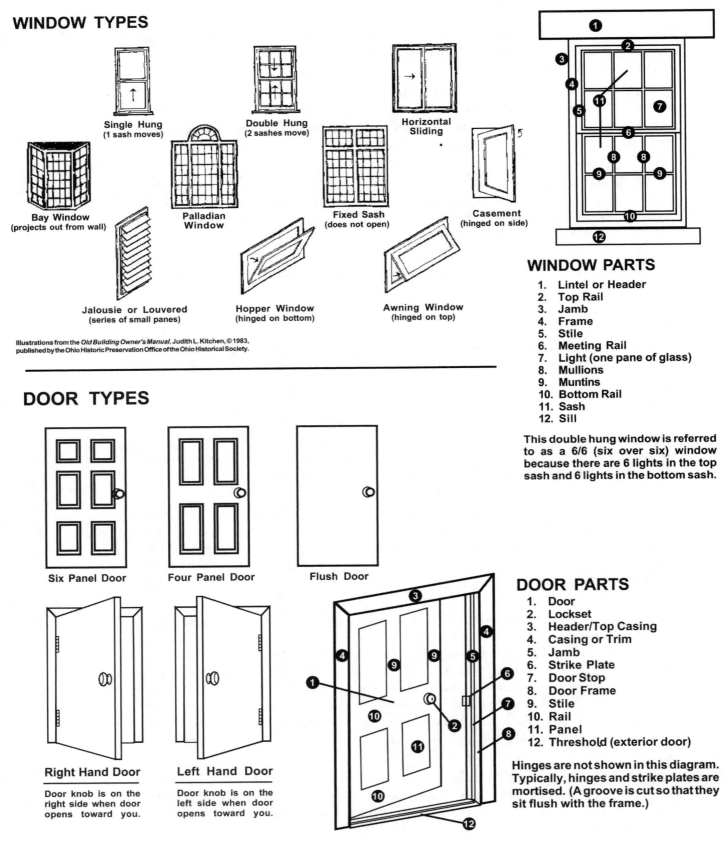

Single Hung
(1 sash moves)

Double Hung
(2 sashes move)

Horizontal
Sliding

Bay Window
(projects out from wall)

Palladian
Window

Fixed Sash
(does not open)

Casement
(hinged on side)

Jalousie or Louvered
(series of small panes)

Hopper Window
(hinged on bottom)

Awning Window
(hinged on top)

Illustrations from the *Old Building Owner's Manual*, Judith L. Kitchen, © 1983,
published by the Ohio Historic Preservation Office of the Ohio Historical Society.

WINDOW PARTS

1. Lintel or Header
2. Top Rail
3. Jamb
4. Frame
5. Stile
6. Meeting Rail
7. Light (one pane of glass)
8. Mullions
9. Muntins
10. Bottom Rail
11. Sash
12. Sill

This double hung window is referred to as a 6/6 (six over six) window because there are 6 lights in the top sash and 6 lights in the bottom sash.

DOOR TYPES

Six Panel Door

Four Panel Door

Flush Door

Right Hand Door

Door knob is on the right side when door opens toward you.

Left Hand Door

Door knob is on the left side when door opens toward you.

DOOR PARTS

1. Door
2. Lockset
3. Header/Top Casing
4. Casing or Trim
5. Jamb
6. Strike Plate
7. Door Stop
8. Door Frame
9. Stile
10. Rail
11. Panel
12. Threshold (exterior door)

Hinges are not shown in this diagram. Typically, hinges and strike plates are mortised. (A groove is cut so that they sit flush with the frame.)

As an appraiser, it should be within the normal course of practice to operate the various plumbing fixtures. Some of the things to look for are faucets that leak, drains that leak, toilets that do not flush properly, drains that are slow, drains that have odors emanating from them, drains that gurgle or make other noises as they empty, and excessive putty on fixtures or pipe joints. Additional warning signs are water damage under fixtures, lack of water pressure when multiple faucets are turned on and/or a toilet is flushed, corroded fixtures or pipes, and lead pipes.

Heating System. The heating system of a house is comprised of several elements, including a boiler, furnace or heat pump, flue, ducts and ductwork, registers, radiators, and thermostat. Depending on the type of fuel the system uses, there may also be electrical connections, gas lines, or oil/fuel storage. For houses with central air conditioning, the air-conditioning system is generally included as part of the heating system because they usually share a common ductwork system. In fact, it's common to refer to all of these system components collectively as **heating and cooling systems** or **HVAC (heating, ventilation, and air conditioning) systems**. "Ventilation" is added to the mix because the systems can also provide fresh air and cleaned air to the house as they circulate the heated or cooled air. In fact, indoor air quality (IAQ) is becoming a hot topic. In addition to standard filters, electronic filters and static filters are cleaning indoor air better than ever.

What Size Furnace or A/C? **Because some variables are unknown, determining the correct size of furnace or air conditioner that a house needs can be a difficult task.** Not only must the size of the house be taken into consideration, but also the number of windows, type of foundation, amount of ventilation, and the biggest unknown—how well the house is insulated. What needs to be determined for a furnace size is how fast heat moves out of the house. A furnace is chosen so it can replace lost heat and keep a house at the desired temperature. Professionals are equipped to make recommendations regarding the appropriate sizing for an HVAC system.

As an example, assume a "normal" 2,000-square-foot house for which it was determined that it loses about 60,000 BTUs per hour. **BTU (British Thermal Unit)** is the *common measurement of heating capacity and is the amount of heat needed to raise the temperature of one pound of water by one degree Fahrenheit.* Since this example house is losing heat at a rate of 60K BTUs/hour, we could install a 60K BTU furnace—but then the furnace would have to run constantly. Instead, HVAC specialists will add 20%-30% to their estimates. So, in this example, the house could comfortably have an 80K BTU furnace installed. Since 60K divided by 80K equals 75%, the furnace would run about 75% of the time.

Air conditioning calculations are different than those for a furnace because additional factors are considered. Since heat rises and tries to escape, a less powerful air conditioner is needed. As a general rule, every 500-1,000 square feet of living area needs one ton of air conditioning capacity. Thus, a "normal" 2,000 square foot home could be cooled adequately by a two-ton air conditioner. (Note: 1 ton = 12,000 BTUs)

Types of Furnaces. There are two basic ways that central furnaces can distribute heat to the house. A forced air furnace has a fan or blower that moves the air through the ductwork. A gravity furnace relies on the natural phenomenon of heat rising to distribute it. Additional types of heat sources can include wall furnaces and electric baseboard heating units. Depending on the geographic area, an appraiser may need to make adjustments in the appraisal if the primary heat source is from something other than a central furnace.

Heat Pumps. Electric heat pumps are an alternative to traditional heating and cooling systems. With heat pumps, the same unit provides heat in the winter and cooled air in the summer. The main advantages are that it uses energy more efficiently than a furnace that burns fuel, and that only one unit is needed instead of two. In recent years, more refined heat pump systems are much improved over early systems, which lacked efficiency once the outside temperature dropped below a certain level. In recent years, it has been common to combine these systems with a traditional forced-air system, creating a dual system. Other variations of the heat pump include the geo-thermal heat pump system, which utilizes outside ground temperature to convert to inside heating and cooling.

Other Non-system Items. Although window air conditioners, space heaters, and fireplaces produce some of the same results as the HVAC system, these items are not included as part of the HVAC system. They're generally considered separate items for inspection purposes.

As an appraiser, it is probably good practice to operate the HVAC system, to the extent that outside temperatures will allow, in an effort to observe any potential problems. Some of these warning signs could be that the furnace runs constantly instead of cycling on and off with the temperature in the room, and loud noises coming from the ductwork, especially after the furnace cycles off. This could indicate that the furnace does not have an adequate cold air return and is trying to receive more air. Both of these problems may be symptoms of an undersized and overworked furnace. A malfunctioning furnace can produce carbon monoxide gas. The gas is a silent killer and should be checked for by an expert.

Other Systems. There are other systems that play a role in maintaining a properly functioning home. These include the roof, foundation, drainage, and may include other items such as built-in appliances, a fireplace, a security system, or the telephone system. Some of these are of more concern to homebuyers than others. Many of them are inspected during a home inspection (but may cost an extra fee).

> **IMPORTANT POINTS...**
> - *There are three basic mechanical systems in a house: 1. Electrical system, 2. Plumbing system, and 3. Heating and cooling system (HVAC).*
> - *Appraisers should observe each system and check its function (e.g., view the distribution box or circuit breaker for obvious warning signs within the electrical system, run sink faucets to check the function of the plumbing system, operate the HVAC system to check heating/cooling cycles).*
> - *Often times, gas lines are included as part of the plumbing system.*
> - *Malfunctioning furnaces can produce carbon monoxide, a silent and deadly gas.*
> - *The checking of additional systems can be requested, but for an extra fee.*

Property Inspection

Property inspection is a *visual examination of the physical structure and systems of a house.* Sometimes the purpose and process of a property inspection and a home inspection become confused to parties outside the appraisal industry. An appraiser inspects a house or other structure as a means of gathering data to be used for analysis and noting the condition, quality, and quantity of improvements. An appraiser typically notes items of concern and recommends inspection by a professional for further determination. On the other hand, a home inspector is typically the professional who is consulted to make that determination. A professional home inspector, in the course of performing a home inspection, is conducting a much more thorough analysis of the structure for quality and condition.

As we discuss home inspections, it will be evident that the discussion focuses upon everything discussed in this chapter. Appraisers and professional home inspectors alike must have knowledge of the building process, components, and systems of a house. As well, a property inspection and a professional home inspection will cover many areas: Roof, mechanicals, and the foundation. A professional home inspection typically is more detailed that an appraiser's property inspection in that property inspectors are much more aware of building codes and compliance issues. They also typically have a greater working knowledge of the individual working components of a structure, such as mechanical systems and can make determinations regarding their adequacy and condition.

A professional home inspection is designed to identify components that are dangerous, faulty, or inoperable. Inspections are not intended to be technically exhaustive and, thus, the purpose of a home inspection is not to find every possible imperfection in the house. Even new homes have imperfections. By concentrating on potential problems, the home inspection is trying to help a homebuyer (or owner) make intelligent choices. Houses cannot "fail" a home inspection. The purpose of the home inspection is information and discovery. On completion of a home inspection, the buyer/owner should know:

- Repairs that need to be done immediately.
- Potential future repairs that may be needed.
- The repair priorities.

- The major repairs that are recommended.
- The minor repairs that are recommended.
- The preventive maintenance steps recommended.
- Significant deficiencies that are present.
- The risks of hidden damage.
- Conditions that are unsafe.
- Areas that may warrant further investigation.

As a course of good practice, appraisers can follow somewhat the same process in conducting analysis and reporting the findings of their property inspection. In some cases, an appraiser will rely upon the determinations made by a professional home inspector within the appraiser's analysis.

Professional Home Inspections

Because appraisers often rely upon professional home inspectors, the home inspection profession should be discussed. Professional home inspections can be performed by anyone who claims to be skilled in the area. This is where potential problems can arise, both in the quality of the inspection and in the area of liability.

Quality of Inspection. In some jurisdictions, home inspectors must be licensed. One can also seek out home inspectors that have a professional certification or are a member of a professional organization. This may indicate a level of training or expertise, and means that the inspector is adhering to the organization's guidelines and ethics. Of course, one should always assure that the home inspector is insured and/or bonded for both general liability and errors and omissions.

The American Society of Home Inspectors® (ASHI) and the National Association of Home Inspectors (NAHI) are well respected as independent professional organizations serving the home inspection industry. Both organizations mandate experience and training requirements to maintain membership, as well as prescribed continuing education. Several other associations also exist.

In some cases, a property condition might warrant that an engineer inspect a house. The National Academy of Building Inspection Engineers (NABIE) is a non-profit, professional society that accepts only state-registered professional engineers specializing in the practice of building inspections as members. In addition to standard home inspection analysis, licensed engineers are also allowed to evaluate overall structural soundness and mechanical system adequacy as of the date of the inspection.

Potential Liability. A home inspection is generally not warranted, and does not provide any type of guarantee on the items or systems inspected. The home inspector provides a report to the buyer or homeowner stating the condition as of the date of the inspection. Typically, though, a buyer can obtain a home warranty, purchased individually or by the seller, at closing. Home warranties, however, typically do not cover pre-existing conditions, and the coverage is usually limited to the mechanical systems of the dwelling.

Where liability can become an issue is if individuals represent themselves as home inspectors and others rely on their opinions, when that individual was not qualified or competent. Such misrepresentation or misunderstanding can lead to serious trouble if a major defect in a house is overlooked. That is why it is very important for appraisers to be careful not to be perceived as giving home inspection advice. The only advice that an appraiser should give to homeowners, buyers, (or sellers) is to urge them to have a professional home inspection performed.

Liability can also be a problem for home inspectors if they miss a serious problem with a house. Since home inspectors are considered to have a higher level of competence, they are held to a higher degree of standard.

Areas Covered By a Professional Home Inspection

A thorough home inspection covers the areas discussed in this chapter, and more. From the roof to the foundation, and all parts and systems in between, home inspections are designed to let homeowners and buyers know what the condition of the property is. The inspection process itself cannot be destructive or invasive. A typical home inspection usually includes site drainage, foundation, exterior components, roof, plumbing, electrical, HVAC systems, interior components, structural components, and any reportable environmental conditions (e.g., mold).

Other items that are usually inspected as part of a home inspection include: Detached garages and other site improvements, fireplaces, chimneys, etc. Some inspectors might also offer additional tests (often at additional cost) for wells, septic systems, drinking water, air quality, termites, lead, radon, and any number of other items. It is important to note, however, that radon inspection and termite inspection is usually regulated and licensed by jurisdictional authorities. Only inspectors with that jurisdiction's credentials may perform those inspections.

Describing Improvements

Once the analysis portion of the appraisal development is completed, the next focus is how to describe the property improvement elements that have been examined. From a reporting perspective, the appraiser's improvement description may be somewhat to the point or a detailed narration, depending upon the reporting option and intended use in the assignment. But, in general, an appraiser's improvement description will focus upon several key areas.

Elements for Describing Improvements

Type of Improvements	• For residential properties, the type of improvement would probably be described as single-family, two-family, etc. • In the description, the appraiser will also discuss if the improvement is attached, detached, common wall, etc.
Design and Style	• The design and style description relates to the number of stories and architectural style of the structure. • In most cases, the description will use commonly recognized references to the particular style. • Basements, attics, and unfinished areas should also be described.
Size	• For residential properties, the gross living area is determined and described using exterior dimensions of the structure. • Below grade areas (finished or unfinished) are typically not included, except in rare circumstances • If rooms are unusually small for the market, have low ceilings, etc., the appraiser should describe the condition and how it might affect value. • The room count is stated, excluding baths, foyers, non-livable rooms (such as walk-in pantries, closets, etc.). The number of baths and bedrooms are described separately.
Overall Condition	• Describes the physical characteristics of the improvements and reflects renovations, maintenance, and deterioration that will be part of the consideration in determining effective age and resulting physical depreciation. • When the appraiser states a condition rating for the improvements, it is reflected against other properties in the subject neighborhood.
Actual Age and Effective Age	• Actual age refers to the year the improvements were constructed. • Effective age is the difference between the total economic life and the remaining economic life, and reflects all forms of deterioration and obsolescence—physical, functional, and external. • If the effective age is more or less than the actual age, the appraiser should fully describe the conditions contributing to the difference.
Mechanical Systems	• Descriptions of the heating and cooling system, plumbing system, and electrical system. • The appraiser should be careful that statements are within the scope of the appraiser's knowledge and expertise. • Heating systems should include the fuel source.

Exterior Materials/ Finishes	• The description of exterior finishes most often addresses the quality and the condition of the finish materials and workmanship.
	• Exterior components described usually include:
	  - Roof
	  - Siding materials
	  - Chimney
	  - Gutters and downspouts
	  - Windows
	  - Foundation
	  - Trim

Interior Materials/ Finishes	• Quality of materials and workmanship, and condition of the interior finish components are described, which typically include:
	  - Ceilings
	  - Walls
	  - Floors
	  - Trim
	  - Cabinetry

Elements for Describing Improvements

Car Storage	• The capacity for car storage is usually described in the context of how many vehicles can be stored in the garage or carport, being able to move in and out without moving another vehicle. • Driveways usually follow the same guideline—if two cars could be parked side by side and either could be moved without moving another, the driveway would be described as having the capacity of two cars. • Garages can be attached, detached, or built-in, while carports are either attached or detached.
Additional Features and Amenities	• Significant items influencing a typical buyer's actions, positively or negatively • These items could include, but are certainly not limited to: - Swimming pools - Spas or hot tubs - Fireplaces - Technology items - Storage sheds and barns (affixed) - Decks - Patios - Fencing - Energy conserving features - Central vacuum systems - Audio and video systems - Security systems
Personal Property	• Any item not considered a fixture but that is being conveyed with a sales transaction, and how the appraiser is considering the item in the appraisal, should be discussed. • The description should include whether the items are being considered in the final value opinion, or possibly, have no affect on value.
Adverse Physical Conditions	• The appraiser should describe any adverse physical conditions noted within the improvements. • In addition to deteriorated items, conditions such as mold, radon, and banned materials such as asbestos and Urea Formaldehyde Foam Insulation (UFFI) should also be described. • If possible, the appraiser should describe any affect on marketability and value—additional professional advice or inspections may be necessary.
Functional Utility	• Functional utility looks at the floor plan and design and how acceptable it is to the typical buyer. • Typical examples might be tandem bedrooms (walking through one bedroom to enter another), unacceptable bedroom/bath ratio, oddly placed stairways, etc. • Poor functional utility most always results in functional obsolescence. • The appraiser should describe the condition and how it will affect marketability and value.
Compliance	• Especially when some (or all) of the improvements are new, recently added, renovated, etc., the appraiser should describe compliance of the improvements with local building and zoning regulations. • In many cases, the appraiser may not be able to confirm whether the improvements are compliant—the appraisal report should describe the steps taken to verify or obtain the information—further investigation or the use of an extraordinary assumption may be required, depending on the scope of work.

IMPORTANT POINTS...
- *Actual age refers to the year the improvements were constructed.*
- *Effective age is the difference between the total economic life and the remaining economic life, and reflects all forms of deterioration and obsolescence—physical, functional, and external.*
- *Any new, recently added, or renovated improvements should be evaluated in regard to their compliance with local building and zoning regulations.*

Calculating Gross Living Area

When performing a cost analysis, it is important that dimensions are correctly calculated. Square footage is always calculated by using the outside dimensions of the structure. The appraiser then follows national standards or locally accepted practices to determine which areas, if any, need to be subtracted from that square footage total. For example, if an upper floor has a balcony, loft, or other open area to the floor below, that open space would be subtracted from the upper floor area. And, it must be remembered to multiply the area times the number of floors in the structure as appropriate for multi-story buildings.

For some properties, such as commercial buildings, the square footage total may be divided by the type of space usage. For example, the square footage may be divided between warehouse space and office space. In such case, a different cost will be assigned to each type of space.

For residential property, non-living areas (e.g., garage space, screened-in porch) are subtracted from the outer dimension totals when figuring square footage. This is referred to as the gross living area. **Gross living area (GLA)** is *residential space that is finished, heated, and above grade. In some warmer climate areas,* GLA must also be cooled. Garages, finished basements, and storage areas do not usually count as part of the GLA, but finished attics can count if they have heat and electricity with finished walls and normal ceiling height. In some parts of the country, it might be customary to include substructure (below grade) space in the GLA. However, this is an exception only when living area below grade is typical for the market and may be in very limited circumstances.

GLA and ANSI

Of course, there may be accepted variations in each local market, but most commonly, national standards adopted by the **American National Standards Institute (ANSI)** are observed for measuring the GLA of single-family, detached homes. Many recognized entities within the appraisal, real estate, and mortgage industry were active in creating what is referred to as American National Standard Z765-2003.

The standards are voluntary but widely accepted because they are constantly revised with input from many sources. When using these standards, appraisers must uniformly apply them. ANSI standards define "finished area" as "an enclosed area in a house suitable for year-round use, embodying walls, floors, and ceilings that are similar to the rest of the house." Garages and spaces below grade are specifically excluded. This is true even if the space is only partially below grade. Areas below grade are not included as finished floor area, according to ANSI standards.

Doing The Math. When calculating square footage, there are two formulas needed: One for the area of a square or rectangle, and one for a triangle.

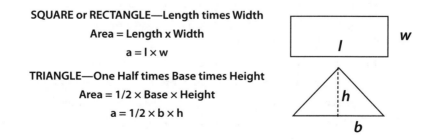

SQUARE or RECTANGLE—Length times Width

Area = Length x Width

$$a = l \times w$$

TRIANGLE—One Half times Base times Height

Area = 1/2 × Base × Height

$$a = 1/2 \times b \times h$$

An appraiser can apply these formulas to each part of the structure until the entire square footage has been calculated. Calculate the area of the individual parts of the structure (usually rectangles), then add them all together, subtracting out the area of overhangs, garages, and other non-living spaces. Remember to double any part of the house designated as "two-story," and do not count finished basements or storage areas. Additionally, do not include second level areas that are open to the main level (e.g., a two-story foyer). (Note that all measurements must be in the same units before doing any calculations.)

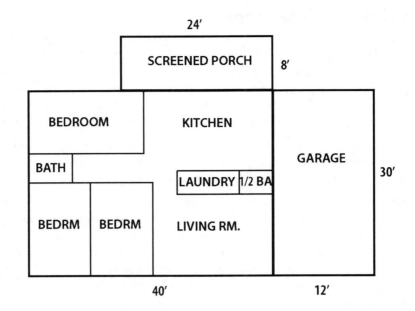

In this example, the house has 1,200 square feet, 5 rooms, 3 bedrooms, and 1½ (1.1) baths. The one-car garage and the screened porch are not counted in the gross living area. The laundry room is considered a utility area and is not included in the room count.

Highest and Best Use

Once the land or site has been analyzed, as well as the improvements, the next analysis which brings all of those efforts together is the highest and best use analysis. Highest and best use was briefly overviewed in Chapter 1, but will be expanded upon here.

Highest and best use is *the legally permitted, physically possible, economically feasible, and most profitable use of a property.* This is one of the most important factors an appraiser considers before forming an opinion of value. As is evident from the comprehensive definition, a number of factors go into making a highest and best use conclusion. Of course, with most appraisals of single-family homes, much thought is not necessary because the homes are in the middle of residential neighborhoods. Still, every appraisal will contain at least a brief description of the property's highest and best use. The analysis of highest and best use for non-residential properties is often much more involved.

Beyond deciding what use of the land would be most profitable, the other parts of the highest and best use definition must be considered as well:

- The zoning laws must permit the intended use of the land.
- The cost to put the land to a new use must make sense economically.
- The owner must be able to build the proposed structure on the land.

All of these factors must be considered when an appraiser forms an opinion of value for a property.

Analyzing Highest and Best Use

Analyzing and concluding upon the highest and best use for the subject property is one of the most important steps in the appraisal process in a market value assignment. In fact, highest and best use is at the heart of the valuation process. The appraiser must look at the use that supports the highest present value for the property (as of the effective date of the appraisal), or the use that develops the highest present value for the property over a reasonable period of time.

Due to zoning and any private regulations, such as subdivision restrictions, homes in the middle of a residential neighborhood often do not present a great issue in the appraiser's conclusion of highest and best use. But what about a house located in a commercially zoned district? Usually, the property would be more profitable if it were generating income from a commercial use (as opposed to being rented as a residence).

With vacant land in an area that is changing, growing, or expanding, highest and best use can be a significant point that needs to be addressed. Sometimes a change of structure is best to maximize the value of the land. In fact, razing one type of commercial structure in favor of another is also a consideration when looking at highest and best use. To determine a property's highest and best use, the appraiser performs two basic steps; then, as a third step, he compares the values derived from each of the first two steps.

Step 1: Value as if the Land Were Vacant

The first step an appraiser takes when analyzing highest and best use is to value the land as if it were vacant and available for any permitted use. Here, the appraiser does not take into account any buildings, structures, or improvements presently on the land (it may be necessary to tear these down if they do not result in the maximum value to the owner). The appraiser must then determine the ideal use of the land that would return the maximum value to the owner. When evaluating ideal use, the appraiser looks at four tests for highest and best use:

Legally Permissible

Here, the appraiser primarily looks at government restrictions, as well as deed or other restrictions. Is the ideal use permitted with the existing zoning on the property? What is the likelihood of a zoning change? A zoning change must be shown to be reasonable or probable—not speculative. Are there other government regulations (e.g., environmental laws) or private restrictions (e.g., deed conditions) that prevent certain uses of the property? Will compliance with regulations add too much to the development costs?

Physically Possible

Here, the appraiser looks at the physical limitations of the land. Is the lot big enough to allow for a structure with required setbacks and other zoning requirements? Does the topography of the land allow for construction? Will the ground support the weight of a building?

Economically Feasible

Here, the appraiser looks at market demand. Can the market support another use of this type in its supply/demand model? Are the other principles of value conducive to this use?

Most Profitable or Maximally Productive

Here, the appraiser might look at net income that could be produced. What uses, building types, etc., produce the greatest net income? When the assignment involves publicly owned land, should other productive uses be considered (i.e., fire station vs. library)?

Value as Currently Improved

The second step an appraiser performs when analyzing highest and best use is to estimate the value of the land as it is currently improved. Here, the appraiser values the property in its present state and condition, with all buildings and structures present. The most common way the appraiser develops this opinion is by comparing the property with other comparable sales that have similar existing buildings.

Final Conclusion of Highest and Best Use

The final step in analyzing highest and best use is to compare the two estimates of value derived in steps one and two. Whichever value is greater is usually said to be the highest and best use for the property. Keep in mind that an appraiser may actually look at several different options in step one before arriving at the ideal use or improvement. Finally, after the value indications from step one and step two are compared, the conclusion of the highest and best use for the property becomes the basis of the valuation process. The final conclusion of highest and best use is an opinion that must always be supported by objective data and facts that have been thoroughly analyzed.

Interim Uses

An **interim use** is a temporary use of property while it awaits conversion to its highest and best use (e.g., waiting for a zoning change, accumulation of investment dollars). An interim use helps the owner achieve maximum value in the future while still receiving some use or income from the property until that time.

When the appraiser is concluding upon an interim use for a property, he must be careful to observe the **principle of consistent use**, which *implies that land cannot be valued for one use while the improvements are valued for another use.* For example, an appraiser is valuing a residential dwelling located on a commercially zoned parcel. The dwelling is deriving rent as a residential rental. The site (as commercial) has greater value than the property, as improved, with a residential structure. However, there is no perceived immediate demand for commercial sites; therefore, an interim use has been concluded to use the property as a residential rental. Thus, in the interim use, the land cannot be valued as commercial while the improvements are valued as residential.

Examples of Highest and Best Use Conclusions

Some possible conclusions of highest and best use for a particular property include:

Conclusion	Example
Leave the property as-is, using the present structure for its intended use.	A residential home in the downtown area of a small town remains used as a home because there is not enough demand for more commercial or retail space.
Leave the property as-is, using the present structure for its current use for as long as that use is viable, being aware that the use is grandfathered as a **non-conforming use**.	A convenience store that has been open for many years does not have enough parking spaces to meet current zoning requirements. Since the business is viable, the appraiser recommends keeping the store open as a legal non-conforming use while advising the client that changes to the property (e.g., adding a drive-thru) or structure (e.g., expanding the store) or business (e.g., installing gas pumps) might invalidate the grandfathered usage and cause the store to have to add parking spaces and conform to all current zoning laws.
Leave the property as-is, *using the present structure temporarily in its current use until the property can be developed to a higher use*. This type of usage is referred to as an **interim use**. The interim use may not be the property's highest and best use now, but this may be the best short-term option so that the land can be developed to its highest and best use later.	A small, independent corner gas station is showing a small profit, but cannot compete with the newer corporate-owned gas stations that have convenience stores attached to them. The appraiser identifies several potential uses for the corner lot (e.g., fast food location, drugstore), but learns that some of the large players are not expanding into the city until the following calendar year. The appraiser recommends continuing to operate the gas station as an interim use until next year when more potential buyers will be looking for land in the market, so that the competition will raise land values.
Alter the present structure on the property, repairing the building so that it can continue to be used for its intended use.	An older strip mall needs some repairs, so the appraiser recommends fixing it with a new roof and new fascia to increase its appeal. The appraiser's market study concludes that there is a shortage of retail space in the area given current demographic trends, and that with these minimal costs, the strip mall can raise rents and help to ward off competition that may be coming from some new development.

(continued on next page)

Conclusion	Example
Alter the present structure on the property, renovating or enlarging it so that it has additional capacity or can serve additional purposes.	A family owns a restaurant and is concerned that it cannot compete with some national restaurant chains, and the family is considering selling the property. The appraiser finds that the business is well-positioned to take advantage of favorable demographic trends that show more blue-collar workers moving to the area with a new company. The data show that business can be increased with newly expanded facilities, including a lounge, carryout counter, and small gift shop added to the premises.
Tear down the present structure, making the land available for another structure or other development.	A small, independent corner gas station is losing money. The appraiser identifies several potential uses for the corner lot (e.g., fast food location, drugstore), but learns that some of the large players are not expanding into the city until the following calendar year. The appraiser recommends tearing down the gas station so it is ready for new uses.
Tear down the present structure, making the land vacant so that it can be held as an investment for speculation or future development.	A run-down house sits on five acres of land beside a property where it has just been announced that ground breaking for a new shopping mall will begin next month. Since the house needs extensive repairs before it could be lived in or rented out, the appraiser recommends tearing down the house and waiting until the mall is finished or other demand factors change.
Leave the property as-is, vacant, waiting for appropriate demand to catch up with the supply of properties available in the marketplace. The property can also be held as an investment for speculation or future development.	A vacant parcel of land sits in a relatively undeveloped area. But demographic trends and data at the city planning office show that future growth and development is moving in that direction. Since there is no real demand for vacant land in that area outside the city limits, the appraiser recommends that the property be held until more business or housing activity is announced for that area.
Apply for a zoning change for the present property so that it can be used in a more productive way.	A house sits on a busy street, where there is a mix of residential and commercial uses. The subject house is actually across the street from a strip mall, but there are other houses on both sides of the subject house. Still, the house sits on two and a half acres, so the appraiser recommends that the owner apply for a zoning change. Even with the added costs of obtaining the zoning change, the property would still be worth much more if it could be developed for commercial use instead of being sold or rented as a house.
Divide the land so that it can be sold off in lots or used for multiple purposes.	A farmhouse sits on a large, 126-acre parcel of land that an investor just bought. The appraiser determines that the land should be divided into several parts. A few parcels should be set aside and sold for retail, fast food, and other commercial uses, while a large tract of the land should be further subdivided and platted into small lots to allow residential homes to be built in a new community.
Acquire additional parcel(s) of land so that the property can accommodate more parking, have more road frontage, or allow a larger structure to be built on it. All of these can increase the value and usefulness of the land.	A doctor's office is for sale, so an investor asks an appraiser to determine value and highest and best use. The appraiser researches the area and finds that there is a relative scarcity of medical facilities in the area. The appraiser's report recommends that the investor acquire the doctor's office, contingent on being able to acquire a neighboring parcel of land at a reasonable cost. This would allow the doctor's office to expand its building and services, plus provide additional parking spaces to conform with current zoning requirements in the area.

Other Considerations of Highest and Best Use

For appraisal purposes, market value of property is always determined as if the land is vacant and available for development to its highest and best use. (Keep in mind, this is often limited by zoning.) Highest and best use implies the right mix of capital improvements and land. Land is at its highest and best use when it has the right *balance* of (**C-E-L-L**):

- **C**apital
- **E**ntrepreneurship/management
- **L**abor
- **L**and

In other words, after considering the previous four cost factors, what balance of these factors results in the best return on investment from the land?

The appraiser must perform a careful analysis of all alternative uses for the property before arriving at a conclusion. If certain uses are not possible, the appraiser should note this in the appraisal report, along with the appropriate reasons. And if it is determined that land would be more valuable if the current structure were torn down and replaced with a new type of building, then the cost of razing the building must be subtracted from the value figure. A valid analysis of highest and best use translates into the most profitable use of the land, which in turn determines the most probable (and highest) price the property can command in the open market.

As a final note, it is important to understand that there are certain assumptions made when discussing the determination of highest and best use:

- There must be potential buyers of a property at its highest and best use if the highest and best use is truly a reflection of the market.
- There is only one highest and best use for land at a given point in time.
- Land not devoted to highest and best use results in a loss of income.
- Highest and best use gives the owner maximum economic advantage.
- Highest and best use allocates land resources efficiently, maximizing economic return.
- Highest and best use gives economic benefits to surrounding land (through the principle of conformity).
- Highest and best use gives economic benefits to the community (because it conserves a scarce resource—land).

Math Exercises

Gross Living Area (GLA) Calculations

The formulas for calculating Gross Living Area (GLA) was discussed earlier in this chapter. As a review, when calculating square footage, the calculations can consist of squares or rectangles, or a triangle. Land area can also be calculated using the same formulas.

SQUARE or RECTANGLE—length x width
> **Area = Length x Width**
> area = l x w

TRIANGLE—One Half x Base x Height
> **Area = 1/2 x Base x Height**
> area = 1/2 x b x h

Appraisers must be able to calculate the area or gross living area of a house, either as a separate problem or as part of a larger problem (such as calculating the cost of a structure using the cost approach). Again, to review, **gross living area (GLA)** is *residential space that is finished, heated, and above grade*. Garages and spaces below grade are specifically excluded.

This means garages, finished basements, and storage areas are typically not counted as part of the total GLA. Finished attics may count as GLA if they have heat and electricity, finished walls, and normal ceiling height. Square footage is always calculated by using the *outside* dimensions of the structure—the building costs need to include the outside walls as well. For residential property, non-living areas (e.g., garage space, screened-in porch) are always subtracted from the outer building dimension totals when calculating square footage.

Work Problems 3.5

1. *What is the gross living area of the house depicted in the diagram below?*

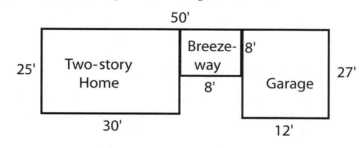

2. *What is the total GLA of the irregularly shaped house illustrated below?*

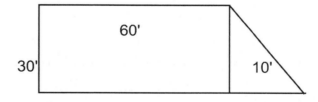

Cubic Foot Calculations

Sometimes, certain types of building area, such as a warehouse, might be stated by *cubic feet*. This method of determining the gross building area will be used when the height of an area is relative to the utility of the building.

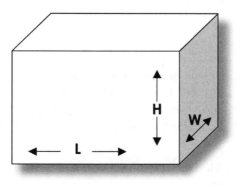

Calculations for a cubic foot are similar to the calculation for gross living area and gross building area, except the height of the structure is also used in the calculation.

Area = Length x Width x Height

Work Problems 3.6

1. *What is the length of a building that has 15,000 cubic feet if the height is 15' and the width is 20'?*

_____

2. *A storage warehouse is 100' long, 75' wide, and 22' tall. What is area of the building in cubic feet?*

_____

Work Problem 3.7

An appraisal is being performed for four commercial lots on Garden Road. Zoning is C-2, general business, which allows both commercial and residential use, depending on lot size. Minimum site size in this township is 1 acre for commercial properties and 0.5 acre for residential properties. The lots are as follows:

Lot 1: 145' x 200'

Lot 2: 145' x 310'

Lot 3: 300' x 500'

Lot 4: 125' x 300'

What is the permitted legal use for each of these lots?

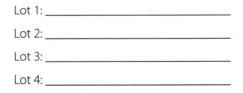

Lot 1: _____

Lot 2: _____

Lot 3: _____

Lot 4: _____

Summary

1. *Steps in building a new house*: Research and planning, pre-construction, site work, foundation, framing, roofing, rough-ins, interior finish, exterior finish, and completion. *Foundations*: Concrete slabs, piers and beams, crawl spaces, or basements. *Framing*: Platform, post and beam, balloon. *Roofing*: Truss, joist and rafters, sloped joist. *Roof styles*: Gable, hip, gambrel, mansard, saltbox, shed, flat.

2. *Building inspections*: Government authorities ensuring compliance with prevailing building codes. *Order of inspections for new builds*: Preliminary (plans), site foundation (before pouring footers), underfloor, close-in, rough, insulation, dry wall/wall cover, final inspection. Occupancy Certification may be required. *Permits*: Government documents allowing work to be performed. *Building permit*: Needed to construct, build, alter, move, destroy, demolish.

3. **Building codes** set construction standards for methods and materials. Codes must be adopted by jurisdictions as exercise of police power for building codes to be enforceable. Old work not up to current code is usually allowed to stay if work was up to code at the time it was performed and is safe now. If remodeling, all work may need to meet code. Commercial buildings usually need to meet current codes, especially health, fire, and ADA. *Electrical deficiencies*: Inadequate electric service (need at least 100 amps), not enough outlets/grounded outlets (need ground fault interrupters), undersized/worn wiring (#12 gauge = 20 amp, #10 gauge = 30 amp). *Plumbing deficiencies*: Traps (S-traps can allow sewer gas to escape; P-traps are better), outdated pipe material (non-copper metal pipes can corrode; lead is dangerous).

4. *Architectural styles*: American Colonial, English Tudor, French Provincial, Spanish Villa, Cape Cod, Traditional Ranch, Modern Contemporary. *Functional layouts*: One-story, one-and-one-half story, and two-story. *Windows*: Single hung, double hung, horizontal sliding, casement, awning, hopper, fixed sash, bay window. *Doors*: 6 panel, 4 panel, flush (solid or hollow).

5. *Mechanical systems* in house are electrical, plumbing, heating. *Electrical system*: Wiring, breaker box, breakers, lights, switches, outlets. *Plumbing system*: Piping, faucets, sinks, toilets, tubs, hot water tank, (and gas lines). Supply water lines are under pressure; sewer lines need gravity, vents. *Heating system*: Furnace, flue, ducts, registers, thermostat, and can include A/C (HVAC). "Normal" 2,000 sq. ft. home might use 80K BTU furnace, 2-ton (24K BTU) A/C. Furnace can be forced air (blower) or gravity. Heat pump is alternative.

6. An appraiser performs a property inspection of a house or other structure as a means of gathering data to be used for analysis and noting the condition, quality, and quantity of improvements. An appraiser typically notes items of concern and recommends inspection by a professional for further determination.

7. *Home inspection*: Visual exam of structure, systems. Objective: Find dangers, damage, non-working items. *Professional home inspectors*: ASHI˚, NAHI˚, NABIE˚, others. Inspection isn't a guarantee, but potential liability exists if something is missed or appraiser acts as an inspector when he is not. Inspection covers systems, foundation, roof, windows, doors, interior, and exterior. May offer tests for well, septic, termites, lead, radon, etc.

8. A site-built house is assembled on the site or lot. A factory-built house is assembled in sections in a factory and delivered to the site to be rolled-off onto a foundation (*not considered a manufactured home*). A manufactured home is built on a permanent chassis and has special requirements to meet Fannie Mae eligibility.

9. Highest and best use is the legally permitted, economically feasible, physically possible, and most profitable use of a property. Highest and best use is important to determine before forming an opinion of value.

10. Sometimes a change of structure is needed for a property to be put to its highest and best use. The first step is for the appraiser to estimate the value of land as if it were vacant; the second step is for the appraiser to estimate the value as the property is currently improved. The third and final step is to compare these two values, with the higher one being the property's highest and best use. When the appraiser considers the land as if it were vacant, he looks at four tests for highest and best use: 1. Is it legally permitted? 2. Is it physically possible? 3. Is it economically feasible? 4. Is it most profitable (or maximally productive)?

Quiz

1. *The first step when building a new house is*

   a. building the foundation.
   b. doing landscaping.
   c. doing research and planning.
   d. doing the rough-ins.

2. *Which type of roof allows for vaulted ceilings?*

   a. joists and rafters
   b. piers and beams
   c. sloped joists
   d. truss roofing

3. *A roof's pitch is the*

   a. rise of the roof.
   b. run of the roof.
   c. vertical rise of the roof in feet per horizontal inches.
   d. vertical rise of the roof in inches per horizontal foot.

4. *A building inspection for the site foundation is performed*

   a. after the footers are poured.
   b. before the footers are poured.
   c. it doesn't matter when it is performed.
   d. while the footers are being poured.

5. *The highest and best use test of "legally permissible" includes which consideration?*

   a. allowable to zoning
   b. hazard insurance could be obtained
   c. police protection is available
   d. title is free of encumbrances

6. *What is NOT a purpose of a ground fault interrupter?*

   a. to prevent electric shock or electrocution of a person
   b. to prevent a malfunctioning device from causing shorts in a house's wiring
   c. to turn off an appliance that falls into a sink full of water
   d. to vary the wattage appliances use

7. *A ranch-style home is typically*

   a. one floor level.
   b. one-and-one-half stories.
   c. a split-level.
   d. two stories.

8. *A Cape Cod style home is typically*

   a. one story.
   b. one-and-one-half stories.
   c. a split-level.
   d. two stories.

9. *Which would NOT be a rationale for concluding on an interim use as the highest and best use?*

   a. anticipated death of a wealthy relative, providing an inheritance to convert the property
   b. anticipated demand for the subject in the near future as something more profitable
   c. anticipated formation of investment interest
   d. anticipated zoning change

10. *The type of construction for which Fannie Mae has specific guidelines is*

    a. factory-engineered.
    b. manufactured.
    c. panelized.
    d. pre-fabricated.

11. *A three-sided building has one side with 30 feet perpendicular to the front of the building which measures 50 linear feet. How many square feet are contained in this building?*

    a. 250
    b. 750
    c. 1,500
    d. 2,250

12. *A warehouse is 65 feet long and 22 feet high. If the structure contains 45,760 cubic feet, how wide is the building?*

    a. 18
    b. 26
    c. 30
    d. 32

13. *A two-story house has exterior dimensions of 52' x 32' and has a full basement. A 20' x 15' one-story addition to the building is being considered. What would be the GLA of the house with the addition?*

    a. 1,964
    b. 2,223
    c. 3,628
    d. 4,139

14. ***Regarding the highest and best use test of "physically possible," which would NOT be considered?***

    a. building materials
    b. building set back lines
    c. parking requirements
    d. size of the building

15. ***Which type of construction framing is assembled one story at a time with each story serving as the base for the next story?***

    a. Balloon
    b. Ledger
    c. Platform
    d. Post and Beam

Chapter 4

Overview of the Sales Comparison Approach

The development of the sales comparison approach requires that sales data be collected and analyzed in the development of the sales comparison analysis. The sales comparison approach is sometimes referred to as the "market approach" due to its reliance upon actual market transaction data for support of the appraiser's opinions and conclusions reached in the methodology. In this chapter, the steps taken by the appraiser in developing the sales comparison approach will be overviewed.

Bracketing A process in which an appraiser identifies a probable value range, most often by identifying values of properties that are inferior and those that are superior. The appraiser then determines where an opinion of value for the subject should fall within that range.

Chattels An item considered personal property.

Comparable Properties Properties that possess many of the same appeal factors, but the buyer for one property may not necessarily be interested in the comparable property.

Competitive Properties Properties that compete head-to-head. A potential buyer for one property would also be interested in the competitive property.

Conditions of Sale Atypical motivations of the parties of a transaction (usually make the sale non-arm's length).

Discount Point An amount paid to a lender when a loan is made to make up the difference between the current market interest rate and the rate a lender gives a borrower on a note. Discount points increase a lender's yield on a note, allowing the lender to give a borrower a lower interest rate.

Economics of Sale A variable often observed through multiple regression; for example, as the size increases, the unit cost decreases.

Elements of Comparison Characteristics of a property or a transaction that can be used to explain differences in the price paid in a transaction.

(Continued on page 109)

Data Collection

As a general practice, the appraiser begins his development of the sales comparison approach by researching and selecting market data of sold and closed transactions for use as comparable data when developing and supporting the conclusions reached in the sales comparison approach. However, it is sometimes appropriate that the appraiser will also gather and analyze pending transactions and current listings as part of the analysis.

Comparable Properties

One of the most challenging steps for many appraisers in the sales comparison approach is choosing data for analysis that is "most comparable" to the subject property. This process requires competency, which relies heavily on the appraiser's experience, judgment skills, and knowledge of the market and/or neighborhood. Which leads to a sometimes complex question: What is a comparable property?

Comparable properties, or comparables, generically can be categorized as *properties that share great, or sometimes subtle, similarities with the subject property*. These similarities could be the location, design, or features. The similarity might also be the typical buyer for these properties—similar buyer mindset and profile. Comparability can be translated to a very broad or a narrowly defined basis.

Competitive Properties

Competitive properties are *those that compete head-to-head*. In other words, *a potential buyer for one property would also be interested in the competitive property*. These properties are not necessarily physically identical. A buyer might be interested in many styles and ages of houses as long as they are located in a particular area.

Properties that are Comparable and Competitive

There would be very little argument that the ideal data to be used for comparable analysis would represent properties that are both *comparable to* and *competitive with* the subject property—properties that are as similar physically, locationally, or legally as possible, and would attract the same buyer. When relevant comparable and competitive data is plentiful, there is little need for the appraiser to venture outside of the market area for his analysis or to instead use a one and one-half story house to compare with a two-story subject. In some assignments, there may be readily available comparable *and* competitive data for subject properties and markets.

Ideally, the data chosen will reflect the most recent, nearest, and physically similar when compared to the subject property. But, the quality and quantity of the data available, as well as any assignment conditions, will dictate this rationale. Client requirements, such as Fannie Mae requirements and guidelines, will be discussed later in this text.

IMPORTANT POINTS...

- *One of the most market-oriented of the appraisal methods given there is relevant data available, the sales comparison approach can be applied to any property type.*

- *The sales comparison approach is typically the most reliable valuation method for non-income producing residential properties.*

- *The biggest advantage is the sales comparison approach relies on information rooted in market activity and most often uses market extracted data as a means to adjust comparable sales.*

- *Sales data from similar properties exposed to a sales transaction is required to develop the sales comparison approach and, thus, it may not provide as useful a method for a value indication for special-purpose properties, such as schools, churches, etc., and other unusual or unique properties for which there isn't sufficient sales data to analyze.*

- *Based on historic data, the sales comparison approach may not reflect any recent changes in the market without the appraiser recognizing, isolating, and applying an appropriate adjustment.*

Choice of Data

The initial choice of data to be used in the sales comparison approach analysis is a decision that requires the appraiser's sound judgment. Experience is required to develop this skill. In many assignments, the appraiser will select several properties for his analysis.

Depending on the assignment and the quantity of data available, the initial gathering of data could exceed that which will eventually be used in his valuation analysis. Once the data has been identified, it can be organized in a manner where the relevance and differences between the properties and the subject can be more easily recognized.

In some assignments, relevant data can be plentiful and the data collection and organization process rather simple. Of course, this also requires the appraiser to be fairly familiar with the particular market and the transactions that have taken place.

Data Analysis

USPAP does not place an obligation on the appraiser to use and analyze a specific number of comparables. Standards Rule 1-4 (a) of USPAP simply requires the appraiser to:

"Analyze such comparable sales data as are available."

A minimum of three comparables are most usually gathered, analyzed, and presented in keeping with the regulations and requirements of many clients and intended users.

Units of Comparison

In each assignment, appraisers select an appropriate *unit of comparison* for which to perform their analysis. The unit of comparison is *the context in which the sale price is stated*. In residential assignments, the unit of comparison is typically the *total sale price of the property*. Depending on the scope of work decided in the assignment, the sale price could also be considered in other ways.

Gross Adjustments The overall total of all adjustments applied, regardless of whether the adjustment is applied as a positive or a negative (for example, a +$1,000 and a -$1,000 adjustment would result in $2,000 gross adjustments).

Mean A statistical value that adds a series of values and then divides the total by the number of values on the set: Commonly known as the average.

Median A statistical value that describes the center or middle number in a set of numbers.

Mode The most frequently occurring number in a number set.

Net Adjustments The sum of the adjustments taking into account whether the adjustment was a positive or a negative. (For example, a +$1,000 and a -$1,000 adjustment would result in $0 net adjustments.)

Paired Data Analysis The process of determining the value of specific property characteristics or features by comparing pairs of similar properties. Also called **Matched Pair Analysis**.

Partial Interest Any interest in real estate that one may have, other than full bundle of rights.

Reconciliation Analyzing the conclusions within each approach that was developed; analyzing the values derived from the different appraisal approaches to arrive at a final opinion of value.

Regression Analysis A statistical measure that attempts to ascertain the source of change in variables.

Unit of Comparison A component with which a property can be divided for the purpose of comparison, such as square foot, living unit, etc.

Key Terms

Units of Comparison Examples

Sale prices of residential properties can be unitized on a *per square foot basis of gross living area:*

Sale price $400,000 / 2,000 square feet = $200 sale price per square foot

Residential apartment buildings can be stated as based on a *price per apartment unit:*

Sale price $400,000 / 4 apartment units = $100,000 per apartment

Or, on a price per room:

Sale price $400,000 / 16 rooms = $25,000 per room

Otherwise, as with the earlier example for single-family properties, the basis can be *per square foot of total gross living area.*

Vacant land can also be considered several different ways. The sale price of smaller residential building lots is often stated in units of square feet. Larger residential tracts may be considered on a per-acre basis. Units of front feet are common when the land parcel's sale price is most influenced by what the parcel faces.

This is similar to how commercial land is considered when its sale price is dependent on the parcel's amount of street frontage.

√ **Note:** The front feet is always the first measurement stated in a dimension.

Sale Price Example

For example, a 100' x 200' residential building lot sold for $40,000. 100' is the front feet since it is the first number in the dimension. Based on a per square foot unit, the sale price was $2.00 per square foot:

100' x 200' = 20,000 square feet

$40,000 / 20,000 = $2.00

A 10-acre residential tract sold for $150,000. Using a per-acre unit of measure, the sale price per acre was $15,000 per acre:

$150,000 / 10 acres = $15,000

A 150' x 100' waterfront parcel sold for $150,000. If front feet were the unit of measure, the unit sale price would be $1,000:

$150,000 / 150 = $1,000

Economics of Scale

When size-related unit prices are used, the appraiser can apply the unit price to comparables of different sizes without making an adjustment for the size difference. The appraiser should strive to apply the unit price to comparable data that is as similar in size as possible. Significantly larger or smaller data may need to be adjusted due to the economics of scale.

Based on the economics of scale, the per square foot price of a 1,500 square foot house may be greater than the per square foot price of a 3,000 square foot house; therefore, the per square foot price unit derived may require an economics of scale adjustment.

Elements of Comparison

Examining the **elements of comparison**, which are *characteristics of a property or a transaction that can be used to explain differences in the price paid in a transaction,* provides the appraiser deeper insight about the similarity of the subject and the properties that have been chosen for comparison.

Appraisers take into account several elements when considering the comparability of a particular property and whether or not to make an adjustment. The elements of comparison reflect similarities of the legal interests, cash equivalency, market conditions, and physical factors between the subject and the comparable data.

The basic elements of comparison that are examined in most transactions are:

1. Property rights conveyed
2. Financing terms
3. Conditions of sale
4. Market conditions
5. Location
6. Physical characteristics

> √ **Note:** Expenditures made immediately after the sale may be considered as an element in some assignments. They will be part of the conditions of sale or listed immediately following. This will be discussed later in this chapter.

When the type of value in an appraisal assignment is market value and if the information is available to the appraiser in the normal course of business, Standards Rule 1-5(a) of USPAP requires the appraiser to:

> *"Analyze all agreements of sale, options, and listings of the subject property current as of the effective date of the appraisal."*

Some may question why appraisers are provided with the current agreement of sale, the details of a pending transaction, or certain listing information. The purpose is fairly simple and directly related to the elements of comparison. Important information regarding key elements can be gained from examining what was being offered in a listing, or what was agreed upon by the parties to a transaction.

Sales contracts specifically alert the appraiser to property rights that are or are not being conveyed. As well, the agreement likely spells out any special financing terms, concessions, and items of value that are included in the transaction. Other considerations noted could have a significant impact as well, such as extended possession periods for the seller or fixtures that the seller is taking with them.

When the elements of a transaction are inconsistent with the data being used for comparison in the sales comparison approach, the appraiser must analyze and consider the potential for adjustments.

Property Rights Conveyed

The appraiser must make certain that the property rights of the subject in the assignment are consistent with the comparable data being used. If the subject of the appraisal is being valued in fee simple and the property rights conveyed are something other than fee simple, such as a partial interest, this would lead to something less than an apples-to-apples comparison. A **partial interest** is *any interest in real estate that one may have, other than the full bundle of rights.*

In reality, in most common residential appraisal assignments, the examination of property rights conveyed is not performed after data has been selected, but rather as a primary consideration of the data's applicability in the initial selection process. In other words, the appraiser determined that the comparable data reflected the same property rights before he chose it for use in the analysis. Therefore, on some common appraisal forms, the appraiser may not actually see "Property Rights Conveyed" as a separate line item. The reasoning for this is that the guidelines and requirements of many clients and intended users of residential appraisals do not allow comparable data to be used where the property rights conveyed in a transaction are something different than the subject of the assignment.

Financing Terms

The underlying premise of the most commonly used definition of market value assumes cash equivalency to the typical market. The assumption is that the subject is not part of a transaction that includes atypical financing terms or financing concessions when the definition of value is market value. Therefore, the effect of any unusual terms or concessions in the transaction of a comparable sale is not reflected by comparison to the subject. Rather, it is reflected in the amount the dollars, the terms, and concessions had on the comparable transaction in relationship to the market.

Unlike the other elements of comparison, financing terms and concessions affect only the comparable data in a market value assignment and have no relationship to the subject. The effect of financing terms should be analyzed to determine if an adjustment is warranted. In addition to seller participation in financing and seller-paid financing concessions, other examples of financing terms that might be considered include:

- Assumption of an existing mortgage
- Buydowns and financial incentives offered by a builder or developer
- Land or installment contracts with the seller retaining legal title until satisfied
- Wraparound loans using existing mortgages
- Program (financing) participation fees required to be paid by the seller

It may be common, depending on the situation, that financing terms are distinguished using a separate analysis and adjustment for financing method and seller-paid fees and concessions, such as seller-paid discount points.

A **discount point** is *an amount paid to a lender when a loan is made to make up the difference between the current market interest rate and the rate a lender gives a borrower on a note. Discount points increase a lender's yield on a note, allowing the lender to give a borrower a lower interest rate. Each discount point equals 1 percent of the loan amount.*

So, if the seller is paying two discount points for the buyer, and the buyer is obtaining a mortgage for $100,000, the discount points would equal $2,000 ($100,000 x 2%). If the purchase price of the property were $105,000, a downward adjustment of $2,000 would be made in the sales comparison approach and the adjusted cash equivalent sale price would be $103,000.

Conditions of Sale

Usually, **conditions of sale** consider *atypical motivations of the parties of a transaction.* Most often, these non-market conditions will be elements that affect the sale price in a transaction that would not be considered arm's length. Some examples of these atypical motivations include:

- Related parties in a transaction where the seller asked for a lower price, due to the relationship
- A seller facing hardship, a tight timeline, or other circumstance that could be interpreted as duress
- Chattels (personal property) included in the transaction
- A transaction of a property where the seller was not necessarily looking out for his own best interest, such as selling for less to a religious entity or a non-profit organization
- Property acquired for assemblage

Some terms of a sales transaction that need to be considered in conditions of sale will evidence themselves in the purchase contract. However, most of these transaction details can be determined only by communication with a party familiar with the comparable transaction.

Expenditures made after the sale can be analyzed either as independent elements of comparison or as part of the conditions of sale. These items could include anticipated costs to cure property condition items, raze all or part of the improvements, or eliminate environmental issues. Most often, these adjustments are addressed in terms of the actual dollars the purchaser anticipated at the time the purchase price was agreed upon.

Market Conditions

An appraiser may need to consider whether an adjustment may be warranted for market conditions when the conditions in which the transaction took place are different from the effective date of the value opinion in an assignment. The date of sale in the comparable transaction evidences to the appraiser the need for the analysis.

Appraisers should be cautious of immediately assuming that although the date of sale is different, an adjustment for market conditions is automatically warranted. In some cases, a few days may account for a measurable difference. In other cases, a period of several months may have very little change in market conditions.

Appraisers seldom locate data in which the comparable data transacted on the effective date in the appraiser's assignment. It is likely that any affect between the market conditions in the comparable data and the subject property will require analysis, but adjustments are not always required. Changes in the conditions of a market are always the purpose for an adjustment for market conditions, not simply the passing of time.

Location

Depending on the availability of data, it is possible that a location element could be found that is different between the comparable data and the subject property. When considering location, the appraiser should be most concerned with the particular location's market preferences and external characteristics, as well as how the subject site compares with the data being analyzed.

Though this list is certainly not all-inclusive, these items could include the following:

- Economic characteristics (including supply and demand)
- External influences
- Zoning
- Access
- View
- Position (i.e., corner vs. interior)

Physical Characteristics

No two properties are *exactly* the same. How the comparable data differs from the subject property and how the market will interpret those differences in dollars could result in a very broad analysis. Therefore, in most residential appraisal assignments, it is likely that there will be some degree of difference in the physical features and characteristics between the data being used for comparison and the subject property.

These differences could be related to the style and design, condition or quality, size and room type, or features of the property. While it is usually easy to recognize differences between properties, determining the necessity of an adjustment and the amount of the adjustment can often be much more painstaking.

Identifying and Supporting Adjustments

Once a difference or differences between the comparable data and the subject property are recognized, the next step is to determine if an adjustment is warranted—and if so, how much. There are several acceptable methods and techniques by which an appraiser can determine the necessity for, and the identification of, an adjustment.

Determining the appropriateness and the amount of an adjustment requires competence that is gained through experience, diligent analytical process, sound judgment, and reasoning skills. The results of the appraiser's analyses *must be based on objective market evidence.*

An appraiser cannot simply "rubber-stamp" adjustments based on unsupported notions. For instance, an appraiser cannot determine that a fireplace will always contribute $500, or that *every* additional bedroom contributes $1,000. Such decisions can only be made when market evidence supports the conclusion.

Adjustments in the sales comparison approach are often identified in the form of quantitative adjustments. Another type of analysis that appraisers employ during the valuation process is qualitative analysis.

Quantitative and Qualitative Adjustments

Making **quantitative adjustments** is *a method that requires the recognition of the differences between the comparable data and the subject property and assigning either a dollar or percentage amount as an adjustment.* In the sales comparison approach, adjustments for most residential appraisal assignments are quantified through data analysis techniques such as paired data analysis.

Qualitative analysis is *a method used after any quantitative adjustments have been applied that employs the appraiser's judgment in forming opinions, relying on such methods as relative comparison analysis, ranking analysis, or personal interviews.* This method requires the appraiser to have good judgment and reasoning skills. This step is used during the reconciliation process or when a quantitative adjustment cannot be reasonably determined. For example, a qualitative technique is when the appraiser recognizes that the subject is inferior to one comparable sale, but superior to another. His supported conclusion might be bracketed (in between) the two indications. Concluding within the indications is interpolation. Or, if the subject is inferior to all properties analyzed, the appraiser's conclusions might be somewhere below the indications or somewhere above the indications if the subject is superior to the properties analyzed. *Concluding above or below the indications of all data analyzed* is known as **extrapolation**.

Paired Data Analysis

Paired data analysis is *the process of determining the value of specific property characteristics or features by comparing pairs of similar properties.* This is also called a matched pair analysis. This process will provide the appraiser with an indication of the particular feature's dollar value.

Ideally, there should be only one different characteristic between the pairs of properties being analyzed so the difference in sale price can be attributed directly to that feature. This will indicate the feature's contributory value.

In selecting paired data, an appraiser ideally looks for comparables with the same features, except one. **Paired data sets** can be deduced from the given information. By finding the difference in price, the feature's contributory value can be determined.

Paired Data Example

An appraiser is trying to find the contributory value of a fireplace for a subject property. In researching recent sales in the area, the appraiser finds two ranch houses with nearly identical features—same number of bedrooms and baths, both with basements, both on a cul-de-sac, and both sold within the past six months after being on the market for about the same amount of time. One sold for $110,000, the other for $112,500. The only difference is one had a fireplace and one did not. From just one analysis, the appraiser may conclude the fireplace has approximately $2,500 in contributory value.

The following market data was gathered on recent sales in an area. (**Note**: These contributory values are examples only and may vary greatly in your area.)

(Continued on next page)

Paired Data Example (continued)

Comparable	Bedrooms	Baths	Sq. Ft.	Garage	Basement	Price
#1	3	1.5	1,250	Yes	Yes	$77,000
#2	3	1.5	1,100	Yes	Yes	$74,000
#3	2	1.0	850	Yes	No	$63,500
#4	4	1.5	1,250	Yes	Yes	$79,000
#5	3	1.5	1,175	No	Yes	$69,500
#6	3	1.0	1,000	No	No	$65,000
#7	2	1.0	950	Yes	No	$65,500
#8	3	1.5	1,175	Yes	Yes	$72,500
#9	3	1.0	1,000	No	Yes	$67,500
#10	3	1.0	1,100	Yes	Yes	$72,500

In picking the pairs, look for comparables with the same features, except one. The following paired data sets were deduced from the given information. By finding the difference in price, the contributory value of the feature can be determined.

Matched Pairs:			VALUE
	Bedrooms	#1 and #4	$2,000
	Baths (Half)	#2 and #10	$1,500
	Square Feet	#3 and #7	$20/sq. ft.
	Garage	#5 and #8	$3,000
	Basement	#6 and #9	$2,500

The paired data analysis is one example of a quantitative adjustment—the dollar amounts revealed through the analysis have been quantified, or extracted as hard numbers, by using market data. The analysis supports the appraiser's action in applying the results in the sales comparison analysis of a subject property. In reality, though, simply performing one paired data analysis to determine the contributory value of a property feature may not be sufficient.

Regression Analysis

Another quantitative technique for analyzing sales comparison data is a regression analysis. A **regression analysis** is *a statistical measure that attempts to ascertain the source of change in variables.* A simple regression analysis can be used whenever there is a relationship between two characteristics of a property, such as a relationship between the sale price of a property and the property's gross living area. A **multiple regression analysis** is *used when more than two variables are being examined.*

Regression analysis is simply an avenue for the appraiser to observe the relationship and to examine the subject property's relevance to the data. It is especially helpful when the data being analyzed is broad and not all of the data is closely comparable to the subject. Regression analysis will be expanded upon in courses focusing on the sales comparison approach, but the following is an example of how the data is arranged in a regression analysis by examining the total gross living area of the paired sales in relationship to the fourth bedroom's contributory value.

Regression Analysis Example

The appraiser has noted that as the paired sets' square footage increases, so does the contributory value of a fourth bedroom. While this may not be the case in every situation, or certainly not always as consistent as is presented by the paired data sets in the example below, this illustration of a simple regression analysis serves to introduce the methodology.

Paired Data Set	GLA	Extracted Contributory Value of a fourth Bedroom
3	1,800 SF	$1,500
1	2,000 SF	$1,800
2	2,200 SF	$2,100
4	2,400 SF	$2,400

If the subject property contains 2,300 square feet of gross living area, the indicated support is at the halfway point between the conclusions of paired data set #2 and #4, which contained 2,200 square feet and 2,400 square feet, respectively.

Thus, the appraiser's conclusion for application to the subject could be bracketed between the $2,100 and $2,400 contributory value indication as $2,250. Bracketing, in this case, *is demonstrated by the value indications that are superior and inferior to the subject, with the subject's relevance positioned in between.*

Graphic Analysis

A **graphic analysis** is *a simple method of displaying data so that it may be visually interpreted.* There are several ways to present data graphically, but as an example, a scatter diagram is *a graph used to study the relationship between two variables.*

In the scatter diagram below, we see the relationship between the gross living area of the data sets and the contributory value of the fourth bedroom. As the total gross living area of the data increases, so does the contributory value of the fourth bedroom. When the data is viewed two-dimensionally, as in this example, the place where the subject best fits within this data becomes obvious.

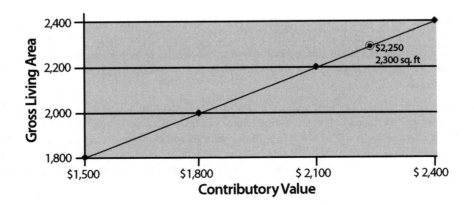

Applying Adjustments

Once the necessity and amount of an adjustment has been determined, the next step for the appraiser is to apply the adjustments to the comparable properties selected for analysis in the sales comparison approach. Theoretically, *the purpose of adjusting comparable properties is to express the differences of the comparable and the subject property as they would be perceived by the market.*

Dollar Adjustments and Percentage Adjustments

In residential appraising, applying dollar adjustments to comparable properties is the most common practice when using the sales comparison approach. Most quantitative adjustments identified for physical characteristics are applied in this manner, as well as others, depending on the specifics of the assignment.

Percentage adjustments are applied more frequently for elements of comparison, such as property rights conveyed, financing terms, conditions of sale, market conditions, and location. In many cases, the percentage may be converted back to a dollar amount for application to a particular comparable. The appraiser must use his judgment as to the appropriateness of the type of adjustment to apply in each assignment.

Direction of Adjustment—Ups and Downs

The purpose of applying an adjustment is to make the comparable as similar to the subject as possible. The subject property is the benchmark for all adjustments; thus, *the subject property is never adjusted!* Adjustments are applied to only the comparable properties.

Comparable Superior

Subject

Comparable Inferior

- When the comparable property is inferior to the subject, an *upward* adjustment is applied to the comparable to align it with the subject.

- When the comparable property is superior to the subject, a *downward* adjustment is applied.

Sequence of Adjustments

In some instances, there could be variations in the order in which the appraiser applies adjustments. However, most residential appraisers follow the progression shown below. Most appraiser examinations use this sequence for testing purposes as well. The order in which adjustments are applied in the sales comparison approach in most residential assignments is similar to the order in which the elements of comparison were discussed:

1. Property rights conveyed
2. Financing terms
3. Conditions of sale
4. Market conditions
5. Location
6. Physical characteristics

Using this sequence allows the appraiser (assuming the data reflects the same property rights conveyed) to adjust for cash equivalency, bring the comparable to the conditions found in an arm's-length transaction, bring the comparable data to the market conditions as of the effective date in the assignment, and mirror the comparable property to the location and physical characteristics if possible or if warranted in the assignment. Adjusting properties in this sequence has a special significance when percentage adjustments are being applied.

Adjustment Application Examples

There are a number of ways that the appraiser can apply either dollar or percentage adjustments. A presentation of an example of dollar adjustments using a market data grid is below.

Dollar Adjustment

FEATURE	SUBJECT	SALE #1	Dollar Adjustment	SALE #2	Dollar Adjustment	SALE #3	Dollar Adjustment
ADDRESS	61 Lake Ave.	127 Dock St.		39 Lake Ave.		168 Shore Dr.	
SALE PRICE	?	$137,900		$149,500		$142,700	
DATE	_____	21 days	0	60 days	+ $1,495	85 days	+ $2,854
1. LOCATION	Waterfront	Waterfront	0	Waterfront	0	Waterfront	0
2. LOT SIZE	100' x 115'	105' x 110'	0	130' x 130'	- $3,000	105' x 125'	- $1,000
3. CONDITION	Good	Average	+ $2,000	Good	0	Good	0
4. AGE	20 years	17 years	0	24 years	0	21 years	0
5. STYLE/CONSTRUCTION	Brick	Brick	0	Stone	- $3,000	Stucco	- $1,000
6. SIZE/SQUARE FEET	1,750 sq. ft.	1,675 sq. ft.	+ $750	1,875 sq. ft.	- $1,250	1,800 sq. ft.	- $500
7. TOTAL ROOMS	7	6	+ $1,000	8	- $1,000	7	0
8. TOTAL BEDROOMS	3	3	0	3	0	3	0
9. TOTAL BATHROOMS	2 ½	2 ½	0	3	- $500	2	+ $500
10. BASEMENT	Full	Full		Full		Full	
11. GARAGE	2-car attached	2-car attached	0	2-car attached	0	2-car attached	0
12. HEATING/COOLING	Gas/Central	Gas/Central		Gas/Central		Gas/Central	
13. OTHER	None	None		Pool	- $2,500	Deck	- $2,000
TOTAL ADJUSTMENTS	_____		+ $3,750		- $9,755		- $1,146
ADJUSTED VALUES	_____		$141,650		$139,745		$141,554

In the following scenario, an example of how percentage adjustments are converted to dollar adjustments and how the dollar adjustments for other elements are applied either in a positive or negative manner is presented. For property rights conveyed, financing terms, conditions of sale, and market conditions, the sale price of the comparable is adjusted after each percentage application as illustrated:

1. Property rights conveyed is adjusted as a percent of the actual sale price.
2. Financing terms are addressed as a percent of the sale price adjusted for property rights conveyed.
3. Conditions of sale is expressed as a percentage of the adjusted sale price after property rights conveyed and financing terms have been addressed.
4. Market conditions are adjusted as a percent of the adjusted sale price after property rights conveyed, financing terms, and conditions of sale have been addressed.

Percentage Adjustment

Once all of these adjustments have been applied, the adjusted sale price of the comparable is revealed. All other adjustments (in this case, location and physical characteristics) are then applied to the adjusted sale price to produce an indication for the price of the subject. Amarket data grid has been provided for examination. The first step of the process is illustrated below.

Element of Comparison	Adjustment %	Adjustment
Sale Price		$400,000
Property Rights Conveyed ($400,000 x 10%)	+10%	+$40,000
Adjusted Price		$440,000
Financing Terms ($440,000 x -5%)	-5%	-$22,000
Adjusted Price		$418,000
Conditions of Sale ($418,000 x -3%)	-3%	-$12,540
Adjusted Price		$405,460
Market Conditions ($405,460 x 9%)	+9%	+$36,491
Adjusted Price		$441,951

There may be times when the appraiser applies all adjustments as percentages, although this may be rare in residential assignments. Property rights conveyed, financing terms, conditions of sale, and market condition adjustments are applied as in the prior example. Location and physical characteristics are applied as a percentage of the price after adjustments for property rights conveyed, financing terms, conditions of sale, and market conditions have been applied. The second part of process, when percentage adjustments are being applied as a percentage is illustrated below.

Element of Comparison	Adjustment %	Adjustment
Sale Price		$400,000
Property Rights Conveyed	+10%	+$40,000
Adjusted Price		$440,000
Financing Terms	-5%	-$22,000
Adjusted Price		$418,000
Conditions of Sale	-3%	-$12,540
Adjusted Price		$405,460
Market Conditions	+9%	+$36,491
Adjusted Price		$441,951
Location (15% x $441,951)	+15%	+$66,293
Physical Characteristics (-10% x $441,951)	-10%	-$44,195
Adjusted Price		$464,049

Reconciliation

In finalizing the development of the sales comparison approach, the appraiser has performed a series of analyses. However, after everything the appraiser has done, the results are without conclusion and somewhat meaningless unless the appraiser reflects on what the analyses revealed. The appraiser needs to perform a final step in order to make sense of the indications produced by the analysis. Thus, the final step in the development process is reconciliation.

After all the individual adjustments are applied and the comparable sales are adjusted, a range of value is revealed. In the sales comparison approach, reconciliation consists of determining the relevance of each comparable and the indications produced.

- Where, in (or in some cases, outside) the value range, is the best value indication for the subject?
- Which comparable, or comparables, provide the best support?

Reconciliation is not purely premised on a mathematical process. The appraiser must use very good logic and reasoning skills when looking at the indications, which lead to sound judgment.

Depending on the scope of work, appraisers can state the final value opinion as a range of value, a single number, or a relationship to a numerical benchmark. Using the indicated value range to support a range of value ($100,000 to $105,000) or even a numerical benchmark (at least as much as…etc.) may be acceptable. However, concluding on a single number opinion should include additional diligence.

Reconciliation in the sales comparison approach brings all the appraiser's analyses together and allows the appraiser to judge the quality and amount of the data examined, as well as the indications the analyses produce.

Simple Reconciliation Example

Suppose that three comparable sales have been used and adjusted in development of the sales comparison analysis. Once adjusted, all of the comparable sales produce the same indication.

	Subject	Comp #1	Comp #2	Comp #3
Sale Price	------	$333,000	$347,000	$335,000
Absolute Adjustments		+$7,000	-$7,000	+$5,000
Adjusted Sale Price	-----	$340,000	$340,000	$340,000

In this scenario, there is little thought that needs to take place in the reconciliation process because the value indication produced in the sales comparison approach is precise, which will seldom (if ever) be seen in the real world. Usually, the indications produced will not be this conclusive. Real estate markets are imperfect. Real estate markets and their participants simply do not typically function in such patterned harmony.

Net and Gross Adjustments

Observing the adjustment total helps the appraiser to recognize the relevance of the data analyzed in the sales comparison approach, given that all differences have been quantified and resulted with a corresponding adjustment. In general, the rationale demonstrated here is that the less a comparable must be adjusted, the more relevant and comparable the data is.

Gross adjustments are *the overall total of all adjustments applied regardless of whether the adjustment is applied as a positive or negative.* In comparison, **net adjustments** are *the sum of the adjustments, taking into account whether the adjustment was a positive or negative.* Net adjustments reflect the percent of adjustments when compared to the sale price of the comparable.

Example

If a comparable requires a +$500 adjustment and a -$500 adjustment, the net adjustments total would be 0% as the two adjustments cancel each other.

Gross adjustments address the sum of all adjustments as a running total. So, the comparable that requires a +$500 adjustment and a -$500 adjustment would have $1,000 in gross adjustments. The dollar amount of gross adjustments would then be divided by the sale price of the comparable to determine the percent of gross adjustments.

Final Reconciliation

There are several techniques available to the appraiser to use during the final reconciliation process, which are discussed in courses specifically focusing on the sales comparison approach. But for now, a simple example of final reconciliation will be presented.

FEATURE	SUBJECT	SALE #1	Dollar Adjustment	SALE #2	Dollar Adjustment	SALE #3	Dollar Adjustment
ADDRESS	61 Lake Ave.	127 Dock St.		39 Lake Ave.		168 Shore Dr.	
SALE PRICE	?	$137,900		$149,500		$142,700	
DATE	_____	21 days	0	60 days	+ $1,495	85 days	+ $2,854
1. LOCATION	Waterfront	Waterfront	0	Waterfront	0	Waterfront	0
2. LOT SIZE	100' x 115'	105' x 110'	0	130' x 130'	- $3,000	105' x 125'	- $1,000
3. CONDITION	Good	Average	+ $2,000	Good	0	Good	0
4. AGE	20 years	17 years	0	24 years	0	21 years	0
5. STYLE/CONSTRUCTION	Brick	Brick	0	Stone	- $3,000	Stucco	- $1,000
6. SIZE/SQUARE FEET	1,750 sq. ft.	1,675 sq. ft.	+ $750	1,875 sq. ft.	- $1,250	1,800 sq. ft.	- $500
7. TOTAL ROOMS	7	6	+ $1,000	8	- $1,000	7	0
8. TOTAL BEDROOMS	3	3	0	3	0	3	0
9. TOTAL BATHROOMS	2 ½	2 ½	0	3	- $500	2	+ $500
10. BASEMENT	Full	Full		Full		Full	
11. GARAGE	2-car attached	2-car attached	0	2-car attached	0	2-car attached	0
12. HEATING/COOLING	Gas/Central	Gas/Central		Gas/Central		Gas/Central	
13. OTHER	None	None		Pool	- $2,500	Deck	- $2,000
NET ADJUSTMENTS	_____	(2.72%) + $3,750		(6.53%) - $9,755		(0.80%) - $1,146	
GROSS ADJUSTMENTS		(2.72%) $3,750		(8.53%) $12,745		(5.50%) $7,845	
ADJUSTED VALUES	_____	$141,650		$139,745		$141,554	

The resulting value range is $139,745 to $141,650. It should be noted that:

- Two of the three comparable sales point to the upper end of the range.
- Most support for the value conclusion is comparable Sale #1—it is the most recent and requires no market condition adjustment, while the other two comparable sales are aging.
- Comparable Sale #1 also has the fewest number of adjustments and the fewest gross adjustments. In addition, comparable Sale #1 is the most similar in bedrooms and baths.

Thus, a value conclusion at the upper end of the value range is fully supported and logical.

Statistical Measures

When appropriate, another technique used by appraisers in reconciling the results of analysis, such as paired data and the final reconciliation is to employ a statistical measure. Use of statistical measures is most often applied when all of the data is of good quality and consistently reliable. Common statistical measures include (but are not limited to) the mean, median, and mode.

Mean

Mean is *the mathematical average of a series of numbers.*

Mean is calculated by adding the numbers together, then dividing the sum by the total number of values in the set.

> **Example:**
>
> Number set given is 27, 76, 43, 19, 55, 80. Find the mean.
>
> 27 + 76 + 43 + 19 + 55 + 80 = 300
>
> 300 / 6 = 50, so 50 is the mean, or average, of this number set.

Median

Median is *the number that appears in the middle of a series of numbers.* Hint: To remember this concept, think of the median in the middle of a road.

To find the median, arrange the numbers from lowest to highest, then simply look at the middle number(s). In an odd set of numbers, there is a single median number in the middle of the set. In an even set of numbers, the average of the two middle numbers is the median.

> **Example #1:**
>
> Number set is 27, 76, 43, 19, 55, 80. Find the median.
>
> Put the numbers in order: 19, 27, 43, 55, 76, 80. Since we have an even number of values, we must average the middle two numbers: 43 + 55 = 98 / 2 = 49, which is the median.
>
> **Example #2:**
>
> Number set is 27, 46, 19, 55, 83. Find the median.
>
> Put the numbers in order: 19, 27, 46, 55, 83. With an odd number count in the set, the middle number (46) is the median.

Mode

Mode is *the number that appears most often in a data set.* If no number occurs more than once, there is no mode for that series of numbers.

> **Example:**
>
> Number set is 27, 76, 27, 43, 86, 19, 27, 80. Find the mode.
>
> The number 27 appears most often (3 times), so 27 is the mode.

Work Problem 4.1: Statistical Measures

Given the following data set, determine the mean, median, and mode.

Sample set: $45,000, $40,000, $40,000, $44,000, $46,000, $41,000

Mean: _____

Median: _____

Mode: _____

Case Study - Applying Adjustments

Apply the following adjustments to a comparable sale that had a sale price of $272,000 using this chart.

Market Conditions:	+6.5%
Property Rights Conveyed:	+2%
Location:	-20%
Physical Characteristics:	+12%
Financing Terms:	5%
Financing Concessions:	-$1,500
Conditions of Sale:	-10%

Element of Comparison	Adjustment %	Adjustment
Sale Price		**$272,000**
Marekt Conditions		
Adjusted Price		
Property Rights Conveyed		
Adjusted Price		
Location		
Adjusted Price		
Physical Characteristics		
Adjusted Price		
Financing Terms		
Adjusted Price		
Financing Concessions		
Adjusted Price		
Conditions of Sale		
Adjusted Price		
Adjusted Sale Price		

1. What is the final adjusted sale price of the comparable sale? _____

2. What was the percent of net and gross adjustments? _____

Summary

1. The sales comparison approach is sometimes referred to as the "market approach" due to its reliance upon actual market transaction data for support of the appraiser's opinions and conclusions.

2. The appraiser begins his development of the sales comparison approach by researching and selecting market data of sold and closed transactions for use as comparable data for analysis.

3. Comparable properties, or comparables, generically can be categorized as properties that share certain similarities with the subject property. Competitive properties are those that compete head-to-head with the subject. The ideal data to be used for comparable analysis would represent properties that are both comparable to and competitive with the subject property.

4. USPAP does not place an obligation on the appraiser to use and analyze a specific number of comparables. A minimum of three comparables are most usually gathered, analyzed, and presented in keeping with the regulations and requirements of many clients and intended users.

5. In each assignment, appraisers select an appropriate unit of comparison for which to perform their analysis. The unit of comparison is the context in which the sale price is stated.

6. An element of comparison represents characteristics of a property or a transaction that can be used to explain differences in the price paid in a transaction.

7. Sales contracts specifically alert the appraiser to property rights that are or are not being conveyed, and also spell out any special financing terms, concessions, and items of value that are included in the transaction.

8. Once a difference or differences between the comparable data and the subject property are recognized, the appraiser must determine if an adjustment is warranted, and if so, the amount of an adjustment.

9. Paired data analysis is the process of determining the value of specific property characteristics or features by comparing pairs of similar properties.

10. Another quantitative technique for analyzing sales comparison data is a regression analysis. A regression analysis is a statistical measure that attempts to ascertain the source of change in variables.

11. The purpose of adjusting comparable properties is to express the differences of the comparable and the subject property as they would be perceived by the market – which can be applied as a dollar amount or a percentage adjustment.

12. When the comparable property is inferior to the subject, an upward adjustment is applied to the comparable to align it with the subject. When the comparable property is superior to the subject, a downward adjustment is applied.

13. The order in which adjustments are applied is: 1) Property rights conveyed; 2) Financing terms; 3) Conditions of sale; 4) Market conditions; 5) Location; and 6) Physical characteristics.

14. After all the individual adjustments are applied and the comparable sales are adjusted, a range of value is revealed. In the sales comparison approach, reconciliation consists of determining the relevance of each comparable and the indications produced.

15. Gross adjustments are the overall total of all adjustments applied, regardless of whether the adjustment is applied as a positive or negative. Net adjustments are the sum of the adjustments, taking into account whether the adjustment was a positive or negative.

Quiz

1. *USPAP requires appraisers to gather, analyze, and present a minimum of _____ comparables in an appraisal report.*

   a. one
   b. two
   c. three
   d. There is no minimum.

2. *Using the data provided, what is the indicated per square foot adjustment for size based on paired data?*

	Comp #1	Comp #2	Comp #3	Comp #4
Sale Price	$300,000	$305,500	$305,000	$322,250
Size	2,800	2,900	3,000	3,250
Bedrooms	5	5	5	6
Baths	3	4	3	5

   a. $10
   b. $25
   c. $40
   d. $55

3. *In terms of elements of comparison, a difference between the subject and comparable in favorability of zoning is addressed in the element of*

   a. location.
   b. market conditions.
   c. physical characteristics.
   d. property rights conveyed.

4. *Which of the following elements of comparison affects only the comparable data in a market value assignment and has no relationship to the subject?*

   a. conditions of sale
   b. financing terms
   c. market conditions
   d. physical characteristics

5. *An element of comparison is a*

   a. characteristic of a property or a transaction that can be used to explain differences in the price paid in a transaction.
   b. demonstration of the proximity of the subject property to common destinations and conveniences.
   c. demonstration of the value using superior and inferior indications to the subject.
   d. device used to compare the price paid for comparable properties of different sizes or with differing features.

6. *A unit of comparison is the*

   a. context with which the sale price of a property is stated for the purpose of comparison.
   b. demonstration of the proximity of the subject property to common destinations and conveniences.
   c. demonstration of the value by using superior and inferior indications to the subject.
   d. property feature that can be used to explain differences in the marketplace.

7. *The following indications have been extracted through paired data. Using the mean of the indications, what is the indicated contributory value of a fireplace?*

Paired Data Set	1	2	3
Extracted Contributory Value of a Fireplace	$500	$1,200	$700

   a. $700
   b. $750
   c. $800
   d. $1,000

8. *What scenario would most likely evidence the conditions of an arm's length transaction?*

   a. After winning the lottery, a man sells his home at a discounted price to a local college he attended that will use it for office space.
   b. A couple getting a divorce quickly sells their home.
   c. A man offers and sells his house to his friend at the appraised market value before he puts it on the market.
   d. A woman accepts a low first offer on her house before she leaves the country for military service.

9. *During an analysis, an appraiser notes that as the size of the houses he is analyzing increases, the sale price per square foot decreases. What term describes this observation?*

   a. economics of scale
   b. functional utility
   c. gentrification
   d. regression

10. **Which would NOT be a factor considered in the element of Conditions of Sale?**

    a. financing concessions being paid by seller
    b. property being acquired for assemblage
    c. related parties
    d. seller not working in his own best interest

11. **A statistical measure that attempts to ascertain the source of change in variables is known as**

    a. graphic analysis.
    b. market analysis.
    c. qualitative analysis.
    d. regression analysis.

12. **Appraiser Paul is finding the contributory value of a third bathroom in a home. The four indications he has derived from comparable paired sales are $1,300, $1,800, $2,000, and $2,100. What is the indicated median contributory value?**

    a. $1,300
    b. $1,800
    c. $1,900
    d. $2,000

13. **A home is found that physically mirrors the subject, but is in a different market and would not appeal to the same buyer. The home is**

    a. comparable to the subject.
    b. competitive with the subject.
    c. inferior to the subject.
    d. superior to the subject.

14. **If a comparable sold for $175,000 and had the adjustments listed, what is the total of gross adjustments (rounded to three places)?**

Location	+ $15,000
Condition	- $7,500
Physical Differences	- $5,000

    a. 1.429%
    b. 6.364%
    c. 10.000%
    d. 15.714%

15. **In a market value appraisal assignment, after the appraiser adjusts a comparable for financing terms, the sale price is said to be**

    a. adjusted normal pricing.
    b. arm's length.
    c. cash equivalent.
    d. conventionally priced.

16. **A 12-acre residential tract sells for $210,000. Using a per-acre unit of measure, the sale price per acre is**

    a. $15,000.
    b. $17,500.
    c. $20,000.
    d. $21,000.

17. **Paired data analysis is one example of a method to determine an adjustment using _____ techniques.**

    a. qualitative
    b. quantitative
    c. reconciliation
    d. regression

18. **In order for the correct application of percentage adjustments, what is the order in which adjustments are applied in the sales comparison approach?**

    a. financing terms, property rights conveyed, conditions of sale, location, market characteristics, and physical characteristics
    b. property rights conveyed, financing terms, conditions of sale, market conditions, location, and physical characteristics
    c. property rights conveyed, location, market conditions, financing terms, conditions of sale, and physical characteristics
    d. property rights conveyed, physical characteristics, financing terms, conditions of sale, market conditions, and location

19. **What is a net adjustment?**

    a. the overall total of all adjustments applied, regardless of whether the adjustment is applied as a positive or negative
    b. the sum of the adjustments taking into account whether the adjustment was a positive or negative
    c. the unit price (per square foot) applied to the subject's square feet to produce an indication of value for the subject
    d. the values derived from the different appraisal approaches to arrive at a final opinion of value

20. *An appraiser has determined that a comparable property, which sold for $185,000, requires the following percentage adjustments. What is the adjusted sale price of the comparable (rounded to the nearest one hundred dollars)?*

Market Conditions	+7%
Financing Terms	-3%
Physical Characteristics	+10%
Location	-15%

a. $157,300
b. $182,400
c. $193,600
d. $207,400

Chapter 5

Overview of the Income Approach

The income approach requires the understanding of numerous principles, terms, and concepts related to its use. This chapter will provide an overview of the important components of developing the income approach. The income approach is closely related to the principle of anticipation, as the methodology analyzes the expectations of the typical investor for the benefit of a particular investment property.

Contract Rent What tenants are actually paying in rent, as stated in the terms of the lease.

Debt Service The amount of funds required to make periodic payments of principal and interest to the lender.

Direct Capitalization An income method that takes a property's single-year net operating income (NOI) into a value indication by applying an overall capitalization rate: NOI / Overall Capitalization Rate = Value.

Effective Gross Income (EGI) Potential gross income, less vacancy and collection losses.

Fixed Expenses Ongoing operating expenses that do not vary based on occupancy levels of the property (e.g., taxes, insurance).

Gross Income Multiplier (GIM) A factor that takes into account income derived from all sources of a property (e.g., vending, storage units).

Gross Rent Multiplier (GRM) A factor derived from comparable rental data, which is then used to develop an opinion of value of the subject property.

Lessee A person who leases property; a tenant.

Lessor A person who leases property to another; a landlord.

Market Rent What the property could rent for in the open market if currently vacant and available.

Key Terms

(Continued on page 131)

Income Concepts and Components

Appraisers must understand several concepts and components before they can effectively apply the income approach in an appraisal assignment. Some of these elements are fundamental to every assignment in which the income approach is applicable, while other elements may be part of a specific technique being applied.

Income vs. Rent

Depending on the particular income technique the appraiser chooses in the scope of work, distinguishing between the terms "income" and "rent" may be critical. In some cases, the rent a particular property generates may be its income. In other circumstances, there may be other types of income aside from the rent the property generates for the living unit or units, such as income from parking spaces, garage spaces, storage spaces, vending machines, etc.

Speaking strictly to rent, there are two defined concepts that must be understood—contract rent and market rent.

Contract Rent

Contract rent is *what the tenants are actually paying in rent, as stated in the terms of the lease*. It is the actual rent that the **lessor** (landlord/property owner) and the **lessee** (tenant/renter) of a particular property have agreed upon. The contract rent, or what a particular property is actually generating, may or may not reflect what a typical lessor would expect, or what a typical lessee would pay. The rent and income basis applied in any technique for which the assignment specifies *market value* would rely on what the typical market participant would do rather than what the parties in a particular agreement are doing.

Market Rent

Market rent (also referred to as **economic rent**) is *what the property could rent for in the open market if currently vacant and available*. It is the amount a property *should* command in an open and competitive market, and as we just mentioned, market rent could be more or less than contract rent. In some cases, the contract rent of a property may reflect, or be the same as, market rent.

Measures of Income and Benefits

Appraisers have several mechanisms that are used as part of some or all income analysis to measure the efficiency of an investment, depending on the scope of work in the assignment. These concepts include:

- Potential gross income (PGI)
- Effective gross income (EGI)
- Net operating income (NOI)
- Reversionary benefit

Potential and Effective Gross Income

Potential gross income (**PGI**) is *the income that could be produced by a property in an ideal situation, with no vacancy or collection losses (e.g., a tenant who failed to pay rent and it could not be collected)*. The key here is that PGI is the income a property *could* generate if the property is fully rented and occupied during the particular period being analyzed. In most cases, PGI is based on an annual amount.

Effective gross income (**EGI**) is *the potential gross income, less vacancy and collection losses*. EGI is the income that could be (or is) realized from an income property after deducting an amount for vacancy and collection losses, but before any operating expenses are considered. If PGI is what the property owner *could* have taken in, EGI can be thought of as what that property owner *did* take in. The formula for EGI is:

PGI - Vacancy and Collection Losses = EGI

Net Operating Income

Net operating income (NOI) is *the income after expenses.* In other words: Net operating income is the effective gross income minus operating expenses. Operating expenses are discussed later in this chapter.

Do not confuse NOI with cash flow. Cash flow considers other obligations, such as payments toward loan debt and income tax obligations that are not considered in the NOI. The formula for NOI is:

PGI - Vacancy and Collection Losses = EGI – Operating Expenses = NOI

As mentioned earlier, PGI and EGI are most commonly expressed in annual terms, as is NOI.

Reversionary Benefit

The **reversionary benefit** is *typically a sum, often stated in a dollar amount, that a property owner will receive when, or if, he sells the property at the end of the investment term.* There are several different methods of measuring the reversionary benefit, but to make it simple, it can be thought of as the net proceeds when and if the property is sold. In most cases, typical investors expect that the value of a property will grow over time for one reason or another.

√ **Note:** Analyses that consider reversionary benefits are not typically associated with most common residential income analyses and are beyond the scope of this course. However, appraisers should be familiar with these terms and concepts, which may be explored in greater detail in more advanced coursework.

Operating Expenses

Operating expenses are *day-to-day costs of operating a property, like repairs and maintenance, but not including debt service or depreciation.* **Debt service** is *the amount of funds required to make periodic payments of principal and interest to the lender.* These are expenses that must be made by the property owner in order to adequately maintain a property at a level that it could continue to produce revenue. When income is analyzed at an annual level (as it usually is), the operating expenses are also considered on an annual basis.

For a market value opinion of the fee simple interest of a property using the income approach, market level expenses are used in the appraiser's analysis. As part of the diligence performed by the appraiser, he will compare the subject's actual expenses to similar properties in the market to determine if the subject's expenses are adequate and at a market level. The primary tool for this analysis is the reconstructed operating income statement reflecting the subject property and comparable income properties.

Key Terms

Multiplier A factor that is derived from market data and applied to the subject's market rent or income to produce a value indication in an income approach.

Net Operating Income (NOI) Income after expenses.

Operating Expenses Day-to-day costs of operating a property, such as repairs and maintenance, but not including debt service or depreciation.

Overall Capitalization Rate Used to interpret a property's single year net operating income to the property's value using direct capitalization,

Potential Gross Income (PGI) The income that could be produced by a property in an ideal situation, with no vacancy or collection losses.

Reserves for Replacement An amount of money set aside for future replacement of major items, such as the roof or heating system. Also called **Reserves**.

Variable Expenses Operating expenses necessary to the property, but usually dependent on the property's occupancy level.

Sample Reconstructed Operating Income Statement

	Subject 121 High St.	Comp #1 232 King Ave.	Comp #2 343 Main Rd.	Comp #3 454 Hill Blvd.
Net Rentable Area (sq. ft.)	35,000	42,500	37,500	40,000
Rent per Square Foot	$23.50	$21.75	$24.25	$22.50
Potential Gross Income	$822,500	$924,375	$909,375	$900,000
Vacancy and Collection =10%	$82,250	$92,438	$90,938	$90,000
Effective Gross Income	$740,250	$831,938	$818,438	$810,000
Expenses: Fixed				
Real Estate Taxes	$91,350	$107,100	$100,125	$99,200
Insurance	$2,450	$3,400	$2,625	$2,800
Expenses: Variable				
Utilities	$81,900	$108,800	$100,125	$92,800
Maintenance/Janitorial	$40,950	$56,525	$45,000	$46,400
Repairs	$14,000	$20,400	$15,375	$17,200
Management Fees	$8,400	$9,350	$9,000	$9,200
Other	$1,750	$2,550	$1,875	$2,400
Reserves (5% of EGI)				
Roof, HVAC	$37,100	$41,650	$40,875	$40,400
Total Expenses	$277,900	$349,775	$315,000	$310,400
Net Operating Income	$462,350	$482,163	$503,438	$499,600

Observing the Sample Reconstructed Operating Income Statement, operating expenses have been defined into three types:

1. Fixed expenses

2. Variable expenses

3. Reserves for replacement

When developing a reconstructed operating income statement, appraisers must identify certain expenses and assign them to the proper category. Therefore, it is important that the characteristics of each are clearly understood.

Fixed Expenses

When one considers **fixed expenses**, the primary thinking should reflect on *ongoing expenses that do not vary based on occupancy levels of the property.* Real estate taxes and insurance on the property are examples of items that are typically considered fixed expenses. Even though the cost of these items might vary from year to year, the change is usually not significant, and is not based upon occupancy.

Other examples of fixed expenses might be services that are contracted at a level rate for, perhaps, a year at a time. A good example might be refuse collection, where the lessor is paying for a certain number of collections per week or month, regardless of how much refuse there is. Another fixed expense might be the cost of a security light for a parking area or other common area where the expense is a reoccurring flat fee. Again, think of costs not associated with the occupancy.

Variable Expenses

Variable expenses are *operating expenses necessary to the property, but dependent on the property's occupancy level.* Maintenance and repairs are typically considered a variable expense, as are any utilities to the living units furnished by the lessor. Another common variable expense is management fees (often expressed as a percent).

Since it is not logical that property managers, or a management company, are rewarded for vacant units or property, the percentage is typically based upon EGI rather than PGI. Thus, management fees are considered a variable expense since the expense varies based on occupancy. Other examples of variable expenses *might* be legal and accounting fees that are charged on a non-consistent basis and other miscellaneous expenses.

Reserves for Replacement

There are certain components or items of any structure that will need to be replaced from time to time throughout the life of the building. For an income-producing property, the anticipated cost of replacing these components or items is addressed by *reserves for replacement*. **Reserves for replacement** (sometimes called just **reserves**) *refers to an amount of money set aside for future replacement of major items*. When used in an income analysis, the replacement reserve is most often applied as an annual dollar (or sometimes as a percentage) amount.

Although there could certainly be others, common components or items for residential income properties for which a replacement reserve is typically considered include roof, heating and/or air conditioning systems, carpeting, and lessor furnished appliances.

Operating expenses encompass all of the expenses that are necessary to adequately maintain a property and its income potential.

Rent and Income Factors

Multipliers are **rent and income factors** frequently used in the valuation of many residential income properties. The use of rent and income factors as a technique in the income approach is an income capitalization method. In order for a meaningful and credible value opinion to result from applying multipliers, the data from which the multiplier is extracted must be very similar to the subject in many ways—physical features, lease terms, and income expense history.

A multiplier is not a percentage. A **multiplier** is identified as *a factor derived by dividing the sale price (or sometimes value) of a comparable property by its gross income or, in some cases, rent*. Multipliers are derived using this formula:

Sale Price (Value) / Gross Income (or Rent) = Multiplier

There are two types of multipliers that can be applied. The type the appraiser will choose depends on the property characteristics and is decided in the scope of work of the assignment. These factors are known as:

- Gross rent multipliers.
- Gross income multipliers.

Gross Rent Multipliers

A **gross rent multiplier,** or **GRM**, is *a factor derived from comparable rental data, which is then used to develop an opinion of value of the subject property*. A GRM is used when the property has income that is derived only from actual rent of the living units. Although the multiplier could be expressed as either a monthly or annual factor, it is most commonly derived on a *monthly* basis. Most residential appraisal forms report the development of the income approach by this technique in such a manner.

Gross Income Multipliers

A **gross income multiplier**, or **GIM**, is *a factor that takes into account income derived from all sources of a property*. It is most often used when there are income-producing capabilities of a property other than rent derived from living units, such as on-premises coin-operated machines, ancillary buildings, or other income sources of a property.

It is most common for GIMs to be derived from and applied to *annual* income. However, the process of derivation and application of the factor is much the same as the GRM.

The basis of income derived from, and applied to, the development of the GIM technique could be based on either potential gross income (PGI) or effective gross income (EGI), which will be discussed in courses expanding on the topic of the income approach.

Rates of Return

There are various **rates of return** that can be used in different techniques for development of a value opinion using an income capitalization method. The overall capitalization rate will be discussed here. Other rates of return are discussed in courses dedicated to the topic of the income approach.

Overall Capitalization Rate

As a component of one of the most common income capitalization methods, the **overall capitalization rate** is *used to interpret a property's single year net operating income to the property's value using direct capitalization.*

The formula in which the rate, stated as a percent, is extracted for application in direct capitalization—known as **IVR**, is as follows:

(Net Operating) Income / Value = Rate

Techniques for determining an overall capitalization rate as well as how the direct capitalization technique is developed will be discussed later in this chapter.

Income Analysis

Although there are numerous income techniques, in this chapter, our discussion will be limited to two particular techniques of income analysis:

1. The use of multipliers, and

2. The use of direct capitalization using an overall capitalization rate.

Both of these techniques are methods of capitalization, and technically, both are categorized by some as being a form of direct capitalization. However, some sources in the industry make a distinction between them. Thus, we will treat these income capitalization techniques separately for ease of presentation and learning. While in most small residential appraisal assignments the use of multipliers is appropriate, in others, the direct capitalization approach (using an overall capitalization rate) will be warranted in the scope of work. There is no standardized or uniform requirement for which approach is used in a particular assignment. However, generally accepted practices suggest that:

• Multipliers are typically used in small residential income properties consisting of one to four units.

• The direct capitalization approach is more often used for properties with more than four units.

Clients and intended users may have guidelines or requirements specifying a particular technique (such as Fannie Mae).

Multipliers

A **multiplier** is *a factor that is derived from market data and applied to the subject's market rent or income to produce a value indication in an income approach.* For the residential appraiser, the use of multipliers will be the most frequently employed income valuation technique in a market value assignment. The **gross rent multiplier (GRM)** and the **gross income multiplier (GIM)** are discussed here. While the use of these multipliers is fairly simple, the derivation and application of a multiplier must be carefully performed. Therefore, there are some very important things to keep in mind when using this technique:

• The GRM and the GIM consider only the *gross* rent or income of the property, and, therefore, do not consider expense items.

• The GRM, and the most common form of the GIM, do not consider any losses attributable to vacancy of the living unit(s) and/or inability to collect rent.

- The market rent used in the application of a GRM to the subject property (or in the case of a GIM, total income) must reflect market level.

- The comparable properties must be *very* similar physically, as well as in lease terms and conditions.

Gross Rent Multiplier—GRM

Developing a value opinion using the **GRM** technique of income capitalization consists of just two primary steps:

1. Determine the appropriate GRM from market data.

2. Apply the GRM to the subject's market rent to indicate a value conclusion.

While the actual steps in using a multiplier are relatively simple in application, the technique can yield misleading or false results if the data being used for the analysis is inconsistent, irrelevant, or not well analyzed.

Determining the GRM from Market Data

To derive a GRM from market data:

- The value of the comparable property is divided by that property's gross market rent to conclude on a multiplier that can be used in later analysis.

When used in a market value appraisal assignment, this data will be extracted from arm's-length transactions of properties that were rented at the time of the sale transaction or rented soon after the sale at a verifiable market level rent. Ideally, this information comes from the appraiser's own files—data collected in the course of other appraisal assignments. However, the data could also come from other appraisers or parties to a transaction, or those who are familiar with a particular transaction (e.g., the real estate broker).

In order for the analysis to be meaningful and produce true results, the market rent applied in the analysis should be consistent with the physical condition of the property. The appraiser must ensure that the sale price in a transaction is consistent with the rent being used in the analysis, or misleading and false conclusions will result. For example, if a property were in poor condition at the time of the transaction but was significantly refurbished after acquisition, the rent amount being generated after refurbishment would not be consistent with the rent potential of the subject at the time of the transaction.

Some other common examples of circumstances where market rent may be different from contract rent could be:

- The agreement was reached in a different market climate with different market conditions.

- The lessee is performing certain repairs or improvements to the property in exchange for reduced rent.

- The lessor is performing or providing specialized improvements, services, or items (that may not be recognized by other potential tenants) required by the specific lessee in exchange for a higher rent.

- The lease agreement could be for a temporary or an extended period of time, thus the contract rent could be higher or lower than that in a typical lease period.

Once there is verification that the transaction is arm's-length and that the rent produced reasonably represents market level, the process of identifying a GRM from the transaction is fairly simple.

1. Collect information from arm's-length transactions of rental properties that are as similar to the subject as possible.

2. Derive the appropriate multiplier from the transaction data by using a formula known as **VIM**, *value divided by income equals multiplier.*

   V (Sale Price) / I (Gross Monthly Rent) = M (Multiplier)

Example

So, if a comparable rental property sold in a recent arm's length transaction for $100,000 and then was immediately rented at market level in the same condition for $1,000 per month, the GRM would be 100.

$100,000 / $1,000 = 100

Applying the GRM to the Subject

To develop a value opinion using the GRM technique, the appraiser:

- Multiplies the monthly market rent of the subject by the selected multiplier.

M (Multiplier) x I (Monthly Market Rent) = V (Value)

Example

The appraiser has chosen $950 per month as a reasonable opinion of market rent for the subject property and a GRM of 100 (from the previous analysis) to apply to the rent. Thus, the results of the appraiser's conclusions are as follows:

100 x $950 = $95,000

In order for the GRM technique to produce meaningful and credible results, the subject property must be located in an area in which there is an established market for rental properties and data is available. When there is a scarcity or lack of relevant data, or where significant dissimilarities exist in available data, the method diminishes in reliability. *In many cases, these circumstances may cause the income approach to be inapplicable in an assignment.*

Gross Income Multipliers

Now that the fundamental concepts of the income approach using the GRM technique have been presented, the development and function of a **gross income multiplier**, or **GIM**, will be much easier to understand. Fundamental concepts of the GIM and the GRM are very similar in many respects, but some things are different.

The use of a GIM is appropriate when the subject property produces income in addition to rent from the living unit(s). With a GIM, both the rent and the other income are used for the analysis, while the GRM considers only rent. There are some special things to know about using the GIM in a market value assignment. Each of these points will be discussed and illustrated:

- Other sources of income must be determined legally permissible and to reasonably have the potential to be ongoing.
- The rent and income derived from comparable data and applied to the subject property is considered on an annual basis.
- The GIM is derived from properties with similar rent and (other) income flows.

The GIM technique could be applied to most nonresidential properties, and may be relevant and ideal for some properties that are primarily residential in nature. In most residential cases, the GIM technique will be used more frequently for properties having two to four units or mixed-use properties, such as a nonresidential use of a lower-floor unit, with a residential use of the upper floor. However, there may be circumstances in which the GIM could be applied to a single-family investment property.

Deriving the GIM from Market Data

Deriving the GIM from market data is performed in much the same way as the GRM is derived using VIM, only using the total income to the property at an annual level:

Example

A single-family residential dwelling in an established neighborhood, which recently was sold in an arm's length transaction for $125,000, includes an extra garage at the rear of the property, which is rented to an outside party. The dwelling rents for $750 per month, and the extra garage rents for $50 per month. The rents appear to be consistent with the market.

Value / (Annual) Income = Multiplier

$125,000 / $9,600 ($9,000 [12 x $750] + $600 [12 x $50]) = 13.02

Of course, in the real world, several comparable income properties would be analyzed before the appraiser concludes upon an appropriate multiplier (GRM or GIM) to be used in an assignment.

Applying the GIM to the Subject

The GIM is applied to the total market income of the subject property in a similar manner as was illustrated for applying a GRM to the subject property's market rent. As a reminder, the appraiser must be careful to apply the GIM consistently with how the multiplier was derived:

Example

The subject property is a single-family dwelling generating $8,200 annually in market rent and has a small storage building at the rear, which produces $600 per year in other income. The indicated GIM derived from the previous example was 13.02.

To develop an indication of the subject's value, the subject's total income is multiplied by the GIM:

$8,400 ($8,200 + $600) x 13.02 = $109,368

Work Problems 5.1

1. If a subject property has a market rent of $625 per month and a GRM of 183.75 is deemed applicable, what is the appraiser's indicated value conclusion (rounded to the nearest one-thousand)? $_____

2. An unfurnished house rents for $8,100 per year, which is determined to represent market level. The property has recently sold for $147,000 in an arm's length transaction. What is the GRM indicated (rounded to two places)? _____

3. A property generates rent from units totaling $2,500 per month and $1,000 per year from revenue from parking spaces at the rear of the property. What is the indicated GIM if the property recently sold for $325,000 and has expenses of $5,700 annually? _____

4. A GIM of 16.87 has been derived from market data. If the subject property has gross income of $1,450 per month and a vacancy rate of 4.35%, what is the indicated value of the subject property (rounded to the nearest one thousand dollars)? $_____

Direct Capitalization Using an Overall Rate

Direct capitalization (using an overall capitalization rate) is *an income method that converts a property's single-year net operating income (NOI) into a value indication by applying an overall capitalization rate:*

NOI / Overall Capitalization Rate = Value

This direct capitalization technique is considered by most to interpret typical investor reactions and motivations of a particular property. Be careful, however, not to confuse direct capitalization with yield capitalization, which considers a series of cash flows rather than a single year's income.

The direct capitalization technique is most relevant when the property's occupancy and net operating income are stabilized or established. There must also be relevant comparable transaction data available that can be analyzed.

The development of the direct capitalization technique requires two major components that are used in the final analysis from which to form conclusions:

1. Net Operating Income
2. Overall Capitalization Rate

Deriving Net Operating Income

The **net income** or **net operating income** (**NOI**) of the subject property is *the estimated amount the property owner or investor should realize (or did realize) after accounting for certain losses and operating expenses (including replacement reserves) for the property.*

The steps in estimating NOI require a systematic and careful analysis. These steps are:

1. Determine PGI
2. Estimate rates of vacancy and collection losses
3. Determine EGI
4. Estimate operating expenses
5. Determine NOI

The method considers all of these components on an *annual* basis. The mathematical formula for NOI is as follows:

PGI - Vacancy and Collection Losses = EGI - Operating Expenses = NOI

Estimating Potential Gross Income (PGI)

PGI is the *amount of income that a property is capable of generating if all the units are occupied without vacancy for the full year and all rents and other anticipated income are received without collection losses* <u>before</u> any operating expenses are deducted. Potential Gross Income is based upon market level rent.

Example

A subject property has four units, which each rent for $600 per month. The calculation of PGI is as follows:

4 units x $600 per month x 12 months = $28,800 (PGI)

Estimating Vacancy Losses

In most cases, both losses due to vacancy and losses due to collection are based on a percentage of the PGI. The percentage applied in the development of NOI is derived through analysis of market level data. The formula is:

Total Number of Days Vacancy of All Units / Total Rentable Days of All Units = % of Vacancy, or Rate

Example

If a comparable property has four units and each unit was vacant during the year for 10 days, the total days vacancy would be 40. Total rentable days would be 1,460 (4 x 365).

40 / 1,460 = 2.74% Vacancy Rate

The vacancy rate should represent an appropriate market level. The appraiser must analyze market data to confirm if the estimate is consistent with the market. Assuming the derived vacancy rate is found to be consistent with the market, the rate can be applied to the PGI of the subject to reveal the loss in dollars.

$28,800 (Subject PGI) x 2.74% = $789 Vacancy Loss (rounded)

Estimating Collection Losses

An estimated amount for collection (or credit) loss is appropriate when the market supports that there is evidence in the market for its use. An allowance for collection losses is most often warranted when the property is large with numerous rental units, or when renters vacating without paying the rent owed is commonplace. When a collection loss is warranted, it is deducted from PGI in the same manner as the percentage for vacancy loss.

Estimating Effective Gross Income (EGI)

Calculations for EGI are not complicated. EGI is the result of subtracting vacancy and any collection losses from PGI.

$28,800 (PGI) - $789 (Vacancy Loss) = $28,011 (EGI)

Estimating Operating Expenses

After EGI is estimated, the next step for the appraiser is to sort out the various operating expenses for the subject property and categorize the expenses. Operating expenses are separated into three categories:

1. Fixed expenses
2. Variable expenses
3. Reserves for replacement

The annual payment for a mortgage (debt service) is voluntary and not every owner would have the same mortgage obligation, or possibly even a mortgage on the property at all. Thus, the amount of debt service has no influence on the value of the property. Depreciation is also not a building expense.

Fixed Expenses

Fixed expenses are *ongoing expenses that do not vary based on occupancy levels of the property, or in some cases services that are contracted at a level rate for, perhaps, a year at a time.* Real estate taxes and property insurance are examples of items that are typically considered fixed expenses.

Example

If the subject property's annual real estate taxes are $1,575 per year and property insurance is $1,600 per year, the fixed expenses are $3,175.

$1,575 + $1,600 = $3,175

Variable Expenses

Variable expenses are *operating expenses necessary to the property, but dependent on the property's occupancy level.* Examples include lessor furnished utilities, management expenses, and most maintenance and repair expenses.

Example

If variable expenses were $1,750 for maintenance and repairs, $750 for lessor furnished utilities, and $1,401 for management fees (5% x $28,011 [EGI]), variable expenses would total $3,901.

$1,750 + $750 + $1,401 = $3,901

Replacement Reserves

Replacement reserves refers to *an amount of money set aside for future replacement of major items.*

Continuing with the example, there are two items for which the appraiser determines it is appropriate to estimate an annual replacement reserve for the four-unit subject property, roof, and HVAC (four units). The appraiser estimates the roof will need to be replaced in 10 years, at a cost of $10,000, and the HVAC systems in 15 years, at a total cost of $24,000 for the four units.

Example

To calculate the annual replacement reserve, the estimated cost of the component as of the point in time the component needs to be replaced is divided by the estimated number of years remaining until replacement is required.

Roof - $10,0000 / 10 years = $1,000 Annual Reserve

HVAC - $24,000/ 15 years = $1,600 Annual Reserve

$1,000 + $1,600 = $2,600 Reserves for Replacement

Final Estimate of Net Operating Income (NOI)

Once the appraiser has estimated the operating expenses for the subject property, the next step is to develop NOI. The total operating expenses are subtracted from EGI.

Example

EGI is $28,011. The operating expenses are $3,175 fixed expenses, $3,901 variable expenses, and $2,600 reserves for expenses, with a total of $9,676.

$3,175 + $3,901 + $2,600 = $9,676

$28,011 - $9,676 = $18,335 NOI

Looking at the entire mathematical formula from PGI through NOI, the calculation is as follows:

$28,800 (PGI)
** - 789 (Vacancy Loss) =**

$28,011 (EGI)
** - 9,676 (Operating Expense) =**

$18,335 (NOI)

Overall Capitalization Rates

After the NOI is estimated for the subject property, the next step in the process is to determine an applicable overall capitalization rate to apply to the subject's NOI. There are several techniques for deriving an overall capitalization rate for use in the income analysis. However, some of these techniques are not common, or often do not lend themselves well to residential appraisal assignments and, thus, are beyond the scope of this course.

Deriving an Overall Capitalization Rate

For the purpose of this course, derivation of an overall capitalization rate utilizing comparable sales of similar investment properties or market data will be illustrated, as it is the most common method. Other common methods of deriving an overall capitalization rate will be discussed and illustrated in course work specific to the income approach.

When employing the comparable sales technique for deriving an overall capitalization rate from income-producing properties that have been transacted, two specific elements must be known:

- Sales price
- NOI of the comparable data

In real world appraising, this information ideally comes from previous appraisal assignments, or from other appraisers who have completed appraisal assignments for similar properties. However, the data can come from other sources as well, such as participants to a transaction, as long as those sources are credible.

In order for market data to be reliable in the comparable sales technique for overall capitalization rate derivation, the appraiser must form certain conclusions about the data:

- NOI calculations of the comparable must be consistent with how the net income of the subject was estimated.
- The lease terms of the comparable must be similar to those of the subject.
- The rents and income generated by the comparables should represent those typical for the market.
- Elements of comparison (e.g., terms of sale, conditions of sale, market conditions) of the comparable data should be consistent with those found in an arm's-length transaction.

In some cases, adjustments could be made to the comparable data to align the data with the subject property in a market value assignment of the fee simple interest. Once the comparable sales data has been gathered and analyzed for its reliability and relevance, the *process of deriving an overall capitalization rate* is fairly simple. Appraisers use a formula or technique known as **IVR**:

Income (NOI) / Value (Sale Price) = Rate

Example

A comparable investment property is being examined, which sold for $225,000 in a recent transaction and had a $18,000 NOI. The overall capitalization rate would be derived as follows:

$18,000 (NOI) / $225,000 (Sales Price) = 8.00% (Rate)

Again, an appraiser would not typically rely on the results of only one analysis for determining an overall capitalization rate to apply to the subject in an assignment.

Applying the Overall Capitalization Rate to the Subject

The final step in the direct capitalization technique is to apply the overall capitalization rate to NOI to produce a value indication. Here, the appraiser divides NOI by the overall capitalization rate. Thus, the formula in this step is commonly known as **IRV**:

(Net Operating) Income / (Overall Capitalization) Rate = Value

Example

Using the results of the previous example in which NOI was estimated, the subject's NOI was estimated to be $18,335. The overall capitalization rate indicated in the previous analysis was 8.00%.

$18,335 / 8.00% = $229,188 (Value Indication of the Subject)

It may have been noted throughout the various analyses performed during income capitalization, whether using a multiplier or a direct capitalization rate, that reconciliation was an ongoing process. At nearly every step, the appraiser was weighing information and forming conclusions about the quality and appropriateness of the information and the resulting indications.

In the final reconciliation, the appraiser will consider the quantity and quality of the data used and the indications produced by the analysis in reaching his final conclusions regarding the relevance of the income approach in the appraisal assignment.

In some cases, the income approach may be the only valuation method developed. However, in most assignments of small residential income properties, the income approach will be developed in concert with at least the sales comparison approach. Even in the case of an income-producing property, some clients and intended users may require, as an assignment condition, that the income approach be used only as a basis of support for the final value opinion by the sales comparison approach.

Work Problems 5.2

1. *A three-unit apartment building that recently sold for $390,000 had net operating income of $24,000. What is the indicated overall capitalization rate (carried to two places) derived from this data? _____*

2. *If net operating income of an investment property for the past 12 months is $56,783, what is the value of the property (rounded to the nearest one hundred dollars) if the overall capitalization rate derived from the market is 10.7654%? _____*

Summary

1. Contract rent, or what a particular property is actually generating, may or may not reflect what a typical lessor would expect, or what a typical lessee would pay. Market rent is the amount a property should command in an open and competitive market.

2. Potential Gross Income, or PGI, is the income a property *could* generate if the property is fully rented and occupied during the particular period being analyzed.

3. Effective Gross Income, or EGI, is the income that could be (or is) realized from an income property after deducting an amount for vacancy and collection losses from potential gross income, but before any operating expenses are considered.

4. Operating expenses are separated into three categories: 1) Fixed expenses, 2) Variable expenses, and 3) Reserves for replacement

5. Net operating income, or NOI, is the effective gross income minus operating expenses, not including debt service, depreciation, or other factors.

6. A Gross Rent Multiplier, or GRM, is a factor used to convert income to a value indication when the property has income that is derived only from actual rent of the living units, and is most commonly derived on a monthly basis.

7. A Gross Income Multiplier, or GIM, is a factor that takes into account income derived from all sources of a property. It is most often used when there are income-producing capabilities of a property other than rent derived from living units.

8. The direct capitalization technique, using an overall capitalization rate, is most relevant when the property's occupancy and net operating income are stabilized or established. There must also be relevant comparable transaction data available that can be analyzed from which the comparable's NOI and sale price can be identified.

QUIZ

1. **When applied to income capitalization, a reserve for replacement is a(n)**
   a. amount of money set aside for future replacement of major items.
   b. fund required to make periodic payments of principal and interest to the lender.
   c. ongoing expense that will vary each year based on occupancy levels of the property.
   d. operating expense necessary to the property, but dependent on the property's occupancy level.

2. **A variable expense is best defined as a(n)**
   a. amount of money set aside for future replacement of major items.
   b. fund required to make periodic payments of principal and interest to the lender.
   c. ongoing expense that does not vary based on occupancy levels of the property.
   d. operating expense necessary to the property, but dependent on the property's occupancy level.

3. **Debt service is a term that describes a(n)**
   a. amount of funds required to make periodic payments of principal and interest to the lender.
   b. amount of money set aside for future replacement of major items.
   c. ongoing expense that does not vary based on occupancy levels of the property.
   d. operating expense necessary to the property, but dependent on the property's occupancy level.

4. **Repairs, maintenance, and real estate taxes are alike in that they are all**
   a. fixed expenses.
   b. operating expenses.
   c. reserves for replacement.
   d. variable expenses.

5. **An investor pays $400,000 for an investment property. Potential gross income is $38,250. Vacancy and collection losses are established at 6.85% and expenses and reserves for replacement are 22.5%. What is the effective gross income?**
   a. $27,613.15
   b. $27,214.88
   c. $35,269.87
   d. $35,629.88

6. **An investor pays $275,000 for an investment property. Gross annual income is $24,000. Vacancy and collection losses are established at 4.9% and expenses and reserves for replacement are 27%. What is the gross rent multiplier?**
   a. 11.5
   b. 16.5
   c. 137.5
   d. 155.5

7. **For a three-unit apartment building, what is the observed vacancy rate (carried to two places) if the total number of days for all units without being rented during a one-year period was 37?**
   a. 2.59%
   b. 3.38%
   c. 4.61%
   d. 5.37%

8. **If a three-unit property generates a total monthly income of $1,975 and sold recently in an arm's length transaction for $185,000, what is the GIM if vacancy loss was estimated at 4.35%?**
   a. 6.74
   b. 7.81
   c. 8.16
   d. 9.47

9. **Calculate the value of an apartment building using direct capitalization. EGI: $150,000; Monthly operating expenses: $2,000; Overall capitalization rate: 9%.**
   a. $1,134,000
   b. $1,400,000
   c. $1,644,444
   d. $1,666,667

10. **A property is valued at $350,000. If it has a PGI of $28,000, a vacancy rate of 5.15%, and operating expenses total $4,700, what is the indicated overall capitalization rate? (rounded to two decimals)**
    a. 5.82%
    b. 5.99%
    c. 6.11%
    d. 6.25%

Chapter 6

Overview of the Cost Approach & Final Reconciliation

6

In this chapter, we will introduce the cost approach and discuss the various components related to its development. Included in the discussion are the concepts and application of replacement cost and reproduction cost, various costing methods that may be applied by an appraiser. as well as methods and techniques for estimating depreciation. In concluding the chapter, the highly important process of final reconciliation will be discussed.

Accrued Depreciation The total accumulated depreciation.

Age-Life Depreciation A calculation that takes the effective age of a property and divides it by the total economic life.

Breakdown Method A method for calculating depreciation by taking a figure for each kind of depreciation and combining them into one number.

Comparative Unit Method A method for determining the cost of a building that uses the cost of recently built comparable buildings as a basis for estimating the cost of replacing the subject property.

Cost Approach An appraisal method used to develop opinons regarding the value of real estate by estimating the cost new of replacing or reproducing the structure on the land minus depreciation and plus the value of the site.

Curable Repairable or able to be fixed; something that can be fixed at a reasonable cost with the value added to the property being more than the cost of the repair.

Deferred Maintenance Physical deterioration created when required repairs are ignored.

Deficiency Property element that is less than necessary, interpreted by the market to be unacceptable, or an element that is functionally inadequate.

Depreciation A loss in value to property improvements for any reason—physical deterioration, functional obsolescence, external obsolescence.

(Continued on page 146)

Key Terms

Concepts and Development of the Cost Approach

The **cost approach** is *an appraisal method used to develop opinions regarding the value of real estate by estimating the cost new of replacing or reproducing the structure on the land minus depreciation and plus the value of the site.*

The three basic steps in developing the cost approach are:

1. Develop an opinion of land value.

2. Estimate cost new of the improvements.

3. Apply depreciation to the cost new.

Typically, the newer the improvements, the more necessary it will be for the appraiser to include development of the cost approach in the scope of work. Although the cost approach is most useful as an valuation method for newer buildings, it can also be used when a replacement cost for an existing building is desired, or for unusual buildings with few comparable sales (e.g., house of worship, school buildings, industrial plants). Moreover, the cost approach is useful to check the value derived from the other appraisal approaches.

When the cost approach is properly developed, there is no reason to doubt that the methodology is just as credible as any other approach to value. In many residential appraisal assignments, the approach is used as a support for the sales comparison approach, typically due to the availability of reliable market sales data. However, the cost approach can be equally reliable when the property's physical characteristics, market conditions, and preferences are adequately addressed.

Costing Concepts

There are several terms and components related to the cost approach, which must be understood and considered by an appraiser prior to commencing development of the methodology. Some of these concepts are related to the estimation of cost new of improvements, while others are specific to estimates of depreciation.

Replacement Cost and Reproduction Cost

Before a specific cost method is chosen, the appraiser must recognize whether the cost estimate is for replacing or reproducing the improvements.

Key Terms

Direct Costs Costs in a project that are not variable, such as labor and materials. Also called **Hard Costs**.

Economic Life The period of time, during the life of an improvement, over which the improvement contributes to the total property value.

Effective Age Considers a structure's physical condition, how acceptably functional a structure is, and the external factors that influence a structure

Entrepreneurial Incentive A dollar value attributable for the expertise and efforts provided in the connection of the development, such as the entrepreneur's expertise, skills, and involvement with development (e.g., leasing, selling) of the project.

Entrepreneurial Profit A figure derived from the market representing an amount received by the entrepreneur for his contributions and risk accepted in a project.

External Obsolescence When something outside the control of a property makes it less desirable. External obsolescence can be locational or economic.

Functional Obsolescence When a building is less desirable because of something inherent in the design of the structure.

Incurable Something that cannot be fixed at a reasonable cost with the cost of the repair being more than the value added to a property.

Index Method A method for determining the cost of a building by taking its original cost and multiplying that number by an index factor based on how long ago the building was constructed.

Indirect Costs Costs in a project that are variable (costs other than labor or materials). Also called **Soft Costs**.

Long-lived Item A component of the property that is not expected to be replaced during the life of a property.

Market Extraction Method A technique for determining depreciation based on comparable sales of similar properties.

Replacement cost is *the estimated cost of building the functional equivalent (substitute) of the original structure using modern materials and workmanship and current day standards of size, layout, quality, and utility.*

Reproduction cost is *the estimated cost of replicating the original building, using identical materials, workmanship, construction standards, size, layout, quality, and utility present in the current structure.*

The appraiser will consider the type and definition of value, intended for use of the appraisal, along with the characteristics of the property to decide whether replacement or reproduction cost will be used in a particular assignment as part of the scope of work decision.

Most frequently, the cost approach uses replacement cost as a building that is built to today's standards is a preferred and often less expensive alternative. Cost estimates for the reproduction of a building are typically done for historical buildings, where it is important for a new structure to have the exact same look and feel as the original.

Building Costs

When using the cost approach, there are several different types of costs that must be calculated. Some of the more obvious costs for a new structure are building materials and labor, but there are numerous other costs involved with construction. The appraiser must be sure to consider all costs for a reliable indication of the cost new of a structure, which are categorized as either direct costs or indirect costs.

Direct Costs

Direct costs are *the costs in a project that are not variable, such as labor and materials.* These are also referred to as **hard costs**. In addition to paying for the labor and buying all the materials needed to build a structure, the contractor has included his profit as part of the direct costs, as it is part of the construction contract.

Indirect Costs

Indirect costs are *the costs in a project that are, in many cases, variable—in other words, all costs for a project other than labor, materials, and equipment.* These are also referred to as **soft costs**. When looking at these costs, there are a number of items that the appraiser should not overlook, such as taxes, insurance, sales commissions, professional fees for legal and accounting work, and many others. These fees are considered "variable," because they often increase as the project moves forward.

Key Terms

Overimprovement An improvement that exceeds the highest and best use for a site and does not increase the value of the real property in proportion to its cost.

Physical Deterioration Wear and tear on something due to age, the elements, or other forces.

Quantity Survey Method A method that specifies the number or quantity of each type of part or material used to build a structure.

Remaining Economic Life The period of usefulness that a building has remaining as of the effective date of the appraisal.

Replacement Cost The estimated cost of building the functional equivalent (substitute) of the original structure, using modern materials and workmanship and current day standards of size, layout, quality, and utility.

Reproduction Cost The estimated cost of replicating the original building, using identical materials, workmanship, construction standards, size, layout, quality, and utility present in the current

structure (including any functional obsolescence, deficiencies, and superadequacies).

Short-lived Item A component of the property that is expected to be replaced during the life of a property.

Superadequacy A feature of an improvement that is more than is necessary for the operation of the improvement.

Underimprovement When property improvements are not sufficient in relation to the highest and best use of the site.

Unit-in-place Method A method that estimates the cost of construction by calculating the unit cost of all component parts of a structure (e.g., framing, roof, HVAC) and adding these costs together.

Useful Life The period of time a structure or a component of the structure can be expected to function for the purpose it was designed for and relates only to physical deterioration.

Direct Costs	Indirect Costs
Materials and labor	Real estate taxes during construction
Building permits	Engineering fees
Equipment cost	Architectural fees
Utility installation and cost	Appraisal fees
Contractor's profit	Accounting fees
Construction site security	Legal fees
	Insurance during construction
	Marketing costs and commissions
	Interest and expenses on any loans during construction

Entrepreneurial Profit and Incentive

Entrepreneurial profit and/or incentive is *an amount of money left after all costs have been paid.* For many residential construction projects, the developer's profit is stated as entrepreneurial incentive. But, in some more complex projects, there could be both. **Entrepreneurial profit** *represents an economic reward received by the entrepreneur for his contributions and risk accepted in a project,* while **entrepreneurial incentive** is an *anticipated economic reward for the entrepreneur's or the developer's contributions of coordination and expertise of a project.*

When entrepreneurial profit and/or entrepreneurial incentive are specified along with the direct and indirect costs, it must be handled appropriately and included with the total cost of the project:

Direct Costs + Indirect Costs + Entrepreneurial Incentive and/or Entrepreneurial Profit = Total Cost

Example

If direct costs of a proposed construction are $375,000 and indirect costs are estimated at $150,000, what is the total estimated cost of the proposed construction if entrepreneurial profit is 10% of direct and indirect costs?

$375,000 (Direct Cost) + $150,000 (Indirect Costs) = $525,000

$525,000 x 0.10 (10% Entrepreneurial Profit) = $52,500

$525,000 + $52,500 = **$577,500** (Total Estimated Cost)

Development of the Cost Approach

As mentioned earlier, the cost approach relies on an opinion of site or land value, estimates of the cost new of the improvement, and an estimation of any accrued depreciation resulting from physical deterioration, functional obsolescence, and external obsolescence. Site and land valuation techniques will be discussed in Chapter 7. Development methodology for estimating cost new and estimating depreciation are discussed here.

Estimating Cost New

There are several different ways of determining the cost of building an improvement on a site. Cost sources used for most residential cost development typically reflect both direct and indirect costs. All of the methods discussed here can be used to estimate the cost of a new structure. When using the cost approach for an existing structure, however, some methods are more appropriate than others.

Again, before a specific cost method is chosen to price an existing structure, the appraiser must know whether the estimate is for replacing or reproducing the building. Remember: *Replacement* of a structure is building the equivalent of the original building using modern materials, workmanship, design, and functional utility; *reproduction* of a structure is building an exact replica of the original building. Reproduction cost also duplicates any negative aspects of the original structure.

Some methods of estimating cost are more appropriate than others, depending on the type and age of the property and whether the improvement already exists or is being proposed. The appraiser's scope of work will set out the costing method appropriate to the appraisal assignment.

The cost approach methods are:

- Comparative unit
- Quantity survey
- Unit-in-place
- Index

Comparative Unit Method

The **comparative unit method** is *a common and relatively simple method for determining the cost of a structure based on known data.* Costs of similar structures are broken down into units of area. For residential dwellings, the unit is typically per square foot. There are several techniques the appraiser can use to develop a cost estimate using the comparative units.

In most appraisals, when using the comparative unit method, the appraiser will rely on cost services for the base or benchmark cost. The appraiser matches the subject property with the most similar type of building and building features that can be found from the costing service, and then makes any necessary adjustments for variations in materials used or for other items or features not reflected in the base cost using the multipliers supplied by the costing service. This particular technique of the comparative unit method is sometimes referred to as the **square-foot method**.

> ### EXAMPLE
> An appraiser is estimating the cost of a 1,500 square foot, one-story house in Indianapolis. Costing information for the Midwest region of the country, in which Indianapolis is located, indicates the cost per square foot is $57.48. The cost per square foot can then be defined further by using a local multiplier for Indianapolis. If the multiplier for Indianapolis is 0.95, then the cost per square foot would be multiplied by the multiplier to determine the cost estimate for the house:
>
> $57.48 x 0.95 = $54.61
>
> 1,500 x $54.61 = **$81,915** (Cost Estimate)
>
> Also, the example assumes the subject building is exactly like the one in the cost manual, so no adjustments were made. Appraisers must take into account differences between buildings described in the cost manual and the subject building.

Quantity Survey Method

Using the **quantity survey method**, the appraiser counts the number of each type of part and material used to construct the subject building. **This method is the most detailed of the cost approaches**, as it requires a thorough itemization of every building component used. This method duplicates the process a contractor goes through when determining a bid for a contract. All direct costs of building the structure are calculated—unit price of each material multiplied by the quantity needed, plus the cost of labor for assembly or installation. Next, the appraiser adds all indirect costs—plans, permits, overhead, interest, taxes, profit, etc. An additional figure for the time value of money is often added to the profit figure, as well as a construction management cost and other costs for additional layers of management and profit—especially when an investor is involved, and the construction company or developer does not own the land. Since the cost is figured so precisely, the appraiser must be able to make accurate estimates for labor and materials, which often entails consultation with building professionals. The quantity survey method is seldom used as a mainstream costing technique.

Unit-In-Place Method

The **unit-in-place method** *estimates the cost of reproducing or replacing a building by determining the unit cost of each of the component parts of the structure, then multiplying the unit costs by the appropriate unit measure, and adding all of these unit costs together based on actual need and usage.*

In the unit-in-place method, rather than calculating the cost of each outlet and outlet cover as in the quantity survey, the method considers the total number of outlets needed for the entire building and uses this to estimate the cost of the electrical service needed. This process is repeated for each main system or component of the building, often relying on cost services as the means of determining the cost figures.

Example

Sample Construction Cost Manual Data: Residential Construction, Midwest			
1-STORY HOUSE			
Economy Grade			
Cost per Square Foot			
Type of Work	**Materials**	**Labor**	**Total**
1. SITE WORK	0.10	0.80	0.90
2. FOUNDATION	3.00	4.10	7.10
3. FRAMING	4.45	3.25	7.60
4. ROOF	0.85	1.35	2.20
5. EXTERIOR WORK	3.75	4.50	8.25
6. MECHANICALS	2.60	1.90	4.50
7. INTERIOR FINISH WORK	4.75	4.85	9.60
8. KITCHEN/BATH	1.50	1.50	3.00
9. OTHER	1.00	1.50	2.50
10. OVERHEAD	1.50	1.50	3.00
TOTALS:	23.40	25.25	**48.65**

NOTE: Numbers are for example purposes only, and may not necessarily reflect current costs in your area.

Index Method

The **index method** *estimates the cost of a building by taking its original cost and multiplying that number by an index factor based on how long ago the building was constructed.* Use of this method is not common and is not broadly considered by many as a reliable method of estimating cost. However, it could be used as a second check against other cost methods.

Example
A building built in 1985 cost $200,000 at the time of construction. A current index factor for that type of building might be 1.15. By multiplying $200,000 x 1.15, the present day cost is estimated at $230,000.

Do the Math

Calculations using square feet of gross living area (GLA) and cubic feet were presented in Chapter 3. There are some additional calculations for which appraisers must be familiar that are typically part of the costing process.

Square Yard Calculations

It is useful to know how to calculate the area, amounts, and costs for various types of common construction materials—especially when completing the cost approach.

Carpet is often sold by the *square yard*, yet appraisers usually measure a room in *square feet*. They must convert from square feet to square yards:

> Length x Width = Square Feet
>
> Square Feet ÷ 9 = Square Yards

For Example

If a room measures 20' x 20', how much carpet is needed?

20' x 20' = 400

400' ÷ 9 = **44.4** square yards of carpet

Work Problem 6.1

The carpet in a 12.5 x 16' room and a 12.25' x 14.75 room needs to be replaced. Rounded to the nearest whole dollar, what will be the total cost of the carpet if it is priced at $26.50 per square yard, including installation? _____

Cubic Yard Calculations

Concrete is typically sold in cubic yards. The formula is:

> Length x Width x Depth = Cubic Feet ÷ 27 = Cubic Yards

Remember these important considerations when working with cubic yards:

1. There is a *depth component* to the measurement, so you will have three numbers to multiply.

2. All numbers must be in the same units. Often, you will have length and width in feet, but the depth in inches—convert inches to percent of a foot.

3. Concrete is usually sold by the cubic yard, so you must convert:

Length x Width x Depth = Cubic Feet

Cubic Feet ÷ 27 = Cubic Yards

For Example

1. A driveway measures 50' x 8' x 3". *How much concrete is needed?*

50' x 8' x 0.25' = 100' (don't forget to convert inches to feet: 3" = 0.25')

100' ÷ 27 = **3.70** Cubic Yards

2. *Find the cost of a sidewalk that is 40' x 8' x 6" if concrete costs $75 per cubic yard?*

Step #1: Calculate sidewalk size:

40' x 8' x 0.5' = 160' (don't forget to convert inches to feet: 6" = 0.5')

160' ÷ 27 = 5.9259 Cubic Yards

Step #2: Calculate total cost as (Size x the Price per Cubic Yard):

5.9259 x $75 = **$444.44**

Work Problem 6.2

How much will concrete cost for a driveway if it is 40' x 8' x 4", and concrete costs $26 per cubic yard? _____

Concepts of Depreciation

Depreciation is a *monetary loss in value of property for any reason.* Although the value of land can fluctuate due to external and economic forces that affect its highest and best use, the land itself is never said to suffer depreciation. Although the enhancements to the land that make it a site, and the improvements that we place on it, could suffer deterioration or obsolescence. Thus, depreciation is only applied to the structure on the land and other site improvements.

Accrued depreciation is the *difference between the current value of an improvement and the cost of replacing the improvement.* This is an important calculation needed for the cost approach. The depreciation amount allows the cost new to be applied to an existing structure that exhibits deterioration or obsolescence. The three forces that cause depreciation are:

- Physical deterioration
- Functional obsolescence
- External obsolescence

The first concept to understand is the important measurements to the life of a structure or other improvement—effective age, useful life, and economic life.

Effective Age, Useful Life, and Economic Life

The most common methods of depreciation revolve around certain measures of time in a structure or an improvement's life. As will be seen later, when the discussion changes to depreciation calculations, the actual age of a structure or improvement is insignificant to depreciation. Rather, most common methods of depreciation examine the structure's effective age in reflection to the economic or useful life of the structure.

The **effective age** of a structure is based on all forces of deterioration and obsolescence (deterioration and obsolescence will be discussed later in this chapter). In other words, the effective age *considers a structure's physical condition, how acceptably functional a structure is, and the external factors that influence a structure.*

Using a house as an example, the moment the house is constructed, the clock accounting for its actual age starts ticking and never stops. At the same time, the clock measuring effective age also begins. However, there are conditions or events that can make the effective age clock set back, or even jump ahead of the actual age clock.

Example

A house is 10 years old (its actual age). The owner replaces the floor coverings, repaints all of the rooms, spruces up the exterior, replaces dated lighting fixtures and otherwise brings the house to current day standards and tastes. Provided there are no other functional or external issues, the effective age clock will be set back—in this case to, say, five years. Now the house has an effective age of five years and an actual age of 10 years. However, once the refurbishments resume being subjected to use and begin to age, the effective age clock ticks ahead as well.

Where did the five-year effective age come from in the previous example? Estimating the effective age of a structure or other improvement requires support by good judgment and reasoning skills that is gained through experience on the part of the appraiser. The results of the cost approach can lack credibility by not reasonably estimating effective age. Appraisers must be thoughtful and use great care, as subjectively estimating the effective age without support of sound reasoning and logic, as well as not communicating the reasoning and logic sufficiently in the appraisal report is an unacceptable practice.

Here are some other examples that could have a significant effect on effective age:

- A house that is neglected, abused, or has suffered damage due to a catastrophic event (e.g., an earthquake, hurricane, tornado) could have an effective age greater than its actual age.

- A poor floor plan or a house built in an undesirable location could actually cause the effective age to be greater than the actual age.

- Left unaddressed, environmental issues such as radon, toxic mold, or site contamination could cause the effective age to be greater than the actual age.

- Changes in property uses external to a particular property (e.g., a factory or toxic waste dump) could cause the effective age of a house to accelerate, even though the house is functionally acceptable and maintained adequately.

These are just a few examples of how the effective age responds, and there certainly are numerous others. In some of these examples, some issues could be resolved, while other issues cannot be reasonably and practically resolved.

Useful life and **economic life** are also important concepts to understand and are best discussed together.

- **Economic life** is *the period of time, during the life of an improvement, over which the improvement contributes to the total property value, and is a reflection of all three of the forces of depreciation.* During this time, the improvement contributes positively to the property value.

- **Useful life** relates to *the period of time a structure or a component of the structure can be expected to function for the purpose it was designed for and relates only to physical deterioration.* An example might be a component of the property, such as a furnace or roof that is expected to be replaced during the lifetime of a property.

Estimation of the total economic life of a particular structure is derived from the market. The market extraction method of depreciation, illustrated later in this chapter, is one way that economic life can be mathematically calculated. Remaining economic life references the period of usefulness a structure has remaining as of the effective date of the appraisal.

- **Effective age** represents *the number of years of the structure's life that has elapsed or has been used.*
- **Remaining economic life** is *the number of year's life that is remaining of the structure.*
- **Total economic life** of a structure is comprised by *the total of the effective age and the remaining economic life.*

Effective Age + Remaining Economic Life = Total Economic Life

Example

If a structure has an effective age of 20 years and a remaining economic life of 40 years, the total economic life of the structure is 60 years.

20 years effective age + 40 years remaining economic life = 60 years total economic life

As deterioration or obsolescence appears and continues, the effective age will become greater and the remaining economic life will become shorter. Likewise, when a property owner refurbishes or renovates a structure, or other curable obsolescence is cured, the effective age will decrease and the remaining economic life will increase.

The effective age is influenced by all forces of depreciation, physical, functional and external. The three forces of depreciation is the next point of discussion, starting with physical deterioration.

Physical Deterioration

Physical deterioration is *the actual wear and tear on something due to age, the elements, or other forces.* This type of depreciation is often observable during the appraiser's personal inspection of the subject property. Regular maintenance can slow this process; deferred maintenance results in items that need immediate attention.

Deferred maintenance is *a physical deterioration that has occurred because of a failure to perform regular maintenance and upkeep.* Most deferred maintenance would be classified as curable (repairable), provided the severity of the condition is not beyond economical repair or replacement; not all physical deterioration is curable.

Curable vs. Incurable Physical Deterioration

The test for deciding if physical deterioration is curable or incurable depends on the contributory value of the item that needs repair or replacement. *If the cost to repair or replace an item exceeds the value that repair or replacement adds to the property value,* then the physical deterioration is said to be **incurable**. *If the item can be repaired or replaced at a reasonable cost and the contributory value added to the property is more than the cost of the repair,* then the physical deterioration is said to be **curable**.

This distinction is fairly clear with deferred maintenance items that are not operational or show advanced signs of neglect and need immediate attention (e.g., a broken furnace or widespread peeling paint). These items, if not repaired, would diminish the value of the property.

Short-lived vs. Long-lived Items

When considering different types of physical deterioration, the deteriorated elements are categorized further as short-lived or long-lived items. **Short-lived items** in a property are *those that are expected to be replaced during the lifetime of the structure.* Short-lived items include things such as:

- Carpet
- HVAC system
- Paint

Long-lived items in a property are *those that are expected to last for the life of the structure.* This would include such things as:

- Foundation
- Framing

Functional Obsolescence

Functional obsolescence is *when a building is less desirable because of something inherent in the design or nature of the structure.* This type of depreciation is observable during an inspection. Examples of functional obsolescence are outdated home styles, out-of-date fixtures, or homes with only one bathroom. Unusual floor plans can also fall under the category of functional obsolescence. These undesirable features may be curable, because they can be fixed at a reasonable cost, like outdated fixtures, or these features may be incurable because they cannot be fixed without major cost or renovations, like a home's style.

Underimprovements and Overimprovements

With functional obsolescence, there are a few additional points that should be made clear. Functional obsolescence must be considered any time the improvements do not lend to the property's highest and best use. An **underimprovement** is *when property improvements are not sufficient in relation to the highest and best use of the site, thus, the property does not achieve maximum value.* An **overimprovement** is a similar example of non-conformity where *the improvements and, likewise the cost of the improvements, exceed the completed market value.*

√ **Note:** Some underimprovements and overimprovements could be related to external factors, which will be discussed later in this chapter.

Deficiencies and Superadequacies

A **deficiency** is when *a feature or component of a property is not adequate in the marketplace and results in a loss of market value.* A **superadequacy** is when *a feature or component of a property is too large, too expensive, or of too high a quality, such that its cost exceeds the contributory value of that item or feature.*

Whether a property feature is deficient or superadequate, it requires particular competency on the part of the appraiser in recognizing what participants within a particular market expect and want. What might be considered deficient or superadequate in one market may not be in another. As well, what might be acceptable at one particular price point might be deficient or superadequate at another price point.

External Obsolescence

External obsolescence is when *something is outside the boundaries of a property and the control of the property owner and makes it less desirable.* The factors causing the obsolescence may be economic or locational factors.

Locational examples will vary depending on the nature of the property and the particular market, but will hold true in most residential applications. Examples of **locational external obsolescence** include:

- Declining neighborhood
- Nearby landfill
- Noise and traffic from a highway
- Nearby railway
- Industrial exposure

Economic external obsolescence can present itself in both residential and non-residential situations. Residential properties are often impacted to a greater degree by economic considerations, such as:

- High interest rates
- Oversupply situations

Economic considerations most often are observed in non-residential applications, such as:

- A structure or facility that can no longer be supported by the market economics
- Some underimprovements and overimprovements

Example

The closing of an industry may cause economic external obsolescence if the industry was vital to an area's economic base. If there is little prospect of another use for the facility, it will create an economic external obsolescence.

External obsolescence is, in almost all instances, incurable—property owners can typically do little to stop or change these conditions.

Estimating Depreciation

There are several recognized methods of depreciation available for an appraiser to use. Some of these techniques are beyond the scope of this course, but will be discussed and illustrated in courses expanding on the topic of the cost approach. There are three methods of depreciation that will be discussed in this section:

- Age-life method
- Breakdown method
- Market extraction method

Age-Life Method

The **age-life method** *estimates depreciation as a ratio of the effective age of improvements to the total economic life*. This is also called **economic age-life method**. The effective age of a structure is based on both physical and economic concepts. Deterioration is a physical concept, while obsolescence is an economic concept. As discussed earlier, the effective age addresses all forms of depreciation by considering the presence of physical deterioration, functional obsolescence, and external obsolescence.

To estimate age-life depreciation, a simple formula is used, whereby the effective age of the improvement is divided by total expected life of the improvement to arrive at a total depreciation amount as a percentage.

Effective Age / Total Expected Economic Life = Depreciation Percentage

Example

An appraiser is estimating the depreciation of a building, with a cost new of $400,000, using the effective age-life method. When built, the building had an expected economic life of 50 years. Its current effective age is 10 years. Given these facts, calculate the building's depreciation.

10 / 50 = .20 = 20% depreciation
$400,000 x 20% = $80,000

It is true that in many residential appraisals, physical deterioration will be the only element addressed in determining effective age. If that is the case, the owners of a well-maintained building can continue to get more useful economic life out of it. In fact, a well-kept building could remain at the same effective age for several years if it is properly maintained and kept to modern standards. Likewise, a building with significant deferred maintenance may demonstrate an effective age greater than its actual age. It may be better to tear down this kind of building rather than invest money to repair it. **The age-life method is the most commonly applied depreciation technique in residential appraisal.**

Work Problem 6.3

A structure building has an expected economic life of 75 years. Its cost new is estimated at $375,000 and effective age is 15 years. Estimate the depreciation using the age-life method.

Breakdown Method

The breakdown method is used when a more comprehensive analysis of various sources of depreciation is necessary. The effective age of the improvements used in the economic age-life method previously discussed considers all sources of depreciation (physical deterioration, functional obsolescence, and external obsolescence), and the rate of depreciation developed by the technique reflects a combined total rate of depreciation from all of the sources. The breakdown method further categorizes the depreciation rate into the various categories.

As a simple example, if the total rate of depreciation indicated by the economic age life method was 10%, the appraiser could break down the total rate into categories:

- 7% - Physical depreciation
- 2% - Functional depreciation
- 1% - External depreciation

Each of these categories could then be broken down further:

Physical depreciation could be defined as either curable or incurable, and then the depreciation could be further assigned as deferred maintenance items, short-lived items, or long-lived items. Each item is analyzed separately using the economic age life method.

Example

The furnace in a house will cost $5,000 when it needs to be replaced. Based on the appraiser's judgment, the furnace's current condition indicates about 30% of its life has been used. The useful remaining life of the furnace is 70%. Therefore, the depreciation would be calculated as:

$5,000 x .30 (30%) = $1,500 (furnace depreciation)

On that same structure, the roof with a 25-year guarantee has approximately 80% of its life left, with about 20 years remaining useful life. Replacement will cost $3,500. Therefore, the depreciation is 20%, or $700.

$3,500 x .20 (20%) = $700

Therefore, the total depreciation calculated for these curable items of physical deterioration is $2,200

As can be seen from this simplistic illustration, each component is considered individually, and is much more comprehensive than applying an overall effective age reflecting all components. In developing physical depreciation indications by using the breakdown method, the appraiser would continue calculating depreciation attributable to other incurable items and adding in the appropriate sum.

For **functional obsolescence and external obsolescence**, the depreciation would be developed separately using methods that will be discussed in course work dedicated to the cost approach. However, for understanding the basic flow of the breakdown method, the following should be recognized:

- Functional obsolescence can be allocated as curable or incurable and can further be broken down as either a deficiency or a superadequacy.

- External obsolescence, while always incurable, can be further defined as external depreciation caused by deficiencies, or depreciation caused by superadequacies.

Work Problem 6.4

Using the breakdown method, calculate the depreciation of a roof that cost $4,000 and has about 90% life left.

Market Extraction Method

The **market extraction method** is *a technique for determining depreciation based on comparable sales of similar properties.* This method is sometimes called the **sales comparison method**, the **market comparison method**, or the **abstraction method**.

The steps for estimating depreciation using the market extraction method are as follows:

- **Step 1**: Identify comparable sold properties that share as many traits as possible with the subject.

- **Step 2**: Make adjustments to the comparable properties for conditions and significant differences, with the exception of market conditions, just like in the sales comparison approach.

- **Step 3**: Subtract an amount for the market value of the site from the adjusted sale price of the comparable; this isolates the improvement value.

- **Step 4**: Calculate the cost of building a replacement structure on the day the comparable property sold. (Cost manuals would be one way to accomplish this.)

- **Step 5**: Take the replacement cost new for the improvement minus the amount extracted for the current improvement contribution, and this will result in the amount of depreciation attributed to the improvement.

Total Market Value - Site Value = Improvement Contribution to Value

Replacement Cost New - Improvement Contribution = Depreciation Amount

Example

A five-year old home sold for $410,000. Sales comparison data for this market reveals that the site is worth about $40,000. The replacement cost new is $295,000. Determine the depreciation amount:

$310,000 (Total Market Value) - $40,000 (Site Value) = $270,000 (Improvement Contribution to Value)

$295,000 (Replacement Cost New) - $270,000 (Improvement Contribution to Value) = $25,000 (Depreciation)

If the improved and vacant land data is more comparable, then the market extraction method will be more reliable. Accuracy is also critical in developing the replacement cost for the comparable property.

The market extraction method is also useful for indicating the economic or remaining economic life of a structure. First, calculate the depreciation amount as shown previously. Then, calculate the remaining economic life.

Depreciation Amount / Actual Age = Annual Depreciation Amount

Replacement Cost New / Annual Depreciation Amount = Total Economic Life

Total Economic Life - Effective Age = Remaining Economic Life

Example

An improved property is 40 years old and is currently valued at $173,000. From market data, the site is worth $42,000. The effective age of the improvements is 20 years. Replacement cost of the structure is $185,000. Using the market extraction method, find the total economic life of the structure.

$173,000 (Market Value) - $42,000 (Site Value) = $131,000 (Improvement Contribution to Value)

$185,000 (Replacement Cost New) - $131,000 (Improvement Contribution) = $54,000 (Depreciation Amount)

$54,000 / 40 (Actual Age) = $1,350 (Annual Depreciation Amount). $185,000 (Replacement Cost New) / $1,350 = **137.0370** or **137** (Total Economic Life)

Note: The remaining economic life is calculated by subtracting the effective age (20) from the total economic life. Thus, the remaining economic life in this example is 117 years.

Work Problem 6.5

A 45-year old home sold for $355,000. Sales comparison data for this market reveals that the site is worth about $60,000. The replacement cost new for the home is $580,000. The effective age of the home is 20 years. What is the remaining economic life of the structure?

Estimating "Other" Site Improvements

There is one final element that is typically associated with most cost analysis—the "as-is" value of "other" site improvements. For existing properties, most often the contributory value of other site improvements will be considered "as-is" or in their depreciated state. In other words, considered on an "as-is" basis, the contributory value is already depreciated and must not be included in the cost new and subject to additional depreciation along with the structure.

Included improvement elements not already considered in the cost calculations include (but are not limited to):

- Driveways
- Landscaping
- Walkways
- Utility provisions

In their "as-is" state, a contributory value of other improvements is typically stated as an aggregate dollar amount as of the effective date of the appraisal.

Final Cost Approach Analysis

Once the conclusions of site value, cost new, depreciation, and the "as-is" value of other site improvements is concluded, the results are assembled to indicate a value conclusion via the cost approach, similar to this sample:

Cost Approach Sample	
Replacement Cost of House	2,400 square feet x $102.00 per square foot $244,800
Depreciation (Physical)	Effective Age 15 years Remaining Economic Life 55 years 15 years ÷ 70 years (15 + 55) 21.4286% depreciation $244,800 x 21.4286% $52,457 (rounded) $244,800 − $52,457 = **$192,343**
Site Value	**$38,000**
Other Site Improvements	**$10,000**
Indicated Value by the Cost Approach	**$240,343**

Final Reconciliation of Value

Now that the recognized approaches to value have been presented, the remaining topic of the discussion is the final reconciliation of value. The final reconciliation is the last step in the appraiser's development process. While the topic appears last in the discussion of valuation methodology and there is no specified coursework dedicated to the topic of the final reconciliation of value, a solid understanding of the critical nature of the process is fundamental to sound appraisal practice.

Process of Reconciliation

USPAP references the reconciliation process for real property appraisal through the obligations of Standards Rule 1-6.

> *In developing a real property appraisal, an appraiser must:*
>
> *(a) reconcile the quality and quantity of data available and analyzed within the approaches used; and*
>
> *(b) reconcile the applicability and relevance of the approaches, methods and techniques used to arrive at the value conclusion(s). (2014-2015 Edition of USPAP).*

As can be seen, USPAP specifies the reconciliation process as consisting of two steps; the first step within each approach to value developed by the appraiser, and the second step reconciling the final conclusion after all valuation approaches necessary in the scope of work have been developed.

As the valuation methods have been presented, it should be clear that an appraiser progressively forms conclusions throughout each approach, beginning early in the development process. In the sales comparison approach, the data chosen, adjustments necessitated, and the appraiser's interpretation of the indicated value by the approach are just a few examples. A similar process is applied to the income approach regarding the data and conclusions of potential income, expenses, and rates of capitalization. In the cost approach, the appraiser forms conclusions regarding elements, such as the appropriate cost new and the estimate of depreciation.

In reconciling the final conclusion of value, the appraiser makes decisions regarding the applicability and relevance of the valuation approaches that were developed in the assignment. Although there are some mathematical techniques that can be employed in developing a final opinion of value, it is not particularly a scientific process. Rather, it is one that necessitates sound logic and reasoning skills, which requires competence.

USPAP indicates, in the definition of the term *appraisal*, that a value opinion can be a single number, a range of numbers, or a relationship to a numerical benchmark or previous value opinion. Simply expressing a value opinion might be confused by newcomers to the industry as reconciliation. While in reality, they are two distinct processes; stating a value opinion is more associated with the reporting aspect of an assignment, while reconciliation is a specific development step. For example:

- The opinion of value is $100,000
- The opinion of value is between $100,000 and $110,000
- The opinion of value is greater (or lesser) than the previous appraisal, what the neighbor's property sold for, etc.

While all of these could be valid final value opinions, reconciliation must take place before the opinion is stated. Appropriateness of each of these forms of expressing value is determined within the scope of work. But reconciliation is the development step that took place leading to these statements. What was the rationale that led the appraiser to the particular value opinion? Appraisers could painstakingly develop the approaches to value and the conclusions could lack credibility if not properly reconciled. Adequate reporting of the steps taken and the appraiser's rationale for his or her conclusions is equally important.

Final Reconciliation Examples

Since the basis of the final reconciliation process requires sound logic and good reasoning, there is no specific formula that is broadly applied for which to perform the process. Therefore, discussion of the final reconciliation of value is best presented through discussion of some common examples and scenarios for most residential appraisers.

Final Value Opinion Based on One Approach to Value

The appraiser's scope of work could necessitate the development of one, two, or three of the approaches to value. For residential appraisals, the scope of work in many assignments may limit the valuation process to only the development of the sales comparison approach. In such case, the final reconciliation process may not require great analysis, and the most credible conclusion would be to agree with the indications produced by the sales comparison approach as the reconciled final opinion of value.

Some may argue that even when only one of the approaches to value has been developed, the reconciled final value conclusion could be lesser or greater than the indication produced in the approach to value (except for rounding, which will be discussed later in this chapter). In some rare cases, this may be true. However, if adequate relevant data were available and selected in the development of the approach, and the approach was developed properly with appropriate adjustments applied to the data, there is little credible rationale for this to occur. The same could be said if only the income approach or the cost approach was developed singularly in an assignment, which is an even rarer occurrence for many residential appraisers.

Example #1

If the conclusion of the sales comparison approach developed in the appraisal of a single-family owner-occupied property was an indicated value of $250,000, the reconciled final opinion of value would most logically be concluded as $250,000.

Final Value Opinion Based on More Than One Approach to Value

The scope of work in some assignments may specify the development of two or three approaches to value. For instance, proposed construction of a new residence may necessitate the sales comparison approach and the cost approach to be developed. Many intended users also may have a similar requirement for certain existing properties. Or, if the highest and best use of an improved property is for income-producing purposes, development of the sales comparison approach and the income approach may be necessary.

Example #2

An appraisal assignment is being performed for the proposed construction of a new dwelling on a residential lot. The appraiser has several recent sales of similar new homes, as well as current construction cost data and lot sales. The sales comparison analysis indicates a value of $249,000, while the cost approach indicates a value of $251,000. In this case, the appraiser finds the indications produced by both approaches to value to be credible and reliable. The final reconciled value conclusion would likely be $250,000.

Example #3

The client has specified the sales comparison approach and the cost approach be developed in a particular assignment. The subject property is a 25-year old residence in a subdivision. The appraiser discovers ample recent comparable data available in the subject market for which to develop the sales comparison approach, with few adjustments required to the data. The cost approach, while developed in an appropriate manner, requires significant adjustments to the data. Substantial estimation of depreciation was also required. Therefore, the appraiser determines that the indication produced by the sales comparison approach, $265,000, is the most reliable indicator, while the results produced via the cost approach, $270,000, is the least reliable. Likely, the most logical and rationale final value opinion produced through the reconciliation is $265,000, which concurs with the indications of the sales comparison approach.

Note: In the example, the appraiser may, or may not, have decided to include development of the cost approach in the scope of work. If the development of the approach at the request of the client does not produce a misleading conclusion, the client's request to develop it is acceptable given the appraiser explains the reasoning for developing the cost approach. If the appraiser believes developing the approach was unnecessary, he should state that it has been given no weight in the final reconciled value. In some cases, the appraiser may choose to use the results of the cost approach as support for other approaches that were developed in the assignment.

These examples provide some introductory insight regarding the rationale and logic involved with the final reconciliation of value. Obviously, there could be many other scenarios not discussed here.

Statistical Measures and Rounding in Reconciliation

It has been a longtime standard within the appraisal profession that an appraiser *never averages* his or her final value opinion – something newcomers to the industry will no doubt hear along the way. The meaning of this concept is that the final value reported in an appraisal is always an opinion, and opinions should not be formed solely through mathematical function.

For example, if the appraiser has developed all three approaches to value in an assignment and the conclusions developed is income approach: $103,000; sales comparison approach: $112,000; and cost approach: $115,000; the final value conclusion, if simply averaged, would be $110,000. As can be seen, there were no conclusions formed by the appraiser in doing such, and therefore, it is premised on mathematics and not an opinion. However, if the appraiser reconciled that the indications produced by all of approaches developed were equally credible, the appraiser may choose to use the mean of those conclusions, giving all equal weight. With that decision, the appraiser has applied logic and reasoning into the opinion – the strength of all results of the approaches developed is equal. The appraiser could also use other statistical measures, such as the median or mode, as well.

Using that same number set, consider that the appraiser has reconciled the indications produced by the three approaches developed and has decided the sales comparison approach and the cost approach possess the greatest strength due to the quality and relevance of the data analyzed. The indications by these two approaches are at the upper end of the range at $112,000 and $115,000. So, these values could be used in reconciling to a final value. As can be seen, the appraiser is using judgment along the way until a final opinion of value has been concluded.

A highly unacceptable practice by an appraiser is to recognize the range of the value indications produced by the approaches to value ($103,000 to $115,000) and select a final number within that range that meets the client's need or expectation. An appraiser may attempt to justify this practice by defending that the "value needed" was within the range of inductions produced by the approaches to value. However, the appraiser did not use his judgment in forming this conclusion, and, if the appraiser's only reasoning for the conclusion was to satisfy the client's needs, the conclusion was not his or her personal opinion. The practice would be a violation of the ETHICS RULE of USPAP.

As a final point, opinions are not typically precise and the dollar amount of any opinion of value is typically rounded. For example, consider that the indicated mean of the conclusions of the three approaches to value that were developed is $247,832. Stating a final opinion of value with such a concise number implies a precision that does not exist in an opinion. At a minimum, the value opinion should be rounded up to $248,000.

Summary

1. The three basic steps in developing the cost approach are: 1.) Develop an opinion of land value; 2.) Estimate cost new of the improvements; 3.) Apply depreciation to the cost new.

2. Although the cost approach is most useful as an valuation method for newer buildings, it can also be used when a replacement cost for an existing building is desired, or for unusual buildings with few comparable sales. The cost approach is also useful to support the value derived from the other appraisal approaches.

3. Before a specific cost method is chosen, the appraiser must recognize whether the cost estimate is for replacing or reproducing the improvements.

4. The appraiser must be sure to consider all costs for a reliable indication of the cost new of a structure, which are categorized as either direct costs or indirect costs.

5. Entrepreneurial profit and/or incentive is *an amount of money left after all costs have been paid.* For many residential construction projects, the developer's profit is stated as entrepreneurial incentive.

6. The cost approach methods for estimating cost new are the comparative unit method, the quantity survey method, the unit-in-place method, and the index method.

7. Depreciation is a monetary loss in value of property for any reason. Accrued depreciation is the difference between the current value of an improvement and the cost of replacing the improvement.

8. The three forces that cause depreciation are physical deterioration, functional obsolescence, and external obsolescence.

9. The effective age of a structure is based on all forces of deterioration and obsolescence. Economic life is the period of time, during the life of an improvement, over which the improvement contributes to the total property value. Useful life relates to the period of time a structure or a component of the structure can be expected to function for the purpose it was designed for, and relates only to physical deterioration.

10. If the cost to repair or replace an item exceeds the value that that repair or replacement adds to the property value, then the physical deterioration is said to be incurable. If the item can be repaired or replaced at a reasonable cost and the contributory value added to the property is more than the cost of the repair, then the physical deterioration is said to be curable.

11. Short-lived items are those that are expected to be replaced during the lifetime of the structure. Long-lived items are those that are expected to last for the life of the structure.

12. An underimprovement is when property improvements are not sufficient in relation to the highest and best use of the site, thus, the property does not achieve maximum value. An overimprovement is a similar example of non-conformity where the improvements and, likewise the cost of the improvements, exceed the completed market value.

13. A deficiency is when a feature or component of a property is not adequate in the marketplace and results in a loss of market value. A superadequacy is when a feature or component of a property is too large, too expensive, or of too high a quality such that its cost exceeds the contributory value of that item or feature.

14. The age-life method is the most commonly applied depreciation technique in residential appraisal. To estimate age-life depreciation, the effective age of the improvement is divided by total expected life of the improvement to arrive at a total depreciation amount as a percentage.

15. The final reconciliation of value is the last step in the appraiser's development process. In reconciling the final conclusion of value, the appraiser is making decisions regarding the applicability and relevance of the valuation approaches that were developed in the assignment, which necessitates sound logic and reasoning.

16. If an appraiser does not use his own judgment in forming his or her conclusions and if the appraiser's only reasoning for the conclusion was to satisfy the client's needs, the conclusion was not his or her personal opinion and the practice would be a violation of the ETHICS RULE of USPAP.

Quiz

1. For which of the following structures would reproduction cost be typically used?

   a. historic cathedral
   b. modern office building
   c. suburban strip mall
   d. vacation condominium

2. A house having outside dimensions of 40' X 70' is being constructed. The regional cost per square foot is $118.00 per square foot. What is the cost new in the local market, if the local multiplier is 1.05?

   a. $310,990
   b. $317,630
   c. $324,410
   d. $346,920

3. If direct costs of a proposed construction are $582,000 and indirect costs are estimated at $300,000, what is the total estimated cost of the proposed construction if entrepreneurial profit is 16% of direct and indirect costs?

   a. $790,460
   b. $896,500
   c. $962,000
   d. $1,023,120

4. Which is most likely to be classified as a long-lived item?

   a. exterior paint
   b. HVAC system
   c. structural framing
   d. wall-to-wall carpet

5. Which of the following is most likely an example of incurable functional obsolescence?

   a. no door on the bathroom
   b. no lighting in the pantry
   c. outdated fixtures
   d. style of the home

6. A 30-year old home sold for $90,000. Sales comparison data for this market reveals that the site is worth about $8,000. The replacement cost new for the home is $112,000. The effective age of the home is 25 years. What is the remaining economic life of the home?

   a. 68
   b. 70
   c. 71
   d. 87

7. A 100-year old building has an expected economic life of 120 years. Its current effective age is 90 years and the cost new is $400,000. Land value is estimated at $50,000. What is the accrued depreciation using the age-life method?

   a. $265,500
   b. $270,000
   c. $285,500
   d. $300,000

8. Damaged drywall is an example of which cause of depreciation?

   a. external obsolescence
   b. functional obsolescence
   c. physical deterioration
   d. short-lived incurable

9. Using the breakdown method, what is the depreciation of a roof with a cost of $15,000 and has about 36% remaining life?

   a. $9,400
   b. $9,600
   c. $10,400
   d. $11,000

10. A building has a total expected economic life of 75 years and an effective age of 25 years. If the replacement cost is $750,000, what is the current value of the building?

    a. $187,500
    b. $250,000
    c. $500,000
    d. $562,000

11. What is the value of the improved property indicated by the cost approach? Site value: $40,000; Dwelling size: 2,600 square feet; Replacement cost: $93 per square feet; Garage: 600 square feet; Replacement cost: $18 per square feet; As-is value of site improvements: $13,000; Effective age: 10 years; Remaining economic life: 90 years

    a. $227,420
    b. $245,570
    c. $267,105
    d. $280,340

12. *A building has a total expected economic life of 62 years and an effective age of 30 years. If the replacement cost is $425,000, what is the current value of the building (rounded)?*

   a. $215,000
   b. $219,000
   c. $242,000
   d. $260,000

13. *When the "as-is" contribution of other site improvements is being estimated in development of the cost approach for an existing property,*

   a. any contribution must be included in the opinion of site value.
   b. contribution to value reflects the cost of the items new on the effective date.
   c. depreciation is already considered in the estimate.
   d. landscaping and driveways are not included.

14. *Whether the reconciled final opinion of value will be expressed as a single number, a range, or a relationship to a benchmark or previous value opinion, is determined by an appraiser*

   a. after he or she has developed their conclusions.
   b. as part of the scope of work decision.
   c. based upon jurisdictional requirements.
   d. in compliance with the reporting standards.

15. *Within the process of final reconciliation, an appraiser's value opinion should be based upon*

   a. the clients needs.
   b. rationalized logic and reasoning.
   c. a simple mathematical calculation.
   d. the type of report in the assignment.

Chapter 7

Overview of Land and Site Valuation

In this chapter, several different methods utilized for site valuation will be overviewed along with important concepts integral to the site valuation process. While it is true that valuing land or site most often precedes development of the approaches to value, this topic is appropriate here as the land and site valuation methods reflect one or more of the sales comparison approach, income approach, or cost approach techniques.

Valuation Methodology for Land and Site

An appraiser determines the specific method or technique appropriate for developing an opinion of value for land or site as part of the scope of work in an assignment. There are five basic methods that the appraiser can use to perform a site valuation:

1. Sales comparison method

2. Allocation method

3. Extraction method

4. Land residual method

5. Ground rent capitalization method

All of these methods will be discussed here. The first three methods (sales comparison, allocation, and extraction) use an analysis of comparable sales, and can be used for almost any type of property or site. The extraction method additionally employs costing methods. The last two methods (land residual and ground rent capitalization) use various income analysis methods to arrive at a value and can only be used for commercial or income properties.

A sixth method, the subdivision analysis method, can also be used for some types of site valuations. The subdivision analysis method is typically used for large tracts of land that will be made into residential lots (although the method could be adapted for use when subdividing land into an office or industrial park). The similarities of the subdivision analysis method to the cost approach will be evident, as the technique employs many of the same components.

Sales Comparison Method

The **sales comparison method** is *a site valuation method that compares the subject land or site to other similar sites that have recently sold.* Adjustments are made to the sales for differences between those properties and the subject property, and the site value opinion is then based on this comparison to other sales.

The first step for a sales comparison is to obtain data on other similar properties that sold recently in the same market area. The comparable sales should be as similar to the subject property as possible and preferably reflect the most current market conditions. Next, market evidence is used to derive and apply adjustments to the sale price of the comparables to address the differences between them and the subject. Finally, the resulting adjusted data is reconciled to arrive at an opinion of value for the subject site or land parcel. The process mirrors the steps taken in the sales comparison approach, which was discussed in Chapter 4.

Example

An appraisal is being performed for a residential building lot. First, adjustments are derived through paired data analysis:

	Sale #1	Sale #2	Sale #3	Sale #4
Sale price	$14,750	$13,750	$13,000	$13,500
Depth	175'	150'	150'	150'
Easement	Yes	Yes	Yes	No
Features	Wooded	Wooded	Not Wooded	Not Wooded

The adjustments derived through the analysis are as follows:

Depth: $1,000 for additional depth, comparing Sales #1 and #2

Easement: $500 for easement influence, comparing Sales #3 and #4

Amenity: $750 for woods, comparing Sales #2 and #3

Example (continued)

Next, the adjustments are applied to the comparables sales, by comparing each comparable sale individually to the subject property:

	Subject	Sale #1	Sale #1 With Adjustments	Sale #2	Sale #2 With Adjustments	Sale #3	Sale #3 With Adjustments
Price	?	$14,000	$14,000	$13,500	$13,500	$14,250	$14,250
Wooded	Yes	No	+ $250	No	+ $250	Yes	0
Location	Inlot	Corner	- $500	Inlot	0	Corner	- $500
Adjusted Sale Price	?		$13,750		$13,750		$13,750

Obviously, the reconciled value indication of the subject property using the sales comparison approach is $13,750.

Allocation Method

The **allocation method** is *a method of site valuation whereby the value of the land is determined by establishing a typical ratio of site value to total property value in an area, then applying that same ratio to the subject property.* In other words, the allocation method recognizes that the utility of the site and the utility of the structure both contribute to the value of a property. Below is an example of the formula:

Site Value (Unimproved) / Market Value of Property (Improved) = Allocation Ratio for Site

Step 1: Identify Comparable Data

- Unimproved sites

- Improved sites

(The improved and unimproved sales should be located within the same market area, such as a subdivision.)

Step 2: Identify the Ratio of Site Value to Improved Value

- Divide the unimproved site value by the improved value.

Step 3: Site Value Indication

- A range of value may be possible if several scenarios are examined.

Example

An appraiser is deriving a land value to apply in a highest and best use analysis in an older, established neighborhood. There have not been any vacant land sales in the subject market for many years. The appraiser found three lot sales in another similar market area, where there are both improved sales and unimproved sales.

	Improved Sale	Unimproved Sale	Allocation Ratio
Sale #1	$400,000	$50,000	12.5%
Sale #2	$395,000	$49,000	12.4%
Sale #3	$410,000	$51,500	12.6%

The appraiser would conclude that 12.5% would be a reasonable allocation ratio to apply to the subject, which he has already concluded has an improved value of $405,000:

$405,000 x 12.5% = $50,625

Work Problem 7.1

Using the mean of the indications from the allocation analysis provided, what is the site value of a property if the improved value is $575,000?

	Improved Sale	Unimproved Sale	Allocation Ratio
Sale #1	$560,000	$84,000	
Sale #2	$570,000	$91,200	
Sale #3	$580,000	$81,200	

The mean of the allocation ratios is _____ .

The indicted site value of the subject is _____ .

Extraction Method

The **extraction method** is *a method of site valuation that takes the depreciated cost of property improvements, and subtracts that cost from the market value of comparable properties to result in land value.* **The extraction method is most commonly used for new construction but is also commonly utilized when the improvements contribute very little value to the sale property.** By taking the market value of a comparable property and subtracting the depreciated cost of the improvement, the resulting amount is the site value.

Step 1: Calculate the Depreciated Value of the Improvements

Step 2: Subtract the Depreciated Improvement Value from the Market Value of the Improved Property

The total property value of a 110-acre farm is $382,000. The farmhouse has been remodeled, but the barns are very old. The volunteer fire department will burn the barns for practice. Reproduction cost of the 2,600 square-foot farmhouse is estimated at $68 per square foot. Depreciation is estimated to be 60% and the "as is" value of the other site improvements is $6,500. Using the extraction method, what is the value of the land?

> 2,600 x $68 = $176,800 (Cost New of Farmhouse)
>
> 60% X $176,800 = $106,080 (Depreciation)
>
> $176,800 – 106,080 = $70,720 (Depreciated Improvement Value)
>
> $382,000 - $70,720 - $6,500 ("As Is" Value of the Other Site Improvements) = $304,780

The land value is **$304,780.**

Work Problem 7.2

A rural property contains 142 acres of woodland and is improved with a 30-year old one-story house that has 1,750 square feet. The reproduction cost of the house is estimated to be $95 per square foot and depreciation is estimated at 35%. The "as is" estimated value of the other site improvements is $9,000. What is the land value if the improved value is $275,000?

The indicated land value would be $_____.

Land Residual Method

The **land residual method** is *a method of site valuation that assigns a certain part of the income produced by a property to the building or other improvement, and then attributes the remaining income (the residual) to the land.* By using an overall capitalization rate, the value of the land is then calculated. As you will recall, a capitalization rate is *a percentage rate of return used to calculate the present value of future income.*

The complexity is determining how much income is contributed by, and thus attributed to, the land compared to the total property. This is a variation of an income method, and primarily used for income producing commercial properties.

Step 1: Identify Net Operating Income Attributable to the Land

- Estimate the value of the improvements.

- Allocate the net operating income attributable to the improvements.

Step 2: Identify Net Operating Income Attributable to the Land

- Subtract the income to the improvements from total net operating income.

- Residual net operating income will be attributable to the land.

Step 3: Indicate Land Value

- Apply direct capitalization of the net operating income to the land.

- Use market derived capitalization rate.

EXAMPLE

An office facility is being appraised. Net operating income is $24,000 per year with 70% being attributable to the building. The market-derived capitalization rate for land is 7.65%.

$24,000 (Net Operating Income to the Property) X 70% = $16,800 (Net Operating Income to Building)

$24,000 - $16,800 = $7,200 (Net Operating Income to Land)

$7,200 / 7.65% (0.0765) = $94,118 (Indicated Land Value)

This method is mainly used as a verification of other income or appraisal methods. Also, the appraiser uses this method as a primary appraisal tool when there are few comparable sales in the area and the market income and capitalization rates can be identified.

Work Problem 7.3

An appraiser is valuing a small industrial building. Net operating income is $47,000 per year. The appraiser estimates that 82% of the income is to the building and that the observed capitalization rate for land is 9.25%.

What is the value of the land? $_____

Ground Rent Capitalization Method

The **ground rent capitalization method** is *a method of valuing land based on the income it generates in a given year and divided by an appropriate overall capitalization rate.* The appropriate overall capitalization rate is determined by examining other comparable sales and using the sale price and the annual net operating income that was generated in a year. Research must be done to obtain comparable sales of leased sites that are similar to the subject site. **This is primarily a method used for commercial properties, but could, in some cases, be used for residential properties built on leased land.** Of course, the overall capitalization rate to be applied is usually derived after examining data from several comparable sales. The technique uses the same components and formula as direct capitalization using an overall capitalization rate discussed in Chapter 5.

Step 1: Analyze Comparable Site or Land Sales

- Lease terms should be similar to the subject.
- Net operating income should reflect a typical market.
- Comparable sales should reflect arm's length transactions.

Step 2: Calculate the Rate of Return (Capitalization Rate) of the Comparables

- Divide the net operating income by the sale price (value) to find the capitalization rate (IVR).

Step 3: Apply the Capitalization Rate to the Subject's Net Operating Income

- Divide the net operating income by the rate to find the value (IRV).

Example

An appraiser is valuing a leased parcel along a busy, high exposure highway. The site is very similar in size to another site from which the appraiser recently gathered data. The comparable site is located just north of the subject site. It was sold for $600,000 and had a net operating income of $48,000 annually. The subject has a net operating income of $42,000 per year, which appears to be in line with the market.

Derive the Rate from the Comparable:

$48,000 Net Operating Income / $600,000 = 0.080

The market derived capitalization rate is 8.0%.

Apply the Derived Rate to the Subject:

$42,000 Net Income / 8.0% (0.080) Rate = $525,000 (Site Value)

Work Problem 7.4

A subject land parcel is producing an annual net operating income of $32,000. A very similar comparable has been located that recently sold for $480,000, with an annual net operating income of $30,000.

What is the value of the subject land parcel? $_____

Subdivision Analysis Method

The **subdivision analysis method** is *a method of valuing raw land that could be developed by taking the total projected sale value of all finished lots and subtracting out all costs of development.* The result is the value of the raw land.

The calculations are very similar to costing methods illustrated in Chapter 6. All direct and indirect costs of development must include many items: Construction of access roads, excavation, providing utilities to each lot, sales people to sell the lots, the interest the property developer must pay to borrow the money, etc. Any cost the developer will incur before all the lots are sold is included as a development cost. In addition, entrepreneurial profit and/or entrepreneurial incentive must also be considered.

Example

A developer expects a land parcel to accommodate 30 lots, which he plans to sell for $25,000 each. If direct costs are $375,000 and indirect costs are $125,000, what is the land value if entrepreneurial profit is 10% of the gross sales?

30 (lots) x $25,000 (Sale Price per Lot) = $750,000 (Total Sales)

$375,000 (Direct Costs) + $125,000 (Indirect Costs) + $75,000 (10% Entrepreneurial Profit) = $575,000 (Total Costs)

$750,000 (Total Sales) - $575,000 (Total Costs) = $175,000 (Land Value)

Other Important Site Valuation Concepts

There are some other concepts that are important to recognize for the valuation of land and site. While the circumstances of these concepts may not present themselves in every assignment, appraisers must be familiar with them. Appraisers must always consider, when appropriate, the potential to combine parcels for greater utility and/or greater value. Also, appraisers must recognize how to address extra land included with property, and how this extra land affects value.

Assemblage

Assemblage is *combining two or more parcels of land into one larger parcel.* This is typically done to increase the usefulness (utility) of the land. By allowing one larger building to be constructed on the larger parcel than could have been built on the smaller individual parcels, the value of the land also increases. In fact, this one large parcel is likely worth more than the sum total of the smaller parcels.

Plottage is *the increase in value (over the cost of acquiring the parcels) by successful assemblage, usually due to a change in use.* By creating a larger parcel with more utility and higher and better use than the individual sites, the owner typically enjoys an increase in value of the land. It should be also noted that on the opposite end of the spectrum, there is also the concept of **reverse plottage** – *when assemblage results in a value decrease of the separate value of the individual parcels assembled,* the amount of decrease in value (below the acquisition cost) is called reverse plottage.

Example

Two side by side parcels are available. The parcels each have 25 feet of frontage and are 100 feet deep. Due to zoning and building regulations, a three-foot setback is required on each side of any building on the lots. Thus, the largest building that could be built on either of the lots would be 19 feet wide (25' – 6'), for which there is a very limited market. If both lots were acquired and their utility were joined, a 43 foot wide building (50' – 6') could be built, which would have much more market appeal.

If the lots were each acquired for $20,000, the total acquisition cost would be $40,000. If the lots assembled were valued at $50,000, plottage is $10,000.

Surplus and Excess Site

Surplus site is the portion over and above what is necessary for the highest and best use of the subject property, and does not have a stand-alone highest and best use. Surplus land is not needed to expand the subject improvements. In other words, it does not have sales potential and value contribution is likely minimal.

For example, consider a house that is built across two lots accommodating a larger yard area. If the extra yard cannot be legally divided or it is not necessary for the highest and best use, or could not be used to significantly contribute to the expansion of the current improvements, the extra yard is likely surplus and would probably have a minimal contributory value.

Example

An appraiser is appraising a house in an older established neighborhood is situated on a 60 x 80 foot lot. Other houses on the street are situated on 40 x 80 foot lots and the size of the dwellings are similar to the subject. Due to its size and local regulations, the extra 20 feet of frontage cannot be sold off. None of the comparable properties in the immediate market evidence an extra large yard. However, the appraiser has located a comparable property that has an extra 15 x 80 feet at one side, similar to the subject, in another similar neighborhood. It sold for $2,000 more than a very similar property on a typical sized lot.

Step 1: Derive the Contributory Value of the Surplus Site from the Comparable Property

18 X 80 = 1,440 Square Feet (Surplus Site of Comparable)

$2,000 / 1,440 = $1.39 Per Square Foot Contribution

Step 2: Apply the Derived Contribution to the Subject

20 X 80 = 1,600 Square Feet (Surplus Site of Subject)

1,600 X $1.39 = $2,224 Contribution

Excess site is *land or site area that is not necessary to support the use of the existing improvements situated on the subject property.* However, it may have its own highest and best use for expansion of the current improvement or for sale for another use.

For example, the owner of a house has an additional lot next to the house, which he uses as a large side yard. If the additional lot has its own unique legal description or could be legally divided from the portion of the site on which the house is situated, the site is likely considered excess.

In such case, the contributory value is probably more inline with what the site could be sold for (minus any cost of subdividing, if applicable).

Summary

1. An appraiser determines the specific method or technique appropriate for developing an opinion of value for land or site as part of the scope of work in an assignment.

2. The sales comparison method is a site valuation method that compares the subject land or site to other similar sites that have recently sold. Adjustments are made to the sales for differences between those properties and the subject property, and the site value opinion is then based on this comparison to other sales.

3. The allocation method recognizes that the utility of the site and the utility of the structure both contribute to the value of a property. The value of the land is indicated by establishing a typical ratio of site value to total property value in an area, then applying that same ratio to the subject property.

4. The extraction method is a method of site valuation that takes the depreciated cost of property improvements and subtracts that cost from the market value of comparable properties, to result in land value.

5. The land residual method is a method of site valuation that assigns a certain part of the income produced by a property to the building or other improvement, and then attributes the remaining income (the residual) to the land. By using an overall capitalization rate, the value of the land is then calculated.

6. The ground rent capitalization method is a method of valuing land based on the income it generates in a given year and dividing by an appropriate overall capitalization rate. The appropriate overall capitalization rate is determined by examining other comparable sales and using the sale price and the annual net operating income that was generated in a year.

7. The subdivision analysis method is a method of valuing raw land that could be developed, by taking the total projected sale value of all finished lots and subtracting out all costs of development. The result is the value of the raw land.

8. Assemblage is combining two or more parcels of land into one larger parcel. This is typically done to increase the usefulness (utility) of the land.

9. Plottage is the increase in value (over the cost of acquiring the parcels) by successful assemblage, usually due to a change in use. By creating a larger parcel with more utility and higher and better use than the individual sites, the owner typically enjoys an increase in value of the land.

10. Surplus site is the portion over and above what is necessary for the highest and best use of the subject property, and does not have a stand-alone highest and best use. Surplus land is not needed to expand the subject improvements. In other words, it does not have sales potential and value contribution is likely minimal.

11. Excess site is land or site area that is not necessary to support the use of the existing improvements situated on the subject property. It may have its own highest and best use for expansion of the current improvement or for sale for another use.

Quiz

1. In analyzing comparable data, if an unimproved vacant lot sold for $30,000 and a lot improved with a dwelling sold for $120,000, the allocation ratio for land is

    a. 20%.
    b. 25%.
    c. 30%.
    d. 40%.

2. A subject land parcel is producing net operating income of $38,000. A very similar comparable has been located that recently sold for $535,000, with net operating income of $45,500. What is the indicated value of the subject land parcel?

    a. $459,254
    b. $465,852
    c. $477,059
    d. $481,068

3. A warehouse facility is being appraised. The appraiser is using the land residual method to verify another income approach. The building is valued at $200,000. Net operating income of the property is $25,000 per year with 48% being attributable to the building. The market-derived capitalization rate for land is 8.75%. What is the total indicated value of the improved property?

    a. $340,479
    b. $348,571
    c. $352,584
    d. $356,482

4. A client purchases two adjacent parcels of land for $20,000 each. The market indicates that the combined larger parcel now has a market value of $40,000. What has occurred?

    a. assemblage
    b. frontage
    c. parcelage
    d. plottage

5. An individual purchases two adjacent parcels of land for $20,000 each. The market indicates that the combined larger parcel is now worth $50,000. Which describes the resulting value increase?

    a. assemblage
    b. frontage
    c. plottage
    d. splittage

6. The subject site is a rectangular shape with a typical eight-foot utility easement. Sale #1 is rectangular in shape, has a 16-foot utility easement, and sold last week for $11,000. Sale #2 is rectangular in shape, has an eight-foot utility easement, and sold last week for $13,000. Sale #3 is irregular in shape, has an eight-foot utility easement, and sold last week for $15,000. What is the adjustment for a utility easement (16 feet versus 8 feet) to be applied in the sales comparison method?

    a. $1,000
    b. $2,000
    c. $2,600
    d. $4,000

7. A developer has direct and indirect development costs of $800,000 to create a residential subdivision with a potential of generating $1,675,000 from sales of the sites. What is the raw land value if the entrepreneurial profit is $300,000?

    a. $275,000
    b. $575,000
    c. $875,000
    d. $1,375,000

8. An appraiser found that in a particular residential subdivision, 0.40-acre lots are selling for $35,000. Another residential lot in the same subdivision sold for $38,000, but contained 0.52 acre (the extra 0.12 acre being deemed surplus site). What per square foot adjustment (rounded to the nearest whole cent) for surplus site is derived from the data?

    a. $0.28
    b. $0.42
    c. $0.47
    d. $0.57

Chapter 8
Real World Residential Appraisal Applications

Residential applications provide the opportunity to illustrate practical examples of appraisal concepts at work. This chapter begins by discussing common regulations and guidelines an appraiser must typically observe in appraisals for residential mortgage transactions for the secondary market. Then, the discussion moves to residential appraisal assignments for purposes other than mortgage lending. The chapter concludes with a discussion of essential non-residential knowledge for residential appraisers, including case examples.

Americans with Disabilities Act (ADA) Legislation passed in 1990 as an extension of civil rights laws that guarantees access to places of public accommodation to people with disabilities. Under the Competency Rule and Standard 1 of USPAP, an appraiser's assignment includes property compliance and how ADA regulations and requirements affect the property's highest and best use value.

Appraisal Review The act or process of developing and communicating an opinion about the quality of another appraiser's work that was performed as part of an appraisal or appraisal review assignment.*

Arm's Length Transaction A transaction that occurred under typical conditions in the marketplace, with each of the parties acting in their own best interests.

Broker Price Opinion (BPO) An opinion of value sought by a lender to determine an appropriate market price for a property in a relocation situation or one that is to be marketed as a short sale (pre-foreclosure) or a bank held property (after foreclosure).

Competitive Market Analysis (CMA) A method of determining a recommended listing price by comparing the subject property to other homes that have sold, are presently for sale, or did not sell in a given area. Also called **Comparative Market Analysis**.

Emblements Crops planted on the land/ property of a tenant, and, therefore, considered an element of personal property.

Fannie Mae (Federal National Mortgage Association) The national's largest privately owned investor in residential mortgages.

* USPAP 2014-2015

Key Terms

(Continued on page 179)

Appraising for Mortgage Lending Transactions

Very commonly, for most residential appraisers, much of their work will be performed in connection with mortgage lending transactions. Residential appraisal for a mortgage lending transaction could occur when someone is purchasing, building, refinancing, or obtaining a second mortgage home equity loan or line of credit.

Appraisers may be engaged in some of these assignments by lenders funding the loans using money deposited in their own institution (known as primary market or portfolio lenders). However, in many (if not most) cases, the appraisal will be used in a secondary market finance transaction; a mortgage originated by the lender/client, but sold to an investor.

Performing Appraisals for the Secondary Market

The nation's largest investor in residential mortgages is **Fannie Mae**. Fannie Mae has very specific regulations and guidelines for appraisal analysis and reporting when they are a participant in the mortgage transaction. Other secondary market participants, such as Freddie Mac and FHA, have similar standards for appraisals performed for their purposes. And it may not be unusual for a primary market or portfolio lender to place conditions upon appraisers in assignments, requiring them to observe guidelines, such as Fannie Mae's, for mortgage appraisals. Having appraisals performed to secondary market standards for these primary or portfolio lenders provides them an option to later sell the loan through the secondary market system.

Secondary market participants, such as Fannie Mae, have numerous guidelines and regulations that must be observed by the appraiser when completing an assignment to their standards. The ETHICS RULE, COMPETENCY RULE, and SCOPE OF WORK of USPAP recognize these standards as assignment conditions, which affect the scope of work. The ETHICS RULE requires that, when any of these special requirements are an element of an assignment, the appraiser must observe them. The COMPETENCY RULE requires the appraiser to recognize the special requirements, know what they are, and how to apply them. There are many regulations and guidelines to be aware of when performing a residential appraisal to Fannie Mae standards. Let's look at some of them, beginning with the expectations of the appraiser.

Appraiser Competency

Fannie Mae does *not* approve individual appraisers, leaving the selection process to the lender. Fannie Mae expects lenders to hire appraisers who are competent and have knowledge and experience with the appraisal subject's particular property type. While USPAP allows appraisers to disclose the lack of competence prior to acceptance of an assignment and then gain competence during the assignment, Fannie Mae asks lenders not to engage an appraiser in an assignment if the appraiser does not already have the knowledge and experience. Further, the appraiser must have experience in the subject's geographic location and access to reliable data sources for the area in which the property is located.

Appraiser Performance

Appraisers must report in factual and specific terms, avoid the use of subjectivity, not violate fair housing and fair lending laws, and provide complete and accurate appraisal reports. These are also good guidelines for all services an appraiser provides. Fannie Mae is very specific about some unacceptable appraiser practices.

Some of these *unacceptable practices* include:

- A value opinion not supported by market data, or one that is misleading
- A value conclusion based on the protected class status of the borrowers, owners, occupants of the subject, or neighborhood
- Misrepresenting the physical characteristics of the subject property or the comparables sales
- Not commenting on negative factors regarding the subject neighborhood, the subject property, or the proximity of the subject property to negative influences
- Failing to sufficiently analyze the prior or current listing, or sale terms, of the subject property or the comparable sales

- Using inappropriate comparable sales data, or data that is not the *most* similar—physically or locationally
- Not *at least* driving by the comparable sales that are used in an appraisal
- Not making an adjustment in the sales comparison approach when it is clearly warranted
- Not basing adjustments to reflect the market's reaction to differences between the subject and the comparable sales
- Using data provided by parties with a financial interest in the subject's transaction, without verifying the information through a disinterested source
- Not complying with USPAP

Mortgage Industry Reporting Forms

Fannie Mae has developed a series of residential appraisal reporting forms that are used for the various types of residential properties for which they participate in loans—single-family (interior/exterior and exterior only), two- to four-family, condominium, and manufactured housing. Freddie Mac also has a mirror version of most of these forms. According to Fannie Mae, the forms *are designed to provide for an objective and unbiased description and analysis of the neighborhood, site, and improvements.* When an appraiser recognizes that Fannie Mae regulations and guidelines are an assignment condition, the appraiser *must* use the applicable Fannie Mae form for reporting the appraisal. The most common Fannie Mae appraisal reporting form is the Uniform Residential Appraisal Report (URAR). The URAR reporting form, along with other industry forms, will be briefly introduced here and overviewed further in Chapter 9. The form in its entirety is included in the Appendix of this course.

Lending institutions and others generally prefer standardized forms, because they provide a sufficient level of detail in a consistent, convenient, and easy-to-read format. However, do not let the apparent simplicity of the forms be deceptive. An extensive amount of diligence is always required when performing an appraisal. The forms should never limit the appraisal process, the amount of data collected, or the explanations of the appraiser's conclusions. *The amount of data collected and the analysis are dictated by the appraisal assignment—not the appraisal form used for the report.*

Additional details and analysis may be required if unusual situations are encountered that must be investigated and reported to the client. Most forms provide spaces for explanations and expanded comments. Additional documentation, exhibits, and, if necessary, addenda may be included beyond those required by the client or the form. Fannie Mae guidelines require the appraiser to provide the lender or client with any information needed to make an informed decision concerning the property.

The latest versions of the Fannie Mae forms detail what is required of the appraiser for each type of report.

Forecasting Adjustment Applied to address how much less the property will eventually sell for if positioned to sell in a less-than-typical period.

Freddie Mac A federally chartered institution that functions as a buyer and seller of savings and loan residential mortgages.

Going Concern Value The market value in use of all property, including real property, trade fixtures, inventory (tangible assets), and the intangible assets of an established and operating business with an indefinite life.

Gross Building Area (GBA) Total floor area of a building measuring from the exterior of the walls—includes the superstructure (floor area) and the substructure (basement area).

Gross Leasable Area (GLA) Total floor area designed to be occupied and used by tenants, measuring from the center of joint partitioning to the outside wall surfaces—includes basements and mezzanines.

Mixed-use Property One property with more than one notable use, such as a mix of residential and non-residential.

Narrative Report A written type of appraisal report. It allows the appraiser to comment fully on the opinions and conclusions of the appraisal.

Trade Fixtures Equipment a tenant installs for use in his or her trade or business and that can be removed by the tenant before the lease expires.

Uniform Residential Appraisal Report (URAR) A standard appraisal report form used by lenders and appraisers; developed and approved by secondary mortgage market participants Fannie Mae and Freddie Mac.

Key Terms

There are some variations depending on the appraisal assignment but, in general, the appraiser must, at a minimum:

1. Perform a complete visual inspection of the interior and exterior areas of the subject property (except for exterior-only appraisals).
2. Inspect the neighborhood.
3. Inspect the comparable sales from, at least, the subject's street.
4. Research, verify, and analyze data from reliable public and/or private sources.
5. Report the analysis, opinions, and conclusions in the appraisal report.

This list is not intended to represent the appraiser's only responsibilities. The scope of work may call for more or less research, analysis, and detail. In every case, though, appraisers should not allow the form to impose any limitation on the scope of their appraisal work. Instead, appraisers must diligently be vigil for potential problems and irregularities so they can account for them in their appraisal assignment. The scope of work (or the certification) within the report cannot be materially altered, or lessened. However, it can be expanded, or added to, when necessary.

This chapter focuses on some real-world situations that may be encountered when appraising residential property. An appraiser must determine the correct course of action so the appraisal report is accurate and relevant. More importantly, though, an appraiser must communicate his thought process and rationale clearly in the report so the lender, client, or other users of the report can follow the logic and reasoning applied to arrive at an opinion of value.

Institutions other than Fannie Mae may also specify that a Fannie Mae form, such as the URAR, be used for appraisals, which is acceptable if the appraisal is being performed for a mortgage finance transaction. However, it is *inappropriate* to use a Fannie Mae reporting form for an appraisal *not* being used for a mortgage transaction, as the scope of work described in the form is specific to that use and assumes the lender is the client. Other forms are available for use in non-mortgage work, or the appraisal could be reported in a narrative format, discussed later in this chapter.

Market Value Definition

There can be many definitions of **market value**. Fannie Mae's specific definition:

Market value is the most probable price a property should bring in a competitive and open market under all conditions requisite to a fair sale, the buyer and seller, each acting prudently, knowledgeably, and assuming the price is not affected by undue stimulus. Implicit in this definition is the consummation of a sale as of a specified date and the passing of title from seller to buyer under conditions whereby:

1. Buyer and seller are typically motivated.
2. Both parties are well informed or well advised, and each is acting in what he considers his own best interest.
3. A reasonable time is allowed for exposure in the open market.
4. Payment is made in terms of cash in U.S. dollars or in terms of financial arrangements comparable thereto.
5. The price represents the normal consideration for the property sold, unaffected by special or creative financing or sales concessions granted by anyone associated with the sale.

Property Description, Development, and Reporting Practices

In previous chapters, USPAP requirements and generally accepted methods for developing an opinion of value have been discussed. The discussions have pointed out that some lending requirements may prohibit or limit the use of certain elements, or require further or specific identification, analysis, or report commentary. It would be impossible to address every difference between basic appraisal practices and Fannie Mae requirements in this course. Many of these practices are guidelines.

One point the appraiser should always be mindful of when applying Fannie Mae standards is *explain, explain, explain*. If there is good reasoning and the appraiser has employed the best data available, a reasonable and thorough explanation is usually sufficient for Fannie Mae. In addition to the items already discussed, there are some elements that illustrate the most specific common requirements and guidelines to follow when performing a residential appraisal according to Fannie Mae standards and guidelines, starting with the general property description:

General Property Description	
Location	Describe the location as *urban, suburban,* or *rural.* Fannie Mae specifically describes that urban refers to a property within a city, suburban is the area adjacent to a city, and rural is the countryside or any area beyond the suburban area.
Marketing Time	USPAP requires the appraiser to identify the exposure time for the subject property. Fannie Mae requires that the marketing time also be stated. **If exposure and marketing time are different**, the appraiser should provide an explanation.
Gross Living Area	Gross living area is calculated using the *exterior* dimensions of each level built *above grade*. If *any part* of a level is below grade, it is *not* included in the gross living area or the room count, regardless of the quality of the interior finish or the presence of windows and exterior doors, such as a walkout basement. A sketch must be included in the report showing the exterior dimensions of each level and the calculations explaining how the appraiser arrived at the gross living area.
Layout and Floor Plan	When the subject's floor plan design is unusual, inadequate, or objectionable to the market, the appraiser must additionally include the interior walls, doorways, etc., in the sketch.

General Valuation Development

Fannie Mae requires the appraiser to develop a value opinion for a property based on one or more of the three approaches to value—sales comparison approach, cost approach, and/or income approach. The sales comparison approach is most heavily relied on by Fannie Mae.

Sales Comparison Approach	
Indicated Value Range	Fannie Mae has no specific guideline for what constitutes an acceptable range of value resulting from the sales comparison approach. However, if there is a large discrepancy among the indicated values, comments should be added to the appraisal report to explain the difference. *Example: Comparable #1 - $150,000 Comparable #2 - $152,000 Comparable #3 - $169,000* An explanation would be necessary as to why Comparable #3 was so different from Comparables #1 and #2.
Sales and Transfer History	In addition to the analysis of all agreements of sale, options, and listings of the subject property as of the effective date of the appraisal, and the analysis of all sales of the subject property within three years prior to the effective date of the appraisal required by USPAP, Fannie Mae has requirements for comparable sales as well. Prior sales for each comparable sale must be reported for the *12 months prior* to the effective date of the appraisal.

Cost Approach	
Applicability	While the cost approach is a good indicator of market value for newer or renovated properties, Fannie Mae will *not* accept appraisals that rely solely on the cost approach as an indicator of market value.
Development	Fannie Mae relies on valid estimates of reproduction cost new.
Value Conclusion	The indicated value conclusion is rounded to eliminate the suggestion of accuracy, which is not factually attainable.

Income Approach	
Applicability	The income approach is generally appropriate in neighborhoods with a prevalence of tenant-occupied properties, and when the subject is a two- to four- family property.
Techniques	The GRM technique is employed using data extracted from other comparable rentals in the neighborhood. The sale prices of comparable properties are divided by their monthly market rent to develop the multiplier. The estimated gross monthly market rent of the subject is then multiplied by the multiplier to indicate a value.

Other Fannie Mae Regulations and Guidelines

Fannie Mae regulations and guidelines also address several other factors which may or may not be applicable in some assignment.

	Other Fannie Mae Valuation Regulations and Guidelines
Conditions of Appraisals	Fannie Mae allows appraisals to be conditioned **three different ways**: 1. **"As is"**—Represents most appraisal assignments for properties that do not have any physical deficiencies or conditions that would affect livability. 2. **Subject to completion**—Usually for new or proposed construction. Sometimes, there are items to be completed in a property that do not affect the ability to obtain an occupancy permit. In that case, the appraisal report must show both the cost of completing the items and the "as completed" value. The cost to complete cannot exceed 2% of the "as completed" value. 3. **Subject to alterations and repairs**—Used when there are conditions or items affecting the livability of the house, or physical conditions posing a risk to the soundness or structural integrity of the improvements. The appraiser must certify completion of the alterations or repairs.
Final Reconciliation	The final opinion of value is stated as a single number with most emphasis being given to the sales comparison approach. The appraiser's conclusions must fall within the range of results indicated by development of more than one approach. In other words, the final reconciliation is interpolated (within a known range), rather than extrapolated (concluding outside of the range).
Rural Properties	Fannie Mae does provide loans for rural properties, but there are some special guidelines for the appraiser to know. The property must be residential in nature and not an agricultural-type property. Barns and outbuildings must have a relatively insignificant value. Fannie Mae will lend on more than five acres; however, the appraiser may not use a physical segment of the property (e.g., five acres of a 20-acre parcel), because Fannie Mae finds this to be an unacceptable practice. Comparable sales may be more than 12 months old and further from the subject than typically preferred. The appraiser must comment, assuring the comparable sales selected represent the best available. If marketing time is longer than six months, the appraiser must comment why—the appraiser must also focus on the reason for the longer marketing time in the report. **Special note:** *Even though Fannie Mae accepts loans on rural properties, some lenders will not underwrite them. If a property is rural but the appraiser complies with a lender's request to indicate the property as suburban, this practice would be misleading and a violation of the Ethics Rule of USPAP.*
Manufactured Housing	Fannie Mae will accept properties that are improved with manufactured homes. The Fannie Mae definition of a manufactured home is discussed in Chapter 6. In addition to meeting the criteria for manufactured housing, the appraisal must be reported on the specified Fannie Mae form. The protocol for developing and reporting manufactured housing is much more complex and detailed. The cost approach must be developed. In the sales comparison approach, at least two comparable sales of manufactured homes must be used, and if the third comparable sale is a site-built house, the appraiser must explain why using it was necessary.

Appraising for Other Purposes

Although maybe not as common, appraisers perform residential appraisals for many purposes other than mortgage transactions. Next, we will briefly discuss the following purposes, along with special considerations for each.

- Estates and probate
- Relocation
- Insurance
- Appraisal review

In most cases, when appraising a property to determine its value for an estate or probate purpose, the appraisal is performed with a *retrospective effective date*. The effective date is usually the date the owner of the property died. The appraisal should reflect market and property conditions as of that date. Some tax appraisals and assignments for litigation may also use the same methodology.

Relocation

Relocation appraisals occur when the property owner is being hired by, or transferred to, an out-of-town destination. The employer typically hires a relocation company to assume the property to some extent. In most cases, the relocation company will advance the owner's equity to the owner, pay off the owner's mortgage, and assume all costs of maintaining and marketing the property.

Because the relocation company is basing the owner's equity advance on the appraiser's value opinion, it is critical that the appraiser be thorough. In addition, the holding period during which the relocation company is paying the bills for maintaining the property is also an important concern. Because of the critical nature of the appraiser's role in relocation transactions, there is often more than one appraiser engaged for each property. Real estate agents may also be engaged by the relocation company to perform a Broker's Price Opinion (BPO). The BPO is very similar to the function of the appraiser, except the *process may be focused more on the marketability of the property.*

Do not confuse a BPO with a Competitive Market Analysis (CMA), which is also performed by real estate agents. The purpose of a CMA is to *determine a recommended listing price based on recent sales and listing data.* Neither a BPO nor a CMA is considered an appraisal. One of the reasons relocation companies consult with both appraisers and real estate agents is to determine marketability. Marketability and the resulting time on the market are important to how long the relocation company must hold the property. Because of this, the relocation appraisal has a few major differences from other appraisals, in that the appraiser will analyze and report current, competitive listings. Also, the appraiser often makes suggestions for aesthetic changes, such as carpeting, color schemes, etc., that should be done to enhance marketability.

Appraisers are usually asked, in relocation assignments, to base their market value opinion on a specified period—for example, 90 days or less. If the appraiser notes competitive properties are requiring longer than the 90-day specified period to sell, the appraiser *must* apply a forecasting adjustment. A **forecasting adjustment** is applied to address *how much less the property will eventually sell for if positioned to sell in a less-than-typical period.* This could represent a liquidation value, or another definition of market value. There is significant additional competence required when performing a relocation appraisal.

When performing an appraisal for relocation, appraisers follow the standards and appraisal forms developed by the Employee Relocation Council (ERC). Formed in 1964, the ERC is a professional membership association of organizations concerned with domestic and international employee transfer. They provide research and statistical support for their members and, early on, adopted USPAP into their standards.

Insurance

Appraisers are often asked to perform an appraisal for insurance purposes—either to establish the amount of coverage that should be carried on the improvements or to settle damage claims. Determining the amount of coverage that should be carried relies on the cost approach—in most cases, replacement cost is used. For damage claims, the appraiser may be using a retrospective effective date (the date of damage or destruction) and, if the property is destroyed, relying on elements other than a physical inspection to identify the improvements. In neither case will the appraiser be considering the site value in the value opinion.

Appraisal Review

Appraisal review is *the act or process of developing and communicating an opinion about the quality of another appraiser's work that was performed as part of an appraisal or appraisal review assignment.* A review appraiser may be engaged to review all of a report, a portion of a report, a workfile, or a combination of these. However, a review by itself does not offer comment by the reviewer on the original appraiser's value conclusion.

When the scope of the review appraiser's work *includes developing an opinion of value*, even if only to agree with the original appraiser's conclusion, the assignment becomes both an *appraisal review and an appraisal*. Fannie Mae has specific forms for reporting a review and an appraisal performed as a result of a review. Appraisal reviews and appraisal are performed for many purposes—quality assurance for lenders probably being the number one purpose. Residential appraisal reporting courses offer additional insight into this segment of appraisal practice.

IMPORTANT POINTS: APPRAISING RESIDENTIAL PROPERTIES FOR OTHER PURPOSES

- *When performing appraisals for estate and probate purposes, a retrospective effective date should be used—most commonly, the date the property owner died.*
- *When performing an appraisal for relocation purposes, appraisers follow the standards and appraisal forms developed by the Employee Relocation Council (ERC).*
- *When performing an appraisal for insurance purposes, appraisers do not consider the site value in their value opinion.*
- *If an appraisal review requires the appraiser to develop his own value opinion, it becomes an appraisal review as well as an appraisal.*

Residential Application Case Studies

Three common scenarios that, if not handled correctly, may lead to problems involve:

1. Questions regarding market value.
2. Transfers not part of an arm's length transaction.
3. Properties with zoning issues.

Each of these potential problem areas must be researched thoroughly to provide a sound basis for the value conclusions reached in an appraisal report. Each applicable concept will first be reviewed. Case examples follow, illustrating how these issues may present themselves, along with practical handling by the appraiser.

Application of Market Value

The *value* of a property should never be confused with its *price*. **Market value** is *what property is expected to sell for;* **market price** is *what the property actually sold for.* Moreover, while the market price represents the final selling price, it is likely this is different from the **listing price** or **asking price** (*price the seller asked for the property when it was first put on the market*).

When appraising residential properties for a sale or refinance transaction, the URAR is typically used. Fannie Mae guidelines require the final value entered on the URAR to represent the appraiser's opinion of market value, as defined in the appraisal report itself.

"**Market value** is the most probable price a property should bring in a competitive and open market under all conditions requisite to a fair sale, the buyer and seller, each acting prudently, knowledgeably, and assuming the price is not affected by undue stimulus."

The objective is to determine what a "typical buyer" would pay for the property.

Fannie Mae expects the final indicated value to represent an opinion of market value. The comprehensive explanation of market value in the URAR form is designed to remind appraisers that all properties chosen should have experienced the same typical conditions in the marketplace. Special attention is paid to sales and financing concessions, because they have the greatest potential to alter the price paid. Fannie Mae requires the appraiser to use good judgment and market-derived data to determine the market's reaction to these concessions.

Case Example 8.1: Property Sells for More than the Asking Price

A listed single-family dwelling is selling for more than the asking price and the appraiser must know why this is the case. The challenge is to discern "market value" from "market price."

Appraiser Darla Cunningham has been engaged by First Continent Mortgage Company to perform an appraisal of a single-family dwelling under contract to sell for $115,000.

What data should be gathered for the appraiser's workfile regarding the assignment and the property and what are the various market indications?

On obtaining the sales contract for the property, appraiser Cunningham notes the seller is paying up to $7,000 of the purchaser's points, closing costs, pre-paid items, and program fees. The buyer has applied for a popular mortgage program that requires the seller to contribute 3.75% of the purchase price as a down payment to help the buyer qualify for the loan. The loan amount will be 100% of the purchase price.

Appraiser Cunningham, as is her normal practice, proceeds to research the property's listing history. The property is currently listed with a local real estate broker for $110,000. It has been listed with this broker for approximately six months. Further research reveals that the property was listed with another broker immediately before for six months as well, with a final listing price of $112,500 after being introduced to the market for $114,900. During the total listing period, the activity of this market segment appears to be steady.

How would this information influence the value indications of the sales comparison analysis?

The transaction is not arm's length. The buyer was influenced by the concessions being paid. A typical buyer who would not require such large concessions would not pay $115,000. The market indicates this buyer may not be a typical buyer. This single-family dwelling is selling for more than the asking price because the seller is paying concessions.

Case Example 8.2:
Property Priced and Being Sold Below Market Value

An FSBO (For Sale By Owner) single-family home is priced (as what will later be found to be) below market value and is in contract for that amount. The challenge is to determine the appraiser's responsibility in this situation.

Appraiser Brett Weller is engaged to appraise a single-family dwelling in a residential neighborhood by Allied-Gulf Mortgage Company. The house is owned by George Cline, an elderly man. Mr. Cline lives in another state and is selling the house on his own without a real estate broker.

The property is under contract to sell for $28,000 to Lisa Wells. When reviewing the transaction documents accompanying the appraisal engagement, appraiser Weller becomes curious. He knows the subject area is a highly desired and established market, and is typically comprised of houses in a price range of $100,000 to $200,000. An appointment to inspect the property is arranged for the following day. On arrival, the property appears to be a well-maintained house, consistent with the other properties in this particular neighborhood.

What question(s) should appraiser Weller ask the owner?

Appraiser Weller interviews Mr. Cline, who reveals he has owned the home for many years, purchasing it for his sister to live in. She is recently deceased and, having no further use for the property, he is disposing of it. Mr. Cline has never had the property appraised and relied on the county auditor's tax appraisal for pricing the property. From this information, he interprets that $28,000 is the auditor's market value of the property. Ms. Wells is the first potential buyer who looked at the property.

(continued on next page)

Case Example 8.2: continued

What should the appraiser investigate based on the information given by Mr. Cline?

Through the interview with Mr. Cline, it was learned that the property was advertised in the local newspaper, along with the price, property address, and a photo of the property. The buyer, Lisa Wells, made an appointment and viewed the property within one hour of the newspaper hitting the newsstands. She wrote a full-price offer on the spot. It was at this point that appraiser Weller looked in his appraisal workfile and noticed that $28,000 was the county auditor's assessed value. Appraiser Weller should include the details of the transaction in his database for future reference in case this property is chosen as a potential comparable for other transactions. This transfer should be avoided as a future comparable sale because the seller's lack of knowledge means this was *not* a typical arm's length transaction.

What can appraiser Weller discuss with Mr. Cline about the transaction and the sale price?

The appraiser is not permitted to say anything to Mr. Cline about the transaction or the sale price because Mr. Cline is not the client. It is not the appraiser's job to educate the seller about the market value of the property because Weller does not have any contractual or fiduciary relationship with the seller. Appraiser Weller should note the entire situation in the appraisal report to explain why the appraised market value is higher than the contracted sale price.

Application of an Arm's Length Transaction

In the Fannie Mae definition of market value, note an important part: *The property was sold in a "competitive and open market."* In fact, the definition considers several conditions that must be present for a transaction to be "typical" within the marketplace. Another way to characterize a "typical" transaction is to say the transfer of property was part of an "arm's length" transaction. This must be the case for the resulting sale price to be considered market value.

An **arm's length transaction** means *the transaction occurred under typical conditions in the marketplace with each of the parties acting in his own best interest.* There are seven specific requirements the appraiser must test for in determining whether a transaction represents a "typical" transaction. If the transfer is truly a typical transaction, another "typical" buyer could be expected to step in and buy the property for the same amount, or another "typical" seller would agree to sell the property under the same terms and conditions.

The seven "typical" conditions that must be present for a transfer to be considered an arm's length transaction are:

1. The buyer paid cash for the property at closing or obtained a conventional mortgage through a lender to pay the seller the agreed upon price at closing.
2. The seller did not grant any unusual payment concessions, such as owner financing or other payment terms.
3. The buyer and seller are not related in any way.
4. The buyer and seller are both acting in their own best interests.
5. The buyer and seller are not acting out of undue haste or duress.
6. The buyer and seller are both reasonably informed about all aspects of the property, its potential uses, market value, and market conditions.
7. The property has been available on the market for a reasonable period.

All of these factors should be taken into consideration when determining a property's value by comparing different sales to arrive at a value opinion. These points affect the sale price of a property and, therefore, its perceived value. If the seller was forced to sell because of a lost job, this could tend to lower the subject's selling price. Or, if the seller agreed to some type of owner financing, this may contribute to a higher selling price. Both the buyer's *and* the seller's actions and motivations must be considered in the transaction.

A competent appraiser must consider all aspects of the transaction. The objective is to determine what a "typical buyer" and "typical seller" would do in a "typical transaction." If a determination cannot be made by the appraiser that a comparable sale was indeed an arm's length transaction, the appraiser should discard it as a potential comparable sale. Furthermore, if the subject property is not part of an arm's length transaction, the appraiser must discuss this in the appraisal report, along with its effect, if any, on the final opinion of value presented in the report.

Case Example 8.3: Property Sells for Less than Market Value

A listed, single-family dwelling sells for (what will later be determined as) less than market value and the appraiser must deduce why this is the case.

Appraiser Jack Swift is considering a comparable property for an assignment for which he is gathering market data. This particular comparable property transferred two weeks ago for $450,000. The property had been listed for $495,000 with a broker and had been on the market for approximately 80 days. The typical **days on market (DOM)** for the subject's area is about 90.

According to this information, does this sale appear to represent an arm's length transaction?

Appraiser Swift recalled a conversation he had with the seller of the property several weeks ago when verifying the listing for a relocation assignment. The seller, who was also the listing agent and one of the area's top-producing agents, told Jack she would not consider selling the property for less than $470,000. She was in the process of building a new house and in no particular hurry to sell, since the new house wouldn't be finished for several months. The seller further stated if she could not obtain her price, she would keep the house and rent it out, as similar properties were renting for about $3,000 per month in the area. Appraiser Swift contacts the agent to verify the terms of the sale.

What information is appraiser Swift looking for?

When asked, the seller relates the details of the transaction to appraiser Swift. The buyer was in a unique circumstance—relocating with an employer, but with temporary housing provided (meaning immediate possession was not necessary). The buyer made the offer of $450,000 with transaction possession terms allowing the seller to remain in the house for five months, which was about when the seller's new house would be completed. The seller also found this term to be attractive, because it meant she and her family would not need to move twice, at an estimated cost of $5,000.

Can this transaction be utilized as an arm's length transaction? How would the concessions be quantified?

The single-family dwelling sold for less than market value due to buyer concessions; therefore, this transaction is *not* an arm's length transaction. The circumstances are far from typical. It can be inferred from the narrative that the seller agreed to a much lower price, because the buyer allowed the seller to remain in the home for the period needed until the new home was completed. The concessions could best be quantified by considering the saved expense from moving only once, instead of twice. Additional adjustments may also need to be made for the rental value of the property during the five months the seller is allowed to remain in the house "rent free."

Application of Zoning Issues

Even when dealing with residential property, there are zoning issues that must be considered. Zoning laws do more than simply state the type of building or activity permitted on the property. There are usually setback and side yard rules, dictating how and where the building may be placed, as well as rules for building size, building use, and other requirements.

Residential properties must conform to these regulations, or fall under one of several exceptions. Failure to comply can result in value loss, so the appraiser must be sure to note any zoning issues in the appraisal report, along with any exceptions applicable. Exceptions generally fall into one of four categories:

1. Area variances
2. Use variances
3. Conditional uses
4. Nonconforming uses

The primary way certain zoning laws or restrictions are deviated from with regard to building size and placement is with variances. **Variances** are *permissions granted by the zoning authority to allow some deviation from strict compliance with zoning laws.* **Area variances** legally *permit deviation regarding building size, height limits, setbacks, side yards, and so on.* **Use variances** *permit a property owner to use land in a way that's not allowed in that zone*—such as a commercial use in a residential zone.

Nonconforming uses *occur when land use does not conform to current zoning laws, but is allowed because the land use was established before the new laws were enacted.* If the property is sold, the new owner may be allowed to continue with the nonconforming use if it is **grandfathered** under the old or pre-zoning laws, usually provided the property is not altered. **Conditional uses** occur *when land usage doesn't comply with the general zoning rules for the property's location, but the use is permitted because it benefits the public good*—such as schools, hospitals, and churches.

Appraisers must address zoning issues as the property currently is classified, or that are based appropriately upon hypothetical condition. Zoning changes or exceptions proposed, but not granted, should *not* be considered when developing a value opinion. If there are zoning violations, or an exception to zoning regulations has been granted, the appraiser must discuss this in the appraisal report, along with its effect, if any, on the final opinion of value.

Case Example 8.4:
Three-Unit Apartment Building with Small Site Area

A three-unit apartment building has a small gross site area, so the appraiser must check for zoning compliance.

Appraiser Jenna Berg is appraising a three-unit apartment building under contract to sell. The building is nearly eighty years old and was converted to three living units in the mid 1960s, long before zoning was imposed for the city in 1974.

The property is located in an R-6, medium-density residential district, which allows up to four units per lot. The subject site contains 9,000 square feet. The current zoning site regulations require 3,500 square feet of site area for each living unit.

How does this regulation affect the property and its value?

The current use of the property is acceptable since it is "grandfathered in" under the old zoning laws. There may be concern over the ability to rebuild the structure if destroyed by fire, but the degree of this concern will vary by jurisdiction. In any event, the appraiser assumes the present nonconforming use will be allowed to continue. She must write an extraordinary assumption in the report, stating the value opinion in the appraisal report is based on the assumption that this nonconforming use will be allowed to continue.

A sample extraordinary assumption comment might be similar to this:

"The subject's current use is considered a grandfathered nonconforming use under local zoning regulations. The site requirement for the subject's R-6 zoning designation is 3,500 square feet of site area for each living unit or, in the case of the subject, 10,500 square feet. The subject's site area is 9,000 square feet. The current use as a three-unit residential property existed prior to the imposition of zoning regulations. Thus, the use is allowed, under the zoning regulation, to continue until such time the use has been vacated for [period specified within the zoning regulations].

"This appraisal and the resulting value opinion are based on the extraordinary assumption the grandfathered nonconforming use will be permitted to continue. The appraiser reserves the right to reconsider the value conclusion should the assumption be found to be false."

Final Thoughts on Residential Applications and Issues

The appraisal process relies on the appraiser making a thorough effort to research all aspects of the subject property and all comparable sales. A credible opinion of market value can be ascertained only by studying actual arm's length transactions in the marketplace, as market participants set the market value of a property.

When a real estate broker is marketing a property, it might be assumed the original listing price is the ceiling of the market, which is not always the case. A seller may have instructed the broker to set the asking price low in order to receive an acceptable offer quickly, which might not be market value. Over time, the listing price becomes an upper limit of value, because the property has been tested and the market has not responded. When the property has been exposed for a reasonable period at one asking price, that price tends to suggest what the property is *not* worth. When this is the case, the listing history turns into a market history of sorts for that property. Once a property has been available for a "reasonable" period in a given market, this activity may even overshadow comparable sales in determining market value for the property based on pure theory. After all, if the market and typical buyers had the opportunity to buy a property at a given price and did not respond with a typical buyer's reaction, it theoretically implies the market (typical buyers) sees that the price as "too high." Thus, the ceiling has been set.

If, during an appraiser's analysis, market data does not appear to support the contract price for a property, the appraiser must look for the underlying cause. Often, there are undue influences on the buyer or seller that result in a contract price higher or lower than the market price of the property. When price does not appear to represent market value, the appraiser must investigate whether the transfer is part of an arm's length transaction. Was the buyer a typical buyer, or were there conditions that motivated or caused this buyer's action?

Finally, the appraiser must discuss these points in the appraisal report, along with any other concerns or irregularities discovered. The appraiser has a duty to convey any such conditions through commentary in the report. Furthermore, the appraiser must analyze whether these conditions affect the value of the property.

Mixed Use and Non-residential Appraisal

Appraising non-residential properties can be an interesting and lucrative business segment for the competent and qualified appraiser. For the purposes here, non-residential land, income-producing agricultural properties, multi-family residential properties with more than four units, mixed-use properties, etc., are included in our reference to non-residential. There are several reasons a residential appraiser should have knowledge of non-residential properties and methods for their valuation. A brief overview is provided of why every appraiser—even one with no aspiration for a career including non-residential appraisal—must know a little about it.

- *Preparation for National Appraiser Examination*—Some methodology and application typically associated with non-residential appraisal is often included in exam content. In addition, some residential appraisers might wish to pursue a higher credential allowing for supervised practice in this area to gain experience.

- *Recognizing Highest and Best Use*—Sometimes, an appraiser does not recognize, or know for sure, when the highest and best use of a property is non-residential. It is important for the residential appraiser to know what to do in this circumstance.

- *Acceptability in Some States*—Some states may allow a licensed and/or certified appraiser to perform appraisal of "other property type" up to a limited transaction amount for certain intended uses. Of course, the appraiser must be in compliance with the COMPETENCY RULE of USPAP in performing this practice. For states allowing the practice of appraisal for other property types by those holding residential credentials, foundational non-residential concepts and applications are essential. Appraisers are advised to inquire with their state regulatory agency for practice limitations applicable to a particular state or jurisdiction.

√ **Reminder:** If an appraiser does not have knowledge or experience with a market, geographic area, property type, or analytical method, the appraiser must disclose the lack of competency prior to accepting the appraisal assignment, take the necessary steps to gain the competence, and disclose the steps taken to gain competency in the appraisal report.

What is Different?

The question is often asked, "What is the difference between appraising residential property and non-residential property?" A common answer might be, "Nothing, but quite a lot." The same fundamental theories and principles of residential property are observed, and the same valuation process discussed in Chapter 1 applies as well. Similar data is collected and analyzed for the physical characteristics of the property as is gathered for a residential dwelling, and most of the same information is described in the appraisal report, but perhaps in a slightly different manner or format.

Highest and Best Use

Determination of highest and best use for residential properties, in many cases, is abbreviated by private and public limitations that could single out only one or two potential property uses. It is not uncommon for a non-residential property to be allowed to have a broad array of permitted potential uses, as zoning and other regulations are usually much broader for non-residential properties than for residential properties. Thus, the appraiser may need to spend a considerable amount of time performing research and analysis to determine the highest and best use.

A residential appraiser may come to the realization he has just stepped into the non-residential world when performing the highest and best use analysis in a market value assignment. The subject might be a residential dwelling located in a commercially zoned area, or a non-zoned vacant site or land parcel. When the residential appraiser recognizes the subject property's highest and best use is something other than residential, he must consider both competency and his practice within the jurisdiction's licensing and certification parameters before proceeding with the assignment.

The residential dwelling located in a commercially zoned area is a good model with which to start our discussion. Consider a residential neighborhood in the process of changing to commercial use. Ongoing conversion of the residential dwellings to commercial uses is taking place and, in some cases, the dwellings are being razed to provide for commercial development. If the dwelling could be converted to a commercial use, such as an office or shop, this potential should be explored. Perhaps, because of the physical condition or design of the residential structure, conversion cannot be economically accomplished.

Many times, the site on which the dwelling is located, while commercially zoned, is not large enough for most of today's commercial uses (and the site zoning requirements) standing alone—the site must be joined with a neighboring site(s). If this were the case, the site's highest and best use would be to assemble it with a contiguous site(s), creating a larger site with greater commercial utility. Of course, the appraiser must analyze how reliable the neighboring property is for successful assemblage. Once this is decided, the appraiser must consider the house located on the site—this requires significant observation and knowledge of the market. If the site would be needed immediately for assemblage, the conclusion would most likely be to raze the house and make the site available for assemblage. If this is not the case, an interim use for the house (e.g., a residential income property) might be concluded.

There are many potential scenarios for determining highest and best use in a non-residential appraisal assignment, depending on whether the site is currently improved or if it is vacant. If the site is improved, the appraiser must first determine if the improvement is bringing the greatest return to the land in terms of market value. On the following pages, an example of typical commercial zoning regulations is presented.

GENERAL COMMERCIAL DISTRICT.

(b) Permitted Uses.

(1) Public or private open land uses, such as arboretums, parks, playgrounds, flood management and storm water detention areas, reservoirs, and wildlife preserves.

(2) Churches and similar places of public assembly.

(3) Public or private schools.

(4) Colleges and/or universities.

(5) Community services, such as community centers, museums, galleries, libraries, and similar facilities.

(6) Public protection facilities, including police, fire, and ambulance facilities and civil defense or storm shelters.

(7) Off-street parking areas and garages as a principal use, subject to the requirements of this Code.

(8) Administrative, business, or professional offices, including:

A. Brokers and dealers in securities, investments and associated services, not including commercial banks and savings institutions.

B. Insurance agents, brokers, and associated services.

C. Real estate sales and associated services.

D. Medical and medical-related activities, but not including veterinary offices or animal hospitals.

E. Professional, legal, engineering, and architectural services, not including the outside storage of equipment.

F. Accounting, auditing, and other bookkeeping services.

(9) Retail Stores primarily engaged in selling merchandise for personal or household consumption, and rendering services incidental to the sale of these goods:

A. Food and food products, consisting of: grocery, meat, fish, fruit or vegetable markets, or combinations thereof, dairy or bakery products, specialty food stores such as candy or confectionery, and miscellaneous food stores.

B. General merchandise, including home furnishings and hardware and similar "hard lines"

C. Apparel, consisting of: clothing, furnishings, and accessory items for men, women and children, custom tailor shops and combined apparel sales and personal service operations, and miscellaneous apparel and accessory stores.

D. Similar retail stores, including: drug stores, florists, gift and novelty stores, books and newspapers, camera, photographic and optical goods, jewelry, antique stores, specialty stores, and other retail stores which conform to the purpose and intent of the CG District.

(10) Personal Services, involving the care of the person and his/her personal effects, including consumer services generally involving the care and maintenance of tangible property or the provision of tangible services for personal consumption including:

A. Restaurants, including establishments with drive-through facilities, but not including outside seating areas.

B. Bars and/or taverns and similar establishments whose principal activity is dispensing intoxicating beverages, but not including outside seating areas.

C. Carry out food and beverage establishments with drive-through facilities

D. Banks, savings and loans, and credit agencies, including establishments with drive-through facilities.

E. Barber and beauty shops.

F. Dry-cleaning establishments.

G. Funeral services.

H. Human medical and dental clinics.

I. Radio, television, or small appliance repair.

J. Public and private parking areas.

K. On-premises duplication facilities.

(11) Business Services engaged in providing services to business establishments on a fee or contract basis, including consulting services, protective services, office equipment rental, lease or purchase, commercial research, and development.

(12) Commercial recreational facilities such as community and public swimming pools, skating rinks, bowling alleys, physical fitness centers.

(13) Lumber and home improvement sales.

(14) Automobile sales and service establishments, including gasoline service stations, but not including truck servicing establishments.

(15) Theatres and similar public assembly facilities.

(16) Hotels and motels.

(17) Garden centers.

(c) Special Exception Uses.

(1) Single-family detached dwellings provided such structures comply with the requirements of all other City codes and ordinances.

(2) Multi-family dwellings, including:

   A. Single-family townhouse units, provided such structures are located on a separate lot within a townhouse development containing at least three lots, are attached by a common party wall to another townhouse unit, are not located above any other dwelling unit, and comply with all other City codes and ordinances.

   B. Apartment

   C. Assisted Living Facility

   D. Convent or Monastery

   E. Rooming or Boarding House

   F. Elderly/Retirement Housing

   G. Life Care Retirement Center, provided the nursing or medical facility meets all applicable licensing requirements by the state health department as an intermediate care facility or as a skilled nursing home.

(3) Child Care Homes.

(4) Group residential facilities.

(6) Structures containing separate small, self-serve storage facilities leased or rented to individuals or businesses.

(7) Restaurants, bars, taverns, and similar facilities with outside seating facilities.

(8) Self-service car washes.

(9) Temporary or seasonal outdoor sales lots having a maximum operating duration of four months, provided all other permits are obtained.

(10) Trade establishments primarily providing business and household maintenance services. Such establishments could offer incidental fabricating, processing, installation and repair, including:

   A. Heating and air conditioning

   B. Appliance repair

   C. Plumbing

   D. Extermination and pest control

   E. Janitorial services

   F. Window cleaning

   G. Contract construction services

(11) Motor vehicle sales and servicing

(12) Intensive open air commercial recreational facilities, including arenas, race tracks, fairgrounds, golf driving ranges, stadiums, and water slides.

(13) Facilities for scientific research, development and testing, within enclosed buildings.

(d) Bulk and Area Requirements.

Bulk and area requirements for the permitted and accessory uses within the General Commercial District are shown:

   Minimum Frontage(feet) 100

   Minimum Setback from Property Line(feet) 50

   Rear and Side Setback(feet) 25

   Parking shall be provided commensurate with the specific use as provided later in this code.

Highest and Best Use Example

The subject property is a one-acre parcel with approximately 250 feet of frontage in a general commercial district observing the same zoning regulations previously illustrated. The site is improved with a 25' x 50' concrete block structure used as a small insurance office. The structure is in good condition and is situated in the center of the parcel. Land values have risen sharply in the immediate vicinity, as the area has recently been annexed into the city.

It is easy to see the site is not improved to its highest and best use, as a considerable amount of the site is not being utilized to its current maximum potential.

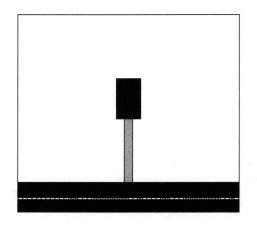

The next step for the appraiser is to analyze the market to determine the ideal use. For our example, there appears to be a demand for professional offices, small retail storefronts, and both one-acre and one-half-acre commercial building tracts.

Given these conclusions, the primary options the appraiser might further analyze include:

- Keeping the site and present structure "as is," allowing for potential expansion of the existing structure to a multi-unit professional and retail facility
- Keeping the site "as is," demolishing the existing structure, and leaving the entire site available for a greater use
- Demolishing the existing structure and dividing the site into two 125-foot frontage parcels

One option not concluded as a possibility is to sell 100 feet of frontage from each side of the parcel and keep the existing structure on the remaining property. Remember, the zoning for this classification requires each parcel to have 100 feet of frontage. Thus, taking 100 feet off each side would not be a legal option, as the remaining site would have only 50 feet of frontage. Unless there is some evidence that a variance could be obtained, this option could not be considered by the appraiser.

The purpose of this example is to illustrate the number of factors the appraiser needs to consider in the assignment. In order to arrive at the conclusion of the property's highest and best use, the appraiser needs to be familiar with the broad range of uses the property could accommodate due to its relatively generous zoning. In addition, the appraiser has to be well acquainted with market conditions and demand. Finally, the resulting land value for each has to be developed, along with costs associated for each option. Significantly more work and competence is required for this type of assignment as opposed to the majority of residential appraisal assignments.

Now, when looking at basic commercial structures that could be adapted to multiple uses, the potential for conversion and related conversion costs must be analyzed. This occurs quite frequently—restaurants are converted to shoe stores; banks are converted to offices, etc. The financial feasibility of conversion, though, is dependent on the conversion costs. Here, the appraiser will usually rely on cost estimates for a credible highest and best use conclusion. Would a conversion be more economical than razing the structure and building from scratch? How adaptable are the existing improvements for the highest and best use?

Functional Obsolescence

One occurrence more unique to commercial (and industrial) properties versus residential property is the economic life of the improvements can virtually be eliminated by functional obsolescence. For residential properties, functional obsolescence certainly occurs, but physical deterioration usually causes the structure to cease lending value. It is possible some commercial structures will experience incurable functional obsolescence much more rapidly than residential structures because they had a shorter expected economic life from the start—structures designed for a specific use. Large chain fast-food restaurants are a good example. Many of these chains use "prototype" buildings and the concept usually has a short life until another design is favored by the chain. Since these business entities prefer to keep facilities up-to-date, they often perform significant modernizations or even raze one design within a relatively short period only to replace it with another.

Example : Functional Obsolescence

Consider the design of an early McDonald's® restaurant. In 1953, when the restaurant began its franchising activities, the structure was a small building featuring the familiar golden arches and walk-up window—patrons stood outside to place an order. A few tables were scattered around the building's exterior. By 1967, the company began replacing the structures with ones featuring interior seating. So, in this case, the original exterior service design had an economic life of approximately 14 years.

*The oldest operating McDonald's® restaurant located in Downey, California.
Photo by Bryan Hong*

Certainly, not all commercial structures are subject to the rapid effects of business change and evolution as dramatically as McDonald's® experienced in its earlier years. However, it is a good example of how commercial structures can become functionally obsolete based on the building's specific use and business trends. Another consideration for uniquely designed structures is their recognizable relation to a commercial entity. How many well-known businesses can you think of for which the business operating inside can be recognized just by looking at the building? In other words, the design of the structure is similar to (or could actually be) its trademark. Businesses that have structures easily associated with their brand often do not allow another entity to use them without significant modifications.

If an appraiser were considering the highest and best use in a market value assignment, conversion to a more common appearance, the physical adaptability, and cost must be considered. Depending on the land value and the value of the building cured, it is possible that a functional obsolescence exists that could be deemed incurable. Obviously, in cases where the structure is functionally incurable, and it is not economically feasible or maybe even physically possible to convert the structure to meet current market expectations or requirements, (or another use altogether), the highest and best use of the site would be as vacant, ready for a better commercial use—thus, the structure should be torn down.

Compliance with the Americans with Disabilities Act

A special concern today for existing structures (often paramount in deciding whether conversion is feasible in the highest and best use analysis of structures for "public accommodation" or "commercial" use) is compliance with the Americans with Disabilities Act (ADA). The ADA defines these structures as falling into one or more of the following categories:

- An inn, hotel, motel, or other place of lodging
- A restaurant, bar, or other establishment serving food or drink
- A theater, concert hall, stadium, or other place of exhibition or entertainment
- An auditorium, convention center, lecture hall, or other place of public gathering
- A bakery, grocery store, clothing store, hardware store, shopping center, or other sales or rental establishment
- A laundromat, dry cleaner, bank, barber shop, hair salon, travel service, shoe repair service, funeral parlor, gas station, office of an accountant or lawyer, pharmacy, insurance office, real estate office, professional office of a health care provider, hospital, or other service establishment
- A terminal, depot, or other station used for specified public transportation
- A museum, library, gallery, or other place of public display or collection
- A park, zoo, amusement park, or other place of recreation
- A nursery, elementary, secondary, undergraduate, or postgraduate private school, or other place of education
- A day care center, senior citizen center, homeless shelter, food bank, adoption agency, or other social service center establishment
- A gymnasium, health spa, bowling alley, golf course, or other place of exercise or recreation
- Commercial facilities whose operations will affect commerce and that are intended for non-residential use by a private entity, which would include just about all commercial uses, including industrial and warehousing facilities

The ADA addresses the areas of existing structures, alteration of existing structures, and new construction, and has specific requirements for various uses, types, and size of structures. Because the Act is so detailed, the appraiser should approach the idea of conversion with great care. Many times, the costs involved with "retrofitting" an existing structure in conjunction with conversion costs to conform to ADA regulations can exceed the cost of razing and starting from scratch. Architecturally speaking, some existing buildings, especially old ones, cannot be feasibly converted. This fact is evidenced commonly throughout the country in central business districts where commercial use of the upper floors of many commercial structures does not meet ADA criteria without modifications. Alternatives for use of these upper floors might include a use that does not need to meet ADA criteria, such as living quarters, or abandoning the use of these levels altogether, leaving only the ground floors as the primary use of the structure.

Speaking strictly about alteration or conversion of existing structures, the ADA addresses specific broad areas of compliance, primarily removal of architectural barriers and special provisions such as:

- Parking
- Exterior accessibility
- Drinking fountains

- Telephones

- Ramps

- Stairs

- Entrances and exits

- Doors and doorways

- Lobbies and corridors

- Elevators

- Room sizes

- Restrooms

- Signage

- Alarms

Many variables exist regarding the application of ADA requirements. The appraiser should use good judgment combined with competent guidance when suggesting conversion or a highest and best use of an existing structure requiring ADA compliance. When reviewing plans and specifications for non-residential new construction, the appraiser should be observant of ADA compliance.

IMPORTANT POINTS: ADA COMPLIANCE AND FUNCTIONAL OBSOLESCENCE

- *Highest and best use of non-residential properties can be more difficult to determine due to zoning regulations and ADA compliance.*

- *Appraisers should be aware of ADA compliance requirements when considering non-residential new construction, alteration, or conversion.*

- *Commercial properties can be more vulnerable to incurable functional obsolescence due to being built for a specific purpose and/or period.*

Valuation Methodology

The same three approaches to value are used, depending on what the appraiser decided was necessary in the scope of work, but *different techniques of developing a value opinion* may be employed in some non-residential assignments. For example, in developing the income approach, techniques using an overall capitalization rate may be more commonly decided on in the scope of work, than using either a gross rent multiplier (GRM) or a gross income multiplier (GIM). An important point to note: *The income approach may likely be concluded as the more credible indicator of value in a commercial appraisal assignment* rather than the sales comparison approach. Of course, the sales comparison approach is still valid in a commercial assignment, given sufficient comparable sales data is available. Commercial properties do not usually transfer as frequently or in the same numbers as residential properties, presenting a major obstacle at times. They also often present numerous physical dissimilarities—truly comparable sales data may be difficult to find for some property types in certain geographic areas. This could, in some cases, lead the appraiser to use older sales data, or data from a different market. Hence, the sales comparison approach may lose reliability as a credible method of developing a value opinion if more reliable methods can be developed. It is not unusual to find the income approach, and sometimes the cost approach, relied on a great deal more in the appraisal of non-residential properties.

Appraising Large Tracts of Land

In Chapter 7, valuation methodology for appraising land was overviewed. Purely for informational purposes, challenges relating to the appraisal of larger tracts of land will be discussed in this chapter. These challenges often present themselves in the course of a residential appraiser's practice and an appraiser should know how to handle them. Specifically, agricultural properties and land with potential for development—either residential or non-residential are discussed here. Competency to proceed with an assignment involving such a land parcel must be carefully considered. There are many licensed and certified appraisers who do not possess the competency to appraise agricultural or development land. In fact, practice in these areas is often considered a specialty.

Agricultural Land

Agricultural land may appear seemingly simple and non-complex and, depending on the scope of work and the presence of truly comparable data, it could be. Many times, instead of something built on the surface of the land, there are things growing on it. Crops, for example, must be addressed and can be considered either personal property or a fixture. *If the crops are planted and are the property of a tenant, the crops are considered an element of personal property* called **emblements**. In this case, the tenant can re-enter the property to harvest the crops until the first crop matures. If the crops are *planted and owned by the property owner*, the crops are considered **fixtures**. Thus, if on the effective date of the appraisal crops are present, the appraiser must consider their contributory value on that date, as the crops would transfer with the property, unless that interest was not being appraised. Such would need to be addressed during problem identification.

However, do not think that simply because there is nothing built on the surface, there is little to consider. Much of the value of agricultural land rests with what is *below* the surface. There are reported to be more than 20,000 different soil types in the United States. Soil quality is measured by its production capability, physical stability, and topographical and physical characteristics. The complexity of soil composition is compounded in that soils tend to run in strains. It is not unusual for a 20-acre parcel to have several types of soil present. From a quality standpoint, the range may run from poor to excellent and one acre may not have the same qualities as an acre located next to it. Appraisers who regularly appraise agricultural properties are keenly aware of the relationship of soil type and classification to value. If the sales comparison approach is used to develop a value opinion of an agricultural property, comparing the soil types among the subject's comparable properties is much like comparing the subject house and a comparable house in a residential assignment.

Methods for Appraising Large Tracts of Land

Tillable land is usually more valuable than pastureland, in many areas. Where that is the case, a *complex income approach* using crop production and yields may be warranted. Another method is the ground rent capitalization method when the farmland is commonly rented. Myriad data are available through public and private sources for research and analysis of agricultural land, income, and production data. These scenarios become complex and are addressed in advanced, specialized appraisal courses.

In the context of highest and best use, many areas of the country are seeing a trend toward agricultural land's highest and best use being development—in many cases, residential development. When this is the case, the subdivision analysis method is often employed and is a process that requires a high and specialized level of competency.

Non-Residential Improvement Description and Analysis

In addition to terminology nuances used to describe non-residential improvements and their components, a notable difference is found in *describing a building's measurements*. The defined area of a residential property is described as gross living area; non-residential improvements are described, commonly, as Gross Building Area (GBA) or Gross Leasable Area (GLA).

Residential appraisers will notice quickly the acronym both for gross living area and gross leasable area is *GLA*. Therefore, care must be taken to determine the context in which the term is being used. In this section, GLA refers to *gross leasable area*. The methods for determining GBA and GLA may differ, depending on custom in various geographic areas. So, to prevent confusion and misunderstanding, the appraiser should carefully describe the techniques used to determine the area and apply all data consistently. The calculation of GBA and GLA are determined somewhat differently than gross living area.

Gross Building Area

Gross building area (GBA) *uses the exterior dimensions of the above grade, or superstructure, and below grade area, or substructure, of a building.* If there are multiple buildings, each should be described separately.

As mentioned earlier, GBA is usually stated as *square feet.* However, for some applications (such as a warehouse), the area might be stated as cubic feet.

Gross Leasable Area

Gross leasable area (GLA) *consists of the total floor area exclusively used by tenants, including below grade areas.* Common areas enjoyed and used by all tenants are *not* considered in the gross leasable area. Thus, the method is primarily used in multi-tenant non-residential structures.

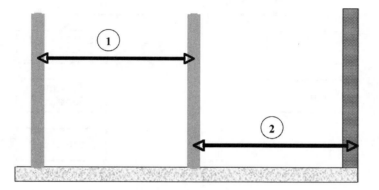

The method for determining gross leasable area is somewhat different than other methods. Here, the area is determined by *calculating the area from mid-point between the partitioning walls* (as shown in measurement 1). In the case that the unit has outside walls, the measurement would extend to the outer surface (as shown in measurement 2).

Trade Fixtures

Trade fixtures are *items usually associated with a business or profession operating in or on a property. They are not like fixtures, in that they are not considered part of the real estate and are considered personal property no matter how they are attached.* Appraisers must be observant to note any trade fixtures in a commercial or industrial property. Specialized knowledge and competence may be required to appraise these items. Sometimes trade fixtures can even be found in residential properties. For example, a homeowner could have operated a small beauty salon in one room of the house—there may be special attached cabinetry, sinks, etc., common to the profession that could be considered trade fixtures. But most often, the appraiser will find trade fixtures in a commercial or industrial property where a tenant is operating. For tenant-occupied properties, the appraiser should review the lease for any terms that address trade fixtures and their provisions for removal, or making the items permanent.

Examples of trade fixtures *might* include:

- Specialized lighting, plumbing, electrical items, and equipment
- Shelving, display cases, and other display items
- Signage and trademarked items
- Hoists, air supply lines, oxygen lines, and controls
- Restaurant equipment, sometimes including walk-in coolers
- Storage tanks and devices
- Service station pumps and canopies

In addition, an appraiser qualified to appraise a commercial property, either by credential or competency, may be asked to appraise an operating business, including real property. This one case truly demonstrates the need for appraiser/client communication during problem identification. Often, the expectation of the appraiser is to include values for three distinct asset types in the appraisal—*tangible real property*, *tangible personal property*, and *intangible business assets*. Sales contracts for businesses often simply state a sale price for the entire enterprise, or the *going concern*.

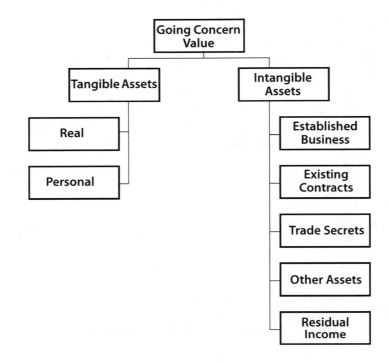

For example, if a small established hardware store was for sale, there would be the real property, trade fixtures (including shelving, display cases, signs, attached equipment, etc.), personal property, inventory, non-attached equipment, office furniture, etc. Other considerations are the business assets, likely to include value of the established business, contracts with others, accounts receivable, franchise (if any), etc. Unless the appraiser can comply with the COMPETENCY RULE of USPAP for appraising the different assets of a going concern, services may be limited to the appraisal only of the real property.

With a **going concern value**, *the appraiser's value opinion for the real property asset would reflect the value of the real property assuming the hardware store is operating in it.* In fact, more than one appraisal may be needed—possibly one for each asset type. Unfortunately, misunderstandings may occur during problem identification without appraiser/client communication—the client could believe the real property appraiser is accepting an assignment including the consideration of all assets.

IMPORTANT POINTS: APPRAISING AND DESCRIBING NON-RESIDENTIAL PROPERTY

- *It is not uncommon for appraisers to encounter large tracts of land and/or trade fixtures in both residential and non-residential assignments. This is another reason general knowledge of non-residential practices is necessary among all appraisers.*

- *It is important to be aware of the content in which GLA is used: Gross living area is a measurement for residential properties; gross leasable area is used for non-residential properties.*

Reporting Methods

Various options for reporting a non-residential appraisal are available both in form and narrative formats. There are software vendors producing programs for each style. Of course, non-residential appraisals can use *either* of the two reporting options:

- Appraisal Report
- Restricted Appraisal Report

As was mentioned earlier in the course, the reporting option is determined with the client, based on the intended user and the intended use of the appraisal. Various land forms are available and are widely used and preferred by many lenders for vacant parcels. In most cases though, a *narrative format* is still the most-used format for presenting a non-residential appraisal. A **narrative appraisal report** will *lead the reader through the important elements of the appraisal, including the conclusions of the appraisal, in an orderly and systematic format.*

USPAP does not dictate the style or suggest a specific method other than the level of content and detail, but generally, a narrative appraisal report will include a written narrative addressing various elements in several sections:

1. Foreword
   - Table of contents
   - Letter of transmittal
   - Executive summary
2. Problem Identification and Scope of Work
   - Reporting option and format
   - Client and other intended users
   - Intended use
   - Type and definition of value
   - Effective date, date of the report, date of inspection
   - Relevant characteristics of the property and rights appraised
   - Assignment conditions, including: General assumptions, limiting conditions, hypothetical conditions, extraordinary assumptions
   - Scope of work
3. Research
   - Property identification, legal description
   - Sales and listing history
   - Neighborhood (market area) description

- Location characteristics
- Description of land
- Description of improvements
- Taxes and assessments
- Zoning and regulations
- Exposure time
- Marketability data

4. Analysis and Conclusions
   - Highest and best use analysis
   - Valuation analysis: Land, cost, sales comparison, income
   - Reconciliation and final value opinion conclusion
   - Appraiser's signed certification
5. Addenda and Exhibits
   - Maps
   - Demographic and statistics data
   - Leases
   - Cost estimates (if applicable)
   - Appraiser's qualifications
   - Other attachments

IMPORTANT POINTS: ASSIGNMENT PURPOSE AND USE OF NARRATIVE FORMAT

- *Client/appraiser communication is important in the problem identification stage to avoid misunderstandings of an assignment and its purpose/use.*
- *A narrative format is the most widely used reporting method for non-residential appraisals.*

Non–Residential Application Case Studies

The purpose of this section is to provide an overview of some of the challenges of non-residential appraisal not typically found with residential assignments, along with problem solving methodology and techniques. Also discussed will be terminology and elements of property description and analysis of non-residential appraisal application. While introducing a few typical non-residential application scenarios, this section should allow for consideration of the problem areas, how the problem can be solved, and application issues relevant to each scenario.

Case Study 8.5: Mixed-use Property

This scenario demonstrates a **mixed-use property**. *Primarily a residential recreation property, non-residential elements are present* that must be considered. Also illustrated is valuation methodology, combining the conclusions of different approaches to reach a conclusion, lease analysis, and interpret an arm's length transaction.

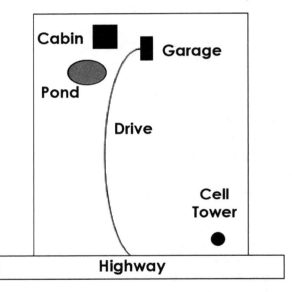

A 9-acre parcel is being appraised. It is improved with a 900 square-foot cabin, a 500 square-foot two-car garage, and a pond at the rear of the property. Other site improvements include a septic system, utilities, 800-foot gravel driveway, and typical landscaping. The cabin is six years old and in average condition. Its economic life is estimated at 60 years. A cell tower is located at the property boundary along the frontage. Similarly sized tracts are selling for around $60,000. Reproduction cost for the cabin is $60 per square foot, and $20 per square foot for the garage. The "as is" value estimate of miscellaneous site improvements is $10,000.

Data indicates sales of similar properties, without a cell tower, are selling for about $100,000. While examining the lease for the cell tower, which is $400 per month, you find it can be renewed by the parties annually for the next 15 years, with no provision for escalation of the rent. It may be terminated by the lessee at any time. Research has revealed similar cell tower leases with a capitalization rate of 10%. The lessee must consent to the assignment of the lease. Currently, the property is in contract to sell for $110,000 between relatives with no broker involved and without being exposed to the market.

Discussion Points

1. *What relevant factors must be considered when valuing this property?*

2. *How should an appraiser address this appraisal assignment?*

3. *What value indications have been formed?*

Case Study 8.6: Zoning Issues

Illustrated here is the result of a grandfathered nonconforming use that has expired due to lack of continued use. The challenge includes determining the highest and best use of the property. As practice, all valuation approaches are developed.

A former corner drug store is being appraised for the purpose of valuing for the owner's personal portfolio. The structure is 100+ years old and located in a historic residential neighborhood. No other commercial uses are in the area. The building contains about 1,800 square feet and is a single story. The site area is about 0.14 acres. Current building regulations restrict new construction to sites of at least 0.25 acres. It has been unused for several years, except as storage by the owner, who lives next door. The drug store operated as a grandfathered nonconforming use, but zoning has now reverted to single-family residential. The exterior is brick and has been maintained and kept in generally good condition. The interior has observable deferred maintenance. A commode and sink are in the back storeroom. The remainder of the building is one large retail area with display windows on the two street sides.

Demand for residential dwellings in the area is strong and they are selling for $82 per square foot. The rental market is also strong, with 3-bedroom rentals bringing about $800 per month. Several rentals were surveyed to determine a GRM, with 165 —plus or minus—being the most frequently observed.

Conversion costs to create a residential dwelling would be about $20 per square foot. There are no similar lot sales in the immediate market.

Discussion Points

1. *What relevant factors must be considered when valuing this property?*

2. *How should an appraiser address this appraisal assignment?*

3. *Based on the analysis performed, what is the highest and best use and the value indication(s) of the property?*

Case Study 8.7:
Income-Producing Properties and Lease Analysis

This scenario provides opportunity to apply the many principles of appraising an income-producing property. Challenges include lease analysis, developing valuation approaches, determining the highest and best use of a non-contiguous property when it is specified by the lease terms, and the impact of zoning and site regulations.

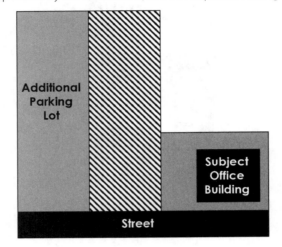

A 2-year old medical office building containing 4,200 square feet is being appraised for refinancing purposes. It is situated on a small lot—0.33 acres—that offers parking for only 15 cars. The subject is leased, with four years remaining on the current term and the option of three additional five-year terms. It generates $4,000 per month, triple net. Likelihood of the lessee renewing the lease is good, as the property was developed for the lessee's use. The lease is considered to reflect the market. The lease also stipulates the lessor will provide parking accommodation for 70 cars. Thus, the lease includes a vacant paved lot, two doors down from the subject accommodating parking for 70 vehicles. It is approximately 0.60 acres. Vacant land is scarce in the area and sells for about $5 per square foot.

City regulations require that with uses such as the subject's, parking for 50 vehicles be provided. Parking spaces in the area rent for $20 per month. Medical office buildings with similar parking are selling for $100 per square foot. Reproduction costs are $80 per square foot. A capitalization rate of 11.25% has been extracted from the market. Vacancy rates of 5% are typical. It is estimated the subject structure has a remaining life of 65 years. "As is" value of other site improvements is estimated to be $25,000.

Discussion Points

1. *What relevant factors must be considered when valuing this property?*

2. *How should an appraiser address this appraisal assignment?*

3. *What are the issues of highest and best use, and the resulting value indications?*

Summary

1. Fannie Mae and others have very specific regulations and guidelines for appraisal analysis and reporting. It may not be unusual for a primary market or portfolio lender to place conditions upon appraisers in assignments, requiring them to observe guidelines, such as Fannie Mae's, for mortgage appraisals, allowing for them to later sell the loan through the secondary market system.

2. Lending institutions and others generally prefer standardized forms, such as the URAR form, because the forms provide a sufficient level of detail in a consistent, convenient, and easy-to-read format. The forms should never limit the appraisal process, the amount of data collected, or the explanations of the appraiser's conclusions.

3. In addition to appraisals performed in connection with a mortgage lending transaction, examples of occasions when an appraisal may be performed for other purposes include relocation, insurance, and appraisal review.

4. Market value is what property is expected to sell for; market price is what the property actually sold for. Fannie Mae expects the final indicated value to represent an opinion of market value, and the comprehensive explanation of market value in the URAR form is designed to remind appraisers that all properties chosen should have experienced the same typical conditions in the marketplace.

5. An arm's length transaction means the transaction occurred under typical conditions in the marketplace with each of the parties acting in his own best interest. A competent appraiser must consider all aspects of the transaction.

6. Appraisers must address zoning issues as the property currently is classified, or that based appropriately upon hypothetical condition. If there are zoning violations, or an exception to zoning regulations has been granted, the appraiser must discuss this in the appraisal report, along with its effect, if any, on the final opinion of value.

7. If, during an appraiser's analysis, market data does not appear to support the contract price for a property, the appraiser must look for the underlying cause. Often, there are undue influences on the buyer or seller that result in a contract price higher or lower than the market value of the property.

8. It is not uncommon for a non-residential property to be allowed to have a broad array of permitted potential uses, as zoning and other regulations are usually much broader for non-residential properties than for residential properties.

9. A special concern today for existing non-residential structures, which is of great concern in deciding whether conversion is feasible in the highest and best use analysis, is compliance with the Americans with Disabilities Act (ADA), which places accessibility and other accommodation requirements for a broad range of property uses.

10. For non-residential properties, the same three approaches to value are used as with residential properties, depending on what the appraiser decided was necessary in the scope of work, but application of different techniques of developing a value opinion may be employed in some non-residential assignments.

11. Competency to proceed with an assignment involving a large land parcel must be carefully considered. There are many licensed and certified appraisers who do not possess the competency to appraise agricultural or development land and the practice is often considered a specialty.

12. Gross building area (GBA) uses the exterior dimensions of the above grade, or superstructure, and below grade area, or substructure, of a building. If there are multiple buildings, each should

be described separately. GBA is usually stated as square feet. However, for some applications (such as a warehouse), the area might be stated as cubic feet.

13. Gross leasable area (GLA) consists of the total floor area exclusively used by tenants, including below grade areas. Common areas enjoyed and used by all tenants are not considered in the gross leasable area.

14. Trade fixtures are items usually associated with a business or profession operating in or on a property. They are not like fixtures, in that they are not considered part of the real estate and are considered personal property no matter how they are attached.

15. In most cases, a narrative format is the most-used format for presenting a non-residential appraisal. A narrative appraisal report will lead the reader through the important elements of the appraisal, including the conclusions of the appraisal, in an orderly and systematic format.

Quiz

1. **Which statement regarding appraisal competency in a Fannie Mae assignment is TRUE?**

   a. The appraiser does not need experience in the subject's geographical location.

   b. The appraiser may disclose the lack of competence prior to acceptance of an assignment and then gain competence during the assignment.

   c. Fannie Mae selects and approves individual competent appraisers.

   d. Lenders cannot engage an appraiser if the appraiser does not already have the necessary knowledge and experience for the assignment.

2. **Which statement regarding an assignment's scope of work for an appraisal using the URAR reporting form is TRUE?**

   a. The scope of work can be applied to both mortgage and non-mortgage transactions; the scope of work is the same in either assignment.

   b. The scope of work contained within the report cannot be materially altered or lessened.

   c. The scope of work may be dictated or limited by the reporting form used.

   d. The scope of work (or the certification) within the report cannot be expanded or added to.

3. **According to Fannie Mae guidelines, which is an unacceptable appraiser practice?**

   a. basing adjustments to reflect the market's reaction to differences between the subject and comparable sales

   b. commenting on negative factors regarding the subject neighborhood, subject property, or proximity of the subject to negative influences

   c. non-compliance with USPAP in developing or reporting an appraisal

   d. not performing an interior inspection of comparable sales used in an appraisal

4. **When working with property owners who are potential sellers, the process used by real estate brokers and agents for establishing a recommended listing price by comparing the subject property to other homes that have sold, are presently for sale, or did not sell in a given area is a(n)**

   a. appraisal.

   b. appraisal review.

   c. broker price opinion.

   d. competitive market analysis.

5. **A wealthy philanthropist owns property zoned as residential. He wants to donate the property for the construction of a charity hospital. Can a hospital be built on this property?**

   a. No, because area variances are illegal in most states.

   b. No, because even a non-profit hospital is considered a commercial use, not a residential use.

   c. Yes, because it is a nonconforming use.

   d. Yes, if the zoning board or planning commission issues a conditional use permit for the project.

6. **A section of the neighborhood has recently been re-zoned for only residential use. Chris' store is located in this section, but she will be allowed to continue use of the property as a store. This is known as a(n)**

   a. area variance.

   b. conditional use.

   c. grandfathered nonconforming use.

   d. variance.

7. **Pat owns an undeveloped property in a commercial zone, which the city later rezones to allow only residential use. The worth of Pat's property for residential development would be $100,000, while its worth for commercial development would have been $500,000. Regarding this situation, what statement is TRUE?**

   a. Pat must apply for an area variance so the land will be grandfathered under the old zoning laws and, thus, permit commercial development.

   b. Since Pat did not develop the land before the zoning change, he can use the property only for residential use.

   c. Since Pat owned the land before the zoning change, he can develop the property commercially as a non-conforming use.

   d. This zoning law is unconstitutional, because it prevents Pat from putting the property to its most profitable use.

8. **When altering or converting existing commercial structures, the ADA does NOT require compliance with regulations regarding**

   a. exterior accessibility.

   b. exterior paint color.

   c. parking.

   d. telephones.

9. *Due to the specialized nature of some commercial structures, they might experience incurable functional obsolescence*

   a. because they deteriorate more quickly due to intensive use.
   b. due to a change in neighborhood use.
   c. more rapidly than residential structures.
   d. very rarely, because they are used only for business purposes.

10. *A tenant planted crops that will not be ready to harvest until September, although the property transferred to new ownership in August. In this case, the crops are considered*

   a. emblements.
   b. fixtures.
   c. intangible assets.
   d. trade fixtures.

11. *Trade fixtures are items*

   a. only found in non-residential properties.
   b. that accompany the property upon transfer.
   c. traded as part of a sale agreement.
   d. usually associated with a business or profession operating in or on a property.

12. *In an appraisal of a commercial property for a going-concern value, which would be considered an intangible asset?*

   a. established business
   b. personal property
   c. real estate
   d. trade fixture

13. *Regarding a building, the superstructure is*

   a. the above-grade area of a building.
   b. built to withstand intense elements.
   c. more than is needed for the highest and best use.
   d. an overimprovement for the area.

14. *Which would most likely NOT be considered a trade fixture?*

   a. floor coverings
   b. shelving
   c. sign
   d. special equipment

15. *If an appraiser has the competency to appraise all tangible assets, he has the knowledge and experience to perform appraisal services for*

   a. all real and personal property.
   b. business assets and equipment.
   c. real property only.
   d. stocks and other business assets.

16. *For an appraisal report in a narrative format, which is a permitted option(s) for an appraiser to use?*

   a. Appraisal Report only
   b. Narrative Appraisal Report only
   c. Restricted Appraisal Report only
   d. Either the Appraisal Report or Restricted Appraisal Report option

17. *A home was listed on September 1st for $159,900. It is sold on December 1st for $154,000. The opinion of value developed by the appraiser is $156,000. What amount is the market price?*

   a. $154,000
   b. $156,000
   c. $159,900
   d. $154,000 to $159,900

18. *What is NOT a characteristic of an arm's length transaction?*

   a. The buyer obtained a mortgage through a lender.
   b. The buyer paid cash at closing.
   c. The buyer was not knowledgeable of the market.
   d. The transaction was made without undue duress or haste.

19. *In addition to appraisals performed by appraisers, relocation companies often engage real estate agents to perform a BPO, which focuses more on the property's marketability. BPO is the synonym for*

   a. Bank Price Opinion.
   b. Bank Principal Offer.
   c. Broker Price Opinion.
   d. Broker Principal Offer.

20. *If an appraiser develops and communicates an opinion regarding the quality of another appraiser's work, he is conducting a(n)*

   a. appraisal review.
   b. broker price opinion.
   c. competitive market analysis.
   d. forecasting analysis.

Chapter 9

Overview of Reporting Forms

I n this chapter, the most commonly used reporting forms will be presented, including the Uniform Residential Appraisal Report (URAR), which was briefly introduced in Chapter 8. Certain components, procedures, and the purposes for its use will be overviewed. Appraisal reporting forms for exterior inspection-only and other property types will also be introduced. Finally, specific reporting forms and reporting compliance obligations for an appraisal review will be discussed.

Recertification of Value Performed to confirm whether or not the conditions of a prior appraisal have been met.

Uniform Appraisal Dataset (UAD) Defines all fields required for an appraisal submission for specific appraisal forms and standardizes definitions and responses for a key subset of fields to enhance data quality and promote consistency.

Residential Appraisal Report Forms

There are numerous appraisal forms available from various sources and integrated with most appraisal software products. Many of these forms were developed collaboratively by Fannie Mae and Freddie Mac for use *only* with a mortgage finance transaction. Other forms may be labeled as "general purpose" forms and may be used for intended uses other than financing. These reporting forms and formats communicate the appraiser's opinions and conclusions in various assignments. Some of the reporting forms used primarily for mortgage lending may be specified by the client and the appraiser may agree to the use, based on the level of risk perceived by the lender. Other forms are specific to a particular appraisal discipline, such as an appraisal review, or for alternative property types, such as manufactured homes or condominiums. While the reporting forms illustrated in this chapter are not all-inclusive of every type of residential reporting form that could be chosen, many of the most common appraisal reporting forms will be highlighted. Only partial illustrations and excerpts are illustrated with this disucssion. The forms discussed in the chapter are presented in their entirety in the Appendix of this textbook.

The Uniform Residential Appraisal Report

As was discussed in Chapter 8, the Uniform Residential Appraisal Report is the most common reporting form employed for appraising residential properties for use by a lender client. The form is a six-page report and provides an orderly and systematic flow of information and commentary. The form is commonly known in the appraisal industry as the URAR, and is more formally referred to as *Fannie Mae Form 1004/ Freddie Mac Form 70*. Many others within the real property lending industry have also adopted use of the form, such as FHA and VA, as well as smaller primary lenders. It is suggested the entire form be reviewed in the Appendix of this textbook to view the entire contents of the reporting form.

Uniform Residential Appraisal Report   File

The purpose of this summary appraisal report is to provide the lender/client with an accurate, and adequately supported, opinion of the market value of the subject property.

SUBJECT

Property Address	City — State — Zip Code
Borrower	Owner of Public Record — County
Legal Description	
Assessor's Parcel #	Tax Year — R.E. Taxes $
Neighborhood Name	Map Reference — Census Tract
Occupant ☐ Owner ☐ Tenant ☐ Vacant	Special Assessments $ — ☐ PUD — HOA $ — ☐ per year ☐ per month
Property Rights Appraised ☐ Fee Simple ☐ Leasehold ☐ Other (describe)	
Assignment Type ☐ Purchase Transaction ☐ Refinance Transaction ☐ Other (describe)	
Lender/Client — Address	

Is the subject property currently offered for sale or has it been offered for sale in the twelve months prior to the effective date of this appraisal? ☐ Yes ☐ No
Report data source(s) used, offering price(s), and date(s).

CONTRACT

I ☐ did ☐ did not analyze the contract for sale for the subject purchase transaction. Explain the results of the analysis of the contract for sale or why the analysis was not performed.

Contract Price $ — Date of Contract — Is the property seller the owner of public record? ☐Yes ☐No Data Source(s)
Is there any financial assistance (loan charges, sale concessions, gift or downpayment assistance, etc.) to be paid by any party on behalf of the borrower? ☐ Yes ☐ No
If Yes, report the total dollar amount and describe the items to be paid.

NEIGHBORHOOD

Note: Race and the racial composition of the neighborhood are not appraisal factors.

Neighborhood Characteristics	One-Unit Housing Trends	One-Unit Housing		Present Land Use %	
Location ☐ Urban ☐ Suburban ☐ Rural	Property Values ☐ Increasing ☐ Stable ☐ Declining	PRICE	AGE	One-Unit	%
Built-Up ☐ Over 75% ☐ 25–75% ☐ Under 25%	Demand/Supply ☐ Shortage ☐ In Balance ☐ Over Supply	$ (000)	(yrs)	2-4 Unit	%
Growth ☐ Rapid ☐ Stable ☐ Slow	Marketing Time ☐ Under 3 mths ☐ 3–6 mths ☐ Over 6 mths	Low		Multi-Family	%
Neighborhood Boundaries		High		Commercial	%
		Pred.		Other	%

Neighborhood Description

Market Conditions (including support for the above conclusions)

SITE

Dimensions — Area — Shape — View	
Specific Zoning Classification — Zoning Description	
Zoning Compliance ☐ Legal ☐ Legal Nonconforming (Grandfathered Use) ☐ No Zoning ☐ Illegal (describe)	
Is the highest and best use of the subject property as improved (or as proposed per plans and specifications) the present use? ☐ Yes ☐ No If No, describe	

Utilities	Public	Other (describe)		Public	Other (describe)	Off-site Improvements—Type	Public	Private
Electricity	☐	☐	Water	☐	☐	Street	☐	☐
Gas	☐	☐	Sanitary Sewer	☐	☐	Alley	☐	☐

FEMA Special Flood Hazard Area ☐ Yes ☐ No FEMA Flood Zone — FEMA Map # — FEMA Map Date
Are the utilities and off-site improvements typical for the market area? ☐ Yes ☐ No If No, describe
Are there any adverse site conditions or external factors (easements, encroachments, environmental conditions, land uses, etc.)? ☐ Yes ☐ No If Yes, describe

The URAR report form is considered an *Appraisal Report,* designed to report an appraisal of a one-unit property or a one-unit property with an accessory unit, including a unit in a planned unit development (PUD), based on an *interior and exterior inspection* of the subject property. This report form is **not** designed to report an appraisal of a manufactured home or a unit in a condominium or cooperative project.

In becoming familiar with the contents of the URAR, the first discussion should evolve around pages 4-6 of the form. This content commences with a discussion of the general use of the form and then continues with the reporting information necessary for USPAP compliance. These sections should be recognizable as some of the major reporting requirements of USPAP:

- Scope of Work
- Intended Use
- Intended User
- Definition of Market Value
- Statement of Assumptions and Limiting Conditions
- Appraiser's Certification
- Supervisory Appraiser's Certification

General Use Provisions of the URAR

The general use provisions of the URAR generally set forth the types of property for which the reporting form is applicable and are an overview of certain aspects of the assignment. The provisions also discuss the unacceptability of modifications, additions, or deletions to those assignment elements with the exception of the scope of work, which may be expanded. Similar limitations are also imposed regarding the appraiser's certification, with the exception of additions to the certification that are required by law or specific requirements of an appraisal organization to which the appraiser must observe membership requirements related to the certification.

> This report form is designed to report an appraisal of a one-unit property or a one-unit property with an accessory unit; including a unit in a planned unit development (PUD). This report form is not designed to report an appraisal of a manufactured home or a unit in a condominium or cooperative project.
>
> This appraisal report is subject to the following scope of work, intended use, intended user, definition of market value, statement of assumptions and limiting conditions, and certifications. Modifications, additions, or deletions to the intended use, intended user, definition of market value, or assumptions and limiting conditions are not permitted. The appraiser may expand the scope of work to include any additional research or analysis necessary based on the complexity of this appraisal assignment. Modifications or deletions to the certifications are also not permitted. However, additional certifications that do not constitute material alterations to this appraisal report, such as those required by law or those related to the appraiser's continuing education or membership in an appraisal organization, are permitted.

Scope of Work

The Scope of Work description establishes the minimum diligence expected of the appraiser regarding inspection, research, verification, analysis, and reporting.

Certainly, the scope of work actually performed by the appraiser will be expanded in many cases from the minimum level described on the form. As well, the disclosure of the scope of work should include additional commentary from the appraiser to sufficiently communicate the extent of the research and analysis performed in the assignment. The Scope of Work Rule of USPAP requires the disclosure in the appraisal report to contain sufficient information to allow intended users to understand the scope of work performed.

Fannie Mae guidelines acknowledge that while the appraisal process may be guided by the form, the form does not limit or control the appraisal process. **The appraiser's analysis should go beyond any limitations of the form, and should be expanded with additional comments and exhibits in the**

report when needed to adequately describe the subject property, document the analysis and valuation process, or support the appraiser's conclusions.

SCOPE OF WORK: The scope of work for this appraisal is defined by the complexity of this appraisal assignment and the reporting requirements of this appraisal report form, including the following definition of market value, statement of assumptions and limiting conditions, and certifications. The appraiser must, at a minimum: (1) perform a complete visual inspection of the interior and exterior areas of the subject property, (2) inspect the neighborhood, (3) inspect each of the comparable sales from at least the street, (4) research, verify, and analyze data from reliable public and/or private sources, and (5) report his or her analysis, opinions, and conclusions in this appraisal report.

Intended Use

The Intended Use statement satisfies the USPAP requirement to state the intended use(s) of the report. The existence of this statement, integral with the form, makes using this form for other non-financing uses (e.g., marketing, estates, litigation) unacceptable.

INTENDED USE: The intended use of this appraisal report is for the lender/client to evaluate the property that is the subject of this appraisal for a mortgage finance transaction.

Intended User

Satisfying USPAP requirements to state the intended user, the Intended User statement, in this case, is predetermined to be the lender/client. Again, this specification eliminates the use of this form for other non-financing uses and users.

INTENDED USER: The intended user of this appraisal report is the lender/client.

Definition of Market Value

There are innumerable ways to define market value. The Definition of Market Value section illustrates the most commonly used and described method. The discussion continues with how adjustments for financing terms and concessions should be handled.

DEFINITION OF MARKET VALUE: The most probable price which a property should bring in a competitive and open market under all conditions requisite to a fair sale, the buyer and seller, each acting prudently, knowledgeably and assuming the price is not affected by undue stimulus. Implicit in this definition is the consummation of a sale as of a specified date and the passing of title from seller to buyer under conditions whereby: (1) buyer and seller are typically motivated; (2) both parties are well informed or well advised, and each acting in what he or she considers his or her own best interest; (3) a reasonable time is allowed for exposure in the open market; (4) payment is made in terms of cash in U. S. dollars or in terms of financial arrangements comparable thereto; and (5) the price represents the normal consideration for the property sold unaffected by special or creative financing or sales concessions* granted by anyone associated with the sale.

*Adjustments to the comparables must be made for special or creative financing or sales concessions. No adjustments are necessary for those costs which are normally paid by sellers as a result of tradition or law in a market area; these costs are readily identifiable since the seller pays these costs in virtually all sales transactions. Special or creative financing adjustments can be made to the comparable property by comparisons to financing terms offered by a third party institutional lender that is not already involved in the property or transaction. Any adjustment should not be calculated on a mechanical dollar for dollar cost of the financing or concession but the dollar amount of any adjustment should approximate the market's reaction to the financing or concessions based on the appraiser's judgment.

Statement of Assumptions and Limiting Conditions

The Statement of Assumptions and Limiting Conditions assists the appraiser in establishing the limitations of responsibility on the part of the appraiser. Some elements also further emphasize the scope of work performed in the assignment, such as providing a sketch of the improvements, research of flood information, and other notes regarding any unfavorable conditions found, or not found, within the subject property.

Appraiser's Certification

The Appraiser's Certification is contained within the URAR form on pages 5 and 6. The Certification satisfies the minimum requirements of USPAP and then expands the certification statements to a more specific and greater level. The Certification contains 25 statements. Examples of those statements include (but are not limited to):

- Specific methodology used in the assignment and, unless otherwise indicated, that the cost approach was not developed
- Analysis and reporting of offerings and any current sales agreement of the subject property
- Research, verification, analysis, and reporting of prior sales of the comparable data
- Process of selecting and analyzing comparable sales data
- Techniques for adjusting comparable sales
- Competency in the assignment

Due to the preprinted and expanded language in the Appraiser's Certification contained in this form (as well as other forms), appraisers should be very familiar with the certification's content and meaning *prior* to affixing their signature. **No content in the certification may be deleted or modified**. However, to accommodate required certifications mentioned in the general provisions and certain disclosures required by USPAP, an "Additional Certifications" page may need to be added to the report.

Items that may need to be added for USPAP compliance include:

- Whether the appraiser has, or has not, provided any services as an appraiser, or in any other capacity, regarding the subject property performed *within the prior three-year period* immediately proceeding acceptance of the assignment
- Specific name(s) of individuals *not* signing the certification who provided significant professional assistance in the assignment
- Any fees, commissions, or things of value that were paid by the appraiser in connection with procurement of the assignment

Required Exhibits

There are several exhibits that are **required** to be attached to the URAR form:

- An exterior building sketch that indicates the dimensions.
- If the floor plan is atypical or functionally obsolete, thus limiting the market appeal for the property in comparison to competitive properties in the neighborhood, a floor plan sketch is required.
- Calculations demonstrating how the estimate for gross living area is derived.
- A street map that shows the location of the subject property and of all comparables that the appraiser used.
- Clear, descriptive, original photographs showing the front, back, and a street scene of the subject property and the front of each comparable sale.
- The subject and all comparables must be appropriately identified. Acceptable photographs include clear, descriptive, original images from photographs or electronic images, copies of photographs from an MLS, or copies from the appraiser's files.
- Interior photographs that must, at a minimum, include:
  - The kitchen
  - All bathrooms
  - Main living area
  - Examples of physical deterioration, if present
  - Examples of recent updates, such as restoration, remodeling, and renovation, if present
- Any other pertinent information related to the property.
- Any other data—as an attachment or addendum to the appraisal report form—that are necessary to provide an adequately supported opinion of market value.

Market Conditions Addendum

A Market Conditions Addendum is required to accompany the URAR form for all appraisals for use by Fannie Mae and Freddie Mac. The form is more formally known as Fannie Mae Form 1004MC and Freddie Mac Form 71. A reproduction of the form can be found in the Appendix of this text.

While the reporting format may exceed the level common in many residential appraisal assignments, the analysis required to develop the appraiser's opinions should not be entirely new. Correctly analyzing most of these factors is embedded in the appraiser's obligation in compliance with Standards Rule 1-3 of USPAP.

The Market Conditions Addendum form is intended to provide the lender with a clear and accurate understanding of the market trends and conditions prevalent in the subject neighborhood. The form provides the appraiser with a structured format to report the data and to more easily identify current market trends and conditions. The appraiser's conclusions are to be reported in the "Neighborhood" section of the appraisal report.

Fannie Mae and Freddie Mac recognize that all of the requested data elements for analysis are not equally available in all markets. In some markets, it may not be possible to retrieve the total number of comparable active listings from earlier periods. If this is the case, the appraiser must explain the attempt to obtain such information. Also, there may be markets in which the data is available in terms of an "average" as opposed to a "median." In this case, the appraiser needs to note that his analysis has been based on an "average" representation of the data. Regardless of whether all requested information is available, the appraiser must provide support for his conclusions regarding market trends and conditions.

Market Conditions Addendum to the Appraisal Report   File No.

The purpose of this addendum is to provide the lender/client with a clear and accurate understanding of the market trends and conditions prevalent in the subject neighborhood. This is a required addendum for all appraisal reports with an effective date on or after April 1, 2009.

Property Address		City		State	ZIP Code
Borrower					

Instructions: The appraiser must use the information required on this form as the basis for his/her conclusions, and must provide support for those conclusions, regarding housing trends and overall market conditions as reported in the Neighborhood section of the appraisal report form. The appraiser must fill in all the information to the extent it is available and reliable and must provide analysis as indicated below. If any required data is unavailable or is considered unreliable, the appraiser must provide an explanation. It is recognized that not all data sources will be able to provide data for the shaded areas below; if it is available, however, the appraiser must include the data in the analysis. If data sources provide the required information as an average instead of the median, the appraiser should report the available figure and identify it as an average. Sales and listings must be properties that compete with the subject property, determined by applying the criteria that would be used by a prospective buyer of the subject property. The appraiser must explain any anomalies in the data, such as seasonal markets, new construction, foreclosures, etc.

Inventory Analysis	Prior 7–12 Months	Prior 4–6 Months	Current – 3 Months	Overall Trend		
Total # of Comparable Sales (Settled)				☐ Increasing	☐ Stable	☐ Declining
Absorption Rate (Total Sales/Months)				☐ Increasing	☐ Stable	☐ Declining
Total # of Comparable Active Listings				☐ Declining	☐ Stable	☐ Increasing
Months of Housing Supply (Total Listings/Ab.Rate)				☐ Declining	☐ Stable	☐ Increasing
Median Sale & List Price, DOM, Sale/List %	Prior 7–12 Months	Prior 4–6 Months	Current – 3 Months	Overall Trend		
Median Comparable Sale Price				☐ Increasing	☐ Stable	☐ Declining
Median Comparable Sales Days on Market				☐ Declining	☐ Stable	☐ Increasing
Median Comparable List Price				☐ Increasing	☐ Stable	☐ Declining
Median Comparable Listings Days on Market				☐ Declining	☐ Stable	☐ Increasing
Median Sale Price as % of List Price				☐ Increasing	☐ Stable	☐ Declining
Seller-(developer, builder, etc.) paid financial assistance prevalent? ☐ Yes ☐ No				☐ Declining	☐ Stable	☐ Increasing

Explain in detail the seller concessions trends for the past 12 months (e.g., seller contributions increased from 3% to 5%, increasing use of buydowns, closing costs, condo fees, options, etc.).

(left margin vertical text: MARKET RESEARCH)

Uniform Appraisal Dataset

At the direction of the Federal Housing Finance Agency, Fannie Mae and Freddie Mac developed the **Uniform Appraisal Dataset (UAD)**. According to Fannie Mae, the Uniform Appraisal Dataset *defines all fields required for an appraisal submission for specific appraisal forms and standardizes definitions and responses for a key subset of fields to enhance data quality and promote consistency.* The purpose of the UAD is to improve the quality and consistency of appraisal data on loans delivered to Fannie Mae and Freddie Mac, which are considered **Government Sponsored Enterprises (GSEs)**. Other lending entities and clients may also require the application of UAD reporting procedures. So, in many, if not most cases, the UAD reporting requirements apply.

UAD Reporting Requirements

The URAR form must be completed in compliance with the UAD standards for the appraisal of single-family residential properties, including condominiums. The requirements apply for appraisal assignments in which there is an interior and exterior inspection, as well as those with only an exterior inspection. The UAD is required when using these four specific appraisal forms:

UAD REQUIRED FORMS		
UAD Form	**Fannie Mae Form**	**Freddie Mac Form**
Uniform Residential Appraisal Report (URAR)	1004	70
Individual Condominium Unit Appraisal Report	1073	465
Exterior-Only Inspection Residential Appraisal Report	2055	2055
Exterior-Only Inspection Individual Condominium Unit Appraisal Report	1075	466

UAD Data Fields

Many of the data fields in the UAD forms are limited to certain choices. There are checkboxes, pick lists, and drop-down boxes populated with prescribed responses or input formats. Appraisal software providers have developed programs that conform to these requirements.

Here are some examples of data entry requirements:

- **Address** – Must conform to United States Postal Service standards
- **Subject Offering Dates and Prices** – Must comply with specific standard
- **Sale Type** – Drop-down list with specific choices
- **View from Property** – Drop-down list with specific choices
- **Condition of Property** – Specific rating from C1 to C6
- **Quality of Construction** – Specific rating from Q1 to Q6

Courses with a concentration on residential report writing fully discuss and illustrate the UAD reporting requirements.

Other Appraisal Forms and Reports

There are several other common appraisal forms used to communicate an appraisal of residential real property for a mortgage finance transaction. In most cases, the key differences between the particular form and the Uniform Residential Appraisal Report (URAR) will be discussed.

Form 2055, Exterior-Only Inspection Residential Appraisal Report

Fannie Mae/Freddie Mac *Form 2055, Exterior-Only Inspection Residential Appraisal Report*, is designed for reporting an exterior-only appraisal of a single-family dwelling, including planned unit developments

(PUDs), but not manufactured homes. The form may **not** be used for condominiums or cooperative units.

Much of Form 2055 is similar to the URAR reporting form; however, there are some key differences.

Exterior-Only Inspection Residential Appraisal Report   File

The purpose of this summary appraisal report is to provide the lender/client with an accurate, and adequately supported, opinion of the market value of the subject property.		

SUBJECT

Property Address	City / State / Zip Code
Borrower	Owner of Public Record / County
Legal Description	
Assessor's Parcel #	Tax Year / R.E. Taxes $
Neighborhood Name	Map Reference / Census Tract
Occupant ☐ Owner ☐ Tenant ☐ Vacant	Special Assessments $ / ☐ PUD HOA $ ☐ per year ☐ per month
Property Rights Appraised ☐ Fee Simple ☐ Leasehold ☐ Other (describe)	
Assignment Type ☐ Purchase Transaction ☐ Refinance Transaction ☐ Other (describe)	
Lender/Client	Address
Is the subject property currently offered for sale or has it been offered for sale in the twelve months prior to the effective date of this appraisal? ☐ Yes ☐ No	
Report data source(s) used, offering price(s), and date(s).	

CON

I ☐ did ☐ did not analyze the contract for sale for the subject purchase transaction. Explain the results of the analysis of the contract for sale or why the analysis was not performed.

Scope of Work

The scope of work required during the development process when Form 2055 is being used for reporting is very similar to that required for the URAR. The form spells out that the appraiser must, at a minimum:

- Perform a visual inspection of the exterior areas of the subject property from the street.

- Inspect the neighborhood.

- Inspect each of the comparable sales from the street.

- Research, verify, and analyze data from reliable public and/or private sources.

- Report the analysis, opinions, and conclusions in the appraisal report.

The scope of work that is integral to Form 2055 indicates that the appraiser is *only* inspecting the exterior of the subject property from the street. There is additional instruction, unique to Form 2055, which specifies requirements for the appraiser in performing an appraisal utilizing the form:

> *"The appraiser must be able to obtain adequate information about the physical characteristics (including, but not limited to, condition, room count, gross living area, etc.) of the subject property from the exterior-only inspection and from reliable public and/or private sources to perform this appraisal. The appraiser should use the same type of data sources that he or she uses for comparable sales such as, but not limited to, multiple listing services, tax and assessment records, prior inspections, appraisal files, information provided by the property owner, etc."*

Since the integrity and accuracy of the data obtained from most of these sources is believed to reflect the actual state of the portions of the property that the appraiser cannot see firsthand, the use of an extraordinary assumption would be appropriate. As we discussed in Chapter 1, when an appraiser employs an extraordinary assumption in the development process, its use must be appropriately disclosed in the appraisal report, per Standards Rule 2-2.

Obtaining Information for the 2055 Exterior-Only Report

The 2055 exterior-only drive-by residential appraisal report has a very specific scope of work that has to be completed. Within the Scope of Work section, it specifies that the appraiser must be able to obtain adequate information about the physical characteristics including, but not limited to, condition, room count, gross living area, etc. of the subject property from the exterior-only inspection and from reliable public or private sources to perform this appraisal. The appraiser should use the same type of data sources that he or she uses for comparable sales data such as, but not limited to, multiple listing services, tax and assessment records, prior inspections, appraisal files, information provided by the property owner, etc. Sometimes, that scope of work needs to be expanded in exterior-only assignments. For example, in a drive-by appraisal, if the appraiser is unable to adequately view the property, such as in a rural setting, and the land characteristics and/or the improvements are not fully visible from the street, credible results may not occur without the appraiser getting more information. The appraiser could consult with the property owner, or obtain information from another source, such as assessment records or the Multiple Listing Service. Of course, in using such information provided by a third party, including the property owner, an extraordinary assumption would likely be needed to address the quality and accuracy of the data. It may be determined that the property owner's word (or other source) may not be relied upon sufficiently to produce credible results. And therefore, in that particular case, the scope of work may need to be expanded to include an interior inspection of the property. Sometimes, the client will readily agree to such a request and other times, they may refuse access for the expanded inspection. In such case, when there is a question regarding assignment results being credible with the use of an extraordinary assumption, the appraiser's only recourse is to withdraw from the assignment.

If data is obtained from the property owner, from public sources, or even from prior appraisal files, the appraiser must be very cautious. One of the appraiser's options is to use an extraordinary assumption. Even if the appraiser is relying on data contained in a prior appraisal file, there is a degree of uncertainty as to whether the property conditions or the information gathered in a prior inspection still reflect the true property characteristics as they are on the effective date of the current assignment. Or, if information is obtained from public sources, sometimes those records are not truly accurate, so extraordinary assumptions may need to be made about their accuracy. In most drive-by exterior assignments, extraordinary assumptions will be required.

Statement of Assumptions and Limiting Conditions

The Statement of Assumptions and Limiting Conditions on page 4 of Form 2055 is very similar to the corresponding section in the URAR. All assumptions and conditions are the same, with the exception of Form 2055, removing the statement regarding the sketch of the subject dwelling. The appraiser is **not** required to provide a sketch, since the appraiser did not enter the premises to determine the exact layout of the property.

As with the URAR, the appraiser is **not** held responsible for legal matters affecting the property, nor is the appraiser expected to give testimony in court about the appraisal, *unless arrangements are made beforehand*. The appraiser must certify that he has examined available flood maps and noted in his appraisal any adverse conditions that may affect the property. Aside from those things noted in the appraisal report, the appraiser makes the assumption that there are no hidden or unapparent deficiencies present that would lower the property's value. If any repairs are noted or required, the appraiser will assume that they will be performed in a professional manner. The appraiser does **not** make *any guarantees about the property*, nor does the appraiser assume any liability for items that are unknown at the time of the appraisal or that could only be discovered by a person with specific expertise in a given discipline.

Appraiser's Certification

The Appraiser's Certification on page 5 of Form 2055 is also very similar to the corresponding section in the URAR. The Appraiser's Certification and the Supervisory Appraiser's Certification are the same, with the exception that Form 2055 removes any statements that refer to inspecting the interior of the subject property. Like the URAR, the certification statements detail actions that the appraiser performed in developing an opinion of value for the subject property.

Small Residential Income Property Appraisal Report

The *Small Residential Income Property Appraisal Report*, Fannie Mae *Form 1025*/Freddie Mac *Form 72*, is the **most common reporting form used for reporting the appraisal of a two- to four-family property** for use by a lender client. This seven-page report form provides an orderly and systematic flow of information and commentary.

While the 1025/72 form was developed for use by Fannie Mae and Freddie Mac, it has been adopted for use by other lending entities such as the FHA, VA, and other lenders. Although some clients and intended users might have guidelines and requirements that are different than Fannie Mae, most of Fannie Mae's guidelines and requirements represent at least a minimum level of expectations by all lenders.

Small Residential Income Property Appraisal Report File

The purpose of this summary appraisal report is to provide the lender/client with an accurate, and adequately supported, opinion of the market value of the subject property.

SUBJECT

Property Address	City	State	Zip Code
Borrower	Owner of Public Record	County	
Legal Description			
Assessor's Parcel #	Tax Year	R.E. Taxes $	
Neighborhood Name	Map Reference	Census Tract	
Occupant ☐ Owner ☐ Tenant ☐ Vacant	Special Assessments $	☐ PUD HOA $	☐ per year ☐ per month
Property Rights Appraised ☐ Fee Simple ☐ Leasehold ☐ Other (describe)			
Assignment Type ☐ Purchase Transaction ☐ Refinance Transaction ☐ Other (describe)			
Lender/Client	Address		
Is the subject property currently offered for sale or has it been offered for sale in the twelve months prior to the effective date of this appraisal? ☐ Yes ☐ No			
Report data source(s) used, offering price(s), and date(s).			

CONTRACT

I ☐ did ☐ did not analyze the contract for sale for the subject purchase transaction. Explain the results of the analysis of the contract for sale or why the analysis was not performed.
Contract Price $ Date of Contract   Is the property seller the owner of public record? ☐Yes ☐No Data Source(s)
Is there any financial assistance (loan charges, sale concessions, gift or downpayment assistance, etc.) to be paid by any party on behalf of the borrower? ☐ Yes ☐ No If Yes, report the total dollar amount and describe the items to be paid.

In the 1025/72 form, the sections on the Scope of Work, Intended Use, Intended User, Definition of Market Value, Appraiser's Certification, and others are consistent with the URAR. **An Operating Income Statement (Fannie Mae Form 216/Freddie Mac Form 998) must be attached to the report** when form 1025/72 is being used. A reproduction of the form is found in the Appendix of this textbook. No UAD reporting requirements are applicable to the Small Residential Income Property Appraisal Report.

Operating Income Statement
One- to Four-Family Investment Property and Two- to Four-Family Owner-Occupied Property

Property Address

Street	City	State	Zip Code

General Instructions: This form is to be prepared jointly by the loan applicant, the appraiser, and the lender's underwriter. The applicant must complete the following schedule indicating each unit's rental status, lease expiration date, current rent, market rent, and the responsibility for utility expenses. Rental figures must be based on the rent for an "unfurnished" unit.

	Currently Rented	Expiration Date	Current Rent Per Month	Market Rent Per Month	Utility Expense	Paid By Owner	Paid By Tenant
Unit No. 1	Yes ____ No ____	_____	$_____	$_____	Electricity............	☐	☐
Unit No. 2	Yes ____ No ____	_____	$_____	$_____	Gas.....................	☐	☐
Unit No. 3	Yes ____ No ____	_____	$_____	$_____	Fuel Oil	☐	☐
Unit No. 4	Yes ____ No ____	_____	$_____	$_____	Fuel (Other)	☐	☐
Total			$_____	$_____	Water/Sewer	☐	☐
					Trash Removal	☐	☐

The applicant should complete all of the income and expense projections and for existing properties provide actual year-end operating statements for the past two years (for new properties the applicant's projected income and expenses must be provided). This Operating

Although much of the contents of the form are similar in content to the URAR form, there are some unique reporting areas:

Comparable Rental Data Section - Much of the data for this section will be derived from comparable market rental data from the appraiser's files, or as part of rent surveys. This analysis is provided in the report to demonstrate support of the appraiser's opinion of market rent for the subject.

The following properties represent the most current, similar, and proximate comparable rental properties to the subject property. This analysis is intended to support the opinion of the market rent for the subject property.

FEATURE	SUBJECT	COMPARABLE RENTAL # 1		COMPARABLE RENTAL # 2		COMPARABLE RENTAL # 3	
Address							
Proximity to Subject							
Current Monthly Rent	$	$		$		$	
Rent/Gross Bldg. Area	$ sq. ft.	$ sq. ft.		$ sq. ft.		$ sq. ft.	
Rent Control	☐ Yes ☐ No	☐ Yes ☐ No		☐ Yes ☐ No		☐ Yes ☐ No	
Data Source(s)							
Date of Lease(s)							
Location							
Actual Age							
Condition							
Gross Building Area							

Unit Breakdown	Rm Count	Size Sq. Ft.	Rm Count	Size Sq. Ft.	Monthly Rent	Rm Count	Size Sq. Ft.	Monthly Rent	Rm Count	Size Sq. Ft.	Monthly Rent
	Tot Br Ba		Tot Br Ba			Tot Br Ba			Tot Br Ba		
Unit # 1					$			$			$
Unit # 2					$			$			$
Unit # 3					$			$			$
Unit # 4					$			$			$
Utilities Included											

Subject Rent Schedule - The reporting here includes the appraiser's opinion of market rent for the subject that is supported from market level comparable rental data. Also in the schedule is the reporting of other sources of income for the subject property in addition to rental income from the living units.

Rent Schedule: The appraiser must reconcile the applicable indicated monthly market rents to provide an opinion of the market rent for each unit in the subject property.

	Leases		Actual Rent			Opinion Of Market Rent		
Unit #	Lease Date		Per Unit		Total	Per Unit		Total
	Begin Date	End Date	Unfurnished	Furnished	Rent	Unfurnished	Furnished	Rent
1			$	$	$	$	$	$
2								
3								
4								
Comment on lease data			Total Actual Monthly Rent		$	Total Gross Monthly Rent		$
			Other Monthly Income (itemize)		$	Other Monthly Income (itemize)		$
			Total Actual Monthly Income		$	Total Estimated Monthly Income		$

Utilities included in estimated rents ☐ Electric ☐ Water ☐ Sewer ☐ Gas ☐ Oil ☐ Cable ☐ Trash collection ☐ Other (describe)

Comments on actual or estimated rents and other monthly income (including personal property)

Sales Comparison Approach Section - This section may seem somewhat similar to that found in the URAR reporting form for single-family properties; however, there are some distinctive differences, including identifying the sale price of the comparable by appropriate unit of comparison (price per square foot, unit, etc.). The appraiser states the gross monthly market rent as well as a gross rent multiplier

(GRM) derived from the data. The appraiser will also report if any rent controls are in place for the subject property or the comparables. Other notable unique elements of the Sales Comparison Approach section of the form are the reporting of gross building area (GBA) and the breakdown of the subject property and the comparable sales by total number of rooms, bedrooms, and baths for each unit. The appraiser states the final adjusted price of the comparable sales per unit, per room, and per bedroom. The appraiser's value indication is then reconciled and stated based upon per unit, per room, per square foot of GBA, and per bedroom by using the quantity of each element present in the subject multiplied by the unit indication produced through analysis of the comparable data.

FEATURE	SUBJECT	COMPARABLE SALE # 1	COMPARABLE SALE # 2	COMPARABLE SALE # 3
Address				
Proximity to Subject				
Sale Price	$	$	$	$
Sale Price/Gross Bldg. Area	$ sq. ft.	$ sq. ft.	$ sq. ft.	$ sq. ft.
Gross Monthly Rent	$	$	$	$
Gross Rent Multiplier				
Price Per Unit	$	$	$	$
Price Per Room	$	$	$	$
Price Per Bedroom	$	$	$	$
Rent Control	☐ Yes ☐ No	☐ Yes ☐ No	☐ Yes ☐ No	☐ Yes ☐ No
Data Source(s)				

Net Adjustment (Total)		☐ + ☐ - $	☐ + ☐ - $	☐ + ☐ - $
Adjusted Sale Price of Comparables		Net Adj. % Gross Adj. % $	Net Adj. % Gross Adj. % $	Net Adj. % Gross Adj. % $
Adj. Price Per Unit (Adj. SP Comp / # of Comp Units)	$	$	$	$
Adj. Price Per Room (Adj. SP Comp / # of Comp Rooms)	$	$	$	$
Adj. Price Per Bedrm (Adj. SP Comp / # of Comp Bedrooms)	$	$	$	$
Value Per Unit	$ _____ X _____ Units = $ _____		Value Per GBA $_____ X _____ GBA = $ _____	
Value Per Rm.	$ _____ X _____ Rooms = $ _____		Value Per Bdrms. $_____ X _____ Bdrms. = $ _____	

Individual Condominium Unit Appraisal Report

Fannie Mae *Form 1073*/Freddie Mac *Form 465*, *Individual Condominium Unit Appraisal Report*, is used for the appraisal of an individual unit in a condominium project, including a condominium that is part of a PUD. This form is **not** designed for valuing cooperative units or for manufactured homes that are part of a project or complex.

The purpose of this summary appraisal report is to provide the lender/client with an accurate, and adequately supported, opinion of the market value of the subject property.
Property Address   Unit #   City   State   Zip Code
Borrower   Owner of Public Record   County
Legal Description
Assessor's Parcel #   Tax Year   R.E. Taxes $
Project Name   Phase #   Map Reference   Census Tract
Occupant ☐ Owner ☐ Tenant ☐ Vacant   Special Assessments $ HOA $ ☐ per year ☐ per month
Property Rights Appraised ☐ Fee Simple ☐ Leasehold ☐ Other (describe)
Assignment Type ☐ Purchase Transaction ☐ Refinance Transaction ☐ Other (describe)
Lender/Client   Address
Is the subject property currently offered for sale or has it been offered for sale in the twelve months prior to the effective date of this appraisal?   ☐ Yes ☐ No
Report data source(s) used, offering price(s), and date(s).
I ☐ did ☐ did not analyze the contract for sale for the subject purchase transaction. Explain the results of the analysis of the contract for sale or why the analysis was not performed.
Contract Price $ Date of Contract   Is the property seller the owner of public record? ☐ Yes ☐ No Data Source(s)

When appraising a condominium unit, the appraiser **performs most of the same steps as in a regular appraisal**. There are some additional project data needed when appraising a condominium, so Fannie Mae and Freddie Mac have developed the Individual Condominium Unit Appraisal Report to ensure that all necessary information is presented in the appraisal report to the lender client.

The Individual Condominium Unit Appraisal Report is similar to the URAR (Form 1004), but the form has additional sections requiring the reporting of details of the entire condominium project. One important difference from the URAR is that *no cost approach is reported (or developed) for condominium units*.

Because of their co-ownership structure, condominium units have unique appraisal requirements. Fannie Mae and Freddie Mac recognize this. **Condominiums** are *properties developed for co-ownership, where each co-owner has a separate interest in an individual unit and an undivided interest in the common areas (grounds, lobby, hallways, etc.) of the property*.

Condominium residents must follow the declarations and bylaws set forth by the founder of the condominium. These bylaws are maintained and enforced by the homeowners association. Most condominiums are designed for residential use. Typical condominiums look like apartments, but residents usually have exclusive ownership of their units. However, as a condominium is a legal concept rather than a design concept, condominiums could also be free-standing units.

Most condominiums have common ownership of some areas. Because of this and the shared external maintenance, the appraiser must report the characteristics of the entire condominium project as a whole, in addition to reporting specific information applicable to subject unit.

Scope of Work

The scope of work specified for Form 1073/465 is similar to that required for the URAR, with some slight variation. The appraiser must, at a minimum:

- Perform a complete visual inspection of the interior and exterior areas of the subject unit.
- Inspect and analyze the condominium project.
- Inspect the neighborhood.
- Inspect each of the comparable sales from the street.
- Research, verify, and analyze data from reliable public and/or private sources.
- Report his or her analysis, opinions, and conclusions in the appraisal report.

Project Information

In addition to specific information about the condominium unit, the appraisal report **requires information related to the project or complex in which the unit is located**. Since the desirability of the unit is also associated with the appeal of the complex, there is an entire section in the appraisal form for clearly reporting sufficient data so that the lender client may understand the subject's project and its characteristics.

Data source(s) for project information				
Project Description ☐ Detached ☐ Row or Townhouse ☐ Garden ☐ Mid-Rise ☐ High-Rise ☐ Other (describe)				
General Description	**General Description**	**Subject Phase**	**If Project Completed**	**If Project Incomplete**
# of Stories	Exterior Walls	# of Units	# of Phases	# of Planned Phases
# of Elevators	Roof Surface	# of Units Completed	# of Units	# o f Planned Units
☐ Existing ☐ Proposed	Total # Parking	# of Units For Sale	# of Units for Sale	# of Units for Sale
☐ Under Construction	Ratio (spaces/units)	# of Units Sold	# of Units Sold	# of Units Sold
Year Built	Type	# of Units Rented	# of Units Rented	# of Units Rented
Effective Age	Guest Parking	# of Owner Occupied Units	# of Owner Occupied Units	# of Owner Occupied Units
Project Primary Occupancy	☐ Principal Residence	☐ Second Home or Recreational	☐ Tenant	

Reporting fields are specific to two categories: *Condition and ownership*. The fields regarding *condition* address the desirability of the subject's condominium project compared to other competing condominium projects in the same market area:

- Was the project created by converting existing buildings into condominiums?
- Are the units, common elements, and recreation facilities complete?
- Is there any commercial space in the project?
- Describe the condition of the project and quality of construction.
- Describe the common elements and recreation facilities.

The reporting fields specific to *ownership* provide the appraiser the opportunity to describe additional measures of desirability within the condominium project. These include the source of fees and the likelihood that they will rise, as well as the owner-occupancy level of the complex. For example:

- Is the developer/builder in control of the homeowners association?
- Does any single entity (individual, investor group, corporation, etc.) own more than 10% of the total number of units in the project?
- Are any common elements leased to or by the homeowners association?
- Is the project subject to ground rent?

Fannie Mae and others will not approve mortgages in condominium complexes where owner-occupancy falls below a specified level. Additionally, details must be reported regarding the current primary occupancy and number of units in various stages of completion for all phases of the condominium project. Finally, fees paid by unit owners are an important aspect of desirability of a condominium. Poor management and budgetary planning or insufficient reserves can lead to sudden fee increases in the future. A major concern of most lender clients is the soundness of the condominium project's management company and that there are enough funds available for future repairs.

Manufactured Home Appraisal Report Form

The *Manufactured Home Appraisal Report* form is known as Fannie Mae *Form 1004C* or Freddie Mac *Form 70B*. The appraisal reporting form is designed for the appraisal of a one-unit manufactured home. This would include a unit located in a planned unit development (PUD). If the manufactured home is part of a condominium project or cooperative, additional information about the project must be supplied on a separate form and attached as an addendum to the reporting form.

Manufactured Home Appraisal Report   File

The purpose of this summary appraisal report is to provide the lender/client with an accurate, and adequately supported, opinion of the market value of the subject property.

(Form fields: Property Address, City, State, Zip Code; Borrower, Owner of Public Record, County; Legal Description; Assessor's Parcel #, Tax Year, R.E. Taxes $; Neighborhood Name, Map Reference, Census Tract; Occupant ☐ Owner ☐ Tenant ☐ Vacant, Project Type (if applicable) ☐ PUD ☐ Condominium ☐ Cooperative ☐ Other (describe); Special Assessments $, HOA $ ☐ per year ☐ per month; Property Rights Appraised ☐ Fee Simple ☐ Leasehold ☐ Other (describe); Assignment Type ☐ Purchase Transaction ☐ Refinance Transaction ☐ Other (describe); Lender/Client, Address; Is the subject property currently offered for sale or has it been offered for sale in the twelve months prior to the effective date of this appraisal? ☐ Yes ☐ No; Report data source(s) used, offering price(s), and date(s).)

Manufactured homes located in either a condominium or cooperative project require the appraiser to inspect the project and complete the Project Information section of the Individual Condominium Unit Appraisal Report or the Individual Cooperative Interest Appraisal Report and attach it as an addendum to this report.

Fannie Mae defines **manufactured housing units** as *single-width or multi-width units constructed off-site and transported to the permanent site*. Once on-site, they are completed and/or attached to the foundation. Under this definition, the dwelling is built to HUD specifications, with a HUD certification label attached and recognized as a manufactured home.

There are no UAD reporting requirements when using the Manufactured Home Appraisal Report. The Scope of Work section as well as the Statement of Assumptions and Limiting Conditions are consistent with other forms that we have discussed, as is the Appraiser's Certification. Required exhibits also are mirrored.

There are several reporting fields on the Manufactured Home Appraisal Report that are unique. These fields require relatively brief "Yes" or "No" responses or explanations, but may have required the appraiser to conduct additional research or investigation during the development process of the appraisal. Most of these fields address the improvements and are focused on having the appraiser **report the permanence of the structure on the site**. These required fields include:

- Is the manufactured home attached to a permanent foundation system?
- Have the towing hitch, wheels, and axles been removed?
- Is the manufactured home permanently connected to a septic tank or sewage system and other utilities?

The appraiser is also asked to **describe any additions or modifications to the structure** (e.g., a deck), and to **rate the quality of construction based on objective criteria**.

The most significant reporting section of the Manufactured Home Appraisal Report form is the HUD Data Plate section. The purpose of this section is to **report data significant to compliance with HUD and local requirements**. The HUD data plate, or compliance certificate, is located on the *interior* of the subject, and the HUD certification label is located on the *exterior* of each section of the home. Both of these contain much of the information needed to complete this section of the form.

One section of Form 1004C that varies from the standard URAR is the Cost section. In calculating the costs of the structure, there is a breakdown of the subject's dimensions by modular section of the home. Thus, the calculations can be performed for each section of single-width or multi-width units independently, with the results added together at the end. There is also a cost field for entering the amount needed for delivery, installation, and setup of the manufactured units. This ensures that all potential replacement costs are considered.

Provide adequate information for the lender/client to replicate the below cost figures and calculations.
Support for the opinion of site value (summary of comparable land sales or other methods for estimating site value)

ESTIMATED ☐ REPRODUCTION OR ☐ REPLACEMENT COST NEW

Source of cost data		Effective date of cost data	Quality rating from cost service		
OPINION OF SITE VALUE		$	Exterior Dimensions of the Subject Unit		
Section One	Sq. ft. @ $	$	X	=	Sq. ft.
Section Two	Sq. ft. @ $	$	X	=	Sq. ft.
Section Three	Sq. ft. @ $	$	X	=	Sq. ft.
Section Four	Sq. ft. @ $	$	X	=	Sq. ft.
		$	Total Gross Living Area:		Sq. ft.
		$	Other Data Identification		
		$	N.A.D.A. Data Identification Info: Edition Mo: Yr:		
Sub-total:		$	MH State: Region: Size: ft. x ft.		
Cost Multiplier (if applicable):		x	Gray pg. White pg. Black SVS pg.		
Modified Sub-total:			15 years and older Conversion Chart pg. Yellow pg.		
Physical Depreciation or Condition Modifier:			Comments		
Functional Obsolescence (not used for N.A.D.A.):					
External Depreciation or State Location Modifier:					
Delivery, Installation, and Setup (not used for N.A.D.A.):		$			
Other Depreciated Site Improvements:		$			
Market Value of Subject Site (as supported above):		$			
Indicated Value by Cost Approach:		$	Estimated Remaining Economic Life (HUD and VA only)		Years
Summary of Cost Approach					

Reporting Forms for Other Purposes

In this section, attention is on the various forms and reporting methods which, while not labeled as an appraisal report, may (or may not) include development of a value opinion by an appraiser.

One-Unit Residential Appraisal Field Review Report Form

Many appraisal review assignments are of the field review variety, which includes an exterior inspection of the subject property, within the review, from the street. The field review form for one-unit residential properties is the *One-Unit Residential Appraisal Field Review Report* (Fannie Mae *Form 2000/*Freddie Mac *Form 1032*). The purpose of this report is to *provide the lender/client with an opinion on the accuracy of the appraisal report under review.*

One-Unit Residential Appraisal Field Review Report   File

The purpose of this appraisal field review report is to provide the lender/client with an opinion on the accuracy of the appraisal report under review.			
Property Address	City	State	Zip Code
Borrower	Owner of Public Record	County	
Legal Description			
Assessor's Parcel #	Map Reference	Census Tract	
Property Rights Appraised ☐ Fee Simple ☐ Leasehold ☐ Other (describe)		Project Type ☐ Condo ☐ PUD ☐ Cooperative	
Loan #	Effective Date of Appraisal Under Review	Manufactured Home ☐ Yes ☐ No	
Lender/Client	Address		

The first page of the form is basically a series of general responses. After completing the information at the top, including the effective date of the original appraisal under review, the appraiser assesses the quality of the original appraisal by filling out Section I on the first page of the review appraisal form. This section consists of a series of "Yes" or "No" responses about the completeness and accuracy of each item on the original appraisal report. Section I must be completed for all review assignments. Many of the "Yes" responses also ask for a brief summary and the "No" responses require an explanation.

One significant difference is found in the certification contained in the report. Per the wording in Certification Statement #10, no individual may provide significant professional assistance to the review appraiser. Thus, an appraisal trainee may **not** gain experience hours if this review form is being used.

Appraisal Update and/or Completion Report

The Appraisal Update and/or Completion Report, *Fannie Mae Form 1004D/Freddie Mac Form 442*, is intended to provide the lender or client with an update of a previously completed appraisal and/or to provide a certificate of completion related to a previous appraisal.

Appraisal Update and/or Completion Report   File

The purpose of this report form is to provide the lender/client with an accurate update of an appraisal and/or to report a certification of completion. The appraiser must identify the service(s) provided by selecting the appropriate report type.		
Property Address		Unit #
City	State	Zip Code
Legal Description		County
Borrower	Contract Price $ Date of Contract	Effective Date of Original Appraisal
Property Rights Appraised ☐ Fee Simple ☐ Leasehold ☐ Other (describe)		Original Appraised Value $
Original Appraiser	Company Name	
Original Lender/Client	Address	

There are a number of situations for which this form is appropriate. Sometimes, this is due to a delayed closing. If a significant amount of time has passed between the effective date of the appraisal and a proposed transaction, the lender or client may require an update to reaffirm the opinion of value presented in the report. There is no set amount of time for this and time limits often vary from one lender to the next.

Another instance where an update appraisal might be provided, instead of a full appraisal, is for recurring valuations. For example, if a lender extends a line of credit based on the value of real estate, a periodic update appraisal may be required as a condition for keeping the line of credit open. This update would be used in lieu of a new appraisal, provided the opinion of value is the same as the original value or falls within a range determined by the lender or client. If the value is thought to have changed significantly, the lender or client might order a new appraisal.

The appraiser performing an appraisal update must complete the information at the top of the form, including the property address, legal description, borrower name, and contract information. The form must also include data referencing the original appraisal report: Effective date, original appraised value, original appraiser, and original lender or client.

The scope of work preprinted in the report form states that the appraiser must, at a minimum:

- Concur with the original appraisal.

- Perform an exterior inspection of the subject property from the street.

- Research, verify, and analyze the current market to determine if the property has declined in value since the effective date of the original appraisal.

If the appraiser indicates that he concurs with the value opinion found in the original appraisal report, that opinion must be developed in compliance with STANDARD 1 of USPAP. The appraisal update report must also include a summary of the development process undertaken by the appraiser to support the concurrence.

The simple act of checking the "Yes or "No" box, in response to any decline in value of the subject property, is the result of the appraiser developing that opinion in compliance with STANDARD 1.

■ SUMMARY APPRAISAL UPDATE REPORT
INTENDED USE: The intended use of this appraisal update is for the lender/client to evaluate the property that is the subject of this report to determine if the property has declined in value since the date of the original appraisal for a mortgage finance transaction.
INTENDED USER: The intended user of this appraisal update is the lender/client.
SCOPE OF WORK: The appraiser must, at a minimum: (1) concur with the original appraisal, (2) perform an exterior inspection of the subject property from at least the street, and (3) research, verify, and analyze current market data in order to determine if the property has declined in value since the effective date of the original appraisal.
HAS THE MARKET VALUE OF THE SUBJECT PROPERTY DECLINED SINCE THE EFFECTIVE DATE OF THE ORIGINAL APPRAISAL? ☐Yes ☐No
APPRAISER'S CERTIFICATION: The appraiser certifies and agrees that: 1. I have, at a minimum, developed and reported this appraisal update in accordance with the scope of work requirements stated in this appraisal update report and concur with the analysis and conclusions in the original appraisal. 2. I performed this appraisal update in accordance with the requirements of the Uniform Standards of Professional Appraisal Practice that were adopted and promulgated by the Appraisal Standards Board of The Appraisal Foundation and that were in place at the time this appraisal update was prepared. 3. I have updated the appraisal by incorporating the original appraisal report. 4. I have summarized my analysis and conclusions in this appraisal update and retained all supporting data in my work file.
SUPERVISORY APPRAISER'S CERTIFICATION: The Supervisory Appraiser certifies and agrees that: 1. I directly supervised the appraiser for this appraisal update assignment, have read the appraisal update report, and agree with the appraiser's analysis, opinions, statements, conclusions, and the appraiser's certification. 2. I accept full responsibility for the contents of this appraisal update report including, but not limited to, the appraiser's analysis, opinions, statements, conclusions, and the appraiser's certification.

The Certificate of Completion section of the report provides for the appraiser to confirm that any requirements or conditions stated in the original appraisal report have been met. Note that the certification statements state the appraiser has performed a "visual inspection" of the property—interior or exterior is not specified, as that depends on the conditions in the original appraisal. Photographs are required addenda for new construction and may be appropriate in other circumstances.

■ CERTIFICATION OF COMPLETION
INTENDED USE: The intended use of this certification of completion is for the lender/client to confirm that the requirements or conditions stated in the appraisal report referenced above have been met.
INTENDED USER: The intended user of this certification of completion is the lender/client.
HAVE THE IMPROVEMENTS BEEN COMPLETED IN ACCORDANCE WITH THE REQUIREMENTS AND CONDITIONS STATED IN THE ORIGINAL APPRAISAL REPORT? ☐ Yes ☐ No If No, describe any impact on the opinion of market value.
APPRAISER'S CERTIFICATION: I certify that I have performed a visual inspection of the subject property to determine if the conditions or requirements stated in the original appraisal have been satisfied.
SUPERVISORY APPRAISER'S CERTIFICATION: I accept full responsibility for this certification of completion.

Often, appraisers are requested to update or recertify the value from an appraisal report that was previously completed. Appraisers should be aware that these concepts are considered to be very different within the context of USPAP. Appraisal updates and recertification of value are discussed in USPAP Advisory Opinion 3. An excerpt from the Advisory Opinion describes the differences:

> The term "Recertification of Value" is often mistakenly used by some clients in lieu of the term "Update." A Recertification of Value is performed to confirm whether or not the conditions of a prior appraisal have been met. A Recertification of Value does not change the effective date of the value opinion. If a client uses this term in an assignment request that includes an updated value opinion, then it constitutes a new appraisal assignment that must be completed as discussed…(in Advisory Opinion 3).

In other words, a recertification of value might be most commonly used during the final completion inspection performed for a property that was appraised "subject to completion," or for repairs that have now been completed, which were only proposed at the time of the appraisal. In an updated appraisal, the value opinion found in the prior appraisal must either be affirmed or a new value opinion is developed. In such case, the appraiser's opinion of concurrence or disagreement must be developed in accordance with STANDARD 1.

Summary

1. Fannie Mae guidelines acknowledge that while the appraisal process may be guided by the URAR (or any appraisal form designed for their use), the form does not limit or control the appraisal process. The appraiser's analysis should go beyond any limitations of the form, and should be expanded with additional comments and exhibits in the report.

2. The Intended Use and Intended Users statements found within the forms satisfy the USPAP requirement to state the intended use(s) and intended user(s) of the report. The existence of this statement, integral with the forms, makes using them for other non-financing related uses unacceptable.

3. Certification statements found in Fannie Mae report forms satisfy the minimum requirements of USPAP, then proceed to expand the certification statements to a more specific and greater level.

4. The Market Conditions Addendum is required to accompany the URAR form for all appraisals for use by Fannie Mae and Freddie Mac. The form is intended to provide the lender with a clear and accurate understanding of the market trends and conditions prevalent in the subject neighborhood in a structured manner.

5. The Uniform Appraisal Dataset (UAD) defines all fields required for an appraisal submission for specific appraisal forms and standardizes definitions and responses for a key subset of fields to enhance data quality and promote consistency. The purpose of the UAD is to improve the quality and consistency of appraisal data on loans delivered to Fannie Mae and Freddie Mac.

6. The 2055 exterior-only drive-by residential appraisal report specifies that the appraiser must be able to obtain adequate information about the physical characteristics of the property. In some cases, an extraordinary assumption regarding the uncertainty of the data is appropriate.

7. The Small Residential Income Property Appraisal Report is the most common reporting form used for reporting the appraisal of a two- to four-family property for use by a lender client. This report form provides an orderly and systematic flow of information and commentary. An Operating Income Statement must be attached to the report.

8. The Individual Condominium Unit Appraisal Report is similar to the URAR (Form 1004), but the form has additional sections requiring the reporting of details of the entire condominium project. One important difference from the URAR is that no cost approach is reported (or developed) for condominium units.

9. Fannie Mae defines manufactured housing units as single-width or multi-width units constructed off-site and transported to the permanent site. Once on-site, they are completed and/or attached to the foundation. Under this definition, the dwelling is built to HUD specifications, with a HUD certification label attached and recognized as a manufactured home.

10. The field review form for one-unit residential properties is the One-Unit Residential Appraisal Field Review Report (Fannie Mae Form 2000/Freddie Mac Form 1032). The purpose of this report is to provide the lender/client with an opinion on the accuracy of the appraisal report under review.

11. Using the Appraisal Update form, if the appraiser indicates that he concurs with the value opinion found in the original appraisal report, that opinion must be developed in compliance with STANDARD 1 of USPAP. An appraisal update is different than a recertification of value, which simply confirms whether or not the conditions of a prior appraisal have been met.

Quiz

1. *Which section of the URAR establishes the minimum diligence expected of the appraiser regarding inspection, research, verification, analysis, and reporting?*
    a. General Use Provisions
    b. Intended Use
    c. Scope of Work
    d. Statement of Assumptions and Limiting Conditions

2. *The existence of which section of the URAR makes it unacceptable to use the form for marketing, estates, or litigation?*
    a. General Use Provisions
    b. Intended Use
    c. Scope of Work
    d. Statement of Assumptions and Limiting Conditions

3. *Appraiser Joe has completed Form 1025/72, Small Residential Income Property Appraisal Report. What form must he also submit with the report?*
    a. 216/998 Operating Income Statement
    b. 1004D/442 Appraisal Update and/or Completion Report
    c. 2000/1032 One-Unit Residential Appraisal Field Review Report
    d. 2055 Exterior-Only Inspection Appraisal Report

4. *Which statement about Fannie Mae Form 1073/ Freddie Mac Form 465, Individual Condominium Unit Appraisal Report form, is FALSE?*
    a. The form contains provisions for the same approaches to value as the URAR form.
    b. The form is not designed for valuing cooperative units or manufactured homes that are part of a complex.
    c. The form is used for the appraisal of a unit in a condominium project.
    d. The form was developed by Fannie Mae/ Freddie Mac to ensure all necessary information is presented in the report.

5. *An appraiser is completing Form 1004C/70B for a manufactured home. Which is NOT a mandatory reporting requirement with which the appraiser must comply when using the form?*
    a. describe any additions or modifications to the structure
    b. rate the quality of construction based on objective criteria
    c. report data using UAD requirements
    d. report the permanence of the structure on the site

6. *Project reporting fields for Form 1073/465, Individual Condominium Unit Appraisal Report, are specific to which two categories?*
    a. condition and ownership
    b. desirability and location
    c. management and funds
    d. owner-occupancy and rentals

7. *An appraiser is reporting an appraisal using Form 2055. The appraiser must, at a minimum, do all the following during the development process EXCEPT*
    a. analyze data from reliable public and/or private sources.
    b. conduct an interior inspection.
    c. inspect each of the comparable sales from the street.
    d. report the analysis, opinions, and conclusions in the appraisal report.

8. *When performing an assignment using only an exterior inspection, conclusions regarding property characteristics not personally observed by an appraiser would typically require the use and disclosure of a(n)*
    a. extraordinary assumption.
    b. jurisdictional exception.
    c. statutory guideline.
    d. unsupported conclusion.

9. *A recertification of value is a*
    a. component of an appraisal review.
    b. confirmation that prior appraisal conditions have been satisfied.
    c. form of an appraisal update.
    d. specific type of value opinion.

10. *In compliance with Fannie Mae reporting regulations, a(n) _____ must accompany any appraisal reported on the URAR form.*

    a. aerial photograph
    b. copy of the appraiser's license
    c. HUD certification
    d. Market Conditions Addendum

Appendix

Uniform Residential Appraisal Report

File #

The purpose of this summary appraisal report is to provide the lender/client with an accurate, and adequately supported, opinion of the market value of the subject property.

SUBJECT

Property Address	City	State	Zip Code

Borrower — Owner of Public Record — County

Legal Description

Assessor's Parcel # — Tax Year — R.E. Taxes $

Neighborhood Name — Map Reference — Census Tract

Occupant ☐ Owner ☐ Tenant ☐ Vacant — Special Assessments $ — ☐ PUD — HOA $ ☐ per year ☐ per month

Property Rights Appraised ☐ Fee Simple ☐ Leasehold ☐ Other (describe)

Assignment Type ☐ Purchase Transaction ☐ Refinance Transaction ☐ Other (describe)

Lender/Client — Address

Is the subject property currently offered for sale or has it been offered for sale in the twelve months prior to the effective date of this appraisal? ☐ Yes ☐ No

Report data source(s) used, offering price(s), and date(s).

CONTRACT

I ☐ did ☐ did not analyze the contract for sale for the subject purchase transaction. Explain the results of the analysis of the contract for sale or why the analysis was not performed.

Contract Price $ — Date of Contract — Is the property seller the owner of public record? ☐ Yes ☐ No Data Source(s)

Is there any financial assistance (loan charges, sale concessions, gift or downpayment assistance, etc.) to be paid by any party on behalf of the borrower? ☐ Yes ☐ No
If Yes, report the total dollar amount and describe the items to be paid.

NEIGHBORHOOD

Note: Race and the racial composition of the neighborhood are not appraisal factors.

Neighborhood Characteristics			One-Unit Housing Trends				One-Unit Housing		Present Land Use %	
Location ☐ Urban ☐ Suburban ☐ Rural			Property Values ☐ Increasing ☐ Stable ☐ Declining				PRICE	AGE	One-Unit	%
Built-Up ☐ Over 75% ☐ 25–75% ☐ Under 25%			Demand/Supply ☐ Shortage ☐ In Balance ☐ Over Supply				$ (000)	(yrs)	2-4 Unit	%
Growth ☐ Rapid ☐ Stable ☐ Slow			Marketing Time ☐ Under 3 mths ☐ 3–6 mths ☐ Over 6 mths				Low		Multi-Family	%
Neighborhood Boundaries							High		Commercial	%
							Pred.		Other	%

Neighborhood Description

Market Conditions (including support for the above conclusions)

SITE

Dimensions	Area	Shape	View

Specific Zoning Classification — Zoning Description

Zoning Compliance ☐ Legal ☐ Legal Nonconforming (Grandfathered Use) ☐ No Zoning ☐ Illegal (describe)

Is the highest and best use of the subject property as improved (or as proposed per plans and specifications) the present use? ☐ Yes ☐ No If No, describe

Utilities	Public	Other (describe)		Public	Other (describe)	Off-site Improvements—Type	Public	Private
Electricity	☐	☐	Water	☐	☐	Street	☐	☐
Gas	☐	☐	Sanitary Sewer	☐	☐	Alley	☐	☐

FEMA Special Flood Hazard Area ☐ Yes ☐ No FEMA Flood Zone — FEMA Map # — FEMA Map Date

Are the utilities and off-site improvements typical for the market area? ☐ Yes ☐ No If No, describe

Are there any adverse site conditions or external factors (easements, encroachments, environmental conditions, land uses, etc.)? ☐ Yes ☐ No If Yes, describe

IMPROVEMENTS

General Description	Foundation	Exterior Description materials/condition	Interior materials/condition
Units ☐ One ☐ One with Accessory Unit	☐ Concrete Slab ☐ Crawl Space	Foundation Walls	Floors
# of Stories	☐ Full Basement ☐ Partial Basement	Exterior Walls	Walls
Type ☐ Det. ☐ Att. ☐ S-Det./End Unit	Basement Area sq. ft.	Roof Surface	Trim/Finish
☐ Existing ☐ Proposed ☐ Under Const.	Basement Finish %	Gutters & Downspouts	Bath Floor
Design (Style)	☐ Outside Entry/Exit ☐ Sump Pump	Window Type	Bath Wainscot
Year Built	Evidence of ☐ Infestation	Storm Sash/Insulated	Car Storage ☐ None
Effective Age (Yrs)	☐ Dampness ☐ Settlement	Screens	☐ Driveway # of Cars
Attic ☐ None	Heating ☐ FWA ☐ HWBB ☐ Radiant	Amenities ☐ Woodstove(s) #	Driveway Surface
☐ Drop Stair ☐ Stairs	☐ Other Fuel	☐ Fireplace(s) # ☐ Fence	☐ Garage # of Cars
☐ Floor ☐ Scuttle	Cooling ☐ Central Air Conditioning	☐ Patio/Deck ☐ Porch	☐ Carport # of Cars
☐ Finished ☐ Heated	☐ Individual ☐ Other	☐ Pool ☐ Other	☐ Att. ☐ Det. ☐ Built-in

Appliances ☐ Refrigerator ☐ Range/Oven ☐ Dishwasher ☐ Disposal ☐ Microwave ☐ Washer/Dryer ☐ Other (describe)

Finished area **above** grade contains: Rooms — Bedrooms — Bath(s) — Square Feet of Gross Living Area Above Grade

Additional features (special energy efficient items, etc.)

Describe the condition of the property (including needed repairs, deterioration, renovations, remodeling, etc.).

Are there any physical deficiencies or adverse conditions that affect the livability, soundness, or structural integrity of the property? ☐ Yes ☐ No If Yes, describe

Does the property generally conform to the neighborhood (functional utility, style, condition, use, construction, etc.)? ☐ Yes ☐ No If No, describe

Uniform Residential Appraisal Report

File #

| There are | comparable properties currently offered for sale in the subject neighborhood ranging in price from $ | | to $ | |
| There are | comparable sales in the subject neighborhood within the past twelve months ranging in sale price from $ | | to $ | |

FEATURE	SUBJECT	COMPARABLE SALE # 1		COMPARABLE SALE # 2		COMPARABLE SALE # 3	
Address							
Proximity to Subject							
Sale Price	$		$		$		$
Sale Price/Gross Liv. Area	$ sq. ft.	$ sq. ft.		$ sq. ft.		$ sq. ft.	
Data Source(s)							
Verification Source(s)							
VALUE ADJUSTMENTS	DESCRIPTION	DESCRIPTION	+(-) $ Adjustment	DESCRIPTION	+(-) $ Adjustment	DESCRIPTION	+(-) $ Adjustment
Sale or Financing Concessions							
Date of Sale/Time							
Location							
Leasehold/Fee Simple							
Site							
View							
Design (Style)							
Quality of Construction							
Actual Age							
Condition							
Above Grade	Total	Bdrms.	Baths	Total	Bdrms.	Baths	
Room Count							
Gross Living Area	sq. ft.	sq. ft.		sq. ft.		sq. ft.	
Basement & Finished Rooms Below Grade							
Functional Utility							
Heating/Cooling							
Energy Efficient Items							
Garage/Carport							
Porch/Patio/Deck							
Net Adjustment (Total)		☐ + ☐ -	$	☐ + ☐ -	$	☐ + ☐ -	$
Adjusted Sale Price of Comparables		Net Adj. % Gross Adj. %	$	Net Adj. % Gross Adj. %	$	Net Adj. % Gross Adj. %	$

I ☐ did ☐ did not research the sale or transfer history of the subject property and comparable sales. If not, explain

My research ☐ did ☐ did not reveal any prior sales or transfers of the subject property for the three years prior to the effective date of this appraisal.

Data source(s)

My research ☐ did ☐ did not reveal any prior sales or transfers of the comparable sales for the year prior to the date of sale of the comparable sale.

Data source(s)

Report the results of the research and analysis of the prior sale or transfer history of the subject property and comparable sales (report additional prior sales on page 3).

ITEM	SUBJECT	COMPARABLE SALE # 1	COMPARABLE SALE # 2	COMPARABLE SALE # 3
Date of Prior Sale/Transfer				
Price of Prior Sale/Transfer				
Data Source(s)				
Effective Date of Data Source(s)				

Analysis of prior sale or transfer history of the subject property and comparable sales

Summary of Sales Comparison Approach

Indicated Value by Sales Comparison Approach $

Indicated Value by: Sales Comparison Approach $ Cost Approach (if developed) $ Income Approach (if developed) $

This appraisal is made ☐ "as is", ☐ subject to completion per plans and specifications on the basis of a hypothetical condition that the improvements have been completed, ☐ subject to the following repairs or alterations on the basis of a hypothetical condition that the repairs or alterations have been completed, or ☐ subject to the following required inspection based on the extraordinary assumption that the condition or deficiency does not require alteration or repair:

Based on a complete visual inspection of the interior and exterior areas of the subject property, defined scope of work, statement of assumptions and limiting conditions, and appraiser's certification, my (our) opinion of the market value, as defined, of the real property that is the subject of this report is $, as of   , which is the date of inspection and the effective date of this appraisal.

(Left vertical margin label: SALES COMPARISON APPROACH / RECONCILIATION)

Uniform Residential Appraisal Report   File

ADDITIONAL COMMENTS

(blank lines)

COST APPROACH TO VALUE (not required by Fannie Mae)			

Provide adequate information for the lender/client to replicate the below cost figures and calculations.

Support for the opinion of site value (summary of comparable land sales or other methods for estimating site value)

COST APPROACH

ESTIMATED ☐ REPRODUCTION OR ☐ REPLACEMENT COST NEW	OPINION OF SITE VALUE .... = $	
Source of cost data	Dwelling Sq. Ft. @ $ .... =$	
Quality rating from cost service Effective date of cost data	Sq. Ft. @ $ .... =$	
Comments on Cost Approach (gross living area calculations, depreciation, etc.)		
	Garage/Carport Sq. Ft. @ $ .... =$	
	Total Estimate of Cost-New .... = $	
	Less Physical | Functional | External	
	Depreciation =$( )	
	Depreciated Cost of Improvements.......................=$	
	"As-is" Value of Site Improvements.......................=$	
Estimated Remaining Economic Life (HUD and VA only) Years	Indicated Value By Cost Approach ....=$	

INCOME APPROACH TO VALUE (not required by Fannie Mae)		

INCOME

Estimated Monthly Market Rent $ _____ X Gross Rent Multiplier _____ = $ _____   Indicated Value by Income Approach

Summary of Income Approach (including support for market rent and GRM)

PROJECT INFORMATION FOR PUDs (if applicable)		

PUD INFORMATION

Is the developer/builder in control of the Homeowners' Association (HOA)? ☐ Yes ☐ No   Unit type(s) ☐ Detached ☐ Attached

Provide the following information for PUDs ONLY if the developer/builder is in control of the HOA and the subject property is an attached dwelling unit.

Legal name of project

Total number of phases _____   Total number of units _____   Total number of units sold _____

Total number of units rented _____   Total number of units for sale _____   Data source(s) _____

Was the project created by the conversion of an existing building(s) into a PUD? ☐ Yes ☐ No If Yes, date of conversion

Does the project contain any multi-dwelling units? ☐ Yes ☐ No Data source(s)

Are the units, common elements, and recreation facilities complete? ☐ Yes ☐ No If No, describe the status of completion.

Are the common elements leased to or by the Homeowners' Association? ☐ Yes ☐ No If Yes, describe the rental terms and options.

Describe common elements and recreational facilities

Uniform Residential Appraisal Report   File

This report form is designed to report an appraisal of a one-unit property or a one-unit property with an accessory unit; including a unit in a planned unit development (PUD). This report form is not designed to report an appraisal of a manufactured home or a unit in a condominium or cooperative project.

This appraisal report is subject to the following scope of work, intended use, intended user, definition of market value, statement of assumptions and limiting conditions, and certifications. Modifications, additions, or deletions to the intended use, intended user, definition of market value, or assumptions and limiting conditions are not permitted. The appraiser may expand the scope of work to include any additional research or analysis necessary based on the complexity of this appraisal assignment. Modifications or deletions to the certifications are also not permitted. However, additional certifications that do not constitute material alterations to this appraisal report, such as those required by law or those related to the appraiser's continuing education or membership in an appraisal organization, are permitted.

SCOPE OF WORK: The scope of work for this appraisal is defined by the complexity of this appraisal assignment and the reporting requirements of this appraisal report form, including the following definition of market value, statement of assumptions and limiting conditions, and certifications. The appraiser must, at a minimum: (1) perform a complete visual inspection of the interior and exterior areas of the subject property, (2) inspect the neighborhood, (3) inspect each of the comparable sales from at least the street, (4) research, verify, and analyze data from reliable public and/or private sources, and (5) report his or her analysis, opinions, and conclusions in this appraisal report.

INTENDED USE: The intended use of this appraisal report is for the lender/client to evaluate the property that is the subject of this appraisal for a mortgage finance transaction.

INTENDED USER: The intended user of this appraisal report is the lender/client.

DEFINITION OF MARKET VALUE: The most probable price which a property should bring in a competitive and open market under all conditions requisite to a fair sale, the buyer and seller, each acting prudently, knowledgeably and assuming the price is not affected by undue stimulus. Implicit in this definition is the consummation of a sale as of a specified date and the passing of title from seller to buyer under conditions whereby: (1) buyer and seller are typically motivated; (2) both parties are well informed or well advised, and each acting in what he or she considers his or her own best interest; (3) a reasonable time is allowed for exposure in the open market; (4) payment is made in terms of cash in U. S. dollars or in terms of financial arrangements comparable thereto; and (5) the price represents the normal consideration for the property sold unaffected by special or creative financing or sales concessions* granted by anyone associated with the sale.

*Adjustments to the comparables must be made for special or creative financing or sales concessions. No adjustments are necessary for those costs which are normally paid by sellers as a result of tradition or law in a market area; these costs are readily identifiable since the seller pays these costs in virtually all sales transactions. Special or creative financing adjustments can be made to the comparable property by comparisons to financing terms offered by a third party institutional lender that is not already involved in the property or transaction. Any adjustment should not be calculated on a mechanical dollar for dollar cost of the financing or concession but the dollar amount of any adjustment should approximate the market's reaction to the financing or concessions based on the appraiser's judgment.

STATEMENT OF ASSUMPTIONS AND LIMITING CONDITIONS: The appraiser's certification in this report is subject to the following assumptions and limiting conditions:

1. The appraiser will not be responsible for matters of a legal nature that affect either the property being appraised or the title to it, except for information that he or she became aware of during the research involved in performing this appraisal. The appraiser assumes that the title is good and marketable and will not render any opinions about the title.

2. The appraiser has provided a sketch in this appraisal report to show the approximate dimensions of the improvements. The sketch is included only to assist the reader in visualizing the property and understanding the appraiser's determination of its size.

3. The appraiser has examined the available flood maps that are provided by the Federal Emergency Management Agency (or other data sources) and has noted in this appraisal report whether any portion of the subject site is located in an identified Special Flood Hazard Area. Because the appraiser is not a surveyor, he or she makes no guarantees, express or implied, regarding this determination.

4. The appraiser will not give testimony or appear in court because he or she made an appraisal of the property in question, unless specific arrangements to do so have been made beforehand, or as otherwise required by law.

5. The appraiser has noted in this appraisal report any adverse conditions (such as needed repairs, deterioration, the presence of hazardous wastes, toxic substances, etc.) observed during the inspection of the subject property or that he or she became aware of during the research involved in performing this appraisal. Unless otherwise stated in this appraisal report, the appraiser has no knowledge of any hidden or unapparent physical deficiencies or adverse conditions of the property (such as, but not limited to, needed repairs, deterioration, the presence of hazardous wastes, toxic substances, adverse environmental conditions, etc.) that would make the property less valuable, and has assumed that there are no such conditions and makes no guarantees or warranties, express or implied. The appraiser will not be responsible for any such conditions that do exist or for any engineering or testing that might be required to discover whether such conditions exist. Because the appraiser is not an expert in the field of environmental hazards, this appraisal report must not be considered as an environmental assessment of the property.

6. The appraiser has based his or her appraisal report and valuation conclusion for an appraisal that is subject to satisfactory completion, repairs, or alterations on the assumption that the completion, repairs, or alterations of the subject property will be performed in a professional manner.

Uniform Residential Appraisal Report   File

APPRAISER'S CERTIFICATION: The Appraiser certifies and agrees that:

1. I have, at a minimum, developed and reported this appraisal in accordance with the scope of work requirements stated in this appraisal report.

2. I performed a complete visual inspection of the interior and exterior areas of the subject property. I reported the condition of the improvements in factual, specific terms. I identified and reported the physical deficiencies that could affect the livability, soundness, or structural integrity of the property.

3. I performed this appraisal in accordance with the requirements of the Uniform Standards of Professional Appraisal Practice that were adopted and promulgated by the Appraisal Standards Board of The Appraisal Foundation and that were in place at the time this appraisal report was prepared.

4. I developed my opinion of the market value of the real property that is the subject of this report based on the sales comparison approach to value. I have adequate comparable market data to develop a reliable sales comparison approach for this appraisal assignment. I further certify that I considered the cost and income approaches to value but did not develop them, unless otherwise indicated in this report.

5. I researched, verified, analyzed, and reported on any current agreement for sale for the subject property, any offering for sale of the subject property in the twelve months prior to the effective date of this appraisal, and the prior sales of the subject property for a minimum of three years prior to the effective date of this appraisal, unless otherwise indicated in this report.

6. I researched, verified, analyzed, and reported on the prior sales of the comparable sales for a minimum of one year prior to the date of sale of the comparable sale, unless otherwise indicated in this report.

7. I selected and used comparable sales that are locationally, physically, and functionally the most similar to the subject property.

8. I have not used comparable sales that were the result of combining a land sale with the contract purchase price of a home that has been built or will be built on the land.

9. I have reported adjustments to the comparable sales that reflect the market's reaction to the differences between the subject property and the comparable sales.

10. I verified, from a disinterested source, all information in this report that was provided by parties who have a financial interest in the sale or financing of the subject property.

11. I have knowledge and experience in appraising this type of property in this market area.

12. I am aware of, and have access to, the necessary and appropriate public and private data sources, such as multiple listing services, tax assessment records, public land records and other such data sources for the area in which the property is located.

13. I obtained the information, estimates, and opinions furnished by other parties and expressed in this appraisal report from reliable sources that I believe to be true and correct.

14. I have taken into consideration the factors that have an impact on value with respect to the subject neighborhood, subject property, and the proximity of the subject property to adverse influences in the development of my opinion of market value. I have noted in this appraisal report any adverse conditions (such as, but not limited to, needed repairs, deterioration, the presence of hazardous wastes, toxic substances, adverse environmental conditions, etc.) observed during the inspection of the subject property or that I became aware of during the research involved in performing this appraisal. I have considered these adverse conditions in my analysis of the property value, and have reported on the effect of the conditions on the value and marketability of the subject property.

15. I have not knowingly withheld any significant information from this appraisal report and, to the best of my knowledge, all statements and information in this appraisal report are true and correct.

16. I stated in this appraisal report my own personal, unbiased, and professional analysis, opinions, and conclusions, which are subject only to the assumptions and limiting conditions in this appraisal report.

17. I have no present or prospective interest in the property that is the subject of this report, and I have no present or prospective personal interest or bias with respect to the participants in the transaction. I did not base, either partially or completely, my analysis and/or opinion of market value in this appraisal report on the race, color, religion, sex, age, marital status, handicap, familial status, or national origin of either the prospective owners or occupants of the subject property or of the present owners or occupants of the properties in the vicinity of the subject property or on any other basis prohibited by law.

18. My employment and/or compensation for performing this appraisal or any future or anticipated appraisals was not conditioned on any agreement or understanding, written or otherwise, that I would report (or present analysis supporting) a predetermined specific value, a predetermined minimum value, a range or direction in value, a value that favors the cause of any party, or the attainment of a specific result or occurrence of a specific subsequent event (such as approval of a pending mortgage loan application).

19. I personally prepared all conclusions and opinions about the real estate that were set forth in this appraisal report. If I relied on significant real property appraisal assistance from any individual or individuals in the performance of this appraisal or the preparation of this appraisal report, I have named such individual(s) and disclosed the specific tasks performed in this appraisal report. I certify that any individual so named is qualified to perform the tasks. I have not authorized anyone to make a change to any item in this appraisal report; therefore, any change made to this appraisal is unauthorized and I will take no responsibility for it.

20. I identified the lender/client in this appraisal report who is the individual, organization, or agent for the organization that ordered and will receive this appraisal report.

Uniform Residential Appraisal Report

File #

21. The lender/client may disclose or distribute this appraisal report to: the borrower; another lender at the request of the borrower; the mortgagee or its successors and assigns; mortgage insurers; government sponsored enterprises; other secondary market participants; data collection or reporting services; professional appraisal organizations; any department, agency, or instrumentality of the United States; and any state, the District of Columbia, or other jurisdictions; without having to obtain the appraiser's or supervisory appraiser's (if applicable) consent. Such consent must be obtained before this appraisal report may be disclosed or distributed to any other party (including, but not limited to, the public through advertising, public relations, news, sales, or other media).

22. I am aware that any disclosure or distribution of this appraisal report by me or the lender/client may be subject to certain laws and regulations. Further, I am also subject to the provisions of the Uniform Standards of Professional Appraisal Practice that pertain to disclosure or distribution by me.

23. The borrower, another lender at the request of the borrower, the mortgagee or its successors and assigns, mortgage insurers, government sponsored enterprises, and other secondary market participants may rely on this appraisal report as part of any mortgage finance transaction that involves any one or more of these parties.

24. If this appraisal report was transmitted as an "electronic record" containing my "electronic signature," as those terms are defined in applicable federal and/or state laws (excluding audio and video recordings), or a facsimile transmission of this appraisal report containing a copy or representation of my signature, the appraisal report shall be as effective, enforceable and valid as if a paper version of this appraisal report were delivered containing my original hand written signature.

25. Any intentional or negligent misrepresentation(s) contained in this appraisal report may result in civil liability and/or criminal penalties including, but not limited to, fine or imprisonment or both under the provisions of Title 18, United States Code, Section 1001, et seq., or similar state laws.

SUPERVISORY APPRAISER'S CERTIFICATION: The Supervisory Appraiser certifies and agrees that:

1. I directly supervised the appraiser for this appraisal assignment, have read the appraisal report, and agree with the appraiser's analysis, opinions, statements, conclusions, and the appraiser's certification.

2. I accept full responsibility for the contents of this appraisal report including, but not limited to, the appraiser's analysis, opinions, statements, conclusions, and the appraiser's certification.

3. The appraiser identified in this appraisal report is either a sub-contractor or an employee of the supervisory appraiser (or the appraisal firm), is qualified to perform this appraisal, and is acceptable to perform this appraisal under the applicable state law.

4. This appraisal report complies with the Uniform Standards of Professional Appraisal Practice that were adopted and promulgated by the Appraisal Standards Board of The Appraisal Foundation and that were in place at the time this appraisal report was prepared.

5. If this appraisal report was transmitted as an "electronic record" containing my "electronic signature," as those terms are defined in applicable federal and/or state laws (excluding audio and video recordings), or a facsimile transmission of this appraisal report containing a copy or representation of my signature, the appraisal report shall be as effective, enforceable and valid as if a paper version of this appraisal report were delivered containing my original hand written signature.

APPRAISER

Signature_____
Name _____
Company Name _____
Company Address_____

Telephone Number _____
Email Address _____
Date of Signature and Report_____
Effective Date of Appraisal _____
State Certification #_____
or State License # _____
or Other (describe) _____ State # _____
State _____
Expiration Date of Certification or License _____

ADDRESS OF PROPERTY APPRAISED

_____
_____

APPRAISED VALUE OF SUBJECT PROPERTY $ _____
LENDER/CLIENT
Name _____
Company Name _____
Company Address_____
_____
Email Address _____

SUPERVISORY APPRAISER (ONLY IF REQUIRED)

Signature_____
Name_____
Company Name _____
Company Address_____
_____
Telephone Number _____
Email Address _____
Date of Signature _____
State Certification #_____
or State License # _____
State _____
Expiration Date of Certification or License _____

SUBJECT PROPERTY

☐ Did not inspect subject property
☐ Did inspect exterior of subject property from street
   Date of Inspection _____
☐ Did inspect interior and exterior of subject property
   Date of Inspection _____

COMPARABLE SALES

☐ Did not inspect exterior of comparable sales from street
☐ Did inspect exterior of comparable sales from street
   Date of Inspection _____

Market Conditions Addendum to the Appraisal Report   File No.

The purpose of this addendum is to provide the lender/client with a clear and accurate understanding of the market trends and conditions prevalent in the subject neighborhood. This is a required addendum for all appraisal reports with an effective date on or after April 1, 2009.

Property Address	City	State	ZIP Code

Borrower

Instructions: The appraiser must use the information required on this form as the basis for his/her conclusions, and must provide support for those conclusions, regarding housing trends and overall market conditions as reported in the Neighborhood section of the appraisal report form. The appraiser must fill in all the information to the extent it is available and reliable and must provide analysis as indicated below. If any required data is unavailable or is considered unreliable, the appraiser must provide an explanation. It is recognized that not all data sources will be able to provide data for the shaded areas below; if it is available, however, the appraiser must include the data in the analysis. If data sources provide the required information as an average instead of the median, the appraiser should report the available figure and identify it as an average. Sales and listings must be properties that compete with the subject property, determined by applying the criteria that would be used by a prospective buyer of the subject property. The appraiser must explain any anomalies in the data, such as seasonal markets, new construction, foreclosures, etc.

Inventory Analysis	Prior 7–12 Months	Prior 4–6 Months	Current – 3 Months	Overall Trend		
Total # of Comparable Sales (Settled)				☐ Increasing	☐ Stable	☐ Declining
Absorption Rate (Total Sales/Months)				☐ Increasing	☐ Stable	☐ Declining
Total # of Comparable Active Listings				☐ Declining	☐ Stable	☐ Increasing
Months of Housing Supply (Total Listings/Ab.Rate)				☐ Declining	☐ Stable	☐ Increasing

Median Sale & List Price, DOM, Sale/List %	Prior 7–12 Months	Prior 4–6 Months	Current – 3 Months	Overall Trend		
Median Comparable Sale Price				☐ Increasing	☐ Stable	☐ Declining
Median Comparable Sales Days on Market				☐ Declining	☐ Stable	☐ Increasing
Median Comparable List Price				☐ Increasing	☐ Stable	☐ Declining
Median Comparable Listings Days on Market				☐ Declining	☐ Stable	☐ Increasing
Median Sale Price as % of List Price				☐ Increasing	☐ Stable	☐ Declining
Seller-(developer, builder, etc.) paid financial assistance prevalent? ☐ Yes ☐ No				☐ Declining	☐ Stable	☐ Increasing

Explain in detail the seller concessions trends for the past 12 months (e.g., seller contributions increased from 3% to 5%, increasing use of buydowns, closing costs, condo fees, options, etc.).

Are foreclosure sales (REO sales) a factor in the market? ☐ Yes ☐ No If yes, explain (including the trends in listings and sales of foreclosed properties).

Cite data sources for above information.

Summarize the above information as support for your conclusions in the Neighborhood section of the appraisal report form. If you used any additional information, such as an analysis of pending sales and/or expired and withdrawn listings, to formulate your conclusions, provide both an explanation and support for your conclusions.

If the subject is a unit in a condominium or cooperative project , complete the following: Project Name:

Subject Project Data	Prior 7–12 Months	Prior 4-6 Months	Current – 3 Months	Overall Trend		
Total # of Comparable Sales (Settled)				☐ Increasing	☐ Stable	☐ Declining
Absorption Rate (Total Sales/Months)				☐ Increasing	☐ Stable	☐ Declining
Total # of Active Comparable Listings				☐ Declining	☐ Stable	☐ Increasing
Months of Unit Supply (Total Listings/Ab. Rate)				☐ Declining	☐ Stable	☐ Increasing

Are foreclosure sales (REO sales) a factor in the project? ☐ Yes ☐ No If yes, indicate the number of REO listings and explain the trends in listings and sales of foreclosed properties.

Summarize the above trends and address the impact on the subject unit and project.

Signature	Signature
Appraiser Name	Supervisory Appraiser Name
Company Name	Company Name
Company Address	Company Address
State License/Certification # State	State License/Certification # State
Email Address	Email Address

Freddie Mac Form 71   March 2009   Page 1 of 1   Fannie Mae Form 1004MC   March 2009

Appendix

Exterior-Only Inspection Residential Appraisal Report File

The purpose of this summary appraisal report is to provide the lender/client with an accurate, and adequately supported, opinion of the market value of the subject property.

SUBJECT

Property Address		City		State	Zip Code
Borrower	Owner of Public Record			County	

Legal Description

Assessor's Parcel #   Tax Year   R.E. Taxes $

Neighborhood Name   Map Reference   Census Tract

Occupant ☐ Owner ☐ Tenant ☐ Vacant   Special Assessments $ ☐ PUD   HOA $ ☐ per year ☐ per month

Property Rights Appraised ☐ Fee Simple ☐ Leasehold ☐ Other (describe)

Assignment Type ☐ Purchase Transaction ☐ Refinance Transaction ☐ Other (describe)

Lender/Client   Address

Is the subject property currently offered for sale or has it been offered for sale in the twelve months prior to the effective date of this appraisal? ☐ Yes ☐ No

Report data source(s) used, offering price(s), and date(s).

CONTRACT

I ☐ did ☐ did not analyze the contract for sale for the subject purchase transaction. Explain the results of the analysis of the contract for sale or why the analysis was not performed.

Contract Price $ Date of Contract   Is the property seller the owner of public record? ☐ Yes ☐ No Data Source(s)

Is there any financial assistance (loan charges, sale concessions, gift or downpayment assistance, etc.) to be paid by any party on behalf of the borrower? ☐ Yes ☐ No
If Yes, report the total dollar amount and describe the items to be paid.

NEIGHBORHOOD

Note: Race and the racial composition of the neighborhood are not appraisal factors.

Neighborhood Characteristics		One-Unit Housing Trends		One-Unit Housing		Present Land Use %	
Location ☐ Urban ☐ Suburban ☐ Rural		Property Values ☐ Increasing ☐ Stable ☐ Declining		PRICE	AGE	One-Unit	%
Built-Up ☐ Over 75% ☐ 25–75% ☐ Under 25%		Demand/Supply ☐ Shortage ☐ In Balance ☐ Over Supply		$ (000)	(yrs)	2-4 Unit	%
Growth ☐ Rapid ☐ Stable ☐ Slow		Marketing Time ☐ Under 3 mths ☐ 3–6 mths ☐ Over 6 mths		Low		Multi-Family	%
Neighborhood Boundaries				High		Commercial	%
				Pred.		Other	%

Neighborhood Description

Market Conditions (including support for the above conclusions)

SITE

Dimensions   Area   Shape   View

Specific Zoning Classification   Zoning Description

Zoning Compliance ☐ Legal ☐ Legal Nonconforming (Grandfathered Use) ☐ No Zoning ☐ Illegal (describe)

Is the highest and best use of the subject property as improved (or as proposed per plans and specifications) the present use? ☐ Yes ☐ No If No, describe

Utilities	Public	Other (describe)		Public	Other (describe)	Off-site Improvements—Type	Public	Private
Electricity	☐	☐	Water	☐	☐	Street	☐	☐
Gas	☐	☐	Sanitary Sewer	☐	☐	Alley	☐	☐

FEMA Special Flood Hazard Area ☐ Yes ☐ No   FEMA Flood Zone   FEMA Map #   FEMA Map Date

Are the utilities and off-site improvements typical for the market area? ☐ Yes ☐ No If No, describe

Are there any adverse site conditions or external factors (easements, encroachments, environmental conditions, land uses, etc.)? ☐ Yes ☐ No If Yes, describe

IMPROVEMENTS

Source(s) Used for Physical Characteristics of Property ☐ Appraisal Files ☐ MLS ☐ Assessment and Tax Records ☐ Prior Inspection ☐ Property Owner
☐ Other (describe)   Data Source(s) for Gross Living Area

General Description	General Description	Heating / Cooling	Amenities	Car Storage
Units ☐ One ☐ One with Accessory Unit	☐ Concrete Slab ☐ Crawl Space	☐ FWA ☐ HWBB	☐ Fireplace(s) #	☐ None
# of Stories	☐ Full Basement ☐ Finished	☐ Radiant	☐ Woodstove(s) #	☐ Driveway # of Cars
Type ☐ Det. ☐ Att. ☐ S-Det./End Unit	☐ Partial Basement ☐ Finished	☐ Other	☐ Patio/Deck	Driveway Surface
☐ Existing ☐ Proposed ☐ Under Const.	Exterior Walls	Fuel	☐ Porch	☐ Garage # of Cars
Design (Style)	Roof Surface	☐ Central Air Conditioning	☐ Pool	☐ Carport # of Cars
Year Built	Gutters & Downspouts	☐ Individual	☐ Fence	☐ Attached ☐ Detached
Effective Age (Yrs)	Window Type	☐ Other	☐ Other	☐ Built-in

Appliances ☐ Refrigerator ☐ Range/Oven ☐ Dishwasher ☐ Disposal ☐ Microwave ☐ Washer/Dryer ☐ Other (describe)

Finished area **above** grade contains: Rooms   Bedrooms   Bath(s)   Square Feet of Gross Living Area Above Grade

Additional features (special energy efficient items, etc.)

Describe the condition of the property and data source(s) (including apparent needed repairs, deterioration, renovations, remodeling, etc.).

Are there any apparent physical deficiencies or adverse conditions that affect the livability, soundness, or structural integrity of the property? ☐ Yes ☐ No
If Yes, describe

Does the property generally conform to the neighborhood (functional utility, style, condition, use, construction, etc.)? ☐ Yes ☐ No If No, describe

Freddie Mac Form 2055 March 2005   Page 1 of 6   Fannie Mae Form 2055 March 2005

239

Exterior-Only Inspection Residential Appraisal Report   File

| There are | comparable properties currently offered for sale in the subject neighborhood ranging in price from $ | | | | | to $ | | . |

| There are | comparable sales in the subject neighborhood within the past twelve months ranging in sale price from $ | | | | | to $ | | . |

FEATURE	SUBJECT	COMPARABLE SALE # 1		COMPARABLE SALE # 2		COMPARABLE SALE # 3	
Address							
Proximity to Subject							
Sale Price	$		$		$		$
Sale Price/Gross Liv. Area	$ sq. ft.	$ sq. ft.		$ sq. ft.		$ sq. ft.	
Data Source(s)							
Verification Source(s)							
VALUE ADJUSTMENTS	DESCRIPTION	DESCRIPTION	+(-) $ Adjustment	DESCRIPTION	+(-) $ Adjustment	DESCRIPTION	+(-) $ Adjustment
Sale or Financing Concessions							
Date of Sale/Time							
Location							
Leasehold/Fee Simple							
Site							
View							
Design (Style)							
Quality of Construction							
Actual Age							
Condition							
Above Grade	Total Bdrms. Baths	Total Bdrms. Baths		Total Bdrms. Baths		Total Bdrms. Baths	
Room Count							
Gross Living Area	sq. ft.	sq. ft.		sq. ft.		sq. ft.	
Basement & Finished Rooms Below Grade							
Functional Utility							
Heating/Cooling							
Energy Efficient Items							
Garage/Carport							
Porch/Patio/Deck							
Net Adjustment (Total)		☐ + ☐ -	$	☐ + ☐ -	$	☐ + ☐ -	$
Adjusted Sale Price of Comparables		Net Adj. % Gross Adj. %	$	Net Adj. % Gross Adj. %	$	Net Adj. % Gross Adj. %	$

I ☐ did ☐ did not research the sale or transfer history of the subject property and comparable sales. If not, explain

My research ☐ did ☐ did not reveal any prior sales or transfers of the subject property for the three years prior to the effective date of this appraisal.
Data source(s)
My research ☐ did ☐ did not reveal any prior sales or transfers of the comparable sales for the year prior to the date of sale of the comparable sale.
Data source(s)
Report the results of the research and analysis of the prior sale or transfer history of the subject property and comparable sales (report additional prior sales on page 3).

ITEM	SUBJECT	COMPARABLE SALE # 1	COMPARABLE SALE # 2	COMPARABLE SALE # 3
Date of Prior Sale/Transfer				
Price of Prior Sale/Transfer				
Data Source(s)				
Effective Date of Data Source(s)				

Analysis of prior sale or transfer history of the subject property and comparable sales

Summary of Sales Comparison Approach

Indicated Value by Sales Comparison Approach $

Indicated Value by: Sales Comparison Approach $	Cost Approach (if developed) $	Income Approach (if developed) $

This appraisal is made ☐ "as is", ☐ subject to completion per plans and specifications on the basis of a hypothetical condition that the improvements have been completed, ☐ subject to the following repairs or alterations on the basis of a hypothetical condition that the repairs or alterations have been completed, or ☐ subject to the following required inspection based on the extraordinary assumption that the condition or deficiency does not require alteration or repair:

Based on a visual inspection of the exterior areas of the subject property from at least the street, defined scope of work, statement of assumptions and limiting conditions, and appraiser's certification, my (our) opinion of the market value, as defined, of the real property that is the subject of this report is
$, as of , which is the date of the inspection and the effective date of this appraisal.

Exterior-Only Inspection Residential Appraisal Report   File

ADDITIONAL COMMENTS

(blank lined area)

COST APPROACH TO VALUE (not required by Fannie Mae)

Provide adequate information for the lender/client to replicate the below cost figures and calculations.

Support for the opinion of site value (summary of comparable land sales or other methods for estimating site value)

ESTIMATED ☐ REPRODUCTION OR ☐ REPLACEMENT COST NEW

OPINION OF SITE VALUE..= $

Source of cost data — Dwelling   Sq. Ft. @ $ ....=$

Quality rating from cost service   Effective date of cost data   Sq. Ft. @ $ ....=$

Comments on Cost Approach (gross living area calculations, depreciation, etc.)

Garage/Carport   Sq. Ft. @ $ ....=$

Total Estimate of Cost-New ....= $

| Less | Physical | Functional | External |

Depreciation   =$(   )

Depreciated Cost of Improvements.......................=$

"As-is" Value of Site Improvements.......................=$

Estimated Remaining Economic Life (HUD and VA only)   Years   Indicated Value By Cost Approach.......................=$

INCOME APPROACH TO VALUE (not required by Fannie Mae)

Estimated Monthly Market Rent $ X Gross Rent Multiplier   = $ Indicated Value by Income Approach

Summary of Income Approach (including support for market rent and GRM)

PROJECT INFORMATION FOR PUDs (if applicable)

Is the developer/builder in control of the Homeowners' Association (HOA)? ☐ Yes ☐ No   Unit type(s) ☐ Detached ☐Attached

Provide the following information for PUDs ONLY if the developer/builder is in control of the HOA and the subject property is an attached dwelling unit.

Legal name of project

Total number of phases   Total number of units   Total number of units sold

Total number of units rented   Total number of units for sale   Data source(s)

Was the project created by the conversion of an existing building(s) into a PUD? ☐ Yes ☐ No If Yes, date of conversion

Does the project contain any multi-dwelling units? ☐ Yes ☐ No Data source(s)

Are the units, common elements, and recreation facilities complete? ☐ Yes ☐ No If No, describe the status of completion.

Are the common elements leased to or by the Homeowners' Association? ☐ Yes ☐ No If Yes, describe the rental terms and options.

Describe common elements and recreational facilities

Freddie Mac Form 2055 March 2005   Page 3 of 6   Fannie Mae Form 2055 March 2005

Exterior-Only Inspection Residential Appraisal Report   File

This report form is designed to report an appraisal of a one-unit property or a one-unit property with an accessory unit; including a unit in a planned unit development (PUD). This report form is not designed to report an appraisal of a manufactured home or a unit in a condominium or cooperative project.

This appraisal report is subject to the following scope of work, intended use, intended user, definition of market value, statement of assumptions and limiting conditions, and certifications. Modifications, additions, or deletions to the intended use, intended user, definition of market value, or assumptions and limiting conditions are not permitted. The appraiser may expand the scope of work to include any additional research or analysis necessary based on the complexity of this appraisal assignment. Modifications or deletions to the certifications are also not permitted. However, additional certifications that do not constitute material alterations to this appraisal report, such as those required by law or those related to the appraiser's continuing education or membership in an appraisal organization, are permitted.

SCOPE OF WORK: The scope of work for this appraisal is defined by the complexity of this appraisal assignment and the reporting requirements of this appraisal report form, including the following definition of market value, statement of assumptions and limiting conditions, and certifications. The appraiser must, at a minimum: (1) perform a visual inspection of the exterior areas of the subject property from at least the street, (2) inspect the neighborhood, (3) inspect each of the comparable sales from at least the street, (4) research, verify, and analyze data from reliable public and/or private sources, and (5) report his or her analysis, opinions, and conclusions in this appraisal report.

The appraiser must be able to obtain adequate information about the physical characteristics (including, but not limited to, condition, room count, gross living area, etc.) of the subject property from the exterior-only inspection and reliable public and/or private sources to perform this appraisal. The appraiser should use the same type of data sources that he or she uses for comparable sales such as, but not limited to, multiple listing services, tax and assessment records, prior inspections, appraisal files, information provided by the property owner, etc.

INTENDED USE: The intended use of this appraisal report is for the lender/client to evaluate the property that is the subject of this appraisal for a mortgage finance transaction.

INTENDED USER: The intended user of this appraisal report is the lender/client.

DEFINITION MARKET VALUE: The most probable price which a property should bring in a competitive and open market under all conditions requisite to a fair sale, the buyer and seller, each acting prudently, knowledgeably and assuming the price is not affected by undue stimulus. Implicit in this definition is the consummation of a sale as of a specified date and the passing of title from seller to buyer under conditions whereby: (1) buyer and seller are typically motivated; (2) both parties are well informed or well advised, and each acting in what he or she considers his or her own best interest; (3) a reasonable time is allowed for exposure in the open market; (4) payment is made in terms of cash in U. S. dollars or in terms of financial arrangements comparable thereto; and (5) the price represents the normal consideration for the property sold unaffected by special or creative financing or sales concessions* granted by anyone associated with the sale.

*Adjustments to the comparables must be made for special or creative financing or sales concessions. No adjustments are necessary for those costs which are normally paid by sellers as a result of tradition or law in a market area; these costs are readily identifiable since the seller pays these costs in virtually all sales transactions. Special or creative financing adjustments can be made to the comparable property by comparisons to financing terms offered by a third party institutional lender that is not already involved in the property or transaction. Any adjustment should not be calculated on a mechanical dollar for dollar cost of the financing or concession but the dollar amount of any adjustment should approximate the market's reaction to the financing or concessions based on the appraiser's judgment.

STATEMENT OF ASSUMPTIONS AND LIMITING CONDITIONS: The appraiser's certification in this report is subject to the following assumptions and limiting conditions:

1. The appraiser will not be responsible for matters of a legal nature that affect either the property being appraised or the title to it, except for information that he or she became aware of during the research involved in performing this appraisal. The appraiser assumes that the title is good and marketable and will not render any opinions about the title.

2. The appraiser has examined the available flood maps that are provided by the Federal Emergency Management Agency (or other data sources) and has noted in this appraisal report whether any portion of the subject site is located in an identified Special Flood Hazard Area. Because the appraiser is not a surveyor, he or she makes no guarantees, express or implied, regarding this determination.

3. The appraiser will not give testimony or appear in court because he or she made an appraisal of the property in question, unless specific arrangements to do so have been made beforehand, or as otherwise required by law.

4. The appraiser has noted in this appraisal report any adverse conditions (such as needed repairs, deterioration, the presence of hazardous wastes, toxic substances, etc.) observed during the inspection of the subject property or that he or she became aware of during the research involved in performing this appraisal. Unless otherwise stated in this appraisal report, the appraiser has no knowledge of any hidden or unapparent physical deficiencies or adverse conditions of the property (such as, but not limited to, needed repairs, deterioration, the presence of hazardous wastes, toxic substances, adverse environmental conditions, etc.) that would make the property less valuable, and has assumed that there are no such conditions and makes no guarantees or warranties, express or implied. The appraiser will not be responsible for any such conditions that do exist or for any engineering or testing that might be required to discover whether such conditions exist. Because the appraiser is not an expert in the field of environmental hazards, this appraisal report must not be considered as an environmental assessment of the property.

5. The appraiser has based his or her appraisal report and valuation conclusion for an appraisal that is subject to satisfactory completion, repairs, or alterations on the assumption that the completion, repairs, or alterations of the subject property will be performed in a professional manner.

Exterior-Only Inspection Residential Appraisal Report   File

APPRAISER'S CERTIFICATION: The Appraiser certifies and agrees that:

1. I have, at a minimum, developed and reported this appraisal in accordance with the scope of work requirements stated in this appraisal report.

2. I performed a visual inspection of the exterior areas of the subject property from at least the street. I reported the condition of the improvements in factual, specific terms. I identified and reported the physical deficiencies that could affect the livability, soundness, or structural integrity of the property.

3. I performed this appraisal in accordance with the requirements of the Uniform Standards of Professional Appraisal Practice that were adopted and promulgated by the Appraisal Standards Board of The Appraisal Foundation and that were in place at the time this appraisal report was prepared.

4. I developed my opinion of the market value of the real property that is the subject of this report based on the sales comparison approach to value. I have adequate comparable market data to develop a reliable sales comparison approach for this appraisal assignment. I further certify that I considered the cost and income approaches to value but did not develop them, unless otherwise indicated in this report.

5. I researched, verified, analyzed, and reported on any current agreement for sale for the subject property, any offering for sale of the subject property in the twelve months prior to the effective date of this appraisal, and the prior sales of the subject property for a minimum of three years prior to the effective date of this appraisal, unless otherwise indicated in this report.

6. I researched, verified, analyzed, and reported on the prior sales of the comparable sales for a minimum of one year prior to the date of sale of the comparable sale, unless otherwise indicated in this report.

7. I selected and used comparable sales that are locationally, physically, and functionally the most similar to the subject property.

8. I have not used comparable sales that were the result of combining a land sale with the contract purchase price of a home that has been built or will be built on the land.

9. I have reported adjustments to the comparable sales that reflect the market's reaction to the differences between the subject property and the comparable sales.

10. I verified, from a disinterested source, all information in this report that was provided by parties who have a financial interest in the sale or financing of the subject property.

11. I have knowledge and experience in appraising this type of property in this market area.

12. I am aware of, and have access to, the necessary and appropriate public and private data sources, such as multiple listing services, tax assessment records, public land records and other such data sources for the area in which the property is located.

13. I obtained the information, estimates, and opinions furnished by other parties and expressed in this appraisal report from reliable sources that I believe to be true and correct.

14. I have taken into consideration the factors that have an impact on value with respect to the subject neighborhood, subject property, and the proximity of the subject property to adverse influences in the development of my opinion of market value. I have noted in this appraisal report any adverse conditions (such as, but not limited to, needed repairs, deterioration, the presence of hazardous wastes, toxic substances, adverse environmental conditions, etc.) observed during the inspection of the subject property or that I became aware of during the research involved in performing this appraisal. I have considered these adverse conditions in my analysis of the property value, and have reported on the effect of the conditions on the value and marketability of the subject property.

15. I have not knowingly withheld any significant information from this appraisal report and, to the best of my knowledge, all statements and information in this appraisal report are true and correct.

16. I stated in this appraisal report my own personal, unbiased, and professional analysis, opinions, and conclusions, which are subject only to the assumptions and limiting conditions in this appraisal report.

17. I have no present or prospective interest in the property that is the subject of this report, and I have no present or prospective personal interest or bias with respect to the participants in the transaction. I did not base, either partially or completely, my analysis and/or opinion of market value in this appraisal report on the race, color, religion, sex, age, marital status, handicap, familial status, or national origin of either the prospective owners or occupants of the subject property or of the present owners or occupants of the properties in the vicinity of the subject property or on any other basis prohibited by law.

18. My employment and/or compensation for performing this appraisal or any future or anticipated appraisals was not conditioned on any agreement or understanding, written or otherwise, that I would report (or present analysis supporting) a predetermined specific value, a predetermined minimum value, a range or direction in value, a value that favors the cause of any party, or the attainment of a specific result or occurrence of a specific subsequent event (such as approval of a pending mortgage loan application).

19. I personally prepared all conclusions and opinions about the real estate that were set forth in this appraisal report. If I relied on significant real property appraisal assistance from any individual or individuals in the performance of this appraisal or the preparation of this appraisal report, I have named such individual(s) and disclosed the specific tasks performed in this appraisal report. I certify that any individual so named is qualified to perform the tasks. I have not authorized anyone to make a change to any item in this appraisal report; therefore, any change made to this appraisal is unauthorized and I will take no responsibility for it.

Exterior-Only Inspection Residential Appraisal Report   File

20. I identified the lender/client in this appraisal report who is the individual, organization, or agent for the organization that ordered and will receive this appraisal report.

21. The lender/client may disclose or distribute this appraisal report to: the borrower; another lender at the request of the borrower; the mortgagee or its successors and assigns; mortgage insurers; government sponsored enterprises; other secondary market participants; data collection or reporting services; professional appraisal organizations; any department, agency, or instrumentality of the United States; and any state, the District of Columbia, or other jurisdictions; without having to obtain the appraiser's or supervisory appraiser's (if applicable) consent. Such consent must be obtained before this appraisal report may be disclosed or distributed to any other party (including, but not limited to, the public through advertising, public relations, news, sales, or other media).

22. I am aware that any disclosure or distribution of this appraisal report by me or the lender/client may be subject to certain laws and regulations. Further, I am also subject to the provisions of the Uniform Standards of Professional Appraisal Practice that pertain to disclosure or distribution by me.

23. The borrower, another lender at the request of the borrower, the mortgagee or its successors and assigns, mortgage insurers, government sponsored enterprises, and other secondary market participants may rely on this appraisal report as part of any mortgage finance transaction that involves any one or more of these parties.

24. If this appraisal report was transmitted as an "electronic record" containing my "electronic signature," as those terms are defined in applicable federal and/or state laws (excluding audio and video recordings), or a facsimile transmission of this appraisal report containing a copy or representation of my signature, the appraisal report shall be as effective, enforceable and valid as if a paper version of this appraisal report were delivered containing my original hand written signature.

25. Any intentional or negligent misrepresentation(s) contained in this appraisal report may result in civil liability and/or criminal penalties including, but not limited to, fine or imprisonment or both under the provisions of Title 18, United States Code, Section 1001, et seq., or similar state laws.

SUPERVISORY APPRAISER'S CERTIFICATION: The Supervisory Appraiser certifies and agrees that:

1. I directly supervised the appraiser for this appraisal assignment, have read the appraisal report, and agree with the appraiser's analysis, opinions, statements, conclusions, and the appraiser's certification.

2. I accept full responsibility for the contents of this appraisal report including, but not limited to, the appraiser's analysis, opinions, statements, conclusions, and the appraiser's certification.

3. The appraiser identified in this appraisal report is either a sub-contractor or an employee of the supervisory appraiser (or the appraisal firm), is qualified to perform this appraisal, and is acceptable to perform this appraisal under the applicable state law.

4. This appraisal report complies with the Uniform Standards of Professional Appraisal Practice that were adopted and promulgated by the Appraisal Standards Board of The Appraisal Foundation and that were in place at the time this appraisal report was prepared.

5. If this appraisal report was transmitted as an "electronic record" containing my "electronic signature," as those terms are defined in applicable federal and/or state laws (excluding audio and video recordings), or a facsimile transmission of this appraisal report containing a copy or representation of my signature, the appraisal report shall be as effective, enforceable and valid as if a paper version of this appraisal report were delivered containing my original hand written signature.

APPRAISER	SUPERVISORY APPRAISER (ONLY IF REQUIRED)
Signature _____	Signature _____
Name _____	Name _____
Company Name _____	Company Name _____
Company Address _____	Company Address _____
Telephone Number _____	Telephone Number _____
Email Address _____	Email Address _____
Date of Signature and Report _____	Date of Signature _____
Effective Date of Appraisal _____	State Certification # _____
State Certification # _____	or State License # _____
or State License # _____	State _____
or Other (describe) _____ State # _____	Expiration Date of Certification or License _____
State _____	
Expiration Date of Certification or License _____	SUBJECT PROPERTY
ADDRESS OF PROPERTY APPRAISED	☐ Did not inspect exterior of subject property
_____	☐ Did inspect exterior of subject property from street
_____	Date of Inspection _____
_____	
APPRAISED VALUE OF SUBJECT PROPERTY $ _____	
LENDER/CLIENT	COMPARABLE SALES
Name _____	☐ Did not inspect exterior of comparable sales from street
Company Name _____	☐ Did inspect exterior of comparable sales from street
Company Address _____	Date of Inspection _____
_____	
Email Address _____	

Freddie Mac Form 2055   March 2005   Page 6 of 6   Fannie Mae Form 2055   March 2005

Small Residential Income Property Appraisal Report   File

The purpose of this summary appraisal report is to provide the lender/client with an accurate, and adequately supported, opinion of the market value of the subject property.

SUBJECT

Property Address	City	State Zip Code
Borrower	Owner of Public Record	County

Legal Description
Assessor's Parcel #   Tax Year   R.E. Taxes $
Neighborhood Name   Map Reference   Census Tract
Occupant ☐ Owner ☐ Tenant ☐ Vacant   Special Assessments $ ☐ PUD   HOA $ ☐ per year ☐ per month
Property Rights Appraised ☐ Fee Simple ☐ Leasehold ☐ Other (describe)
Assignment Type ☐ Purchase Transaction ☐ Refinance Transaction ☐ Other (describe)
Lender/Client   Address
Is the subject property currently offered for sale or has it been offered for sale in the twelve months prior to the effective date of this appraisal? ☐ Yes ☐ No
Report data source(s) used, offering price(s), and date(s).

CONTRACT

I ☐ did ☐ did not analyze the contract for sale for the subject purchase transaction. Explain the results of the analysis of the contract for sale or why the analysis was not performed.

Contract Price $ Date of Contract   Is the property seller the owner of public record? ☐ Yes ☐ No Data Source(s)
Is there any financial assistance (loan charges, sale concessions, gift or downpayment assistance, etc.) to be paid by any party on behalf of the borrower? ☐ Yes ☐ No
If Yes, report the total dollar amount and describe the items to be paid.

NEIGHBORHOOD

Note: Race and the racial composition of the neighborhood are not appraisal factors.

Neighborhood Characteristics	2-4 Unit Housing Trends	2-4 Unit Housing	Present Land Use %
Location ☐ Urban ☐ Suburban ☐ Rural	Property Values ☐ Increasing ☐ Stable ☐ Declining	PRICE AGE	One-Unit %
Built-Up ☐ Over 75% ☐ 25–75% ☐ Under 25%	Demand/Supply ☐ Shortage ☐ In Balance ☐ Over Supply	$ (000) (yrs)	2-4 Unit %
Growth ☐ Rapid ☐ Stable ☐ Slow	Marketing Time ☐ Under 3 mths ☐ 3–6 mths ☐ Over 6 mths	Low	Multi-Family %
Neighborhood Boundaries		High	Commercial %
		Pred.	Other %

Neighborhood Description

Market Conditions (including support for the above conclusions)

SITE

Dimensions   Area   Shape   View
Specific Zoning Classification   Zoning Description
Zoning Compliance ☐ Legal ☐ Legal Nonconforming (Grandfathered Use) ☐ No Zoning ☐ Illegal (describe)
Is the highest and best use of the subject property as improved (or as proposed per plans and specifications) the present use? ☐ Yes ☐ No If No, describe

Utilities	Public	Other (describe)		Public	Other (describe)	Off-site Improvements—Type	Public	Private
Electricity	☐	☐	Water	☐	☐	Street	☐	☐
Gas	☐	☐	Sanitary Sewer	☐	☐	Alley	☐	☐

FEMA Special Flood Hazard Area ☐ Yes ☐ No FEMA Flood Zone   FEMA Map #   FEMA Map Date
Are the utilities and off-site improvements typical for the market area? ☐ Yes ☐ No If No, describe
Are there any adverse site conditions or external factors (easements, encroachments, environmental conditions, land uses, etc.)? ☐ Yes ☐ No If Yes, describe

IMPROVEMENTS

General Description	Foundation	Exterior Description materials/condition	Interior materials/condition
Units ☐ Two ☐ Three ☐ Four	☐ Concrete Slab ☐ Crawl Space	Foundation Walls	Floors
☐ Accessory Unit (describe below)	☐ Full Basement ☐ Partial Basement	Exterior Walls	Walls
# of Stories # of bldgs.	Basement Area sq. ft.	Roof Surface	Trim/Finish
Type ☐ Det. ☐ Att. ☐ S-Det./End Unit	Basement Finish %	Gutters & Downspouts	Bath Floor
☐ Existing ☐ Proposed ☐ Under Const.	☐ Outside Entry/Exit ☐ Sump Pump	Window Type	Bath Wainscot
Design (Style)	Evidence of ☐ Infestation	Storm Sash/Insulated	**Car Storage**
Year Built	☐ Dampness ☐ Settlement	Screens	☐ None
Effective Age (Yrs)	**Heating/Cooling**	**Amenities**	☐ Driveway # of Cars
Attic ☐ None	☐ FWA ☐ HWBB ☐ Radiant	☐ Fireplace(s) # ☐ Woodstove(s) #	Driveway Surface
☐ Drop Stair ☐ Stairs	☐ Other Fuel	☐ Patio/Deck ☐ Fence	☐ Garage # of Cars
☐ Floor ☐ Scuttle	☐ Central Air Conditioning	☐ Pool ☐ Porch	☐ Carport # of Cars
☐ Finished ☐ Heated	☐ Individual ☐ Other	☐ Other	☐ Att. ☐ Det. ☐ Built-in

# of Appliances Refrigerator   Range/Oven   Dishwasher   Disposal   Microwave   Washer/Dryer   Other (describe)
Unit # 1 contains: Rooms   Bedroom(s)   Bath(s)   Square feet of Gross Living Area
Unit # 2 contains: Rooms   Bedroom(s)   Bath(s)   Square feet of Gross Living Area
Unit # 3 contains: Rooms   Bedroom(s)   Bath(s)   Square feet of Gross Living Area
Unit # 4 contains: Rooms   Bedroom(s)   Bath(s)   Square feet of Gross Living Area
Additional features (special energy efficient items, etc.)

Describe the condition of the property (including needed repairs, deterioration, renovations, remodeling, etc.).

Small Residential Income Property Appraisal Report — File

IMPROVEMENTS

Are there any physical deficiencies or adverse conditions that affect the livability, soundness, or structural integrity of the property? ☐ Yes ☐ No If Yes, describe

Does the property generally conform to the neighborhood (functional utility, style, condition, use, construction, etc.)? ☐ Yes ☐ No If No, describe

Is the property subject to rent control? ☐ Yes ☐ No If Yes, describe

The following properties represent the most current, similar, and proximate comparable rental properties to the subject property. This analysis is intended to support the opinion of the market rent for the subject property.

COMPARABLE RENTAL DATA

FEATURE	SUBJECT	COMPARABLE RENTAL # 1	COMPARABLE RENTAL # 2	COMPARABLE RENTAL # 3
Address				
Proximity to Subject				
Current Monthly Rent	$	$	$	$
Rent/Gross Bldg. Area	$ sq. ft.	$ sq. ft.	$ sq. ft.	$ sq. ft.
Rent Control	☐ Yes ☐ No	☐ Yes ☐ No	☐ Yes ☐ No	☐ Yes ☐ No
Data Source(s)				
Date of Lease(s)				
Location				
Actual Age				
Condition				
Gross Building Area				

Unit Breakdown

	Rm Count	Size Sq. Ft.	Rm Count	Size Sq. Ft.	Monthly Rent	Rm Count	Size Sq. Ft.	Monthly Rent	Rm Count	Size Sq. Ft.	Monthly Rent
	Tot Br Ba		Tot Br Ba			Tot Br Ba			Tot Br Ba		
Unit # 1					$			$			$
Unit # 2					$			$			$
Unit # 3					$			$			$
Unit # 4					$			$			$
Utilities Included											

Analysis of rental data and support for estimated market rents for the individual subject units reported below (including the adequacy of the comparables, rental concessions, etc.)

SUBJECT RENT SCHEDULE

Rent Schedule: The appraiser must reconcile the applicable indicated monthly market rents to provide an opinion of the market rent for each unit in the subject property.

	Leases		Actual Rent			Opinion Of Market Rent		
	Lease Date		Per Unit		Total Rent	Per Unit		Total Rent
Unit #	Begin Date	End Date	Unfurnished	Furnished		Unfurnished	Furnished	
1			$	$	$	$	$	$
2								
3								
4								

Comment on lease data

Total Actual Monthly Rent	$	Total Gross Monthly Rent	$
Other Monthly Income (itemize)	$	Other Monthly Income (itemize)	$
Total Actual Monthly Income	$	Total Estimated Monthly Income	$

Utilities included in estimated rents ☐ Electric ☐ Water ☐ Sewer ☐ Gas ☐ Oil ☐ Cable ☐ Trash collection ☐ Other (describe)

Comments on actual or estimated rents and other monthly income (including personal property)

PRIOR SALE HISTORY

I ☐ did ☐ did not research the sale or transfer history of the subject property and comparable sales. If not, explain

My research ☐ did ☐ did not reveal any prior sales or transfers of the subject property for the three years prior to the effective date of this appraisal.

Data source(s)

My research ☐ did ☐ did not reveal any prior sales or transfers of the comparable sales for the year prior to the date of sale of the comparable sale.

Data source(s)

Report the results of the research and analysis of the prior sale history of the subject property and comparable sales (report additional prior sales on page 4).

ITEM	SUBJECT	COMPARABLE SALE # 1	COMPARABLE SALE # 2	COMPARABLE SALE # 3
Date of Prior Sale/Transfer				
Price of Prior Sale/Transfer				
Data Source(s)				
Effective Date of Data Source(s)				

Analysis of prior sale history for the subject property and comparable sales

Small Residential Income Property Appraisal Report File

There are _____ comparable properties currently offered for sale in the subject neighborhood ranging in price from $ _____ to $ _____ .

There are _____ comparable sales in the subject neighborhood within the past twelve months ranging in sale price from $ _____ to $ _____ .

FEATURE	SUBJECT	COMPARABLE SALE # 1		COMPARABLE SALE # 2		COMPARABLE SALE # 3	
Address							
Proximity to Subject							
Sale Price	$		$		$		$
Sale Price/Gross Bldg. Area	$ sq. ft.	$ sq. ft.		$ sq. ft.		$ sq. ft.	
Gross Monthly Rent	$	$		$		$	
Gross Rent Multiplier							
Price Per Unit	$	$		$		$	
Price Per Room	$	$		$		$	
Price Per Bedroom	$	$		$		$	
Rent Control	☐ Yes ☐ No	☐ Yes ☐ No		☐ Yes ☐ No		☐ Yes ☐ No	
Data Source(s)							
Verification Source(s)							
VALUE ADJUSTMENTS	DESCRIPTION	DESCRIPTION	+ (-) Adjustment	DESCRIPTION	+ (-) Adjustment	DESCRIPTION	+ (-) Adjustment
Sale or Financing Concessions							
Date of Sale/Time							
Location							
Leasehold/Fee Simple							
Site							
View							
Design (Style)							
Quality of Construction							
Actual Age							
Condition							
Gross Building Area							
Unit Breakdown	Total Bedrooms Baths	Total Bdrms Baths		Total Bdrms Baths		Total Bdrms Baths	
Unit # 1							
Unit # 2							
Unit # 3							
Unit # 4							
Basement Description							
Basement Finished Rooms							
Functional Utility							
Heating/Cooling							
Energy Efficient Items							
Parking On/Off Site							
Porch/Patio/Deck							
Net Adjustment (Total)		☐ + ☐ -	$	☐ + ☐ -	$	☐ + ☐ -	$
Adjusted Sale Price of Comparables		Net Adj. % / Gross Adj. %	$	Net Adj. % / Gross Adj. %	$	Net Adj. % / Gross Adj. %	$
Adj. Price Per Unit (Adj. SP Comp / # of Comp Units)	$	$		$		$	
Adj. Price Per Room (Adj. SP Comp / # of Comp Rooms)	$	$		$		$	
Adj. Price Per Bedrm (Adj. SP Comp / # of Comp Bedrooms)	$	$		$		$	

Value Per Unit $ _____ X _____ Units = $ _____   Value Per GBA $ _____ X _____ GBA = $ _____
Value Per Rm. $ _____ X _____ Rooms = $ _____   Value Per Bdrms. $ _____ X _____ Bdrms. = $ _____

Summary of Sales Comparison Approach including reconciliation of the above indicators of value.

Indicated Value by Sales Comparison Approach $ _____

Total gross monthly rent $ _____ X gross rent multiplier (GRM) _____ = $ _____ Indicated value by the Income Approach

Comments on income approach including reconciliation of the GRM

Indicated Value by: Sales Comparison Approach $ _____   Income Approach $ _____   Cost Approach (if developed) $ _____

This appraisal is made ☐ "as is", ☐ subject to completion per plans and specifications on the basis of a hypothetical condition that the improvements have been completed, ☐ subject to the following repairs or alterations on the basis of a hypothetical condition that the repairs or alterations have been completed, or ☐ subject to the following required inspection based on the extraordinary assumption that the condition or deficiency does not require alteration or repair:

Based on a complete visual inspection of the interior and exterior areas of the subject property, defined scope of work, statement of assumptions and limiting conditions, and appraiser's certification, my (our) opinion of the market value, as defined, of the real property that is the subject of this report is $ _____ , as of _____ , which is the date of inspection and the effective date of this appraisal.

Small Residential Income Property Appraisal Report   File

ADDITIONAL COMMENTS

COST APPROACH TO VALUE (not required by Fannie Mae)

Provide adequate information for the lender/client to replicate the below cost figures and calculations.

Support for the opinion of site value (summary of comparable land sales or other methods for estimating site value)

COST APPROACH

ESTIMATED ☐ REPRODUCTION OR ☐ REPLACEMENT COST NEW | OPINION OF SITE VALUE..= $

Source of cost data | Dwelling   Sq. Ft. @ $ ....=$

Quality rating from cost service   Effective date of cost data | Sq. Ft. @ $ ....=$

Comments on Cost Approach (gross building area calculations, depreciation, etc.)

Garage/Carport   Sq. Ft. @ $ ....=$

Total Estimate of Cost-New ....= $

Less   Physical   Functional   External

Depreciation =$( )

Depreciated Cost of Improvements ....=$

"As-is" Value of Site Improvements...................=$

Estimated Remaining Economic Life (HUD and VA only)   Years | Indicated Value By Cost Approach......................=$

PROJECT INFORMATION FOR PUDs (if applicable)

Is the developer/builder in control of the Homeowners' Association (HOA)? ☐ Yes ☐ No   Unit type(s) ☐ Detached ☐ Attached

Provide the following information for PUDs ONLY if the developer/builder is in control of the HOA and the subject property is an attached dwelling unit.

Legal name of project

Total number of phases   Total number of units   Total number of units sold

Total number of units rented   Total number of units for sale   Data source(s)

Was the project created by the conversion of an existing building(s) into a PUD? ☐ Yes ☐ No   If Yes, date of conversion

Does the project contain any multi-dwelling units? ☐ Yes ☐ No   Data source(s)

Are the units, common elements, and recreation facilities complete? ☐ Yes ☐ No   If No, describe the status of completion.

Are the common elements leased to or by the Homeowners' Association? ☐ Yes ☐ No   If Yes, describe the rental terms and options.

Describe common elements and recreational facilities.

Small Residential Income Property Appraisal Report   File

This report form is designed to report an appraisal of a two- to four-unit property, including a two- to four-unit property in a planned unit development (PUD). A two- to four-unit property located in either a condominium or cooperative project requires the appraiser to inspect the project and complete the project information section of the Individual Condominium Unit Appraisal Report or the Individual Cooperative Interest Appraisal Report and attach it as an addendum to this report.

This appraisal report is subject to the following scope of work, intended use, intended user, definition of market value, statement of assumptions and limiting conditions, and certifications. Modifications, additions, or deletions to the intended use, intended user, definition of market value, or assumptions and limiting conditions are not permitted. The appraiser may expand the scope of work to include any additional research or analysis necessary based on the complexity of this appraisal assignment. Modifications or deletions to the certifications are also not permitted. However, additional certifications that do not constitute material alterations to this appraisal report, such as those required by law or those related to the appraiser's continuing education or membership in an appraisal organization, are permitted.

SCOPE OF WORK: The scope of work for this appraisal is defined by the complexity of this appraisal assignment and the reporting requirements of this appraisal report form, including the following definition of market value, statement of assumptions and limiting conditions, and certifications. The appraiser must, at a minimum: (1) perform a complete visual inspection of the interior and exterior areas of the subject property, (2) inspect the neighborhood, (3) inspect each of the comparable sales from at least the street, (4) research, verify, and analyze data from reliable public and/or private sources, and (5) report his or her analysis, opinions, and conclusions in this appraisal report.

INTENDED USE: The intended use of this appraisal report is for the lender/client to evaluate the property that is the subject of this appraisal for a mortgage finance transaction.

INTENDED USER: The intended user of this appraisal report is the lender/client.

DEFINITION OF MARKET VALUE: The most probable price which a property should bring in a competitive and open market under all conditions requisite to a fair sale, the buyer and seller, each acting prudently, knowledgeably and assuming the price is not affected by undue stimulus. Implicit in this definition is the consummation of a sale as of a specified date and the passing of title from seller to buyer under conditions whereby: (1) buyer and seller are typically motivated; (2) both parties are well informed or well advised, and each acting in what he or she considers his or her own best interest; (3) a reasonable time is allowed for exposure in the open market; (4) payment is made in terms of cash in U. S. dollars or in terms of financial arrangements comparable thereto; and (5) the price represents the normal consideration for the property sold unaffected by special or creative financing or sales concessions* granted by anyone associated with the sale.

*Adjustments to the comparables must be made for special or creative financing or sales concessions. No adjustments are necessary for those costs which are normally paid by sellers as a result of tradition or law in a market area; these costs are readily identifiable since the seller pays these costs in virtually all sales transactions. Special or creative financing adjustments can be made to the comparable property by comparisons to financing terms offered by a third party institutional lender that is not already involved in the property or transaction. Any adjustment should not be calculated on a mechanical dollar for dollar cost of the financing or concession but the dollar amount of any adjustment should approximate the market's reaction to the financing or concessions based on the appraiser's judgment.

STATEMENT OF ASSUMPTIONS AND LIMITING CONDITIONS: The appraiser's certification in this report is subject to the following assumptions and limiting conditions:

1. The appraiser will not be responsible for matters of a legal nature that affect either the property being appraised or the title to it, except for information that he or she became aware of during the research involved in performing this appraisal. The appraiser assumes that the title is good and marketable and will not render any opinions about the title.

2. The appraiser has provided a sketch in this appraisal report to show the approximate dimensions of the improvements, including each of the units. The sketch is included only to assist the reader in visualizing the property and understanding the appraiser's determination of its size.

3. The appraiser has examined the available flood maps that are provided by the Federal Emergency Management Agency (or other data sources) and has noted in this appraisal report whether any portion of the subject site is located in an identified Special Flood Hazard Area. Because the appraiser is not a surveyor, he or she makes no guarantees, express or implied, regarding this determination.

4. The appraiser will not give testimony or appear in court because he or she made an appraisal of the property in question, unless specific arrangements to do so have been made beforehand, or as otherwise required by law.

5. The appraiser has noted in this appraisal report any adverse conditions (such as needed repairs, deterioration, the presence of hazardous wastes, toxic substances, etc.) observed during the inspection of the subject property or that he or she became aware of during the research involved in performing this appraisal. Unless otherwise stated in this appraisal report, the appraiser has no knowledge of any hidden or unapparent physical deficiencies or adverse conditions of the property (such as, but not limited to, needed repairs, deterioration, the presence of hazardous wastes, toxic substances, adverse environmental conditions, etc.) that would make the property less valuable, and has assumed that there are no such conditions and makes no guarantees or warranties, express or implied. The appraiser will not be responsible for any such conditions that do exist or for any engineering or testing that might be required to discover whether such conditions exist. Because the appraiser is not an expert in the field of environmental hazards, this appraisal report must not be considered as an environmental assessment of the property.

6. The appraiser has based his or her appraisal report and valuation conclusion for an appraisal that is subject to satisfactory completion, repairs, or alterations on the assumption that the completion, repairs, or alterations of the subject property will be performed in a professional manner.

Small Residential Income Property Appraisal Report   File

APPRAISER'S CERTIFICATION: The Appraiser certifies and agrees that:

1. I have, at a minimum, developed and reported this appraisal in accordance with the scope of work requirements stated in this appraisal report.

2. I performed a complete visual inspection of the interior and exterior areas of the subject property, including all units. I reported the condition of the improvements in factual, specific terms. I identified and reported the physical deficiencies that could affect the livability, soundness, or structural integrity of the property.

3. I performed this appraisal in accordance with the requirements of the Uniform Standards of Professional Appraisal Practice that were adopted and promulgated by the Appraisal Standards Board of The Appraisal Foundation and that were in place at the time this appraisal report was prepared.

4. I developed my opinion of the market value of the real property that is the subject of this report based on the sales comparison and income approaches to value. I have adequate market data to develop reliable sales comparison and income approaches to value for this appraisal assignment. I further certify that I considered the cost approach to value but did not develop it, unless otherwise indicated in this report.

5. I researched, verified, analyzed, and reported on any current agreement for sale for the subject property, any offering for sale of the subject property in the twelve months prior to the effective date of this appraisal, and the prior sales of the subject property for a minimum of three years prior to the effective date of this appraisal, unless otherwise indicated in this report.

6. I researched, verified, analyzed, and reported on the prior sales of the comparable sales for a minimum of one year prior to the date of sale of the comparable sale, unless otherwise indicated in this report.

7. I selected and used comparable sales that are locationally, physically, and functionally the most similar to the subject property.

8. I have not used comparable sales that were the result of combining a land sale with the contract purchase price of a home that has been built or will be built on the land.

9. I have reported adjustments to the comparable sales that reflect the market's reaction to the differences between the subject property and the comparable sales.

10. I verified, from a disinterested source, all information in this report that was provided by parties who have a financial interest in the sale or financing of the subject property.

11. I have knowledge and experience in appraising this type of property in this market area.

12. I am aware of, and have access to, the necessary and appropriate public and private data sources, such as multiple listing services, tax assessment records, public land records and other such data sources for the area in which the property is located.

13. I obtained the information, estimates, and opinions furnished by other parties and expressed in this appraisal report from reliable sources that I believe to be true and correct.

14. I have taken into consideration the factors that have an impact on value with respect to the subject neighborhood, subject property, and the proximity of the subject property to adverse influences in the development of my opinion of market value. I have noted in this appraisal report any adverse conditions (such as, but not limited to, needed repairs, deterioration, the presence of hazardous wastes, toxic substances, adverse environmental conditions, etc.) observed during the inspection of the subject property or that I became aware of during the research involved in performing this appraisal. I have considered these adverse conditions in my analysis of the property value, and have reported on the effect of the conditions on the value and marketability of the subject property.

15. I have not knowingly withheld any significant information from this appraisal report and, to the best of my knowledge, all statements and information in this appraisal report are true and correct.

16. I stated in this appraisal report my own personal, unbiased, and professional analysis, opinions, and conclusions, which are subject only to the assumptions and limiting conditions in this appraisal report.

17. I have no present or prospective interest in the property that is the subject of this report, and I have no present or prospective personal interest or bias with respect to the participants in the transaction. I did not base, either partially or completely, my analysis and/or opinion of market value in this appraisal report on the race, color, religion, sex, age, marital status, handicap, familial status, or national origin of either the prospective owners or occupants of the subject property or of the present owners or occupants of the properties in the vicinity of the subject property or on any other basis prohibited by law.

18. My employment and/or compensation for performing this appraisal or any future or anticipated appraisals was not conditioned on any agreement or understanding, written or otherwise, that I would report (or present analysis supporting) a predetermined specific value, a predetermined minimum value, a range or direction in value, a value that favors the cause of any party, or the attainment of a specific result or occurrence of a specific subsequent event (such as approval of a pending mortgage loan application).

19. I personally prepared all conclusions and opinions about the real estate that were set forth in this appraisal report. If I relied on significant real property appraisal assistance from any individual or individuals in the performance of this appraisal or the preparation of this appraisal report, I have named such individual(s) and disclosed the specific tasks performed in this appraisal report. I certify that any individual so named is qualified to perform the tasks. I have not authorized anyone to make a change to any item in this appraisal report; therefore, any change made to this appraisal is unauthorized and I will take no responsibility for it.

20. I identified the lender/client in this appraisal report who is the individual, organization, or agent for the organization that ordered and will receive this appraisal report.

Small Residential Income Property Appraisal Report   File

21. The lender/client may disclose or distribute this appraisal report to: the borrower; another lender at the request of the borrower; the mortgagee or its successors and assigns; mortgage insurers; government sponsored enterprises; other secondary market participants; data collection or reporting services; professional appraisal organizations; any department, agency, or instrumentality of the United States; and any state, the District of Columbia, or other jurisdictions; without having to obtain the appraiser's or supervisory appraiser's (if applicable) consent. Such consent must be obtained before this appraisal report may be disclosed or distributed to any other party (including, but not limited to, the public through advertising, public relations, news, sales, or other media).

22. I am aware that any disclosure or distribution of this appraisal report by me or the lender/client may be subject to certain laws and regulations. Further, I am also subject to the provisions of the Uniform Standards of Professional Appraisal Practice that pertain to disclosure or distribution by me.

23. The borrower, another lender at the request of the borrower, the mortgagee or its successors and assigns, mortgage insurers, government sponsored enterprises, and other secondary market participants may rely on this appraisal report as part of any mortgage finance transaction that involves any one or more of these parties.

24. If this appraisal report was transmitted as an "electronic record" containing my "electronic signature," as those terms are defined in applicable federal and/or state laws (excluding audio and video recordings), or a facsimile transmission of this appraisal report containing a copy or representation of my signature, the appraisal report shall be as effective, enforceable and valid as if a paper version of this appraisal report were delivered containing my original hand written signature.

25. Any intentional or negligent misrepresentation(s) contained in this appraisal report may result in civil liability and/or criminal penalties including, but not limited to, fine or imprisonment or both under the provisions of Title 18, United States Code, Section 1001, et seq., or similar state laws.

SUPERVISORY APPRAISER'S CERTIFICATION: The Supervisory Appraiser certifies and agrees that:

1. I directly supervised the appraiser for this appraisal assignment, have read the appraisal report, and agree with the appraiser's analysis, opinions, statements, conclusions, and the appraiser's certification.

2. I accept full responsibility for the contents of this appraisal report including, but not limited to, the appraiser's analysis, opinions, statements, conclusions, and the appraiser's certification.

3. The appraiser identified in this appraisal report is either a sub-contractor or an employee of the supervisory appraiser (or the appraisal firm), is qualified to perform this appraisal, and is acceptable to perform this appraisal under the applicable state law.

4. This appraisal report complies with the Uniform Standards of Professional Appraisal Practice that were adopted and promulgated by the Appraisal Standards Board of The Appraisal Foundation and that were in place at the time this appraisal report was prepared.

5. If this appraisal report was transmitted as an "electronic record" containing my "electronic signature," as those terms are defined in applicable federal and/or state laws (excluding audio and video recordings), or a facsimile transmission of this appraisal report containing a copy or representation of my signature, the appraisal report shall be as effective, enforceable and valid as if a paper version of this appraisal report were delivered containing my original hand written signature.

APPRAISER

Signature _____
Name _____
Company Name_____
Company Address _____
_____
Telephone Number _____
Email Address _____
Date of Signature and Report _____
Effective Date of Appraisal_____
State Certification # _____
or State License # _____
or Other (describe)_____ State # _____
State_____
Expiration Date of Certification or License _____

ADDRESS OF PROPERTY APPRAISED

_____
_____

APPRAISED VALUE OF SUBJECT PROPERTY $ _____

LENDER/CLIENT

Name _____
Company Name_____
Company Address _____
_____
Email Address _____

SUPERVISORY APPRAISER (ONLY IF REQUIRED)

Signature _____
Name _____
Company Name_____
Company Address _____
_____
Telephone Number_____
Email Address _____
Date of Signature _____
State Certification # _____
or State License # _____
State_____
Expiration Date of Certification or License_____

SUBJECT PROPERTY

☐ Did not inspect subject property
☐ Did inspect exterior of subject property from street
    Date of Inspection_____
☐ Did inspect interior and exterior of subject property
    Date of Inspection_____

COMPARABLE SALES

☐ Did not inspect exterior of comparable sales from street
☐ Did inspect exterior of comparable sales from street
    Date of Inspection_____

Operating Income Statement

One- to Four-Family Investment Property and Two- to Four-Family Owner-Occupied Property

Property Address

	Street	City	State	Zip Code

General Instructions: This form is to be prepared jointly by the loan applicant, the appraiser, and the lender's underwriter. The applicant must complete the following schedule indicating each unit's rental status, lease expiration date, current rent, market rent, and the responsibility for utility expenses. Rental figures must be based on the rent for an "unfurnished" unit.

	Currently Rented	Expiration Date	Current Rent Per Month	Market Rent Per Month	Utility Expense	Paid By Owner	Paid By Tenant
Unit No. 1	Yes ___ No ___	_____	$_____	$_____	Electricity............	☐	☐
Unit No. 2	Yes ___ No ___	_____	$_____	$_____	Gas....................	☐	☐
Unit No. 3	Yes ___ No ___	_____	$_____	$_____	Fuel Oil	☐	☐
Unit No. 4	Yes ___ No ___	_____	$_____	$_____	Fuel (Other)	☐	☐
Total			$_____	$_____	Water/Sewer	☐	☐
					Trash Removal	☐	☐

The applicant should complete all of the income and expense projections and for existing properties provide actual year-end operating statements for the past two years *(for new properties the applicant's projected income and expenses must be provided)*. This Operating Income Statement and any previous operating statements the applicant provides must then be sent to the appraiser for review, comment, and/or adjustments next to the applicant's figures *(e.g., Applicant/Appraiser 288/300)*. If the appraiser is retained to complete the form instead of the applicant, the lender must provide to the appraiser the aforementioned operating statements, mortgage insurance premium, HOA dues, leasehold payments, subordinate financing, and/or any other relevant information as to the income and expenses of the subject property received from the applicant to substantiate the projections. The underwriter should carefully review the applicant's/appraiser's projections and the appraiser's comments concerning those projections. The underwriter should make any final adjustments that are necessary to more accurately reflect any income or expense items that appear unreasonable for the market. *(Real estate taxes and insurance on these types of properties are included in PITI and not calculated as an annual expense item.)* Income should be based on current rents, but should not exceed market rents. When there are no current rents because the property is proposed, new, or currently vacant, market rents should be used.

Annual Income and Expense Projection for Next 12 months

Income *(Do not include income for owner-occupied units)*	By Applicant/Appraiser	Adjustments by Lender's Underwriter
Gross Annual Rental *(from unit(s) to be rented)*	$_____	$_____
Other Income *(include sources)*	+_____	+_____
Total	$_____	$_____
Less Vacancy/Rent Loss	−_____ (%)	−_____ (%)
Effective Gross Income	$_____	$_____

Expenses *(Do not include expenses for owner-occupied units)*

	By Applicant/Appraiser	Adjustments by Lender's Underwriter
Electricity	_____	_____
Gas	_____	_____
Fuel Oil	_____	_____
Fuel ....(Type - _____)	_____	_____
Water/Sewer	_____	_____
Trash Removal	_____	_____
Pest Control	_____	_____
Other Taxes or Licenses	_____	_____
Casual Labor	_____	_____
This includes the costs for public area cleaning, snow removal, etc., even though the applicant may not elect to contract for such services.		
Interior Paint/Decorating	_____	_____
This includes the costs of contract labor and materials that are required to maintain the interiors of the living units.		
General Repairs/Maintenance	_____	_____
This includes the costs of contract labor and materials that are required to maintain the public corridors, stairways, roofs, mechanical systems, grounds, etc.		
Management Expenses	_____	_____
These are the customary expenses that a professional management company would charge to manage the property.		
Supplies	_____	_____
This includes the costs of items like light bulbs, janitorial supplies, etc.		
Total Replacement Reserves - See Schedule on Pg. 2.................	_____	_____
Miscellaneous	_____	_____
....	_____	_____
....	_____	_____
....	_____	_____
....	_____	_____
....	_____	_____
....	_____	_____
Total Operating Expenses	$_____	$_____

Freddie Mac
Form 998 Aug 88

This Form Must Be Reproduced By Seller
Page 1 of 2

Fannie Mae
Form 216 Aug 88

252

Replacement Reserve Schedule

Adequate replacement reserves must be calculated regardless of whether actual reserves are provided for on the owner's operating statements or are customary in the local market. This represents the total average yearly reserves. Generally, all equipment and components that have a remaining life of more than one year—such as refrigerators, stoves, clothes washers/dryers, trash compactors, furnaces, roofs, and carpeting, etc.—should be expensed on a replacement cost basis.

Equipment	Replacement Cost	Remaining Life		By Applicant/ Appraiser	Lender Adjustments
Stoves/Ranges	@ $ _____ ea.	÷ ___ Yrs. x	_____ Units =$	_____	$ _____
Refrigerators	@ $ _____ ea.	÷ ___ Yrs. x	_____ Units =$	_____	$ _____
Dishwashers	@ $ _____ ea.	÷ ___ Yrs. x	_____ Units =$	_____	$ _____
A/C Units	@ $ _____ ea.	÷ ___ Yrs. x	_____ Units =$	_____	$ _____
C. Washer/Dryers	@ $ _____ ea.	÷ ___ Yrs. x	_____ Units =$	_____	$ _____
HW Heaters	@ $ _____ ea.	÷ ___ Yrs. x	_____ Units =$	_____	$ _____
Furnace(s)	@ $ _____ ea.	÷ ___ Yrs. x	_____ Units =$	_____	$ _____
(Other)	@ $ _____ ea.	÷ ___ Yrs. x	_____ Units =$	_____	$ _____
Roof	@ $ _____	÷ ___ Yrs. x One Bldg. =		$ _____	$ _____

Carpeting (Wall to Wall)   Remaining Life

			By Applicant/Appraiser	Lender Adjustments
(Units)	___ Total Sq. Yds. @ $___ Per Sq. Yd. ÷ ___Yrs. =		$ _____	$ _____
(Public Areas)	___ Total Sq. Yds. @ $___ Per Sq. Yd. ÷ ___Yrs. =		$ _____	$ _____

Total Replacement Reserves. (Enter on Pg. 1) $ _____ $ _____

Operating Income Reconciliation

$ _____ − $ _____ = $ _____ ÷12 = $ _____
Effective Gross Income   Total Operating Expenses   Operating Income   Monthly Operating Income

$ _____ − $ _____ = $ _____
Monthly Operating Income   Monthly Housing Expense   Net Cash Flow

(Note: Monthly Housing Expense includes principal and interest on the mortgage, hazard insurance premiums, real estate taxes, mortgage insurance premiums, HOA dues, leasehold payments, and subordinate financing payments.)

Underwriter's instructions for 2-4 Family Owner-Occupied Properties

- If Monthly Operating Income is a positive number, enter as "Net Rental Income" in the "Gross Monthly Income" section of Freddie Mac Form 65/Fannie Mae Form 1003. If Monthly Operating Income is a negative number, it must be included as a liability for qualification purposes.

- The borrower's monthly housing expense-to-income ratio must be calculated by comparing the total Monthly Housing Expense for the **subject property** to the borrower's stable monthly income.

Underwriter's instructions for 1-4 Family Investment Properties

- If Net Cash Flow is a positive number, enter as "Net Rental Income" in the "Gross Monthly Income" section of Freddie Mac Form 65/Fannie Mae Form 1003. If Net Cash Flow is a negative number, it must be included as a liability for qualification purposes.

- The borrower's monthly housing expense-to-income ratio must be calculated by comparing the total monthly housing expense for the borrower's **primary residence** to the borrower's stable monthly income.

Appraiser's Comments (Including sources for data and rationale for the projections)

_____   _____   _____
Appraiser Name   Appraiser Signature   Date

Underwriter's Comments and Rationale for Adjustments

_____   _____   _____
Underwriter Name   Underwriter Signature   Date

Freddie Mac
Form 998 Aug 88   Page 2 of 2   Fannie Mae
                                                                  Form 216 Aug 88

Individual Condominium Unit Appraisal Report

File #

The purpose of this summary appraisal report is to provide the lender/client with an accurate, and adequately supported, opinion of the market value of the subject property.

SUBJECT

Property Address	Unit #	City	State	Zip Code

Borrower   Owner of Public Record   County

Legal Description

Assessor's Parcel #   Tax Year   R.E. Taxes $

Project Name   Phase #   Map Reference   Census Tract

Occupant ☐ Owner ☐ Tenant ☐ Vacant   Special Assessments $ HOA $ ☐ per year ☐ per month

Property Rights Appraised ☐ Fee Simple ☐ Leasehold ☐ Other (describe)

Assignment Type ☐ Purchase Transaction ☐ Refinance Transaction ☐ Other (describe)

Lender/Client   Address

Is the subject property currently offered for sale or has it been offered for sale in the twelve months prior to the effective date of this appraisal? ☐ Yes ☐ No

Report data source(s) used, offering price(s), and date(s).

CONTRACT

I ☐ did ☐ did not analyze the contract for sale for the subject purchase transaction. Explain the results of the analysis of the contract for sale or why the analysis was not performed.

Contract Price $ Date of Contract   Is the property seller the owner of public record? ☐ Yes ☐ No   Data Source(s)

Is there any financial assistance (loan charges, sale concessions, gift or downpayment assistance, etc.) to be paid by any party on behalf of the borrower? ☐ Yes ☐ No
If Yes, report the total dollar amount and describe the items to be paid.

NEIGHBORHOOD

Note: Race and the racial composition of the neighborhood are not appraisal factors.

Neighborhood Characteristics			Condominium Unit Housing Trends				Condominium Housing		Present Land Use %	
Location ☐ Urban	☐ Suburban	☐ Rural	Property Values ☐ Increasing	☐ Stable	☐ Declining		PRICE	AGE	One-Unit	%
Built-Up ☐ Over 75%	☐ 25–75%	☐ Under 25%	Demand/Supply ☐ Shortage	☐ In Balance	☐ Over Supply		$ (000)	(yrs)	2-4 Unit	%
Growth ☐ Rapid	☐ Stable	☐ Slow	Marketing Time ☐ Under 3 mths	☐ 3–6 mths	☐ Over 6 mths		Low		Multi-Family	%
Neighborhood Boundaries							High		Commercial	%
							Pred.		Other	%

Neighborhood Description

Market Conditions (including support for the above conclusions)

PROJECT SITE

Topography   Size   Density   View

Specific Zoning Classification   Zoning Description

Zoning Compliance ☐ Legal ☐ Legal Nonconforming – Do the zoning regulations permit rebuilding to current density? ☐ Yes ☐ No
☐ No Zoning ☐ Illegal (describe)

Is the highest and best use of the subject property as improved (or as proposed per plans and specifications) the present use? ☐ Yes ☐ No If No, describe

Utilities	Public	Other (describe)		Public	Other (describe)	Off-site Improvements—Type	Public	Private
Electricity	☐	☐	Water	☐	☐	Street	☐	☐
Gas	☐	☐	Sanitary Sewer	☐	☐	Alley	☐	☐

FEMA Special Flood Hazard Area ☐ Yes ☐ No FEMA Flood Zone   FEMA Map #   FEMA Map Date

Are the utilities and off-site improvements typical for the market area? ☐ Yes ☐ No If No, describe

Are there any adverse site conditions or external factors (easements, encroachments, environmental conditions, land uses, etc.)? ☐ Yes ☐ No If Yes, describe

PROJECT INFORMATION

Data source(s) for project information

Project Description ☐ Detached ☐ Row or Townhouse ☐ Garden ☐ Mid-Rise ☐ High-Rise ☐ Other (describe)

General Description	General Description	Subject Phase	If Project Completed	If Project Incomplete	
# of Stories	Exterior Walls	# of Units	# of Phases	# of Planned Phases	
# of Elevators	Roof Surface	# of Units Completed	# of Units	# o f Planned Units	
☐ Existing ☐ Proposed	Total # Parking	# of Units For Sale	# of Units for Sale	# of Units for Sale	
☐ Under Construction	Ratio (spaces/units)	# of Units Sold	# of Units Sold	# of Units Sold	
Year Built	Type	# of Units Rented	# of Units Rented	# of Units Rented	
Effective Age	Guest Parking	# of Owner Occupied Units	# of Owner Occupied Units	# of Owner Occupied Units	

Project Primary Occupancy ☐ Principal Residence ☐ Second Home or Recreational ☐ Tenant

Is the developer/builder in control of the Homeowners' Association (HOA)? ☐ Yes ☐ No

Management Group – ☐ Homeowners' Association ☐ Developer ☐ Management Agent – Provide name of management company.

Does any single entity (the same individual, investor group, corporation, etc.) own more than 10% of the total units in the project? ☐ Yes ☐ No If Yes, describe

Was the project created by the conversion of an existing building(s) into a condominium? ☐ Yes ☐ No If Yes, describe the original use and the date of conversion.

Are the units, common elements, and recreation facilities complete (including any planned rehabilitation for a condominium conversion)? ☐ Yes ☐ No If No, describe

Is there any commercial space in the project? ☐ Yes ☐ No If Yes, describe and indicate the overall percentage of the commercial space.

Individual Condominium Unit Appraisal Report

File #

Describe the condition of the project and quality of construction.

Describe the common elements and recreational facilities.

Are any common elements leased to or by the Homeowners' Association? ☐ Yes ☐ No If Yes, describe the rental terms and options.

Is the project subject to ground rent? ☐ Yes ☐ No If Yes, $ per year (describe terms and conditions)

Are the parking facilities adequate for the project size and type? ☐ Yes ☐ No If No, describe and comment on the effect on value and marketability.

I ☐ did ☐ did not analyze the condominium project budget for the current year. Explain the results of the analysis of the budget (adequacy of fees, reserves, etc.), or why the analysis was not performed.

Are there any other fees (other than regular HOA charges) for the use of the project facilities? ☐ Yes ☐ No If Yes, report the charges and describe.

Compared to other competitive projects of similar quality and design, the subject unit charge appears ☐ High ☐ Average ☐ Low If High or Low, describe

Are there any special or unusual characteristics of the project (based on the condominium documents, HOA meetings, or other information) known to the appraiser? ☐ Yes ☐ No If Yes, describe and explain the effect on value and marketability.

Unit Charge $ per month X 12 = $ per year   Annual assessment charge per year per square feet of gross living area = $

Utilities included in the unit monthly assessment ☐ None ☐ Heat ☐ Air Conditioning ☐ Electricity ☐ Gas ☐ Water ☐ Sewer ☐ Cable ☐ Other (describe)

General Description	Interior materials/condition	Amenities	Appliances	Car Storage
Floor #	Floors	☐ Fireplace(s) #	☐ Refrigerator	☐ None
# of Levels	Walls	☐ Woodstove(s) #	☐ Range/Oven	☐ Garage ☐ Covered ☐ Open
Heating Type Fuel	Trim/Finish	☐ Deck/Patio	☐ Disp ☐ Microwave	# of Cars
☐ Central AC ☐ Individual AC	Bath Wainscot	☐ Porch/Balcony	☐ Dishwasher	☐ Assigned ☐ Owned
☐ Other (describe)	Doors	☐ Other	☐ Washer/Dryer	Parking Space #

Finished area **above** grade contains: Rooms   Bedrooms   Bath(s)   Square Feet of Gross Living Area Above Grade

Are the heating and cooling for the individual units separately metered? ☐ Yes ☐ No If No, describe and comment on compatibility to other projects in the market area.

Additional features (special energy efficient items, etc.)

Describe the condition of the property (including needed repairs, deterioration, renovations, remodeling, etc.).

Are there any physical deficiencies or adverse conditions that affect the livability, soundness, or structural integrity of the property? ☐ Yes ☐ No If Yes, describe

Does the property generally conform to the neighborhood (functional utility, style, condition, use, construction, etc.)? ☐ Yes ☐ No If No, describe

I ☐ did ☐ did not research the sale or transfer history of the subject property and comparable sales. If not, explain

My research ☐ did ☐ did not reveal any prior sales or transfers of the subject property for the three years prior to the effective date of this appraisal.
Data source(s)

My research ☐ did ☐ did not reveal any prior sales or transfers of the comparable sales for the year prior to the date of sale of the comparable sale.
Data source(s)

Report the results of the research and analysis of the prior sale or transfer history of the subject property and comparable sales (report additional prior sales on page 3).

ITEM	SUBJECT	COMPARABLE SALE # 1	COMPARABLE SALE # 2	COMPARABLE SALE # 3
Date of Prior Sale/Transfer				
Price of Prior Sale/Transfer				
Data Source(s)				
Effective Date of Data Source(s)				

Analysis of prior sale or transfer history of the subject property and comparable sales.

Individual Condominium Unit Appraisal Report

File #

There are _____ comparable properties currently offered for sale in the subject neighborhood ranging in price from $_____ to $_____.
There are _____ comparable sales in the subject neighborhood within the past twelve months ranging in sale price from $_____ to $_____.

FEATURE	SUBJECT	COMPARABLE SALE # 1		COMPARABLE SALE # 2		COMPARABLE SALE # 3	
Address and Unit #							
Project Name and Phase							
Proximity to Subject							
Sale Price	$	$		$		$	
Sale Price/Gross Liv. Area	$ sq. ft.	$ sq. ft.		$ sq. ft.		$ sq. ft.	
Data Source(s)							
Verification Source(s)							
VALUE ADJUSTMENTS	DESCRIPTION	DESCRIPTION	+(-) $ Adjustment	DESCRIPTION	+(-) $ Adjustment	DESCRIPTION	+(-) $ Adjustment
Sale or Financing Concessions							
Date of Sale/Time							
Location							
Leasehold/Fee Simple							
HOA Mo. Assessment							
Common Elements and Rec. Facilities							
Floor Location							
View							
Design (Style)							
Quality of Construction							
Actual Age							
Condition							
Above Grade	Total Bdrms. Baths	Total Bdrms. Baths		Total Bdrms. Baths		Total Bdrms. Baths	
Room Count							
Gross Living Area	sq. ft.	sq. ft.		sq. ft.		sq. ft.	
Basement & Finished Rooms Below Grade							
Functional Utility							
Heating/Cooling							
Energy Efficient Items							
Garage/Carport							
Porch/Patio/Deck							
Net Adjustment (Total)		☐ + ☐ -	$	☐ + ☐ -	$	☐ + ☐ -	$
Adjusted Sale Price of Comparables		Net Adj. % Gross Adj. %	$	Net Adj. % Gross Adj. %	$	Net Adj. % Gross Adj. %	$

Summary of Sales Comparison Approach

Indicated Value by Sales Comparison Approach $

INCOME APPROACH TO VALUE (not required by Fannie Mae)

Estimated Monthly Market Rent $ _____ X Gross Rent Multiplier _____ = $ _____ Indicated Value by Income Approach

Summary of Income Approach (including support for market rent and GRM)

Indicated Value by: Sales Comparison Approach $ _____ Income Approach (if developed) $

This appraisal is made ☐ "as is", ☐ subject to completion per plans and specifications on the basis of a hypothetical condition that the improvements have been completed, ☐ subject to the following repairs or alterations on the basis of a hypothetical condition that the repairs or alterations have been completed, or ☐ subject to the following required inspection based on the extraordinary assumption that the condition or deficiency does not require alteration or repair:

Based on a complete visual inspection of the interior and exterior areas of the subject property, defined scope of work, statement of assumptions and limiting conditions, and appraiser's certification, my (our) opinion of the market value, as defined, of the real property that is the subject of this report is $ _____, as of _____, which is the date of inspection and the effective date of this appraisal.

Individual Condominium Unit Appraisal Report

File #

This report form is designed to report an appraisal of a unit in a condominium project or a condominium unit in a planned unit development (PUD). This report form is not designed to report an appraisal of a manufactured home or a unit in a cooperative project.

This appraisal report is subject to the following scope of work, intended use, intended user, definition of market value, statement of assumptions and limiting conditions, and certifications. Modifications, additions, or deletions to the intended use, intended user, definition of market value, or assumptions and limiting conditions are not permitted. The appraiser may expand the scope of work to include any additional research or analysis necessary based on the complexity of this appraisal assignment. Modifications or deletions to the certifications are also not permitted. However, additional certifications that do not constitute material alterations to this appraisal report, such as those required by law or those related to the appraiser's continuing education or membership in an appraisal organization, are permitted.

SCOPE OF WORK: The scope of work for this appraisal is defined by the complexity of this appraisal assignment and the reporting requirements of this appraisal report form, including the following definition of market value, statement of assumptions and limiting conditions, and certifications. The appraiser must, at a minimum: (1) perform a complete visual inspection of the interior and exterior areas of the subject unit, (2) inspect and analyze the condominium project, (3) inspect the neighborhood, (4) inspect each of the comparable sales from at least the street, (5) research, verify, and analyze data from reliable public and/or private sources, and (6) report his or her analysis, opinions, and conclusions in this appraisal report.

INTENDED USE: The intended use of this appraisal report is for the lender/client to evaluate the property that is the subject of this appraisal for a mortgage finance transaction.

INTENDED USER: The intended user of this appraisal report is the lender/client.

MARKET VALUE: The most probable price which a property should bring in a competitive and open market under all conditions requisite to a fair sale, the buyer and seller, each acting prudently, knowledgeably and assuming the price is not affected by undue stimulus. Implicit in this definition is the consummation of a sale as of a specified date and the passing of title from seller to buyer under conditions whereby: (1) buyer and seller are typically motivated; (2) both parties are well informed or well advised, and each acting in what he or she considers his or her own best interest; (3) a reasonable time is allowed for exposure in the open market; (4) payment is made in terms of cash in U. S. dollars or in terms of financial arrangements comparable thereto; and (5) the price represents the normal consideration for the property sold unaffected by special or creative financing or sales concessions* granted by anyone associated with the sale.

*Adjustments to the comparables must be made for special or creative financing or sales concessions. No adjustments are necessary for those costs which are normally paid by sellers as a result of tradition or law in a market area; these costs are readily identifiable since the seller pays these costs in virtually all sales transactions. Special or creative financing adjustments can be made to the comparable property by comparisons to financing terms offered by a third party institutional lender that is not already involved in the property or transaction. Any adjustment should not be calculated on a mechanical dollar for dollar cost of the financing or concession but the dollar amount of any adjustment should approximate the market's reaction to the financing or concessions based on the appraiser's judgment.

STATEMENT OF ASSUMPTIONS AND LIMITING CONDITIONS: The appraiser's certification in this report is subject to the following assumptions and limiting conditions:

1. The appraiser will not be responsible for matters of a legal nature that affect either the property being appraised or the title to it, except for information that he or she became aware of during the research involved in performing this appraisal. The appraiser assumes that the title is good and marketable and will not render any opinions about the title.

2. The appraiser has provided a sketch in this appraisal report to show the approximate dimensions of the improvements. The sketch is included only to assist the reader in visualizing the property and understanding the appraiser's determination of its size.

3. The appraiser has examined the available flood maps that are provided by the Federal Emergency Management Agency (or other data sources) and has noted in this appraisal report whether any portion of the subject site is located in an identified Special Flood Hazard Area. Because the appraiser is not a surveyor, he or she makes no guarantees, express or implied, regarding this determination.

4. The appraiser will not give testimony or appear in court because he or she made an appraisal of the property in question, unless specific arrangements to do so have been made beforehand, or as otherwise required by law.

5. The appraiser has noted in this appraisal report any adverse conditions (such as needed repairs, deterioration, the presence of hazardous wastes, toxic substances, etc.) observed during the inspection of the subject property or that he or she became aware of during the research involved in performing this appraisal. Unless otherwise stated in this appraisal report, the appraiser has no knowledge of any hidden or unapparent physical deficiencies or adverse conditions of the property (such as, but not limited to, needed repairs, deterioration, the presence of hazardous wastes, toxic substances, adverse environmental conditions, etc.) that would make the property less valuable, and has assumed that there are no such conditions and makes no guarantees or warranties, express or implied. The appraiser will not be responsible for any such conditions that do exist or for any engineering or testing that might be required to discover whether such conditions exist. Because the appraiser is not an expert in the field of environmental hazards, this appraisal report must not be considered as an environmental assessment of the property.

6. The appraiser has based his or her appraisal report and valuation conclusion for an appraisal that is subject to satisfactory completion, repairs, or alterations on the assumption that the completion, repairs, or alterations of the subject property will be performed in a professional manner.

Individual Condominium Unit Appraisal Report

APPRAISER'S CERTIFICATION: The Appraiser certifies and agrees that:

1. I have, at a minimum, developed and reported this appraisal in accordance with the scope of work requirements stated in this appraisal report.

2. I performed a complete visual inspection of the interior and exterior areas of the subject property. I reported the condition of the improvements in factual, specific terms. I identified and reported the physical deficiencies that could affect the livability, soundness, or structural integrity of the property.

3. I performed this appraisal in accordance with the requirements of the Uniform Standards of Professional Appraisal Practice that were adopted and promulgated by the Appraisal Standards Board of The Appraisal Foundation and that were in place at the time this appraisal report was prepared.

4. I developed my opinion of the market value of the real property that is the subject of this report based on the sales comparison approach to value. I have adequate comparable market data to develop a reliable sales comparison approach for this appraisal assignment. I further certify that I considered the cost and income approaches to value but did not develop them, unless otherwise indicated in this report.

5. I researched, verified, analyzed, and reported on any current agreement for sale for the subject property, any offering for sale of the subject property in the twelve months prior to the effective date of this appraisal, and the prior sales of the subject property for a minimum of three years prior to the effective date of this appraisal, unless otherwise indicated in this report.

6. I researched, verified, analyzed, and reported on the prior sales of the comparable sales for a minimum of one year prior to the date of sale of the comparable sale, unless otherwise indicated in this report.

7. I selected and used comparable sales that are locationally, physically, and functionally the most similar to the subject property.

8. I have not used comparable sales that were the result of combining a land sale with the contract purchase price of a home that has been built or will be built on the land.

9. I have reported adjustments to the comparable sales that reflect the market's reaction to the differences between the subject property and the comparable sales.

10. I verified, from a disinterested source, all information in this report that was provided by parties who have a financial interest in the sale or financing of the subject property.

11. I have knowledge and experience in appraising this type of property in this market area.

12. I am aware of, and have access to, the necessary and appropriate public and private data sources, such as multiple listing services, tax assessment records, public land records and other such data sources for the area in which the property is located.

13. I obtained the information, estimates, and opinions furnished by other parties and expressed in this appraisal report from reliable sources that I believe to be true and correct.

14. I have taken into consideration the factors that have an impact on value with respect to the subject neighborhood, subject property, and the proximity of the subject property to adverse influences in the development of my opinion of market value. I have noted in this appraisal report any adverse conditions (such as, but not limited to, needed repairs, deterioration, the presence of hazardous wastes, toxic substances, adverse environmental conditions, etc.) observed during the inspection of the subject property or that I became aware of during the research involved in performing this appraisal. I have considered these adverse conditions in my analysis of the property value, and have reported on the effect of the conditions on the value and marketability of the subject property.

15. I have not knowingly withheld any significant information from this appraisal report and, to the best of my knowledge, all statements and information in this appraisal report are true and correct.

16. I stated in this appraisal report my own personal, unbiased, and professional analysis, opinions, and conclusions, which are subject only to the assumptions and limiting conditions in this appraisal report.

17. I have no present or prospective interest in the property that is the subject of this report, and I have no present or prospective personal interest or bias with respect to the participants in the transaction. I did not base, either partially or completely, my analysis and/or opinion of market value in this appraisal report on the race, color, religion, sex, age, marital status, handicap, familial status, or national origin of either the prospective owners or occupants of the subject property or of the present owners or occupants of the properties in the vicinity of the subject property or on any other basis prohibited by law.

18. My employment and/or compensation for performing this appraisal or any future or anticipated appraisals was not conditioned on any agreement or understanding, written or otherwise, that I would report (or present analysis supporting) a predetermined specific value, a predetermined minimum value, a range or direction in value, a value that favors the cause of any party, or the attainment of a specific result or occurrence of a specific subsequent event (such as approval of a pending mortgage loan application).

19. I personally prepared all conclusions and opinions about the real estate that were set forth in this appraisal report. If I relied on significant real property appraisal assistance from any individual or individuals in the performance of this appraisal or the preparation of this appraisal report, I have named such individual(s) and disclosed the specific tasks performed in this appraisal report. I certify that any individual so named is qualified to perform the tasks. I have not authorized anyone to make a change to any item in this appraisal report; therefore, any change made to this appraisal is unauthorized and I will take no responsibility for it.

20. I identified the lender/client in this appraisal report who is the individual, organization, or agent for the organization that ordered and will receive this appraisal report.

Individual Condominium Unit Appraisal Report

File #

21. The lender/client may disclose or distribute this appraisal report to: the borrower; another lender at the request of the borrower; the mortgagee or its successors and assigns; mortgage insurers; government sponsored enterprises; other secondary market participants; data collection or reporting services; professional appraisal organizations; any department, agency, or instrumentality of the United States; and any state, the District of Columbia, or other jurisdictions; without having to obtain the appraiser's or supervisory appraiser's (if applicable) consent. Such consent must be obtained before this appraisal report may be disclosed or distributed to any other party (including, but not limited to, the public through advertising, public relations, news, sales, or other media).

22. I am aware that any disclosure or distribution of this appraisal report by me or the lender/client may be subject to certain laws and regulations. Further, I am also subject to the provisions of the Uniform Standards of Professional Appraisal Practice that pertain to disclosure or distribution by me.

23. The borrower, another lender at the request of the borrower, the mortgagee or its successors and assigns, mortgage insurers, government sponsored enterprises, and other secondary market participants may rely on this appraisal report as part of any mortgage finance transaction that involves any one or more of these parties.

24. If this appraisal report was transmitted as an "electronic record" containing my "electronic signature," as those terms are defined in applicable federal and/or state laws (excluding audio and video recordings), or a facsimile transmission of this appraisal report containing a copy or representation of my signature, the appraisal report shall be as effective, enforceable and valid as if a paper version of this appraisal report were delivered containing my original hand written signature.

25. Any intentional or negligent misrepresentation(s) contained in this appraisal report may result in civil liability and/or criminal penalties including, but not limited to, fine or imprisonment or both under the provisions of Title 18, United States Code, Section 1001, et seq., or similar state laws.

SUPERVISORY APPRAISER'S CERTIFICATION: The Supervisory Appraiser certifies and agrees that:

1. I directly supervised the appraiser for this appraisal assignment, have read the appraisal report, and agree with the appraiser's analysis, opinions, statements, conclusions, and the appraiser's certification.

2. I accept full responsibility for the contents of this appraisal report including, but not limited to, the appraiser's analysis, opinions, statements, conclusions, and the appraiser's certification.

3. The appraiser identified in this appraisal report is either a sub-contractor or an employee of the supervisory appraiser (or the appraisal firm), is qualified to perform this appraisal, and is acceptable to perform this appraisal under the applicable state law.

4. This appraisal report complies with the Uniform Standards of Professional Appraisal Practice that were adopted and promulgated by the Appraisal Standards Board of The Appraisal Foundation and that were in place at the time this appraisal report was prepared.

5. If this appraisal report was transmitted as an "electronic record" containing my "electronic signature," as those terms are defined in applicable federal and/or state laws (excluding audio and video recordings), or a facsimile transmission of this appraisal report containing a copy or representation of my signature, the appraisal report shall be as effective, enforceable and valid as if a paper version of this appraisal report were delivered containing my original hand written signature.

APPRAISER

Signature _____
Name _____
Company Name _____
Company Address _____

Telephone Number _____
Email Address _____
Date of Signature and Report _____
Effective Date of Appraisal _____
State Certification # _____
or State License # _____
or Other _____ State # _____
State _____
Expiration Date of Certification or License _____

ADDRESS OF PROPERTY APPRAISED
_____
_____
APPRAISED VALUE OF SUBJECT PROPERTY $ _____
LENDER/CLIENT
Name _____
Company Name _____
Company Address _____
Email Address _____

SUPERVISORY APPRAISER (ONLY IF REQUIRED)

Signature _____
Name _____
Company Name _____
Company Address _____
_____
Telephone Number _____
Email Address _____
Date of Signature _____
State Certification # _____
or State License # _____
State _____
Expiration Date of Certification or License _____

SUBJECT PROPERTY
☐ Did not inspect subject property
☐ Did inspect exterior of subject property from street
   Date of Inspection _____
☐ Did inspect interior and exterior of subject property
   Date of Inspection _____

COMPARABLE SALES
☐ Did not inspect exterior of comparable sales from street
☐ Did inspect exterior of comparable sales from street
   Date of Inspection _____

Manufactured Home Appraisal Report

File #

The purpose of this summary appraisal report is to provide the lender/client with an accurate, and adequately supported, opinion of the market value of the subject property.

SUBJECT

Property Address		City		State	Zip Code

Borrower | Owner of Public Record | County

Legal Description

Assessor's Parcel # | Tax Year | R.E. Taxes $

Neighborhood Name | Map Reference | Census Tract

Occupant ☐ Owner ☐ Tenant ☐ Vacant | Project Type (if applicable) ☐ PUD ☐ Condominium ☐ Cooperative ☐ Other (describe)

Special Assessments $ | HOA $ ☐ per year ☐ per month

Property Rights Appraised ☐ Fee Simple ☐ Leasehold ☐ Other (describe)

Assignment Type ☐ Purchase Transaction ☐ Refinance Transaction ☐ Other (describe)

Lender/Client | Address

Is the subject property currently offered for sale or has it been offered for sale in the twelve months prior to the effective date of this appraisal? ☐ Yes ☐ No

Report data source(s) used, offering price(s), and date(s).

CONTRACT

Manufactured homes located in either a condominium or cooperative project require the appraiser to inspect the project and complete the Project Information section of the Individual Condominium Unit Appraisal Report or the Individual Cooperative Interest Appraisal Report and attach it as an addendum to this report.

I ☐ did ☐ did not analyze the contract for sale for the subject purchase transaction. Explain the results of the analysis of the contract for sale or why the analysis was not performed.

Contract Price $ | Date of Contract | Is the property seller the owner of public record? ☐ Yes ☐ No Data Source(s)

Is there any financial assistance (loan charges, sale concessions, gift or downpayment assistance, etc.) to be paid by any party on behalf of the borrower? ☐ Yes ☐ No
If Yes, report the total dollar amount and describe the items to be paid.

I ☐ did ☐ did not analyze the manufacturer's invoice. Explain the results of the analysis of the manufacturer's invoice or why the analysis was not performed.

Retailer's Name (New Construction)

NEIGHBORHOOD

Note: Race and the racial composition of the neighborhood are not appraisal factors.

Neighborhood Characteristics			Manufactured Housing Trends			Manufactured Housing		Present Land Use %	
Location ☐ Urban	☐ Suburban	☐ Rural	Property Values ☐ Increasing	☐ Stable	☐ Declining	PRICE	AGE	One-Unit	%
Built-Up ☐ Over 75%	☐ 25–75%	☐ Under 25%	Demand/Supply ☐ Shortage	☐ In Balance	☐ Over Supply	$ (000)	(yrs)	2-4 Unit	%
Growth ☐ Rapid	☐ Stable	☐ Slow	Marketing Time ☐ Under 3 mths	☐ 3–6 mths	☐ Over 6 mths	Low		Multi-Family	%
Neighborhood Boundaries						High		Commercial	%
						Pred.		Other	%

Neighborhood Description

Market Conditions (including support for the above conclusions)

SITE

Dimensions | Area | Shape | View

Specific Zoning Classification | Zoning Description

Zoning Compliance ☐ Legal ☐ Legal Nonconforming (Grandfathered Use) ☐ No Zoning ☐ Illegal (describe)

Is the highest and best use of the subject property as improved (or as proposed per plans and specifications) the present use? ☐ Yes ☐ No If No, describe

Utilities	Public	Other (describe)		Public	Other (describe)	Off-site Improvements—Type	Public	Private
Electricity	☐	☐	Water	☐	☐	Street	☐	☐
Gas	☐	☐	Sanitary Sewer	☐	☐	Alley	☐	☐

FEMA Special Flood Hazard Area ☐ Yes ☐ No FEMA Flood Zone | FEMA Map # | FEMA Map Date

Are the utilities and off-site improvements typical for the market area? ☐ Yes ☐ No If No, describe

Is the site size, shape and topography generally conforming to and acceptable in the market area? ☐ Yes ☐ No If No, explain

Is there adequate vehicular access to the subject property? ☐ Yes ☐ No If No, describe

Is the street properly maintained? ☐ Yes ☐ No If No, describe

Are there any adverse site conditions or external factors (easements, encroachments, environmental conditions, land uses, etc.)? ☐ Yes ☐ No If Yes, describe

HUD DATA PLATE

The HUD Data Plate/Compliance Certificate is located on the interior of the subject and contains, among other things, the manufacturer's name, trade/model name, year manufactured and serial number. The HUD Certification Label is located on the exterior of each section of the home.

Is the HUD Data Plate/Compliance Certificate attached to the dwelling? ☐ Yes ☐ No If Yes, identify the location. If No, provide the data source(s) for the HUD Data Plate/Compliance Certificate information.

Is a HUD Certification Label attached to the exterior of each section of the dwelling? ☐ Yes ☐ No If No, provide the data source(s) for the HUD Certification Label #'s

Manufacturer's Serial #(s)/VIN #(s)

HUD Certification Label #(s)

Manufacturer's Name | Trade/Model | Date of Manufacture

Do the Wind, Roof Load, and Thermal Zones meet the minimum HUD requirements for the location of the subject property? ☐ Yes ☐ No If No, explain

Manufactured Home Appraisal Report

File #

General Description	Foundation	Exterior Description — materials/condition	Interior — materials/condition
# of Units ☐ One ☐ Additions	☐ Poured Concrete ☐ Concrete Runners	Skirting	Floors
# of Stories ☐ 1 ☐ 2 ☐ Other	☐ Block & Pier ☐ Other-att. description	Exterior Walls	Walls
Design (Style)	☐ Full Basement ☐ Partial Basement	Roof Surface	Trim/Finish
# of Sections ☐ 1 ☐ 2 ☐ 3	Basement Area sq. ft.	Gutters & Downspouts	Bath Floor
☐ Other	Basement Finish %	Window Type	Bath Wainscot
Type ☐ Det. ☐ Att. ☐ S-Det./End Unit	☐ Outside Entry/Exit ☐ Sump Pump	Storm Sash/Insulated	Car Storage ☐ None
☐ Existing ☐ Proposed ☐ Under Const.	Evidence of ☐ Infestation	Screens	☐ Driveway # of Cars
Year Built Effective Age (Yrs)	☐ Dampness ☐ Settlement	Doors	Driveway Surface
Attic ☐ None	Heating ☐ FWA ☐ HWBB ☐ Radiant	Amenities ☐ WoodStove(s) #	☐ Garage # of Cars
☐ Drop Stair ☐ Stairs	☐ Other Fuel	☐ Fireplace(s) # ☐ Fence	☐ Carport # of Cars
☐ Floor ☐ Scuttle	Cooling ☐ Central Air Conditioning	☐ Patio/Deck ☐ Porch	☐ Attached ☐ Detached
☐ Finished ☐ Heated	☐ Individual ☐ Other	☐ Pool ☐ Other	☐ Built-in

Appliances ☐ Refrigerator ☐ Range/Oven ☐ Dishwasher ☐ Disposal ☐ Microwave ☐ Washer/Dryer ☐ Other (describe)

Finished area **above** grade contains: Rooms   Bedrooms   Bath(s)   Square Feet of Gross Living Area Above Grade

Describe any additions or modifications (decks, rooms, remodeling, etc.)

Installer's Name   Date Installed   Model Year

Is the manufactured home attached to a permanent foundation system? ☐ Yes ☐ No If No, describe the foundation sytem and the manner of attachment.

Have the towing hitch, wheels, and axles been removed? ☐ Yes ☐ No If No, explain

Is the manufactured home permanently connected to a septic tank or sewage system and other utilities? ☐ Yes ☐ No If No, explain

Does the dwelling have sufficient gross living area and room dimensions to be acceptable to the market? ☐ Yes ☐ No If No, explain

Additional features (special energy efficient items, non-realty items, etc.)

The appraiser must rate the quality of construction for the subject unit based on objective criteria (such as N.A.D.A. Manufactured Housing Appraisal Guide®, Marshall & Swift Residential Cost Handbook®, or other published cost service). The appraiser must also report the source used for this quality of construction rating determination.

Quality ☐ Poor ☐ Fair ☐ Average ☐ Good ☐ Excellent   Identify source of quality rating

Describe the condition of the property (including needed repairs, deterioration, renovations, remodeling, etc.).

Are there any physical deficiencies or adverse conditions that affect the livability, soundness, or structural integrity of the property? ☐ Yes ☐ No If Yes, describe

Does the property generally conform to the neighborhood (functional utility, style, condition, use, construction, etc.)? ☐ Yes ☐ No If No, describe

Provide adequate information for the lender/client to replicate the below cost figures and calculations.

Support for the opinion of site value (summary of comparable land sales or other methods for estimating site value)

ESTIMATED ☐ REPRODUCTION OR ☐ REPLACEMENT COST NEW

Source of cost data	Effective date of cost data	Quality rating from cost service		
OPINION OF SITE VALUE	$	**Exterior Dimensions of the Subject Unit**		
Section One Sq. ft. @ $	$	X	=	Sq. ft.
Section Two Sq. ft. @ $	$	X	=	Sq. ft.
Section Three Sq. ft. @ $	$	X	=	Sq. ft.
Section Four Sq. ft. @ $	$	X	=	Sq. ft.
	$	Total Gross Living Area:		Sq. ft.
	$	**Other Data Identification**		
	$	N.A.D.A. Data Identification Info: Edition Mo: Yr:		
Sub-total:	$	MH State: Region: Size: ft. x ft.		
Cost Multiplier (if applicable):	x	Gray pg. White pg. Black SVS pg.		
Modified Sub-total:		15 years and older Conversion Chart pg. Yellow pg.		
Physical Depreciation or Condition Modifier:		Comments		
Functional Obsolescence (not used for N.A.D.A.):				
External Depreciation or State Location Modifier:				
Delivery, Installation, and Setup (not used for N.A.D.A.):	$			
Other Depreciated Site Improvements:	$			
Market Value of Subject Site (as supported above):	$			
Indicated Value by Cost Approach:	$	Estimated Remaining Economic Life (HUD and VA only) Years		
Summary of Cost Approach				

Manufactured Home Appraisal Report

File #

There are	comparable properties currently offered for sale in the subject neighborhood ranging in price from $					to $			.
There are	comparable sales in the subject neighborhood within the past twelve months ranging in sale price from $					to $			.

FEATURE	SUBJECT	COMPARABLE SALE # 1		COMPARABLE SALE # 2		COMPARABLE SALE # 3	
Address							
Proximity to Subject							
Sale Price	$	$		$		$	
Sale Price/Gross Liv. Area	$ sq. ft.	$ sq. ft.		$ sq. ft.		$ sq. ft.	
Manufactured Home		☐ Yes ☐ No		☐ Yes ☐ No		☐ Yes ☐ No	
Data Source(s)							
Verification Source(s)							
VALUE ADJUSTMENTS	DESCRIPTION	DESCRIPTION	+(-) $ Adjustment	DESCRIPTION	+(-) $ Adjustment	DESCRIPTION	+(-) $ Adjustment
Sale or Financing Concessions							
Date of Sale/Time							
Location							
Leasehold/Fee Simple							
Site							
View							
Design (Style)							
Quality of Construction							
Actual Age							
Condition							
Above Grade	Total Bdrms. Baths	Total Bdrms. Baths		Total Bdrms. Baths		Total Bdrms. Baths	
Room Count							
Gross Living Area	sq. ft.	sq. ft.		sq. ft.		sq. ft.	
Basement & Finished Rooms Below Grade							
Functional Utility							
Heating/Cooling							
Energy Efficient Items							
Garage/Carport							
Porch/Patio/Deck							
Net Adjustment (Total)		☐ + ☐ - $		☐ + ☐ - $		☐ + ☐ - $	
Adjusted Sale Price of Comparables		Net Adj. % Gross Adj. % $		Net Adj. % Gross Adj. % $		Net Adj. % Gross Adj. % $	

I ☐ did ☐ did not research the sale or transfer history of the subject property and comparable sales. If not, explain

My research ☐ did ☐ did not reveal any prior sales or transfers of the subject property for the three years prior to the effective date of this appraisal.

Data source(s)

My research ☐ did ☐ did not reveal any prior sales or transfers of the comparable sales for the year prior to the date of sale of the comparable sale.

Data source(s)

Report the results of the research and analysis of the prior sale or transfer history of the subject property and comparable sales (report additional prior sales on page 4).

ITEM	SUBJECT	COMPARABLE SALE # 1	COMPARABLE SALE # 2	COMPARABLE SALE # 3
Date of Prior Sale/Transfer				
Price of Prior Sale/Transfer				
Data Source(s)				
Effective Date of Data Source(s)				

Analysis of prior sale or transfer history of the subject property and comparable sales

Summary of Sales Comparison Approach

Indicated Value by Sales Comparison Approach $

Indicated Value by: Sales Comparison Approach $ **Cost Approach $**   **Income Approach (if developed) $**

This appraisal is made ☐ "as is", ☐ subject to completion per plans and specifications on the basis of a hypothetical condition that the improvements have been completed, ☐ subject to the following repairs or alterations on the basis of a hypothetical condition that the repairs or alterations have been completed, or ☐ subject to the following required inspection based on the extraordinary assumption that the condition or deficiency does not require alteration or repair.

Based on a complete visual inspection of the interior and exterior areas of the subject property, defined scope of work, statement of assumptions and limiting conditions, and appraiser's certification, my (our) opinion of the market value, as defined, of the real property that is the subject of this report is $, as of   , which is the date of inspection and the effective date of this appraisal.

(vertical label left: SALES COMPARISON APPROACH)
(vertical label left: RECONCILIATION)

Freddie Mac Form 70B   March 2005   Page 3 of 7   Fannie Mae Form 1004C March 2005

Manufactured Home Appraisal Report

File #

ADDITIONAL COMMENTS

(blank ruled lines)

INCOME | **INCOME APPROACH TO VALUE (not required by Fannie Mae.)**

Estimated Monthly Market Rent $ _____ X Gross Rent Multiplier _____ = $ _____ Indicated Value by Income Approach

Summary of Income Approach (including support for market rent and GRM)

PROJECT INFORMATION FOR PUDs (if applicable)

PUD INFORMATION

Is the developer/builder in control of the Homeowners' Association (HOA)? ☐ Yes ☐ No   Unit type(s) ☐ Detached ☐ Attached

Provide the following information for PUDs ONLY if the developer/builder is in control of the HOA and the subject property is an attached dwelling unit.

Legal name of project

Total number of phases	Total number of units	Total number of units sold
Total number of units rented	Total number of units for sale	Data source(s)

Was the project created by the conversion of existing building(s) into a PUD? ☐ Yes ☐ No If Yes, date of conversion

Does the project contain any multi-dwelling units? ☐ Yes ☐ No Data source(s)

Are the units, common elements, and recreation facilities complete? ☐ Yes ☐ No If No, describe the status of completion.

Are the common elements leased to or by the Homeowners' Association? ☐ Yes ☐ No If Yes, describe the rental terms and options.

Describe common elements and recreational facilities.

Manufactured Home Appraisal Report

This report form is designed to report an appraisal of a one-unit manufactured home; including a manufactured home in a planned unit development (PUD). A Manufactured home located in either a condominium or cooperative project requires the appraiser to inspect the project and complete the project information section of the Individual Condominium Unit Appraisal Report or the Individual Cooperative Interest Appraisal Report and attach it as an addendum to this report.

This appraisal report is subject to the following scope of work, intended use, intended user, definition of market value, statement of assumptions and limiting conditions, and certifications. Modifications, additions, or deletions to the intended use, intended user, definition of market value, or assumptions and limiting conditions are not permitted. The appraiser may expand the scope of work to include any additional research or analysis necessary based on the complexity of this appraisal assignment. Modifications or deletions to the certifications are also not permitted. However, additional certifications that do not constitute material alterations to this appraisal report, such as those required by law or those related to the appraiser's continuing education or membership in an appraisal organization, are permitted.

SCOPE OF WORK: The scope of work for this appraisal is defined by the complexity of this appraisal assignment and the reporting requirements of this appraisal report form, including the following definition of market value, statement of assumptions and limiting conditions, and certifications. The appraiser must, at a minimum: (1) perform a complete visual inspection of the interior and exterior areas of the subject property, (2) inspect the neighborhood, (3) inspect each of the comparable sales from at least the street, (4) research, verify, and analyze data from reliable public and/or private sources, and (5) report his or her analysis, opinions, and conclusions in this appraisal report.

INTENDED USE: The intended use of this appraisal report is for the lender/client to evaluate the property that is the subject of this appraisal for a mortgage finance transaction.

INTENDED USER: The intended user of this appraisal report is the lender/client.

DEFINITION OF MARKET VALUE: The most probable price which a property should bring in a competitive and open market under all conditions requisite to a fair sale, the buyer and seller, each acting prudently, knowledgeably and assuming the price is not affected by undue stimulus. Implicit in this definition is the consummation of a sale as of a specified date and the passing of title from seller to buyer under conditions whereby: (1) buyer and seller are typically motivated; (2) both parties are well informed or well advised, and each acting in what he or she considers his or her own best interest; (3) a reasonable time is allowed for exposure in the open market; (4) payment is made in terms of cash in U. S. dollars or in terms of financial arrangements comparable thereto; and (5) the price represents the normal consideration for the property sold unaffected by special or creative financing or sales concessions* granted by anyone associated with the sale.

*Adjustments to the comparables must be made for special or creative financing or sales concessions. No adjustments are necessary for those costs which are normally paid by sellers as a result of tradition or law in a market area; these costs are readily identifiable since the seller pays these costs in virtually all sales transactions. Special or creative financing adjustments can be made to the comparable property by comparisons to financing terms offered by a third party institutional lender that is not already involved in the property or transaction. Any adjustment should not be calculated on a mechanical dollar for dollar cost of the financing or concession but the dollar amount of any adjustment should approximate the market's reaction to the financing or concessions based on the appraiser's judgment.

STATEMENT OF ASSUMPTIONS AND LIMITING CONDITIONS: The appraiser's certification in this report is subject to the following assumptions and limiting conditions:

1. The appraiser will not be responsible for matters of a legal nature that affect either the property being appraised or the title to it, except for information that he or she became aware of during the research involved in performing this appraisal. The appraiser assumes that the title is good and marketable and will not render any opinions about the title.

2. The appraiser has provided a sketch in this appraisal report to show approximate dimensions of the improvements. The sketch is included only to assist the reader in visualizing the property and understanding the appraiser's determination of its size.

3. The appraiser has examined the available flood maps that are provided by the Federal Emergency Management Agency (or other data sources) and has noted in this appraisal report whether any portion of the subject site is located in an identified Special Flood Hazard Area. Because the appraiser is not a surveyor, he or she makes no guarantees, express or implied, regarding this determination.

4. The appraiser will not give testimony or appear in court because he or she made an appraisal of the property in question, unless specific arrangements to do so have been made beforehand, or as otherwise required by law.

5. The appraiser has noted in this appraisal report any adverse conditions (such as needed repairs, deterioration, the presence of hazardous wastes, toxic substances, etc.) observed during the inspection of the subject property or that he or she became aware of during the research involved in performing this appraisal. Unless otherwise stated in this appraisal report, the appraiser has no knowledge of any hidden or unapparent physical deficiencies or adverse conditions of the property (such as, but not limited to, needed repairs, deterioration, the presence of hazardous wastes, toxic substances, adverse environmental conditions, etc.) that would make the property less valuable, and has assumed that there are no such conditions and makes no guarantees or warranties, express or implied. The appraiser will not be responsible for any such conditions that do exist or for any engineering or testing that might be required to discover whether such conditions exist. Because the appraiser is not an expert in the field of environmental hazards, this appraisal report must not be considered as an environmental assessment of the property.

6. The appraiser has based his or her appraisal report and valuation conclusion for an appraisal that is subject to satisfactory completion, repairs, or alterations on the assumption that the completion, repairs, or alterations of the subject property will be performed in a professional manner.

Manufactured Home Appraisal Report

File #

APPRAISER'S CERTIFICATION: The Appraiser certifies and agrees that:

1. I have, at a minimum, developed and reported this appraisal in accordance with the scope of work requirements stated in this appraisal report.

2. I performed a complete visual inspection of the interior and exterior areas of the subject property. I reported the condition of the improvements in factual, specific terms. I identified and reported the physical deficiencies that could affect the livability, soundness, or structural integrity of the property.

3. I performed this appraisal in accordance with the requirements of the Uniform Standards of Professional Appraisal Practice that were adopted and promulgated by the Appraisal Standards Board of The Appraisal Foundation and that were in place at the time this appraisal report was prepared.

4. I developed my opinion of the market value of the real property that is the subject of this report based on the sales comparison approach to value. I also developed the cost approach to value as support for the sales comparison approach. I have adequate comparable market and cost data to develop reliable sales comparison and cost approaches for this appraisal assignment. I further certify that I considered the income approach to value but did not develop it, unless otherwise indicated in this report.

5. I researched, verified, analyzed, and reported on any current agreement for sale for the subject property, any offering for sale of the subject property in the twelve months prior to the effective date of this appraisal, and the prior sales of the subject property for a minimum of three years prior to the effective date of this appraisal, unless otherwise indicated in this report.

6. I researched, verified, analyzed, and reported on the prior sales of the comparable sales for a minimum of one year prior to the date of sale of the comparable sale, unless otherwise indicated in this report.

7. I selected and used comparable sales that are locationally, physically, and functionally the most similar to the subject property.

8. I have not used comparable sales that were the result of combining a land sale with the contract purchase price of a home that has been built or will be built on the land.

9. I have reported adjustments to the comparable sales that reflect the market's reaction to the differences between the subject property and the comparable sales.

10. I verified, from a disinterested source, all information in this report that was provided by parties who have a financial interest in the sale or financing of the subject property.

11. I have knowledge and experience in appraising this type of property in this market area.

12. I am aware of, and have access to, the necessary and appropriate public and private data sources, such as multiple listing services, tax assessment records, public land records and other such data sources for the area in which the property is located.

13. I obtained the information, estimates, and opinions furnished by other parties and expressed in this appraisal report from reliable sources that I believe to be true and correct.

14. I have taken into consideration the factors that have an impact on value with respect to the subject neighborhood, subject property, and the proximity of the subject property to adverse influences in the development of my opinion of market value. I have noted in this appraisal report any adverse conditions (such as, but not limited to, needed repairs, deterioration, the presence of hazardous wastes, toxic substances, adverse environmental conditions, etc.) observed during the inspection of the subject property or that I became aware of during the research involved in performing this appraisal. I have considered these adverse conditions in my analysis of the property value, and have reported on the effect of the conditions on the value and marketability of the subject property.

15. I have not knowingly withheld any significant information from this appraisal report and, to the best of my knowledge, all statements and information in this appraisal report are true and correct.

16. I stated in this appraisal report my own personal, unbiased, and professional analysis, opinions, and conclusions, which are subject only to the assumptions and limiting conditions in this appraisal report.

17. I have no present or prospective interest in the property that is the subject of this report, and I have no present or prospective personal interest or bias with respect to the participants in the transaction. I did not base, either partially or completely, my analysis and/or opinion of market value in this appraisal report on the race, color, religion, sex, age, marital status, handicap, familial status, or national origin of either the prospective owners or occupants of the subject property or of the present owners or occupants of the properties in the vicinity of the subject property or on any other basis prohibited by law.

18. My employment and/or compensation for performing this appraisal or any future or anticipated appraisals was not conditioned on any agreement or understanding, written or otherwise, that I would report (or present analysis supporting) a predetermined specific value, a predetermined minimum value, a range or direction in value, a value that favors the cause of any party, or the attainment of a specific result or occurrence of a specific subsequent event (such as approval of a pending mortgage loan application).

19. I personally prepared all conclusions and opinions about the real estate that were set forth in this appraisal report. If I relied on significant real property appraisal assistance from any individual or individuals in the performance of this appraisal or the preparation of this appraisal report, I have named such individual(s) and disclosed the specific tasks performed in this appraisal report. I certify that any individual so named is qualified to perform the tasks. I have not authorized anyone to make a change to any item in this appraisal report; therefore, any change made to this appraisal is unauthorized and I will take no responsibility for it.

20. I identified the lender/client in this appraisal report who is the individual, organization, or agent for the organization that ordered and will receive this appraisal report.

Manufactured Home Appraisal Report

File #

21. The lender/client may disclose or distribute this appraisal report to: the borrower; another lender at the request of the borrower; the mortgagee or its successors and assigns; mortgage insurers; government sponsored enterprises; other secondary market participants; data collection or reporting services; professional appraisal organizations; any department, agency, or instrumentality of the United States; and any state, the District of Columbia, or other jurisdictions; without having to obtain the appraiser's or supervisory appraiser's (if applicable) consent. Such consent must be obtained before this appraisal report may be disclosed or distributed to any other party (including, but not limited to, the public through advertising, public relations, news, sales, or other media).

22. I am aware that any disclosure or distribution of this appraisal report by me or the lender/client may be subject to certain laws and regulations. Further, I am also subject to the provisions of the Uniform Standards of Professional Appraisal Practice that pertain to disclosure or distribution by me.

23. The borrower, another lender at the request of the borrower, the mortgagee or its successors and assigns, mortgage insurers, government sponsored enterprises, and other secondary market participants may rely on this appraisal report as part of any mortgage finance transaction that involves any one or more of these parties.

24. If this appraisal report was transmitted as an "electronic record" containing my "electronic signature," as those terms are defined in applicable federal and/or state laws (excluding audio and video recordings), or a facsimile transmission of this appraisal report containing a copy or representation of my signature, the appraisal report shall be as effective, enforceable and valid as if a paper version of this appraisal report were delivered containing my original hand written signature.

25. Any intentional or negligent misrepresentation(s) contained in this appraisal report may result in civil liability and/or criminal penalties including, but not limited to, fine or imprisonment or both under the provisions of Title 18, United States Code, Section 1001, et seq., or similar state laws.

SUPERVISORY APPRAISER'S CERTIFICATION: The Supervisory Appraiser certifies and agrees that:

1. I directly supervised the appraiser for this appraisal assignment, have read the appraisal report, and agree with the appraiser's analysis, opinions, statements, conclusions, and the appraiser's certification.

2. I accept full responsibility for the contents of this appraisal report including, but not limited to, the appraiser's analysis, opinions, statements, conclusions, and the appraiser's certification.

3. The appraiser identified in this appraisal report is either a sub-contractor or an employee of the supervisory appraiser (or the appraisal firm), is qualified to perform this appraisal, and is acceptable to perform this appraisal under the applicable state law.

4. This appraisal report complies with the Uniform Standards of Professional Appraisal Practice that were adopted and promulgated by the Appraisal Standards Board of The Appraisal Foundation and that were in place at the time this appraisal report was prepared.

5. If this appraisal report was transmitted as an "electronic record" containing my "electronic signature," as those terms are defined in applicable federal and/or state laws (excluding audio and video recordings), or a facsimile transmission of this appraisal report containing a copy or representation of my signature, the appraisal report shall be as effective, enforceable and valid as if a paper version of this appraisal report were delivered containing my original hand written signature.

APPRAISER

Signature _____
Name _____
Company Name_____
Company Address _____
_____

Telephone Number _____
Email Address _____
Date of Signature and Report _____
Effective Date of Appraisal _____
State Certification # _____
or State License # _____
or Other _____
State _____
Expiration Date of Certification or License _____

ADDRESS OF PROPERTY APPRAISED

_____
_____

APPRAISED VALUE OF SUBJECT PROPERTY $ _____

LENDER/CLIENT
Name_____
Company Name_____
Company Address _____
Email Address _____

SUPERVISORY APPRAISER (ONLY IF REQUIRED)

Signature _____
Name _____
Company Name_____
Company Address _____
_____

Telephone Number _____
Email Address _____
Date Signature_____
State Certification # _____
or State License # _____
State_____
Expiration Date of Certification or License _____

SUBJECT PROPERTY

☐ Did not inspect subject property
☐ Did inspect exterior of subject property from street
  Date of Inspection_____
☐ Did inspect interior and exterior of subject property
  Date of Inspection_____

COMPARABLE SALES

☐ Did not inspect exterior of comparable sales from street
☐ Did inspect exterior of comparable sales from street
  Date of Inspection_____

One-Unit Residential Appraisal Field Review Report

File #

The purpose of this appraisal field review report is to provide the lender/client with an opinion on the accuracy of the appraisal report under review.

Property Address		City		State	Zip Code
Borrower	Owner of Public Record		County		
Legal Description					

Assessor's Parcel #   Map Reference   Census Tract

Property Rights Appraised ☐ Fee Simple ☐ Leasehold ☐ Other (describe)   Project Type ☐ Condo ☐ PUD ☐ Cooperative

Loan #   Effective Date of Appraisal Under Review   Manufactured Home ☐ Yes ☐ No

Lender/Client   Address

SECTION I — COMPLETE FOR ALL ASSIGNMENTS

1. Is the information in the subject section complete and accurate? ☐ Yes ☐ No If Yes, provide a brief summary. If No, explain

2. Is the information in the contract section complete and accurate? ☐ Yes ☐ No ☐ Not Applicable If Yes, provide a brief summary. If No, explain

3. Is the information in the neighborhood section complete and accurate? ☐ Yes ☐ No If Yes, provide a brief summary. If No, explain

4. Is the information in the site section complete and accurate? ☐ Yes ☐ No If Yes, provide a brief summary. If No, explain

5. Is the data in the improvements section complete and accurate? ☐ Yes ☐ No If Yes, provide a brief summary. If No, explain

6. Are the comparable sales selected locationally, physically, and functionally the most similar to the subject property? ☐ Yes ☐ No If Yes, provide a brief summary. If No, provide a detailed explanation as to why they are not the best comparable sales.

7. Are the data and analysis (including the individual adjustments) presented in the sales comparison approach complete and accurate? ☐ Yes ☐ No If Yes, provide a brief summary. If No, explain

8. Are the data and analysis presented in the income and cost approaches complete and accurate? ☐ Yes ☐ No ☐ Not developed If No, explain

9. Is the sale or transfer history reported for the subject property and each of the comparable sales complete and accurate? ☐ Yes ☐ No If Yes, provide a brief summary. If No, analyze and report the correct sale or transfer history and the data source(s).

10. Is the opinion of market value in the appraisal report under review accurate as of the effective date of the appraisal report? ☐ Yes ☐ No If No, complete Section II.

Freddie Mac Form 1032 March 2005   Page 1 of 4   Fannie Mae Form 2000 March 2005

One-Unit Residential Appraisal Field Review Report

File #

SECTION II — COMPLETE ONLY IF REVIEW APPRAISER ANSWERS "NO" TO QUESTION 10 IN SECTION I.

1. Provide detailed reasoning for disagreement with the opinion of value in the appraisal report under review.

2. State all extraordinary assumptions used (i.e. gross living area, room count, condition, etc.).

3. Provide a new opinion of value as of the effective date of the appraisal report under review using the below sales comparison analysis grid.
(NOTE: This may or may not include the use of the same comparable sales in the appraisal report under review.)

FEATURE	SUBJECT	COMPARABLE SALE # 1		COMPARABLE SALE # 2		COMPARABLE SALE # 3	
Address							
Proximity to Subject							
Sale Price	$		$		$		$
Sale Price/Gross Liv. Area	$ sq.ft.	$ sq.ft.		$ sq.ft.		$ sq.ft.	
Data Source(s)							
Verification Source(s)							
VALUE ADJUSTMENTS	DESCRIPTION	DESCRIPTION	+(-) $ Adjustment	DESCRIPTION	+(-) $ Adjustment	DESCRIPTION	+(-) $ Adjustment
Sale or Financing Concessions							
Date of Sale/Time							
Location							
Leasehold/Fee Simple							
Site							
View							
Design (Style)							
Quality of Construction							
Actual Age							
Condition							
Above Grade Room Count	Total Bdrms Baths	Total Bdrms Baths		Total Bdrms Baths		Total Bdrms Baths	
Gross Living Area	sq. ft.	sq. ft.		sq. ft.		sq. ft.	
Basement & Finished Rooms Below Grade							
Functional Utility							
Heating/Cooling							
Energy Efficient Items							
Garage/Carport							
Porch/Patio/Deck							
Net Adjustment (Total)		☐ + ☐ -	$	☐ + ☐ -	$	☐ + ☐ -	$
Adjusted Sale Price of Comparables		Net Adj. % Gross Adj. %	$	Net Adj. % Gross Adj. %	$	Net Adj. % Gross Adj. %	$

I ☐ did ☐ did not research the sale or transfer history of the above comparable sales. If not, explain

My research ☐ did ☐ did not reveal any prior sales or transfers of the comparable sales for the year prior to the date of sale of the comparable sale.

Data source(s)

Report the results of the research and analysis of the prior sale or transfer history of the above comparable sales (report additional prior sales on an addendum).

ITEM	COMPARABLE SALE # 1	COMPARABLE SALE # 2	COMPARABLE SALE # 3
Date of Prior Sale/Transfer			
Price of Prior Sale/Transfer			
Data Source(s)			
Effective Date of Data Source(s)			

Analysis of prior sale or transfer history for the comparable sales.

Summary of Value Conclusion (including detailed support for the opinion of value and reasons why the new comparable sales are better that the sales used in the appraisal report under review).

REVIEW APPRAISER'S OPINION OF MARKET VALUE (Required only if review appraiser answered "No" to Question 10 in Section 1)

Based on a ☐ visual inspection of the exterior areas of the subject property from at least the street or ☐ complete visual inspection of the interior and exterior areas of the subject property, defined scope of work, statement of assumptions and limiting conditions, and appraiser's certification, my opinion of the market value, as defined, of the real property that is the subject of this report is $, as of   , which is the effective date of the appraisal report under review.

Freddie Mac Form 1032 March 2005   Page 2 of 4   Fannie Mae Form 2000 March 2005

One-Unit Residential Appraisal Field Review Report

File #

SCOPE OF WORK

The scope of work for this appraisal field review is defined by the complexity of the appraisal report under review and the reporting requirements of this report form, including the following statement of assumptions and limiting conditions, and certifications. The review appraiser must, at a minimum: (1) read the entire appraisal report under review, (2) perform a visual inspection of the exterior areas of the subject property from at least the street, (3) inspect the neighborhood, (4) inspect each of the comparable sales from at least the street, (5) perform data research and analysis to determine the appropriateness and accuracy of the data in the appraisal report, (6) research, verify, and analyze data from reliable public and/or private sources, (7) determine the accuracy of the opinion of value, and (8) assume the property condition reported in the appraisal report is accurate unless there is evidence to the contrary.

If the review appraiser determines that the opinion of value in the report under review is not accurate, he or she is required to provide an opinion of market value. The review appraiser is not required to replicate the steps completed by the original appraiser that the review appraiser believes to be reliable and in compliance with the applicable real property appraisal development standards of the Uniform Standards of Professional Appraisal Practice. Those items in the appraisal report under review are extended to this report by the use of an extraordinary assumption, which is identified in Section II, Question 2. If the review appraiser determines that the opinion of value is not accurate, he or she must present additional data that has been researched, verified, and analyzed to produce an accurate opinion of value in accordance with the applicable sections of Standard 1 of the Uniform Standards of Professional Appraisal Practice.

INTENDED USE

The intended use of this appraisal field review report is for the lender/client to evaluate the accuracy and adequacy of support of the appraisal report under review.

INTENDED USER

The intended user of this appraisal field review report is the lender/client.

GUIDANCE FOR COMPLETING THE ONE-UNIT RESIDENTIAL APPRAISAL FIELD REVIEW REPORT

The appraisal review function is important to maintaining the integrity of both the appraisal and loan underwriting processes. The following guidance is intended to aid the review appraiser with the development and reporting of an appraisal field review:

1. The review appraiser must be the individual who personally read the entire appraisal report, performed a visual inspection of the exterior areas of the subject property from at least the street, inspected the neighborhood, inspected each of the comparable sales from at least the street, performed the data research and analysis, and prepared and signed this report.

2. The review appraiser must focus his or her comments on the appraisal report under review and not include personal opinions about the appraiser(s) who prepared the appraisal.

3. The lender/client has withheld the identity of the appraiser(s) who prepared the appraisal report under review, unless otherwise indicated in this report.

4. The review appraiser must assume that the condition of the property reported in the appraisal report is accurate, unless there is evidence to the contrary.

5. This One-Unit Residential Appraisal Field Review Report is divided into two sections. Section I must be completed for all assignments. Section II must be completed only if the answer to Question 10 in Section I is "No."

6. The review appraiser must determine whether the opinion of market value is accurate and adequately supported by market evidence. When the review appraiser disagrees with the opinion of value, he or she must complete Section II. Because appraiser's opinions can vary, the review appraiser must have conclusive evidence that the opinion of value is not accurate.

7. The review appraiser must explain why the comparable sales in the appraisal report under review should not have been used. Simply stating: "see grid" is unacceptable. The review appraiser must explain and support his or her conclusions.

8. The review appraiser must form an opinion about the overall accuracy and quality of the data in the appraisal report under review. The objective is to determine whether material errors exist and what effect they have on the opinions and conclusions in the appraisal report under review. When the review appraiser agrees that the data is essentially correct (although minor errors may exist), he or she must summarize the overall findings. When the review appraiser determines that material errors exist in the data, he or she must identify them, comment on their overall effect on the opinions and conclusions in the appraisal report under review, and include the correct information.

9. The Questions in Section I are intended to identify both the positive and negative elements of the appraisal under review and to report deficiencies. The review appraiser must make it clear to the reader what effect the deficiencies have on the opinions and conclusions in the appraisal report. Simple "Yes" and "No" answers are unacceptable.

10. The review appraiser must provide specific, supportable reasons for disagreeing with the opinion of value in the appraisal report under review in response to Question 1 in Section II.

11. The review appraiser must identify any extraordinary assumptions that were necessary in order to arrive at his or her opinion of market value. Extraordinary assumptions include the use of information from the appraisal report under review that the review appraiser concludes is reliable (such as an assumption that the reported condition of the subject property is accurate).

12. The review appraiser must include the rationale for using new comparable sales. The following question must be answered: Why are these new comparable sales better than the sales in the appraisal report under review?

13. The new comparable sales provided by the review appraiser and reported in the sales comparison analysis grid must have closed on or before the effective date of the appraisal report under review. It may be appropriate to include data that was not available to the original appraiser as of the effective date of the original appraisal; however, that information should be reported as "supplemental" to the data that would have been available to the original appraiser.

14. The review appraiser must provide a sale or transfer history of the new comparable sales for a minimum of one year prior to the date of sale of the comparable sale. The review appraiser must analyze the sale or transfer data and report the effect, if any, on the review appraiser's conclusions.

15. A review of an appraisal on a unit in a condominium, cooperative, or PUD project requires the review appraiser to analyze the project information in the appraisal report under review and comment on its completeness and accuracy.

16. An appraisal review of a manufactured home requires the review appraiser to assume that the HUD data plate information is correct, unless information to the contrary is available. In such cases, the review appraiser must identify the source of the data.

17. The review appraiser's opinion of market value must be "as of" the effective date of the appraisal report under review.

One-Unit Residential Appraisal Field Review Report

File #

STATEMENT OF ASSUMPTIONS AND LIMITING CONDITIONS

1. The review appraiser will not be responsible for matters of a legal nature that affect either the property that is the subject of the appraisal under review or the title to it, except for information that he or she became aware of during the research involved in performing this appraisal review. The review appraiser assumes that the title is good and marketable and will not render any opinions about the title.

2. The review appraiser will not give testimony or appear in court because he or she performed a review of the appraisal of the property in question, unless specific arrangements to do so have been made beforehand, or as otherwise required by law.

3. Unless otherwise stated in this appraisal field review report, the review appraiser has no knowledge of any hidden or unapparent physical deficiencies or adverse conditions of the property (such as but not limited to, needed repairs, deterioration, the presence of hazardous wastes, toxic substances, adverse environmental conditions, etc.) that would make the property less valuable, and has assumed that there are no such conditions and makes no guarantees or warranties, expressed or implied. The review appraiser will not be responsible for any such conditions that do exist or for any engineering or testing that might be required to discover whether such conditions exist. Because the review appraiser is not an expert in the field of environmental hazards, this appraisal field review report must not be considered as an environmental assessment of the property.

REVIEW APPRAISER'S CERTIFICATION

The Review Appraiser certifies and agrees that:

1. I have, at a minimum, developed and reported this appraisal field review in accordance with the scope of work requirements stated in this appraisal field review report.

2. I performed this appraisal field review in accordance with the requirements of the Uniform Standards of Professional Appraisal Practice that were adopted and promulgated by the Appraisal Standards Board of The Appraisal Foundation and that were in place at the time this appraisal field review report was prepared.

3. I have the knowledge and experience to perform appraisals and review appraisals for this type of property in this market area.

4. I am aware of, and have access to, the necessary and appropriate public and private data sources, such as multiple listing services, tax assessment records, public land records and other such data sources for the area in which the property is located.

5. I obtained the information, estimates, and opinions furnished by other parties and expressed in this appraisal field review report from reliable sources that I believe to be true and correct.

6. I have not knowingly withheld any significant information from this appraisal field review report and, to the best of my knowledge, all statements and information in this appraisal field review report are true and correct.

7. I stated in this appraisal field review report my own personal, unbiased, and professional analysis, opinions, and conclusions, which are subject only to the assumptions and limiting conditions in this appraisal field review report.

8. I have no present or prospective interest in the property that is the subject of this report, and I have no present or prospective personal interest or bias with respect to the participants in the transaction. I did not base, either partially or completely, my analysis and/or opinion of market value (if any) in this appraisal field review report on the race, color, religion, sex, age, marital status, handicap, familial status, or national origin of either the prospective owners or occupants of the subject property or of the present owners or occupants of the properties in the vicinity of the subject property or on any other basis prohibited by law.

9. My employment and/or compensation for performing this appraisal field review or any future or anticipated appraisals or appraisal field reviews was not conditioned on any agreement or understanding, written or otherwise, that I would report (or present analysis supporting) a predetermined specific value, a predetermined minimum value, a range or direction in value, a value that favors the cause of any party, or the attainment of a specific result or occurrence of a specific subsequent event (such as approval of a pending mortgage loan application).

10. I personally prepared all conclusions and opinions about the real estate that were set forth in this appraisal field review report. I further certify that no one provided significant professional assistance to me in the development of this appraisal field review report. I have not authorized anyone to make a change to any item in this appraisal field review report; therefore, any change made to this appraisal field review report is unauthorized and I will take no responsibility for it.

11. I identified the lender/client in this appraisal field review report who is the individual, organization, or agent for the organization that ordered and will receive this appraisal field review report.

12. The lender/client may disclose or distribute this appraisal field review report to: the mortgagee or its successors and assigns; mortgage insurers; government sponsored enterprises; other secondary market participants; professional appraisal organizations; any department, agency, or instrumentality of the United States; and any state, the District of Columbia, or other jurisdictions; without having to obtain the review appraiser's consent. Such consent must be obtained before this appraisal field review report may be disclosed or distributed to any other party (including, but not limited to, the public through advertising, public relations, news, sales, or other media).

13. The mortgagee or its successors and assigns, mortgage insurers, government sponsored enterprises, and other secondary market participants may rely on this appraisal field review report as part of any mortgage finance transaction that involves any one or more of these parties.

14. If this appraisal field review report was transmitted as an "electronic record" containing my "electronic signature," as those terms are defined in applicable federal and/or state laws (excluding audio and video recordings), or a facsimile transmission of this appraisal field review report containing a copy or representation of my signature, the appraisal field review report shall be as effective, enforceable and valid as if a paper version of this appraisal field review report were delivered containing my original hand written signature.

15. Any intentional or negligent misrepresentation(s) contained in this appraisal field review report may result in civil liability and/or criminal penalties including, but not limited to, fine or imprisonment or both under the provisions of Title 18, United States Code, Section 1001, et seq., or similar state laws.

REVIEW APPRAISER	LENDER/CLIENT
Signature _____	Name _____
Name _____	Company Name _____
Company Name _____	Company Address _____
Company Address _____	_____
Telephone Number _____	**LENDER/CLIENT OF THE APPRAISAL UNDER REVIEW**
Email Address _____	Name _____
Date of Signature and Report _____	Company Address _____
State Certification # _____	_____
Or State License # _____	
State _____	Reviewer's Opinion of Market Value $ ___ Date
Expiration Date of Certification or License _____	Only ff review appraiser answered "No" to Questions 10, in Section I.

Instructions

One-Unit Residential Appraisal Field Review Report

A lender uses this form for the spot-check appraisal component of its quality control process. This appraisal field review report is intended to provide the lender/client with an opinion on the accuracy of the appraisal report under review.

Scope of Work

The scope of work for this appraisal field review is defined by the complexity of the appraisal report under review and the reporting requirements of this report form, including the following statement of assumptions and limiting conditions, and certifications. The review appraiser must, at a minimum: (1) read the entire appraisal report under review, (2) perform a visual inspection of the exterior areas of the subject property from at least the street, (3) inspect the neighborhood, (4) inspect each of the comparable sales from at least the street, (5) perform data research and analysis to determine the appropriateness and accuracy of the data in the appraisal report, (6) research, verify, and analyze data from reliable public and/or private sources, (7) determine the accuracy of the opinion of value, and (8) assume the property condition reported in the appraisal report is accurate unless there is evidence to the contrary.

If the review appraiser determines that the opinion of value in the report under review is not accurate, he or she is required to provide an opinion of market value. The review appraiser is not required to replicate the steps completed by the original appraiser that the review appraiser believes to be reliable and in compliance with the applicable real property appraisal development standards of the Uniform Standards of Professional Appraisal Practice. Those items in the appraisal report under review are extended to this report by the use of an extraordinary assumption, which is identified in Section II, Question 2. If the review appraiser determines that the opinion of value is not accurate, he or she must present additional data that has been researched, verified, and analyzed to produce an accurate opinion of value in accordance with the applicable sections of Standard 1 of the Uniform Standards of Professional Appraisal Practice.

Required Exhibits

- A street map that shows the location of the subject property and of all comparables included in the appraisal report under review and any additional comparable sales provided by the review appraiser;

- Clear, descriptive, appropriately identified photographs that show the front and a street scene of the subject property. (Photographs must be originals that are produced either by photography or electronic imaging);

- Clear, descriptive, appropriately identified photographs that show the front of each comparable sale included in the appraisal report under review and any additional comparable sales described in the appraisal field review report. Acceptable photographs include originals that are produced by photography or electronic imaging; however, copies of photographs from a multiple listing service or from the appraiser's files are acceptable if they are clear and descriptive.

Appraisal Update and/or Completion Report

File #

Property Address	Unit #
City	State	Zip Code
Legal Description	County

The purpose of this report form is to provide the lender/client with an accurate update of an appraisal and/or to report a certification of completion. The appraiser must identify the service(s) provided by selecting the appropriate report type.

Property Address	Unit #
City State	Zip Code
Legal Description	County
Borrower Contract Price $ Date of Contract	Effective Date of Original Appraisal
Property Rights Appraised ☐ Fee Simple ☐ Leasehold ☐ Other (describe)	Original Appraised Value $
Original Appraiser Company Name	
Original Lender/Client Address	

■ SUMMARY APPRAISAL UPDATE REPORT

INTENDED USE: The intended use of this appraisal update is for the lender/client to evaluate the property that is the subject of this report to determine if the property has declined in value since the date of the original appraisal for a mortgage finance transaction.

INTENDED USER: The intended user of this appraisal update is the lender/client.

SCOPE OF WORK: The appraiser must, at a minimum: (1) concur with the original appraisal, (2) perform an exterior inspection of the subject property from at least the street, and (3) research, verify, and analyze current market data in order to determine if the property has declined in value since the effective date of the original appraisal.

HAS THE MARKET VALUE OF THE SUBJECT PROPERTY DECLINED SINCE THE EFFECTIVE DATE OF THE ORIGINAL APPRAISAL? ☐ Yes ☐ No

APPRAISER'S CERTIFICATION: The appraiser certifies and agrees that:

1. I have, at a minimum, developed and reported this appraisal update in accordance with the scope of work requirements stated in this appraisal update report and concur with the analysis and conclusions in the original appraisal.

2. I performed this appraisal update in accordance with the requirements of the Uniform Standards of Professional Appraisal Practice that were adopted and promulgated by the Appraisal Standards Board of The Appraisal Foundation and that were in place at the time this appraisal update was prepared.

3. I have updated the appraisal by incorporating the original appraisal report.

4. I have summarized my analysis and conclusions in this appraisal update and retained all supporting data in my work file.

SUPERVISORY APPRAISER'S CERTIFICATION: The Supervisory Appraiser certifies and agrees that:

1. I directly supervised the appraiser for this appraisal update assignment, have read the appraisal update report, and agree with the appraiser's analysis, opinions, statements, conclusions, and the appraiser's certification.

2. I accept full responsibility for the contents of this appraisal update report including, but not limited to, the appraiser's analysis, opinions, statements, conclusions, and the appraiser's certification.

■ CERTIFICATION OF COMPLETION

INTENDED USE: The intended use of this certification of completion is for the lender/client to confirm that the requirements or conditions stated in the appraisal report referenced above have been met.

INTENDED USER: The intended user of this certification of completion is the lender/client.

HAVE THE IMPROVEMENTS BEEN COMPLETED IN ACCORDANCE WITH THE REQUIREMENTS AND CONDITIONS STATED IN THE ORIGINAL APPRAISAL REPORT? ☐ Yes ☐ No If No, describe any impact on the opinion of market value.

APPRAISER'S CERTIFICATION: I certify that I have performed a visual inspection of the subject property to determine if the conditions or requirements stated in the original appraisal have been satisfied.

SUPERVISORY APPRAISER'S CERTIFICATION: I accept full responsibility for this certification of completion.

SIGNATURES

ADDITIONAL CERTIFICATION: I/we certify that if this report was transmitted as an "electronic record" containing my "electronic signature," as those terms are defined in applicable federal and/or state laws (excluding audio and video recordings), or a facsimile transmission of this report containing a copy or representation of my signature, the report shall be as effective, enforceable and valid as if a paper version of this appraisal report were delivered containing my original hand written signature.

APPRAISER
Signature _____
Name _____
Company Name _____
Company Address _____
Telephone Number _____
Date of Signature and Report _____
Effective Date of Appraisal Update _____
Date of Inspection _____
State Certification # _____
or State License # _____
or Other (describe) _____ State # _____
State _____
Expiration Date of Certification or License _____

CURRENT LENDER/CLIENT
Name _____
Company Name _____
Company Address _____

SUPERVISORY APPRAISER (ONLY IF REQUIRED)
Signature _____
Name _____
Company Name _____
Company Address _____
Telephone Number _____
Date of Signature _____
State Certification # _____
or State License # _____
State _____
Expiration Date of Certification or License _____

SUPERVISORY APPRAISER
☐ Did not inspect subject property
☐ Did inspect exterior of subject property from street
　Date of Inspection _____
☐ Did inspect interior and exterior of subject property
　Date of Inspection _____

Instructions

Appraisal Update and/or Completion Report

This report form is intended to provide the lender/client with an accurate update of a prior appraisal and/or to report a certification of completion. The appraiser must identify the service(s) provided by selecting the appropriate report type.

Learn How to Use the New Market Conditions Addendum

Gain an understanding of and recognize the sources of market information necessary to analyze market conditions. Our new recorded training is organized to address the Market Conditions Addendum (Form 1004MC), effective April 1, 2009, section by section.

View Recorded Training

Scope of Work for an Appraisal Update

The appraiser must, at a minimum:
1. concur with the original appraisal,
2. perform an exterior inspection of the subject property from at least the street, and
3. research, verify, and analyze current market data in order to determine if the property has declined in value since the effective date of the original appraisal.

Required Exhibits

*   For new or proposed construction, clear, descriptive photographs (either in black and white or color) of the completed improvements must accompany this report form

*   Any other data--as an attachment or addendum to the appraisal report form--that are necessary to provide an adequately supported opinion ofmarket value

Glossary

A

Abandonment The failure to occupy and use property, which may result in a loss of rights.

Absorption Analysis A study to determine how many property units can be sold or rented in the marketplace during a certain period of time.

Absorption Period The period of time it will take a property unit to be sold or rented in the marketplace.

Absorption Rate The relationship between the marketplace and the time required to absorb a specific type of property.

Abstract of Title A brief, chronological summary of the recorded documents affecting the title to a particular parcel of real property.

Abutting Property Properties which are directly contiguous, sharing at least one common boundary.

Acceptance 1. Agreeing to the terms of an offer to enter into a contract, thereby creating a binding contract. 2. Taking delivery of a deed.

Access A means of entry to a property.

Accession The acquisition of title to land by its addition to real estate already owned, through human actions or natural processes.

Accretion A gradual addition to dry land by the forces of nature, mostly used for property abutting a body of water where such addition is made by the deposits of waterborne sediment carried by rivers, winds, tides, etc. to the shoreline property.

Accrued Depreciation The total accumulated depreciation.

Acquisition Cost The total cost to purchase a property, including such items as closing costs, appraisal fees, origination fees, inspection fees, title insurance, etc.

Acre A unit of land equaling 43,560 square feet, or 4,840 square yards, or 160 square rods, or 1/640th of a square mile.

Actual Age The total number of years since the completion of a structure. Also called **Chronological Age**.

Ad Valorem A Latin phrase meaning "according to value," used to refer to taxes assessed on the value of real property.

Ad Valorem Tax A proportional tax that is based on real property's assessed value.

Addenda Additional parts of an appraisal report. Addenda usually consist of photos of the subject improvements and comparable properties, a sketch of the subject's floor plan, a table for calculating the area of the subject, a location map, or additional necessary comments..

Adjustable Rate Mortgage A mortgage that permits the lender to periodically adjust the interest rate to reflect fluctuations in the cost of money. Also called **ARM**.

Adjusted Basis An accounting process that takes the acquisition cost, adds capital improvements, and subtracts depreciation.

Adjusted Sale Price The final, estimated price of a comparable property after all additions and subtractions have been made for differences between the comparable and the subject.

Adverse Possession Acquiring title to someone else's real property through possession of it. The possession must be open and notorious, hostile and adverse, exclusive, and continuous for a period of years as per state law.

Advocacy Representing the cause or interest of another, even if that cause or interest does not necessarily coincide with one's own beliefs, opinions, conclusions, or recommendations.

Age-Life Depreciation A calculation that takes the effective age of a property and divides it by the total economic life.

Agents of Production Theoretically, the **four agents of production**: Capital, Entrepreneurship, Land, and Labor (C-E-L-L) together create real estate, and the total costs to develop a property is a basic measure of real property value.

Air Rights The right to undisturbed use and control of the airspace over a parcel of land, within reasonable limits for air travel. Air rights may be transferred separately from the land.

Alienation Clause A contract clause that gives the lender certain stated rights when a transfer of property ownership takes place. Upon the sale of, or even transfer of, significant interest in the property, the lender often has the right to accelerate the debt, change the interest rate, or charge a hefty assumption fee. FHA and VA loans cannot contain this clause.

Allocation Method A site valuation method that separates the value of the land from the structures that sit on it by taking a ratio of the land or site value to the total property value, based on a typical property in the area.

Amenity A tangible or intangible feature that enhances and adds value to real estate.

American Craftsman Style American architecture that was popular from the last years of the nineteenth century through the early years of the twentieth century. Also known as the **American Arts and Crafts Movement**.

Amortization Elimination of a debt with a series of equal payments (principal and interest) at regular time intervals.

Amortization Factor A periodic constant (number) used to calculate the required fixed even payment to retire all interest and principal over the full loan term.

Amortized Loan A loan with payments applied to principal and interest.

Anchor Tenant The main store in a shopping center, expected to draw the most people.

Annexation Attaching personal property to land so the law views it as part of real property.

Annexer A person who owns an item as personal property and brings it onto real property, making it a part of the real property.

Annual Percentage Rate (APR) The relationship between the cost of borrowing money and the total amount financed, represented as a percentage. The APR is the total cost of financing a loan in percentage terms, as a relationship of the total finance charges to the total amount financed.

ANSI American National Standards Institute; responsible for GLA standards.

Anticipation An economic theory that says value is created by the expectation of future benefits (appreciation, tax benefits, income, etc.).

Appraisal (noun) The act or process of developing an opinion of value; an opinion of value. (adjective) of or pertaining to appraising and related functions such as appraisal practice or appraisal services. (corresponding comments have not been presented) (USPAP 2014-2015 Edition, p. U-1).

Appraisal Foundation A nonprofit private organization which is recognized by Congress as the authority for professional appraisal standards and appraiser qualifications.

Appraisal Management Company (AMC) A third party vendor who orders and receives appraisals on behalf of the lender client. The appraisal management fee negotiates turn around time and fees with the appraisers.

Appraisal Plan A preliminary survey identifying the scope, character, and amount of work needed to complete an appraisal.

Appraisal Practice Valuation services performed by an individual acting as an appraiser, including but not limited to appraisal or appraisal review. (corresponding comments have not been presented) (USPAP 2014-2015 Edition, p. U-1)

Appraisal Report A report containing the minimum level of reporting necessary for an appraisal assignment that which permits other intended user(s) in addition to the client, and for an assignment in which the client may need to understand the appraiser's rationale, or the client may not have specialized knowledge about the subject property.

Appraisal Review The act or process of developing and communicating an opinion about the quality of another appraiser's work that was performed as part of an appraisal or appraisal review assignment. (corresponding comments have not been presented) (USPAP 2014-2015 Edition, p. U-1)

Appraiser One who is expected to perform valuation services competently and in a manner that is independent, impartial, and objective. (corresponding comments have not been presented). (USPAP 2014-2015 Edition, p. U-1)

Appraiser Assisted Valuation Models (AAVM) A statistical model based on multiple regression analysis that assists an appraiser in data collection for use with geographic information systems (GIS) data to calculate the estimated value of the subject for underwriting purposes.

Appraiser's Peers Other appraisers who have expertise and competency in a similar type of assignment. (USPAP 2014-2015 Edition, p. U-1)

Appreciation Increase to the value of property.

Appropriative Rights Water rights allocated by government permit, according to an appropriation system. It is not necessary to own property beside the body of water to apply for an appropriation permit.

Appurtenance A right that goes with ownership of real property. It is usually transferred with the property but may be sold separately. This is a legal term referring to both physical and nonphysical appurtenances.

Appurtenance, Intangible An appurtenant right that does not involve ownership of physical objects, i.e., easements.

Appurtenant Rights Rights that go with ownership of real property. They are usually transferred with the property, but may be sold separately. This is a legal term referring to both physical and non-physical appurtenances.

Argon The most commonly used gas between panes in a thermal window.

Arm's Length Transaction A transaction that occurred under typical conditions in the marketplace, with each of the parties acting in their own best interests.

"As-Is" The value of the property without completing repairs or updates.

"As-Is" Clause A provision in a purchase agreement stating that the buyer accepts the property in its present condition.

Asking Price The price the seller sets for the property when first put on the market.

"As-Repaired" A value determined by adding in the repair costs to bring the subject to similar condition as a comp in good condition.

Assemblage The combining of two or more parcels of land into one larger parcel.

Assessed Value The value established by a government agency for the purpose of real estate taxation.

Assessment 1. A government's valuation of property for tax purposes. 2. A special tax, usually used to pay for community improvements.

Assessment Ratio The ratio of a property's tax assessed value to its market value.

Assessor An official who determines the value of property for taxation.

Asset Management Company A company that offers services from pre-foreclosure to the end of the foreclosure process when the property is sold.

Assignment 1) An agreement between an appraiser and a client to provide a valuation service; 2) the valuation service that is provided as a consequence of such as agreement. (USPAP 2014-2015 Edition, p. U-1)

Assignment Conditions 1. Specific requirements of a client that are applicable in an appraisal review assignment. 2. Conditions above and beyond USPAP imposed by the client on the appraiser at the time the appraisal is ordered. Assignment conditions can be "conform to Fannie Mae guidelines." They can also be "perform an exterior-only inspection."

Assignment Elements Factors identified as part of problem identification and scope of work determination for an appraisal review.

Assignment Results An appraiser's opinions and conclusions developed specific to an assignment. (corresponding comments have not been presented) (USPAP 2014-2015 Edition, p. U-1)

Assumption That which is taken to be true. (USPAP 2014-2015 Edition, p. U-2)

Attachment 1. Things connected to the land, whether natural or man-made. Man-made attachments are called improvements. 2. Court-ordered seizure of property belonging to a defendant in a lawsuit so it will be available to satisfy a judgment. In the case of real property, attachment creates a lien.

Attachments, Natural Things growing on land, such as trees, shrubs, or crops.

Automated Valuation Models (AVM) A statistical model based on multiple regression analysis along with geographic information systems (GIS) data to calculate the estimated value of the subject for underwriting purposes.

B

Balance 1. A condition that exists in the real estate market when there are slightly more homes available than buyers. 2. The right mix of capital, entrepreneurship/management, labor, and land—C-E-L-L (the four agents of production) that results in best return on investment from land. Highest and best use occurs when the four agents of production are in balance.

Balloon (Framing) A type of framing with long studs up the entire length of the house, from the foundation to the roof. No longer permitted as a construction method by most building codes.

Balloon Mortgage A mortgage where there is a series of fixed payments that do not fully reduce the debt, with one larger final payment (balloon payment) that pays off the debt in full.

Balloon Payment A final payment at the end of a loan term (usually larger than previous payments) that pays off the entire remaining balance of principal and interest not covered by scheduled payments during the loan term.

Band of Investment A method for deriving an overall capitalization rate for use in an income approach that relies on a weighted average of the equity component and a weighted average of the mortgage component.

Base Companies Companies and industries that bring new business and jobs to an area.

Base Lines Primary east-west lines designated and named throughout the country for use with the government survey system.

Base Multiplier A number used to show how many service (non-basic) jobs are affected by one base job.

Basement Part of a house or building that is partially or entirely below grade (ground level), and is used to support the rest of the structure.

Basis An accounting procedure used to determine the capital gain or loss after the sale of a property. It is equal to purchase price, plus capital improvements, less depreciation.

Bearing Wall A wall that carries the load for the roof, ceiling, and/or floors.

Bell-shaped Curve The graphic representation of data in the general shape of a bell

Berm House A type of earth shelter dwelling that rests into an incline or hill and has a conventional roof.

Bias A preference or inclination that precludes an appraiser's impartiality, independence, or objectivity in an assignment. (USPAP 2014-2015 Edition, p. U-2)

Biased Sample When the data process collection produces a statistical error by systematically choosing some results over others.

Bill of Sale A document used to transfer title to personal property from one person to another.

Blanket Mortgage A mortgage instrument that covers more than one property.

Blockbusting Illegal practice of inducing owners to sell their homes, often at a deflated price, by suggesting the ethnic or racial composition of the neighborhood is changing, with the implication that property values will decline as a result.

Blower Door Test An energy test performed on a house by putting a large, calibrated fan in an exterior door, reducing the air pressure inside, and then noting where air flows into the house.

Blueprints Detailed building plans used to evaluate design, determine feasibility, and guide construction of a structure.

Book Value The value of property for accounting purposes, based on cost, less accrued depreciation.

Boundary 1. The perimeter or border of a parcel of land. 2. The dividing line between one piece of property and another.

Bracketing A process in which an appraiser identifies a probable value range, most often by identifying values of properties that are inferior and those that are superior. The appraiser then determines where an opinion of value for the subject should fall within that range.

Break Even The amount of operating income needed to pay operating expenses and debt service.

Breakdown Method A method for calculating depreciation by taking a figure for each kind of depreciation and combining them into one number.

Bridge Loan A short term loan to fill the gap between the end of one loan and the placement of a new, long-term loan.

Broker Price Opinion (BPO) A method used by lenders and others to determine elements of value and marketability for a property.

BTU (British Thermal Unit) The amount of heat needed to raise the temperature of one pound of water by one degree Fahrenheit. It is used as a measure of furnace or air conditioner capacity.

Building Code A means of setting construction standards, requiring builders to use particular methods and materials; regulations establishing minimum standards for construction and materials. (There are different building codes for different systems: Electric, plumbing, etc.)

Building envelope Refers to the entire building, from basement to roof.

Building Inspection A process whereby local government employees, often engineers, are charged with ensuring compliance with state and local building codes.

Building Permits Official documents from a local government or other authority that allow the beginning of a construction or remodeling project.

Built-up The percentage of available land that has been improved.

Bundle of Rights All real property rights conferred with ownership including, but not limited to, right of use, right of enjoyment, and right of disposal.

Business Cycles General swings in business, resulting in expanding and contracting activity during different phases of the cycle.

Business Enterprise An entity pursuing an economic activity. (USPAP 2014-2015 Edition, p. U-2)

Business Equity The interests, benefits, and rights inherent in the ownership of a business enterprise or a part thereof in any form (including, but not necessarily limited to, capital stock, partnership interests, cooperatives, sole proprietorships, options, and warrants). (USPAP 2014-2015 Edition, p. U-2)

Buydown When additional funds, in the form of points, are paid to a lender at the beginning of a loan to lower the interest rate and monthly payments on the loan.

Buyer's Market A situation in the real estate market where buyers have a large selection of properties from which to choose.

C

Capital Improvement Any addition to real property in which an effort is made to increase the usefulness or value of the property.

Capital Market A place where buying and selling of financial instruments occurs.

Capitalization A way to convert a property's income figure into an estimated value.

Capitalization of Ground Rents Method A site valuation method that takes an estimated value of improvements and subtracts it from the total sales price to derive a figure for the land value.

Capitalization Rate A percentage rate of return used to calculate the present value of future income. It is used for the income approach to appraisal. Also called **Cap Rate** or **Rate.**

Carbon footprint "The total set of greenhouse gas (GHG) emissions caused by an organization, event, product, or person."[Source: Wikipedia]

Cash Equivalent The value of financing, notes, securities, etc., expressed in only cash terms.

Cash Equivalency Adjustment An adjustment applied to the sale price of a comparable sale, to address atypical financing terms.

Cash Flow The cash available after "cash" expenses have been paid. Non-cash expenses, such as depreciation, are not considered.

Categorical Data Data grouped by common properties not associated with numbers, such as hair color, race, or marital status.

Caveat Emptor A Latin phrase meaning "let the buyer beware." The rule says a buyer is expected to examine property carefully, instead of relying on the seller to identify problems.

CC&Rs A declaration of **C**ovenants, **C**onditions, and **R**estrictions, usually recorded by a developer to create a general plan of private restrictions for a subdivision.

Census Tract Relatively small areas used to track the population of the United States by the Census Bureau.

Certificate of Occupancy A permit that is issued to the builder after all inspections have been made and the property is deemed fit for occupancy.

Certified Green Professional Designation available from NAHB (National Association of Home Builders) for persons with experience in building and contracting who fulfill the requirements.

Change A principle affecting value in real estate that says all factors that influence real estate—physical, economic, governmental, and social—are constantly changing, and thus property value itself is subject to constant change.

Characteristics of Value The characteristics of value are **D**emand (desire), **U**tility, **S**carcity, and **T**ransferability (effective purchasing power). Also known as **D-U-S-T**.

Chattel A piece of personal property.

Chattel Mortgage A mortgage for which personal property is used to secure the note.

Chink The space between logs in log cabins and other log-walled structures.

Chinking The mortar/infill material between the logs in the construction of log cabins and other log-walled structures.

Civil Rights Fundamental humanitarian rights guaranteed to all persons by law.

Client The party or parties who engage, by employment or contract, an appraiser in a specific assignment. (corresponding comments have not been presented) (USPAP 2014-2015 Edition, p. U-2)

Climate The weather conditions of a given area.

Closing Transfer of ownership of real property from seller to buyer, according to terms and conditions in sales contracts or escrow agreements. Final stage in a real estate transaction.

Closing Costs Expenses incurred in the transfer of real estate in addition to the purchase price; for example, the appraisal fee, title insurance premiums, broker's commission, and transfer tax.

Cloud on the Title A claim, encumbrance, or defect that makes the title to real property unmarketable.

Collection Loss An amount stated as a percent or a dollar amount reflecting the risk anticipated for nonpayment of rent by tenants. Also called **Credit Loss.**

Commercial Property Property zoned and used for business purposes, such as warehouses, restaurants, and office buildings, as distinguished from residential, industrial, or agricultural property.

Common Areas The land and improvements in a condominium, planned unit development, or cooperative that all residents use and own as tenants in common, such as the parking lot, hallways, and recreational facilities. These areas do not include individual apartment units or homes.

Comparable Properties Properties that possess many of the same appeal factors, but the buyer for one property may not necessarily be interested in the comparable property.

Comparative Unit Method A method for determining the cost of a building that uses the cost of recently built comparable buildings as a basis for estimating the cost of replacing the subject property.

Competency Rule A USPAP rule that requires appraisers to have knowledge and experience necessary to complete assignments competently, and also contains procedures for appraisers who do not have sufficient competence.

Competition Two or more parties, properties, etc., trying to obtain the same thing.

Competition, Principal of In a free marketplace, this principal states that if excess profits are being generated by a particular product or service, then additional competition will develop

Competitive Market Analysis (CMA) A method of determining the approximate market value of a home by comparing the subject property to other homes that have sold, are presently for sale, or did not sell in a given area.

Competitive Properties Properties that compete head to head. A potential buyer for one property would also be interested in the competitive property.

Competitive Supply Available properties that a buyer would accept as ready substitutes because they share the same features and utility as the subject.

Competitive Use A property that offers the same products or services as other properties in the immediate area, and thus will compete against them for customers.

Complementary Use A property that offers different products or services than other properties in the immediate area, and thus will benefit from the traffic and customers that patronize the other businesses.

Complex Property A property that is considered deficient, deteriorated, functionally obsolete, etc.

Compound Interest Interest earned/charged on the principal amount, as well as interest on any previously earned/charged interest that has been added to the principal.

Concrete Siding A mixture of cellulose, concrete and sand which forms a highly durable (estimated life span is 50 years) product which can have the color "baked" into the concrete. It is low maintenance and offers a high R-value.

Condemnation 1. Taking private property for public use through the government's power of eminent domain. Also called **Appropriation**. 2. A declaration that a structure is unfit for occupancy and must be closed or demolished.

Condition 1. Provisions in a deed or other document that make the parties' rights and obligations depend on the occurrence or non-occurrence of some event. 2. The state of repair or disrepair of an item, structure, etc.

Conditional Use A land use that does not comply with the general zoning rules for the zone in which it is located, but is permitted because it benefits the public (e.g., a hospital in a residential neighborhood). Also called **Special Exception**.

Conditions of Sale Atypical motivations of the parties of a transaction (usually make the sale non-arm's length).

Condominium A property developed for co-ownership, where each co-owner has a separate interest in an individual unit and an undivided interest in the common areas of the property.

Confidence Interval A number represented as a percentage, i.e. 95%, used to estimate where a single datum point from the population is likely to fall based on a sample of the population.

Confidential Information Information that is either: identified by the client as confidential when providing it to an appraiser and that is not available from any other source; or classified as confidential or private by applicable law or regulation. (USPAP 2014-20153 Edition, p. U-2)

Conforming Loans Loans that meet qualifying standards, and thus can be sold on the secondary market.

Conformity The theory that says a particular property achieves its maximum value when it is surrounded by properties that are similar in style, function, and utility. Also called **Homogeneity**.

Conformity, External How a property and its characteristics conform to the market and the demands of market participants.

Conformity, Internal A state of four agents of production in relation to land use and improvements.

Consideration Anything of value, such as money, goods, services, or promises, given in exchange for something from another party.

Construction Cost The dollar amount of material, labor, etc., required to build a structure.

Consumer Price Index (CPI) A measure of the fixed cost of a market basket of goods and services used as an inflation indicator.

Contract An agreement between two or more parties to do or not do a certain thing. The requirements for an enforceable contract are **capacity, mutual consent, lawful objective**, and **consideration**. In addition, certain contracts must be in writing to be enforceable.

Contract, Land A real estate installment agreement where the buyer makes payments to the seller in exchange for the right to occupy and use property. No deed or title is transferred until all, or a specified portion of, the payments have been made. Also called **Installment Land Contract, Installment Sales Contract, Land Sales Contract, Real Estate Contract**, and other names.

Contract Rent What tenants are actually paying in rent, as stated in the terms of the lease.

Contractor's Profit Profit earned by the manager of a construction project.

Contribution The theory that a particular item or feature of a property is only worth what it actually contributes in value to that parcel of real estate. This is known as the feature's **Contributory Value**.

Contributory Value The theory that a particular item or feature of a property is worth only what it actually contributes in value to that parcel of real estate.

Conventional Loan A loan that is not insured or guaranteed by a government entity.

Cooperative A building owned by a corporation, where the residents are shareholders in the corporation. Each shareholder receives a proprietary lease on an individual unit and the right to use the common areas.

Co-ownership Any form of ownership with two or more people sharing title to real property.

Corner Influence Value change in a property because it sits on a corner lot.

Cost The amount required to create, produce, or obtain a property. (corresponding comment is not presented) (USPAP 2014-2015 Edition, p. U-2)

Cost Approach An appraisal method that estimates the value of real estate by establishing the cost new of replacing or reproducing the improvements, minus depreciation, plus the value of the site.

Cost Estimating Determining the price to replace or reproduce a structure.

Cost Inflation An increase in the cost of goods or services.

Cost of Living Index A government index that reflects the increase cost to consumers to purchase a specific list of items.

Cost of Money The interest rate that people or businesses pay to use another's money for their own purposes.

Cost Manuals—Books, electronic media, and online sources that give estimated construction costs for various types of buildings in different areas of the country.

Cost to Cure The amount, in dollars, that it will cost to cure some forms of depreciation.

Cost Services Companies that provide appraisers with accurate, up-to-date data on building costs for labor and materials.

Covenant 1. A contract. 2. A promise. 3. A guarantee (express or implied) in a document such as a deed or lease. 4. A restrictive covenant.

Covenant of Quiet Enjoyment A guarantee that a buyer or tenant has the right to exclusive, undisturbed possession of a leasehold estate, and will not be disturbed by the previous owner, the lessor, or anyone else claiming an interest in the property.

Crawl Space The unfinished space below the first floor of a house or other structure that is less than a full story in height.

Credible Worthy of belief. (corresponding comment is not presented) (USPAP 2014-2015 Edition, p. U-2)

Cul-de-Sac A short dead-end street that has a circular area at the end allowing cars to turn around.

Curable Repairable or able to be fixed; something that can be fixed at a reasonable cost, with the value added to the property being more than the cost of the repair.

Curb Appeal Visual impression that buyers and others get from a property before entering it.

Current Appraisal An appraisal with an effective date that is contemporaneous with the date of the report.

D

Data Information collected from various resources.

Data Collection Process of collecting and recording the data.

Data Organization How the appraiser arranges or lays out the collected data for his eventual analysis.

Data Set Group of individual datum points collected, usually for the purpose of statistical analysis.

Data Selection Process of deciding what data is required for analysis.

Database A list of information sources.

Date of Appraisal (effective date) Calendar date for which property value has been established. It is not always the same as the date of inspection.

Date of Inspection Date on which the appraiser physically visited the subject property.

Date of Report Indicates whether the perspective of the appraiser on the market and property as of the effective date of the appraisal is prospective, current, or retrospective.

Day Lighting The use of natural light, via positioning, skylights, etc. to reduce the use of artificial light in a building.

Datum Point A single piece of data.

Days on Market (DOM) The amount of time that a property has been available for sale or lease.

Debt Service The amount of funds required to make periodic payments of principal and interest to the lender.

Decline The third stage a neighborhood goes through in its life cycle, when property values begin to fall as demand falls.

Deed An instrument that conveys the grantor's interest in real property.

Deed, Fiduciary A deed executed by a trustee, executor, or other fiduciary, conveying property that the fiduciary does not own but is authorized to manage.

Deed, General Warranty A deed in which the grantor warrants title against defects that might have arisen before or during his or her period of ownership.

Deed, Limited Warranty A deed in which the grantor warrants title only against defects arising during the time he or she owned the property, and not against defects arising before his or her time of ownership. Also called **Special Warranty Deed**.

Deed, Quitclaim A deed that conveys any interest in a piece of real property the grantor has at the time the deed is executed. This type of deed is often used to clear up a cloud on the title. It contains no warranties of any kind.

Deed Restrictions
Limitations on real property use, imposed by a former owner (or developer) through language included in the deed. There are two types of deed restrictions: Restrictive conditions, and restrictive covenants.

Deed, Warranty A deed carrying warranties (guarantees) of clear title and the grantor's right to convey.

Deed in Lieu of Foreclosure A deed given by a borrower to the lender to satisfy the debt and avoid foreclosure.

Deed of Trust An instrument held by a third party as security for the payment of a note. Like a mortgage, it creates a voluntary lien on real property to secure repayment of a debt. The parties to a deed of trust are the grantor or trustor (borrower), beneficiary (lender), and trustee (neutral third party). Unlike a mortgage, a deed of trust includes a power of sale, allowing the trustee to foreclose non-judicially. Used In some states.

Deferred Maintenance A physical deterioration that has occurred because of a failure to perform regular maintenance and upkeep.

Deficiency Property element that is less than necessary, interpreted by the market to be unacceptable, or an element that is functionally inadequate.

Deficit Rent The resulting difference when the market rent exceeds the contract rent.

Demand The need or desire for a specific good or service by others.

Demand Inflation Too much money chasing too few goods. *Compare:* **Cost Inflation.**

De Minimis PUD A planned unit development with the available level of amenities and/or services being so low or minimal they have little, if any, effect on the property.

Demographic Data Information about the people in a given area.

Depreciate To decline in value.

Depreciation A loss in value to property for any reason—physical deterioration, functional obsolescence, external obsolescence.

Depreciation, External A loss in value from forces or elements outside the property's boundaries.

Depreciation, Functional A loss in value from design features that are longer competitive with current market demands.

Depreciation, Observable Any loss of value the appraiser can attribute to physical deterioration, functional obsolescence, or economic obsolescence.

Depreciation Physical A loss in value from deterioration of the physical structure or from deferred maintenance.

Design Refers to how it functions to enhance the overall efficiency and livability of the house. Houses must be both attractive and comfortable to attract buyers.

Desktop BPO Assignments BPO assignments that are performed by utilizing property information from tax records and from the MLS.

Developer's Profit Money above costs earned by the person or entity undertaking a real estate project.

Diminishing Returns Principle that says that beyond a certain point, the added value of an additional feature, addition, repair, etc., is less than the actual cost of the item. Also called **Law of Decreasing Returns**.

Direct Capitalization An income method that converts a property's single-year net operating income (NOI) into a value indication by applying an overall capitalization rate: NOI / Overall Capitalization Rate = Value.

Direct Costs Costs in a project that are not variable, such as labor and materials. Also called **Hard Costs**.

Disaggregation A process that involves separating different users and different uses for property in the real estate market, focusing on real estate products on the supply side of the market.

Discount Points An amount paid to a lender when a loan is made to make up the difference between the current market interest rate and the rate a lender gives a borrower on a note. Discount points increase a lender's yield on a note, allowing the lender to give a borrower a lower interest rate.

Discount Rate The interest rate charged by the Federal Reserve Banks on loans to member commercial banks. Also called **Federal Discount Rate**.

Discounted Cash Flow An appraisal procedure that is used in the income analysis of a property. Cash flows are converted to present values using a rate of return that would be required to attract an investor.

Discounting The process, by some investors, that uses the principles of TVM to convert future income or cash flows into present value, at a specified interest rate.

Discrimination Treating people unequally because of race, religion, sex, national origin, age, or some other characteristic of a protected class, in violation of civil rights laws.

Disposable Income That amount of money on an annual basis which is left and available to be spent, after all taxes have been paid.

Distinguishing Terms Indicate the level of information communicated by each specific reporting option permitted by USPAP: an Appraisal Report summarizes; and a Restricted Appraisal Report states.

District The narrowest of definitions of a market area. A district is an area consisting of one particular land use, such as multi-family residential, commercial, industrial, etc. There could be several districts within a neighborhood and several neighborhoods comprising a market area.

Dominant Tenant A person who has easement rights on another's property; either the owner of a dominant tenement or someone who has an easement in gross.

Dominant Tenement A property that benefits from an easement.

Double Hung A window style with two moving sashes.

E

Earth Shelter Dwelling An earth-covered home built into flatland.

Easement A right to use some part of another person's real property for a particular purpose. An easement is irrevocable and creates an interest in the property.

Easement, Appurtenant An easement that burdens one piece of land for the benefit of another.

Easement by Express Grant An easement granted to another in a deed or other document.

Easement by Express Reservation An easement created in a deed when a landowner is dividing property, transferring the servient tenement but retaining the dominant tenement.

Easement by Implication An easement created by operation of law instead of express grant or reservation when land is divided, if there is a long-standing, apparent use that is reasonably necessary for enjoyment of the dominant tenement. Also called **Implied Easement**.

Easement by Necessity A special kind of easement by implication that occurs when the dominant tenement would be completely useless without an easement, even if it is not a long-standing, apparent use.

Easement by Prescription An easement acquired by prescription. Also called **Prescriptive Easement**.

Easement in Gross An easement that benefits a person instead of a piece of land; there is a dominant tenant but no dominant tenement.

Economic Age-Life Method A simple depreciation method that divides the effective age by the economic life to reveal the percent of depreciation to be applied.

Economic Base The main business or industry in an area that a community uses to support and sustain itself.

Economic Base Analysis A study of the present business and employment situation in an area to determine the likelihood of continued stability, growth, or decline.

Economic Forces One of the broad forces of value, which reflects the health of a market area's economy and the economic state overall, including national and regional factors.

Economic Life The time during which a building can be used for its intended purpose and generate more income than is paid out for operating expenses. Also called **Useful Life**.

Economics of Scale - A variable often observed through multiple regression. Example: As the size increases, the unit cost decreases. Also called **Economies of Scale** or **Economy of Scale**.

Effective Age The age of a dwelling estimated by an appraiser and based on all forces of physical deterioration and functional and external obsolescence.

Effective Age-Life Method A simple depreciation method that divides the effective age by the economic life to reveal the percent of depreciation to be applied.

Effective Date The context for the appraiser's opinions and conclusions. Effective dates can be current, retrospective, or prospective.

Effective Demand The prospective buyer having enough disposable income available to satisfy his or her needs, wants, and desires. Also called **Effective Purchasing Power**.

Effective Gross Income (EGI) Potential gross income, less vacancy and collection losses.

Effective Gross Income Multiplier (EGIM) A factor derived and applied using EGI—the amount after estimated vacancy has been deducted from potential gross income (PGI).

Effective Purchasing Power The ability found in a market to afford a property. Also called **Effective Demand**.

Egress Means of exiting a property.

Electrical System A house system comprised of several elements, including such things as the wiring, distribution box, circuit breaker box, circuit breakers, fuses, lights and lighting fixtures, light switches, and wall outlets.

Elements of Comparison Characteristics of a property or a transaction that can be used to explain differences in the price paid in a transaction.

Eminent Domain The government's constitutional power to appropriate or condemn private property for public use, as long as the owner is paid just compensation. The government's taking of private land is called **Condemnation**. Condemnation is the *action*; eminent domain is the *right*.

Encroachment A physical object intruding onto neighboring property, often due to a mistake regarding the boundary.

Encumbrance A non-possessory interest in property; a lien, easement, or restrictive covenant, burdening the property owner's title.

Energy Audit A process of examining the structure and systems of a house to determine its overall energy efficiency.

Energy Efficiency Are the systems and appliances that provide the most output for the least cost.

Energy Efficient Mortgages (EEMs) Mortgages offered by HUD which take into account the energy costs of the house, and allow the borrower to extend his/her debt to income ratios to take into account the lower energy costs.

Energy Rating Labels Yellow stickers affixed to products to advise the consumer of the projected energy consumption of that particular product and the average energy consumption for other products like it.

ENERGY STAR One of the rating systems available to evaluate homes for energy efficiency. ENERGY STAR Certified Raters are RESNET approved raters.

Entrepreneurial Incentive A dollar value attributable for the expertise and efforts provided in the connection of the development, such as the entrepreneur's expertise, skills, and involvement with development (e.g., leasing, selling) of the project.

Entrepreneurial Profit A figure derived from the market representing an amount received by the entrepreneur for his contributions and risk accepted in a project.

Environmental Hazard A situation that exists in which there is potential for harm to persons or property from conditions that exist in a property or the surrounding area.

Environmental Impact Statement (EIS) A study required for all federal and federally related projects by the National Environmental Policy Act, which details a development project's impact on energy use, sewage systems, drainage, water facilities, schools, and other environmental, economic, and social areas.

Environmental Protection Laws Regulations that can block or restrict the use of land.

Equal Credit Opportunity Act (ECOA) A federal law that prohibits discrimination in granting credit to people based on sex, age, marital status, race, color, religion, national origin, or receipt of public assistance.

Equitable Title An interest created in property with the execution of a valid sales contract, with actual title being transferred by deed at a future date. Also, the vendee's (buyer's) interest in property under a land contract. Also called **Equitable Interest**.

Equity Capitalization Rate The capitalization rate applied to the expectation of return on equity (symbolized by R_E). Also referred to as an **equity dividend rate**.

Equity Divided Rate The rate used to capitalize equity income. The equity dividend rate is the ratio of equity dividend to the amount of equity.

Equity Yield Rate The rate of return on an investment, considering all income cash flow plus money invested in the property and eventual sale proceeds.

Escheat When property reverts to the state after a person dies without leaving a valid will and without heirs. Property also reverts to the state after abandonment.

Estate 1. A possessory interest in real property; either a freehold estate or a leasehold estate. 2. The real and personal property left by someone who has died.

Estate For Years A leasehold estate that is specified as a defined period (e.g., year, month, week). Also called **Term Tenancy**.

Ethics Rule A USPAP rule that (among other things) requires appraisers to avoid actions that could be considered misleading or fraudulent.

Excess Rent The amount of contract rent over and above market level rent.

Excess Site Land or site that is not needed to support the existing improvements or highest and best use. Could have sell-off potential or be needed for future expansion of the existing or anticipated improvements.

Exposure Time The estimated length of time that the property interest being appraised would have been offered on the market prior to the hypothetical consummation of a sale at market value on the effective date of the appraisal. (corresponding comment is not presented) (USPAP 2014-2015 Edition, p. U-2)

Exterior BPO Assignments Require the individual undertaking the BPO to drive by the property and take specific pictures of the exterior.

External Conformity How a property and its characteristics conform to the market and the demands of market participants.

External Obsolescence When something outside the control of a property makes it less desirable. External obsolescence can be locational or economic.

Externalities Any event, item, etc., outside the boundaries of a property.

Extraction Method A site valuation method that takes an estimated value of improvements and subtracts it from the total sales price to derive a figure for the land value.

Extraordinary Assumption An assumption, directly related to a specific assignment, as of the effective date of the assignment results, which, if found to be false, could alter the appraiser's opinions or conclusions. (corresponding comment is not presented) (USPAP 2014-2015 Edition, p. U-3)

Extrapolation Concluding outside (higher or lower) the known range of data.

F

Feasibility Analysis A study of the cost-benefit relationship of an economic endeavor. (USPAP 2014-2015 Edition, p. U-3) Also referred to as a **Feasibility Study**.

Federal Fair Housing Act Title VIII of the Civil Rights Act of 1968; this law makes it illegal to discriminate based on **race**, **color**, **religion**, **sex**, **national origin**, **disability**, or **familial status** in the sale or lease of residential property, including vacant land intended for residential housing. The law also prohibits discrimination in advertising, brokerage, lending, appraisal, and other housing services, and specifically prohibits **blockbusting**, **steering**, and **redlining**.

Federal Home Loan Mortgage Corporation (Freddie Mac) A stockholder-owned corporation chartered by Congress in 1970 to keep money flowing to mortgage lenders in support of homeownership and rental housing.

Federal Housing Administration (FHA) A government agency that insures mortgage loans.

Federal National Mortgage Association (Fannie Mae) A privately held stockholder corporation and the largest purchaser of mortgages in the United States.

Federal Reserve System The central banking authority for the United States.

Fee An estate of inheritance; title to real property that can be willed or descend to heirs.

Fee Simple The greatest estate (ownership) one can have in real property; it is freely transferable and inheritable, and of indefinite duration, with no conditions on the title. Also called **Fee Simple Absolute** or **Fee Title**.

Fee Simple Conditional (defeasible) A conditional ownership that will terminate when certain conditions are not maintained.

Fenestration The number, design, and location of doors and windows in a structure.

Fiduciary One who is in an appointed position of trust, and is acting on another's behalf.

Financial Calculator An electronic calculator specifically designed to solve the six functions of a dollar equations.

Financial Institutions Reform, Recovery and Enforcement Act (FIRREA) An act passed in 1989 as a comprehensive savings and loan bailout and preventive measure against future S&L insolvency. This act recognizes USPAP as the industry standard for appraisals, and identifies the Appraisal Foundation as the authority for professional appraisal standards.

First Mortgage The mortgage with the highest lien priority.

Fiscal Policy The government's plan for spending, taxation, and debt management.

Fixed Expenses Ongoing operating expenses that do not vary based on occupancy levels of the property (e.g., taxes and insurance).

Fixed-rate Loan A loan that has an interest rate that remains constant for the duration of the loan.

Fixture A man-made attachment; an item of personal property that has been attached to or closely associated with real property in such a way that it legally becomes part of the real property. Major fixtures are called **Improvements**.

Flashing Material used to cover joints where two or more different types of materials join together for the purpose of preventing water from penetrating the joint (e.g., metal over the seam between a brick chimney and a shingle roof).

Forecasting Creating future assumptions based on current data models and trends.

Foreclosure When a lienholder causes property to be sold so unpaid debt secured by the lien can be satisfied from the sale proceeds.

Foundation The basic structure on which the rest of the building will sit. A foundation can be **concrete slab**, **pier and beams**, **crawl spaces**, or **basement**.

Four Unities The unities of time, title, interest, and possession that are required for a joint tenancy.

Fractile A fractile divides data into fractions.

Framing The basic load bearing skeleton of the house to which interior walls, exterior walls, and roof are attached. The framing can be **platform**, **post and beam**, or **balloon**.

Fraud An intentional or negligent misrepresentation or concealment of a material fact; making statements that a person knows, or should realize, are false or misleading.

Freehold A possessory interest in real property of uncertain (and often unlimited) duration; an ownership estate in real property, either a fee simple or life estate. The holder of a freehold estate has title.

Frontage The linear dimensions across the access (road) side of a parcel of land. (The first number of a lot dimension is the frontage.)

Fructus Industriales Plants planted and cultivated by people ("fruits of industry").

Fructus Naturales Naturally occurring plants ("fruits of nature").

Fully Amortized Loans Loans in which the total payments over the life of the loan will pay off the entire balance of principal and interest due at the end of the loan term.

Functional Obsolescence When a building is less desirable because of something inherent in the design of the structure.

Functional Utility When a building has the adequate design and features to be used as intended.

Future Value 1. Worth of something at some later point in time. 2. Amount of money that an investment (either a single payment or an annuity) at a fixed interest rate, for a specified period of time, will grow to in the future.

Future Value of $1 The future amount of $1, based on the effects of compound interest.

G

General Analysis An analysis covering the conditions in the marketplace for the area where the property is located. Also called a **Market Study** or **Market Analysis**.

General Data Information that covers the forces that affect property values but are not directly related to a particular piece of property. General data covers physical, economic, governmental, and social factors (**P-E-G-S**) and can be local or national.

Gentrification The process of rapid revitalization of properties in a neighborhood, which causes current residents to be displaced.

Geo-Thermal Energy Energy that is generated and stored in the earth. About 20% of the geothermal energy of the earth's crust is from the origins of the planet; 80% is from the radioactive decay of minerals. A common example of geo-thermal energy is a hot spring, or geyser.

Geographic Competency The USPAP Competency rule speaks to an appraiser's level of familiarity with a specific type of property, a market, or **geographical area**, In an assignment where geographic competency is necessary, an appraiser preparing an appraisal in an unfamiliar location must spend sufficient time to understand the nuances of the local market and the supply and demand factors relating to the specific property type and the location involved.

Geographic information systems (GIS) An emerging computer technology used to collect, store, view, and analyze mapped geographical information.

Gingerbread House A term used to refer to highly decorated houses in Victorian Architecture.

Going Concern Value The market value in use of all property, including real property, trade fixtures, inventory (tangible assets), and the intangible assets of an established and operating business with an indefinite life.

Gothic Revival An architectural movement that originated in England in the mid-eighteenth century.

Governmental Forces One of the broad forces of value, which reflects the federal, state, or local jurisdictional right to impose laws, regulations, or taxes that affect property.

Government National Mortgage Association (Ginnie Mae) A wholly owed government corporation of the Department of Housing and Urban Development (HUD) that uses MBS to provided funding for low- to moderate-income borrowers.

Government Sponsored Enterprises (GSEs) A financial services corporation created by the United States Congress. Their function is to enhance the flow of credit to targeted sectors of the economy and to make those segments of the capital market more efficient and transparent.

Government Survey System A legal description for land, referencing principal meridians and base lines designated throughout the country. Also called **Rectangular Survey** or **Township System**.

Grade The slope of land, especially used when discussing land sloping away from the foundation of a structure.

Grantee Person receiving title to real property (buyer).

Grantor Person conveying title to real property (seller).

Green MLS A Multiple Listing Service (MLS) which has added sufficient fields so that energy efficient items can be reported, and therefore, appraisers can find them and make appropriate adjustments for them.

Greenwashing Practice of claiming that a house or other building has more green features than it actually has.

Grey Water Water which has been used in a household for washing or showering, but not for flushing toilets.

Gross Adjustments The overall total of all adjustments applied regardless of whether the adjustment is applied as a positive or a negative (for example, a +$1,000 and a -$1,000 adjustment would result in $2,000 gross adjustments).

Gross Building Area (GBA) Total area of a building measured from the exterior walls that include common areas (e.g., hallways, entryways, common laundry rooms).

Gross Income Income before expenses.

Gross Income Multiplier (GIM) A factor that takes into account income derived from all sources of a property (e.g., vending, storage units). A GIM can be stated as a PGIM or an EGIM.

Gross Leasable Area An area specified by the lease. Usually for non-residential properties, gross leasable area is calculated from within, or to the mid-point of perimeter walls.

Gross Lease A property lease where the landlord pays all utilities and expenses.

Gross Living Area (GLA) Residential space that is finished, livable, and above grade. Garages, finished basements, and storage areas usually do not count as GLA.

Gross Rent Multiplier (GRM) A number derived from comparable rental property in an area, which is then used in an income method for indicating a value conclusion.

Ground Fault Interrupter (GFI) A specially grounded outlet that turns off the outlet's power instantaneously if the device or appliance that is plugged in gets wet, shorts out, or malfunctions.

Ground Lease A property lease that only covers the land, often with the lessee owning the building on the land.

Ground Rent Income earned from a ground lease.

Ground Rent Capitalization Method A method of valuing land based on the rent it generates in a given year, divided by an appropriate capitalization rate.

Ground Source Heat Pump A heating and cooling system which uses the constant temperature of the ground beneath the surface for heating and cooling. Ground temperatures in the lower 48 states of the United States vary from a low of 42° F in North Dakota to a high of 102° F in Idaho. In the western United States, the geology provides natural hot springs, which are used to heat homes. In many northwestern states, air conditioning is not commonly found in homes.

Growth 1. The first stage a neighborhood goes through in its life cycle, when property values rise as development activity begins and continues. 2. Refers to the growth rate.

H

Hard Costs Costs in a project that are not variable, such as labor and materials. Also called **Direct Costs**.

Heat Pump An alternative to traditional heating and cooling systems, whereby one unit provides heat in the winter and cooled air in the summer.

Heating and Cooling System A house system comprised of several elements, including such things as a furnace or heat pump, flue, ducts and ductwork, registers, and thermostat. Also called **HVAC**.

Highest and Best Use The most profitable, legally permitted, economically feasible, and physically possible use of a property.

Home Energy Rating Systems (HERS) Index used by ENERGY STAR Certified Raters. In the HERS rating system, 0 = zero net energy home. The higher the score, the less efficient the home is.

Home Inspection A visual examination of the physical structure and systems of a home.

Homeowners Association A nonprofit association made up of homeowners in a subdivision, responsible for enforcing the subdivision's CC&Rs and managing other community affairs.

Homogeneity A characteristic of being similar or comparable in composition or structure.

Household A group of people living in one unit of housing.

HUD The Department of Housing and Urban Development; a government agency that deals with housing issues.

HVAC A heating, ventilation, and air conditioning system.

Hypothetical Condition A condition, directly related to a specific assignment, which is contrary to what is known by the appraiser to exist on the effective date of the assignment results, but is used for the purpose of analysis. (corresponding comment is not presented) (USPAP 2014-2015 Edition, p. U-3)

I

Illegal Flipping Occurs when successive transfer and mortgage transactions are facilitated in a short time period for fraudulent and criminally profitable purposes.

Immobility A physical characteristic of real estate referring to the fact that real estate cannot move from one place to another.

Improvements Additions to real property; they can be natural (e.g., trees or a lot feature), but usually are man-made, substantial fixtures, such as buildings.

Income Money derived from an activity, such as the exertion of labor or investment of capital.

Income Approach An appraisal method that indicates the value of real estate by analyzing the amount of income the property potentially could generate and applying income techniques.

Income Capitalization A method used to convert a single year's estimate of income into a value indicated in the income capitalization approach.

Income Factors Include the potential gross income multiplier (PGIM), gross rent multiplier (GRM), and the effective gross income multiplier (EGIM).

Income Rates Rates used in income capitalization which include the overall (property) capitalization rate, mortgage capitalization rate, equity dividend rate, land capitalization rate, and the building capitalization rate.

Increasing Returns Principle that says the added value of an additional feature, addition, repair, etc., is more than the actual cost of the item.

Incurable Something that cannot be fixed at a reasonable cost, with the cost of the repair being more than the value added to a property.

Indestructibility A physical characteristic of real estate referring to the fact that it cannot be destroyed.

Index Method A method for determining the cost of a building by taking its original cost and multiplying that number by an index factor based on how long ago the building was constructed.

Indirect Costs Costs in a project that are variable (costs other than labor or materials) Also called **Soft Costs**.

Inflation An increase in the cost of goods or services; too much money chasing too few goods.

Infra-Red Thermal Camera A camera used in home inspection that can reveal "hot" and "cold" spots in a house, as well as water infiltration and leaks.

Infrastructure The support facilities and services for a community, such as roads, parks, sewers, water, schools, trash disposal, etc.

Ingress Means of entry or access to a property.

Insulation Material used in construction to keep buildings warmer in winter and cooler in summer, by blocking the flow of conditioned air (hot or cold) from the structure. Insulation is available in many forms.

Insurance Value The amount that the property can be insured for, usually only representing the replacement costs of the structure and disregarding any value for the land.

Intangible Property (Intangible Assets) Nonphysical assets, including but not limited to franchises, trademarks, patents, copyrights, goodwill, equities, securities, and contracts as distinguished from physical assets such as facilities and equipment. (USPAP 2014-2015 Edition, p. U-3)

Intended Use The use or uses of an appraiser's reported appraisal or appraisal review assignment opinions and conclusions, as identified by the appraiser based on communication with the client at the time of the assignment. (USPAP 2014-2015 Edition, p. U-3)

Intended User The client and any other party as identified, by name or type, as users of the appraisal or appraisal review report by the appraiser on the basis of communication with the client at the time of the assignment. (USPAP 2014-2015 Edition, p. U-3)

Interior BPO Assignments Performed on vacant properties and sometimes, occupied properties.

Investment Value The value of a property to a specific investor or type of investor based on a typical investor's investment expectation and criteria

Interest 1. A right or share in something, such as a piece of real estate. 2. The charge a borrower pays to a lender for the use of the lender's money.

Interest-only Loan A loan in which only the interest is paid; the entire principal is still owed.

Interest Rate The cost of money; the additional percentage of a borrowed sum that a borrower must repay to the lender for use of the lender's money.

Interim Use Temporary use of a property while it awaits conversion to its highest and best use (e.g., waiting for a zoning change, accumulation of investment dollars, etc.)

Internal Conformity A state of four agents of production in relation to land use and improvements.

International Code Council (ICC) "A member-focused association dedicated to helping the building safety community and construction industry provide safe, sustainable and affordable construction through the development of codes and standards used in the design, build and compliance process. Most U.S. communities and many global markets choose the International Codes." (per ICC website)

Interpolation Concluding within a known value range.

Intestate An individual who dies and has not written a will, or one who has prepared a will that is defective and considered invalid.

Italianate Style Introduced in the United States by architect Alexander Jackson Davis in the 1840s as an alternative to Gothic or Greek Revival styles.

Investment The use of capital designed to produce income and/or profit.

Investment Value The value of a property to a particular investor based on that investor's specific investment expectation and criteria.

IVR A formula or technique that derives an overall capitalization rate: Income (NOI) / Value (Sale Price) = Rate.

J

Joint and Several The ability of a creditor to collect all debts due from any party or from all parties to a contract.

Joist and Rafters (Roofing) A type of roof frame with joists supported by the outer load bearing walls and a central load bearing wall that acts as the beams do for the floor joists. The ceiling joists run horizontally, parallel to the floor; the ceiling rafters begin on the outer load bearing walls, but rise as they come to center peak of the roof.

Joists Long beams of wood or steel that span the piers of a foundation or the load bearing walls of a roof.

Jurisdictional Exception An assignment condition established by applicable law or regulations, which precludes an appraiser from complying with a part of USPAP. (USPAP 2014-2015 Edition, p. U-3).

Just Compensation Appropriate or fair value for private land taken by the government for public use. *See:* **Eminent Domain.**

K

Knob and Tube Wiring An older method of wiring property where wires are insulated form the structure with porcelain devices

Known Adjustments Adjustments that the appraiser has developed over time.

L

Land The surface of the earth: Actual dirt on the ground, part of a waterway that is owned, or even a swampy marsh. From a legal standpoint, land also refers to everything under the ground to the center of the earth, and everything over the land into the air (within limits to allow for air traffic).

Land Residual Method An income method of site valuation that attributes a certain part of the income produced by a property to the building or other improvement, then attributes the remaining income to the land.

Land Use Controls Public or private restrictions on how land may be used.

Landlocked Property 1. Land without access to a road or highway. 2. Land not beside water.

Landlord A landowner who has leased his or her property to another. Also called **Lessor.**

Latent Defect A defect that is not visible or apparent; a hidden defect that would not be discovered in a reasonably thorough inspection of property.

Law of Diminishing Returns Law that says beyond a certain point, the added value of an additional feature, addition, repair, etc., is less than the actual cost of the item. Also called the **Law of Decreasing Returns.**

Law of Increasing Returns Law that says the added value of an additional feature, addition, repair, etc., is more than the actual cost of the item.

Leach Field An area that is part of a waste disposal system to distribute waste water into the soil.

Lease Conveyance of a leasehold estate from the fee owner to a tenant; a contract where one party pays the other rent in exchange for possession of real estate.

Lease/Option When a seller leases property to someone for a specific term, with an option to buy the property at a predetermined price during the term. Usually, a portion of the lease payments is applied to the purchase price.

Lease/Purchase When a seller leases property to someone for a specific term, with the tenant agreeing to buy the property at a predetermined price during or following the lease term, usually with a portion of the lease payments applied to the purchase price.

Leased Fee Interest The landlord's ownership interest in leased property. Defined by the amount of contract rent over and above market rent. Also, called **Leased Fee Estate.**

Leasehold Estate An estate that gives the holder (tenant) a temporary right to possession, without title. Also called **Less-than-Freehold Estate.**

Leasehold Interest Defined by the amount of rent that is less than market rent (amount of difference between contract and market rent).

LEED® (Leadership in Energy Efficiency and Design) Third party rating system for energy efficiency. The USGBC® (United States Green Building Council) confers LEED® designations.

Legal Description A precise description of a parcel of property.

Legally Permissible A use of land available to the owner under current laws and zoning regulations.

Lessee A person who leases property; a tenant.

Lessor A person who leases property to another; a landlord.

Leverage Using borrowed capital as part or all of the purchase price of real estate.

Levy 1. Verb: To impose a tax. 2. Noun: The tax itself.

License 1. Official permission to do a particular thing that the law does not allow everyone to do. 2. Revocable, non-assignable permission to enter another person's land for a particular purpose.

Lien 1. A non-possessory interest in property, giving a lienholder the right to foreclose if the owner does not pay a debt owed to lienholder. 2. A financial encumbrance on the owner's title.

Lien, General A lien against all property of a debtor, instead of a particular piece of property.

Lien, Involuntary A lien that arises by operation of law, without the consent of the property owner. Also called **Statutory Lien.**

Lien, Specific A lien that attaches only to a specific property (as opposed to a general lien, which attaches to all of the debtor's property.

Lien, Voluntary A lien placed against property with consent of the owner (e.g., mortgages and derivatives, such as home equity credit lines). In some states, called a **deed of trust.**

Life Estate A freehold estate that lasts only as long as a specified person lives. That person is referred to as the **life tenant** or **measuring life**.

Life Tenant Someone who owns a life estate; the person entitled to possession of the property during the measuring life.

Limiting Conditions Statement by the appraiser explaining the framework used to reach the appraisal value and establishing the report's limitations.

Linear Foot A measurement that has only one dimension which is length. An 8′ board has 8 linear feet.

Linkages The time-distance relationship to services between properties and services that people in the market rely on such as schools, employment, and shopping, etc.

Liquidation Value The value of a property if sold under duress or in a must-sell situation with less than typical market exposure.

Littoral Property Land that abuts a body of water, lakes, oceans, and seas.

Littoral Rights The water rights of a landowner whose property is adjacent to a lake or contains a lake; also called **Riparian Rights**, although that term literally refers only to the water rights of a landowner on a river.

Loan Constant A periodic payment expressed as a decimal equivalent of the periodic principal and interest payment required to amortize a loan

Loan-to-Value Ratio (LTV) The loan amount compared to the market value of the property (loan amount / market value amount = %).

Loan Value The amount of money a lender is willing to loan to someone to finance a property.

Location 1. Exact position of real estate. 2. The type of area surrounding the subject property.

Location Survey The process of verifying that an improvement properly sits within the boundaries of the property and there are no encroachments from neighboring land onto the subject property.

Long-lived Item A component of the property that is **not** expected to be replaced during the life of a property

Lot A parcel of land; especially, a parcel in a subdivision.

Lot and Block Type of legal description used for platted property. Description states only the property's lot and block number in a particular subdivision; to find out the exact location of property boundaries, the plat map for that subdivision must be consulted at the county recorder's office.

Low-E, or Low Emittance A coating put on windows which stops some rays of the sun, but allows others to penetrate-allowing sunlight in but keeping the heat or cooling in the house.

M

Macroeconomic Elements Economic elements that affect the entire market.

Macroeconomics Examines the behavior of the general economy of an overall area, taking into consideration such factors as income, employment, interest rates, and inflation.

Management Fee Money collected by an individual or company for overseeing a project, rental properties, etc.

Manufactured Housing Any dwelling unit built on a permanent chassis and attached to a permanent foundation system. Factory built housing, such as modular, pre-fabricated, panelized or sectional housing is not considered manufactured, per Fannie Mae.

Margin of Error The likely difference between sample data sets, if the data were collected multiple times relative to the population of the data.

Market A place where goods are exchanged, often between buyers and sellers.

Market Analysis A study of supply and demand, as well as other economic conditions in an area. Also called **Market Study**.

Market Area The broadest of all terms identifying the boundaries of a particular area. Market area takes into account the land uses and characteristics of typical market participants within the defined area.

Market Disaggregation A process that involves separating different users and different uses for property in the real estate market, focusing on real estate products on the supply side of the equation.

Market Extraction Method A method of depreciating that is based on sales of comparable properties with comparable traits.

Market Price The price that property sold for in an actual transaction.

Market Rent What the property could rent for in the open market if it were currently vacant and available.

Market Segmentation A process that involves identifying and categorizing the various sub-markets that exist within a larger market, focusing on market participants on the demand side of the equation.

Market Study A study of supply and demand, as well as other economic conditions in an area. Also called **Market Analysis**.

Market Value A type of value, stated as an opinion, that presumes the transfer of a property (i.e., a right of ownership or a bundle of such rights), as of a certain date, under specific conditions set forth in the definition of the term identified by the appraiser as applicable in an appraisal. (corresponding comment is not presented) (USPAP 2014-2015 Edition, p. U-3)

Marketability The ability of a product to attract buyers.

Marketability Study Analysis of the likelihood that a particular product will sell.

Marketable Title A title free and clear of objectionable encumbrances or defects, so that a reasonably prudent person with full knowledge of the facts would not hesitate to purchase the property.

Marketing Time The estimated period of time required to market the property after the effective date in order to consummate a sale at market value.

Mass Appraisal The process of valuing a universe of properties as of a given date using standard methodology, employing common data, and allowing for statistical testing. (USPAP 2014-2015 Edition, p. U-3)

Mass Appraisal Model A mathematical expression of how supply and demand factors interact in a market. (USPAP 2014-2015 Edition, p. U-3)

Matched Pair Analysis Process of determining the value of specific property characteristics or features by comparing pairs of similar properties. Also called **Paired Data Analysis**.

Mean A statistical value which adds a series of values and then divides the total by the number of values on the set: commonly known as the average.

Mechanical Systems The plumbing, electrical, and heating/cooling systems of a structure.

Mechanics Lien A lien provided for by some states' laws that may be placed against a property when work has been performed on the property but the work or materials have not been paid for.

Median A statistical value that describes the center or middle number in a set of numbers.

Measurements of Central Tendencies Methods and calculations to determine the center points of the data set.

Metes and Bounds A legal description that starts at an easily identifiable point of beginning (POB), then describes the property's boundaries in terms of courses (compass directions) and distances, ultimately returning to the POB.

Microeconomic Elements Economic elements that affect a narrow portion of the market.

Microeconomics Examines the behavior of smaller economic models on a local level, such as individual consumers, local lending, local employment, and terms of sale typical for the area.

Mile A unit of measure equaling 5,280 feet.

Mills A factor used for calculating property taxes. Mills are dollars per thousand of assessed value.

Mineral Rights Rights to the minerals located beneath the surface of a property.

Mixed-Use Property Combines more than one use for a common property

Mode The most frequently occurring number in a number set.

Modified Age-Life Method A combination of the age-life method and the breakdown method of depreciation. This method can be employed when curable depreciation is attributable to obsolescence for which the depreciation can be readily recognized and calculated.

Mold Organic spores that grow where moisture is present.

Monetary Policy The means by which the government can exert control over the supply and cost of money.

Monuments Fixed physical objects used in a metes and bounds description as points of reference. Also called **Markers**.

Mortgage An instrument that pledges and creates a voluntary lien on real property to secure repayment of a debt. The parties to a mortgage are the mortgagor (borrower) and mortgagee (lender).

Mortgage, Construction A temporary loan used to finance the construction of a building on land. Replaced with a takeout loan.

Mortgage, Purchase Money A mortgage for which the seller finances all or part of the sale price of a piece of property.

Mortgage Back Securities (MBS) Real Estate asset-backed securities whose cash flows are backed by the principal and interest payments of a group of pooled mortgages.

Mortgage Brokers Entities who, for a fee, place loans with investors, but typically do not service such loans. Mortgage brokers generally do not fund their loans.

Mortgage Capitalization Rate A return on the money lent in an investment (symbolized by R_M).

Mortgage Companies Institutions that function as the originators and servicers of loans on behalf of large investors, such as insurance companies, pension plans, or secondary market participants.

Mortgage Constant The ratio between annual debt service and loan principal.

Mortgagee A lender who accepts a mortgage as security for repayment of the loan.

Mortgagor The borrower in a loan who gives a mortgage to the lender as security.

Most Probable Sales Price The most likely price a property will bring in a typical (arm's length) transaction.

Most Probable Use The most likely use for a property given its current condition, position, configuration, etc.

Most Profitable Use The use of a property that will maximize the owner's capital investment.

Multiple Listing Service (MLS) A listing service whereby local member brokers agree to share listings, and agree to share commissions on properties sold jointly.

Multiple Regression Analysis A statistical measure that attempts to ascertain the source of change in multiple variables.

Multiple Use Property A property that has a limited number of unique uses that may or may not be used simultaneously or with little modification to the property. Also called **Multiple Purpose Property**.

Multiplier A factor that is derived from market data and applied to the subject's market rent or income to produce a value indication in an income approach.

N

Narrative Report A written type of appraisal report. It allows the appraiser to comment fully on the opinions and conclusions of the appraisal.

National Association of Home Builders (NAHB®) A large trade group of home builders. They also have a research center which helped the ICC develop standards for green building.

National Register of Historic Places The nation's official list of cultural resources worthy of preservation. Also known as the **National Register.**

Negative Leasehold When contract rent is more than market rent (an advantage to the lessor).

Negative Leverage The use of borrowed capital that decreases the overall yield of an investment.

Neighborhood Any constant, contiguous area that may be identified by similar characteristics of physical boundaries.

Net Adjustments The sum of the adjustments taking into account whether the adjustment was a positive or a negative. (For example, a +$1,000 and a -$1,000 adjustment would result in $0 net adjustments.)

Net Household Formations The number of new households being formed or moving into the area, minus the number of households leaving the area.

Net Income Ratio (NIR) Expressed as a percentage; net operating income divided by effective gross income.

Net Lease A property lease where the tenant pays some or all utilities and expenses, in addition to rent payments.

Net Operating Income (NOI) Income after expenses.

Net Rentable Area In multi-tenant buildings, the gross area less all common areas and set-aside areas for the building's use (e.g., maintenance rooms, etc.).

Non-conforming Loan A loan in which the amount, LTV, term, or characteristics exceeds specific underwriting guidelines.

Non-conforming Use Property use that does not conform to current zoning laws, but is allowed because the property was being used that way before the new zoning law was passed.

Non-possessory Interest 1. An interest in property that does not include the right to possess and occupy the property. 2. An encumbrance, such as a lien or easement.

Normal Distribution Indicates that most datum points in a data set are close to the "mean" of the data, while relatively few numbers are off to one end or the other.

Nuisance Anything outside property boundaries that interferes with the right of enjoyment and use of a person's land.

Numerical Data Data associated with a numerical value, such as height, weight speed, or the number of jelly beans in a glass jar.

O

Observable Depreciation Method of determining depreciation based on inspection of the structure, study of demographics, and analysis of the market or other external conditions.

Obsolescence A loss in value because of inherent design flaws or other defects not easily corrected.

Operating Expenses Day-to-day costs of running a building, such as repairs and maintenance, but not including debt service or depreciation.

Operating Expense Ratio (OER) Expressed as a percentage, it is the operating expenses divided by effective gross income.

Opportunity Cost The loss in value or potential value that occurs because one action is chosen over another.

Option A contract giving one party the right to do something within a designated time period, without obligation to do so.

Ordinance A law passed by a local legislative body, such as a city or village council.

Over Improvement An improvement that exceeds the highest and best use for the site and does not increase the value of the real property in proportion to its cost.

Overage Rent A percentage of business sales a tenant's business has generated paid in addition to rent payments.

Overall Capitalization Rate Used to interpret a property's single year net operating income to the property's value using direct capitalization (symbolized by R_o).

Overall Yield Rate Considers a series of annual figures over the entire investment period as well as reversion.

Ownership Title to and dominion over property; the rights of possession and control of real or personal property.

Ownership in Severalty Ownership by a single individual or entity (such as a corporation), as opposed to co-ownership; interests are severed (cut) from the interests of all others.

P

Paired Data Analysis The process of determining the value of specific property characteristics or features by comparing pairs of similar properties. Also called **Matched Pair Analysis**.

Paired Sale Adjustment In appraisal, the theory that an appraiser can find two sales which are identical in every respect except one, and from that one difference, derive the appropriate, market based adjustment for the difference.

Parameter A numerical quantity that expresses some characteristic of a population, such as the mean, median, and mode.

Parcel A lot or tract of real estate, particularly a specified part of a larger tract.

Partial Interest Any interest in real estate that one may have, other than full bundle of rights.

Party Wall A wall built along the boundary line between two parcels of land, where part of the wall rests on each side.

Pass-through Zoning When zoning laws are set up in a hierarchical fashion, such that all uses above the current zoning are permitted.

Patent Defect A visible, apparent defect that can be seen in a reasonably thorough inspection of property.

Percentage Adjustments Adjustment applied to the sale price of a comparable sale whereby the appraiser translates a dollar figure from a paired-data analysis into a percentage change in value.

Percentage Lease A type of lease that requires the lessee to make rental payments based (either in whole or in part) on a percentage of the gross sales, net sales, income, profit or some other value.

Percentage Rent Lease payment that is based on the sales of the tenant, with the landlord receiving a percentage of the tenant's sales, often in addition to a minimum rent amount.

Periodic Tenancy A leasehold estate that continues for successive periods of equal length (e.g., month-to-month, week-to-week) until terminated by either party.

Permits Official government documents that acknowledge work that a person wants to do on a property and allow it to be done.

Personal Property Identifiable tangible objects that are considered by the general public as being "personal" - for example, furnishings, artwork, antiques, gems and jewelry, collectibles, machinery and equipment; all tangible property that is not classified as real estate. (USPAP 2014-2015 Edition, p. U-4) Also called **Chattel** or **Personalty**.

Personalty Personal property.

Photovoltaic Shingles These are made from crystalline silicone-based materials, or in some cases, thin-film solar cells which are made of semiconductor materials. They are flexible and much less noticeable than standard solar panels. They absorb energy from the sun.

Physical Characteristics Indestructibility-Immobility-Uniqueness-Scarcity; the four physical characteristics of real estate.

Physical Deterioration The diminishment of condition of a structure or other improvement; or a component of the structure or improvement due to age, the elements, or other forces.

Physical Forces One of the broad forces of value, which applies to the land and any natural or man-made features or characteristics.

Pin A rod driven into the ground to serve as a marker for a metes and bounds legal description.

Pitch A roof's vertical rise in inches, divided by its horizontal span in feet.

PITI (**P**rincipal, **I**nterest, **T**axes and **I**nsurance); The typical payment on a mortgage loan.

Planned Unit Development (PUD) A special type of subdivision that may combine nonresidential uses with residential uses, or otherwise depart from ordinary zoning and subdivision regulations; some PUDs have lot owners co-own recreational facilities or open spaces as tenants in common.

Planning Commission A local government agency responsible for preparing a community's comprehensive development plan.

Plans and Specifications Construction blueprints.

Plat A detailed survey map of a subdivision or other grouped lots of land, recorded in the county where the land is located. Subdivided property is often called **Platted Property**. Also called **Plat Map**.

Plat Book A large book containing subdivision plats, kept at the county recorder's office.

Platform (Framing) A type of framing used to build a house or building one story at a time, with each story serving as a platform for the next story to be built.

Plot Plan A drawing showing the layout of the subject site, including the positioning of the improvements. Also called **Plot Map**.

Plottage Combining two or more parcels into one, with an increase in value over the value of the two parcels individually.

Plottage Increment An increase in total land value when two or more parcels are joined. (e.g., if two $50,000 parcels are joined and now sell for $125,000, the plottage increment is $25,000.)

Plumbing System A house system comprised of several elements including piping, drains, clean outs, vents, valves, faucets, sinks, toilets, tubs, showers, and hot water tank. Gas lines may also be included.

Point of Beginning (POB) The starting and ending point for a metes and bounds description. Also called **Point of Origin**.

Points One percent of a loan amount. Points can be charged for any reason, but often are used for buydowns. Also called **Discount Points**.

Pole A land measurement equaling 16.5 feet.

Police Power The constitutional power of state and local governments to enact and enforce laws that protect the public's health, safety, morals, and general welfare.

Population All datum points available for study in a particular set.

Portfolio Lenders Financial institutions that make real estate loans, which they keep and service in-house instead of selling on the secondary markets. Also called **Primary Lenders**.

Positive Leasehold When contract rent is less than market rent (an advantage to the lessee).

Positive Leverage The use of borrowed capital that increases the overall yield of an investment.

Possession 1. Holding and enjoying property. 2. Actual physical occupation of real property.

Possessory Interest An interest in property that entitles the holder to possess and occupy the property, now or in the future; an estate, which may be either a freehold or leasehold.

Post and Beam (Framing) A type of framing with the floor for higher stories (and the roof) supported by beams that sit on top of posts and the outside wall perimeter.

Potential Gross Income (PGI) The income that could be produced by a property in an ideal situation, with no vacancy or collection losses.

Potential Gross Income Multiplier (PGIM) A factor derived from, and applied to, the total gross income generated by the property without vacancy being considered.

Prairie Style A style of architecture that features open horizontal floor plans and natural materials.

Prepaid Interest Interest paid before it is earned. Often found as points paid to increase the yield. It is also the interest paid at closing to cover the period from the time the lender funds a loan, (closing date) to the date the first payment is due (usually 30 to 45 days later).

Prescription Acquiring an interest in property (usually an easement) by using it openly and without the owner's permission for a period of time as prescribed by law (from 5-30 years in most states). In contrast to adverse possession, prescriptive use does not have to be exclusive and the user does not acquire title to the property.

Present Value The discounted value of future income. Based on the principle that money has a time value.

Present Value of $1 An amount today that is equivalent to a future payment, or series of payments (annuity), based on a specified interest rate, for a specific period of time.

Preserve To maintain a structure's existing form through careful maintenance and repair.

Price The amount asked, offered, or paid for a property. (corresponding comment is not presented) (USPAP 2014-2015 Edition, p. U-4)

Primary Data Data that is obtained directly by the appraiser.

Primary Mortgage Market The market where purchasers obtain loans from mortgage originators.

Principal Meridians Main north-south lines designated and named throughout the country for use with the government survey system.

Principle of Consistent Use An economic principle that holds that land cannot be valued for one use, while the improvements are valued at another use.

Private Mortgage Insurance (PMI) Insurance offered by private companies to insure a lender against default on a loan by a borrower.

Probability A number stated as a percentage that expresses the likelihood that a specific event will occur.

Productivity Analysis A means of determining the current position of a property in relation to the marketplace. Also called **Property Productivity Analysis** or **Productivity Market Analysis**.

Progression A principle that says the value of a home is helped by the other homes in an area. Usually said about the "worst" home in the "best" area.

Property 1. The rights of ownership in a thing, such as the right to use, possess, transfer, or encumber real estate. 2. Something that is owned, real or personal.

Property Characteristics Physical, legal, economic, and descriptive attributes of the property and may include personal property, fixtures, intangible items, and such things as easements, encumbrances, covenants, and contracts.

Property-Specific Analysis An analysis comparing the subject property to all the other properties against which it competes in the market. Also called a **Marketability Study** or **Marketability Analysis**.

Proprietary Lease An exclusive, longer-term lease given to a person who lives in and owns stock in the cooperative.

Prospective Appraisal An appraisal with an effective date in the future.

Public An improvement dedicated to and accepted by a unit of government.

Public Limitations The effects of governmental police powers.

Public Record The official collection of legal documents that individuals have filed with the county recorder to make the information contained in them public.

Purchase Ability The prospective buyer having enough disposable income available to satisfy his or her needs, wants, and desires. Also called **Effective Demand** or **Effective Purchasing Power**.

Purchase Agreement A contract in which a seller promises to convey title to real property to a buyer in exchange for the purchase price.

Purpose of the Appraisal A statement of the type of value defined in an assignment.

Q

Qualitative Analysis A method used after any quantitative adjustments have been applied that employs the appraiser's judgment in forming opinions relying on such methods as relative comparison analysis (bracketing), ranking analysis, and/or personal interviews. The method requires good judgment and reasoning skills of the appraiser.

Quantitative Adjustments A method that requires the recognition of the differences between the comparable data and the subject property and assigning either a market derived dollar or percentage amount as an adjustment.

Quantitative Analysis A method that determines dollar adjustments that have been "quantified" through techniques such as paired data, cost or income methods, or statistics and trending.

Quantity Survey Method A cost approach appraisal method in which the appraiser counts the number and type of each part and material used to construct the building, adding costs for labor, profit, permits, etc.

Quiet Enjoyment The use and possession of real property without interference from a previous owner, the lessor, or anyone else claiming title.

R

Radon Gas A naturally occurring radioactive gas that emanates from the earth; it is odorless, colorless, and tasteless but has been identified as a cancer-causing agent.

Rafters Sloped support beams that follow the pitch of the roof and serve to hold the outer roof covering.

Range The difference between the lowest and highest numbers in a number set.

Range Lines In the government survey system, north-south lines that run parallel to principal meridians at six-mile intervals.

Real Estate An identified parcel or tract of land, including improvements, if any. (USPAP 2014-2015 Edition, p. U-4)

Real Estate Contract 1. A purchase agreement. 2. A land contract. 3. Any contract having to do with real property.

Real Estate Cycles General swings in real estate activity, resulting in increasing or decreasing activity and property values during different phases of the cycle.

Real Estate Owned (REO) Property acquired by a lending institution through foreclosure, or deed in lieu, and held in inventory.

Real Estate Settlement Procedures Act (RESPA) A federal law dealing with real estate closings that sets forth specific procedures and guidelines for disclosure of settlement costs. RESPA lets buyers compare cost of services, requires specific statements/disclosures, prevents kickbacks, and limits lender-held escrows.

Real Property The interests, benefits, and rights inherent in the ownership of real estate. (corresponding comment is not presented) (USPAP 2014-2015 Edition, p. U-4) Also called **Realty**.

Realty Real property.

Recertification of Value A process performed to confirm whether or not the conditions of a prior appraisal have been met. A Recertification of Value does not change the effective date of the value opinion.

Reconciliation Analyzing the conclusions within each approach that was developed; Analyzing the values derived from the different appraisal approaches to arrive at a final opinion of value.

Reconstructed Operating Income Statement Prepared by the appraiser, a reconstructed operating income statement reflects anticipated net operating income.

Recording Filing a document at the county recorder's office, so it will be placed in the public record.

Redlining When a lender refuses to make loans secured by property in a certain neighborhood because of the racial or ethnic composition of the neighborhood.

Regression A principle that says the value of a home is held down by the other homes in an area. Usually said about the "best" home in the "worst" area.

Regression Analysis Statistical measure that attempts to ascertain the source of change in variables.

Regulation 1. A rule adopted by an administrative agency. 2. Any governmental order having the force of law.

Rehabilitate To repair a structure and make it usable again while preserving those portions or features that are historically and culturally significant.

Release 1. To give up a legal right. 2. A document in which a legal right is given up.

Relevant Characteristics Those characteristics of a property, whether location, physical, legal, or economic, which affect value.

Reliction An increase in land size by the withdrawal of a body of water.

Remainderman The party in a life estate who is entitled to the remainder of the property interest after the life estate is terminated.

Remaining Economic Life The period of usefulness that a building has remaining as of the effective date of the appraisal.

Rent Consideration paid by tenant to landlord in exchange for possession and use of property.

Rent Roll Briefly details the unit information, such as lease terms, contract rent, as well as the effective date of the leases that are in place for the property.

Rent Survey A compilation of the rents being generated (and often rent history) in a particular market for a particular property type.

Replacement Building the functional equivalent (substitute) of the original building, using modern materials, usually with one that is the same size, layout, quality, and utility as the original. *Compare:* **Reproduction.**

Replacement Cost The estimated cost new of building the functional equivalent (substitute) of the original structure, using modern materials and workmanship and current day standards of size, layout, quality, and utility.

Report Any communication, written or oral, of an appraisal or appraisal review that is transmitted to the client upon completion of an assignment. (corresponding comment is not presented) (USPAP 2014-2015 Edition, p. U-4)

Reporting Options The two reporting options permitted by USPAP are Appraisal Report and Restricted Appraisal Report.

Reproduction Building an exact duplicate (replica) of the original building, giving the new structure the exact look and feel of the original.

Reproduction Cost The estimated cost new of replicating the original building, using identical materials, workmanship, construction standards, size, layout, quality, and utility that is present in the current structure; including any functional obsolescence, deficiencies, and superadequacies.

Reserves for Replacement An amount of money set aside for future replacement of major items, such as the roof or heating system. Also called **Reserves**.

Residential Energy Services Network (RESNET) Non-profit membership corporation, which has established national standards for energy efficiency ratings. Inspectors must be RESNET certified.

Restricted Appraisal Report A type of appraisal report that is for the use of the client only, with no other intended users. It might be stated in a more brief manner, identifying the facts and conclusions of the appraisal with the utilized data contained in the appraiser's workfile.

Restriction A limitation on the use of real property.

Restriction, Deed Limitations on real property use, imposed through language included in the deed.

Restriction, Private Restriction imposed on property by a previous owner or subdivision developer.

Restriction, Public A law or regulation limiting or regulating the use of real property, such as zoning.

Restrictive Covenant 1. A limitation on real property use, imposed by a former owner. 2. A promise to do or not do an act relating to real property, usually the owner's promise to not use property in a particular way. Cannot cause forfeiture of title.

Restore To return a building to its form and condition as represented by a specified time period using materials as similar as possible to the original materials.

Retrospective Appraisal An appraisal with an effective date in the past.

Return on Investment Expressed as a percentage, it is the amount of interest earned by an investor for use of his or her money for a specific period of time.

Revenue Generating Laws Laws enacted by government consisting of taxation and specific tax policies.

Reverse Mortgage A loan used when a qualified senior citizen mortgages his or her home to a lender and, in return, receives a monthly check from the lender. The borrower must have a substantial amount of equity in the home to make this option viable. The mortgage is repaid when the home is sold or when the borrower dies.

Reverse Polish Notation (RPN) A formal logic system used in the HP-12C calculator that allows mathematical equations to be expressed by pressing the arithmetic operations key (+, -, x, /) after the numbers or variables have been keyed.

Reversionary Benefit Typically a sum, often stated in a dollar amount, that a property owner will receive when or if he sells the property at the end of the investment term.

Revitalization The final stage a neighborhood goes through in its life cycle, when property values rise again as demand increases, resulting in increased renovation and rehabilitation.

Rezoning A revision in zoning law, usually changing an entire zone or area from permitted use to another permitted use.

Right Hand Door A door with the door knob on the right side when is opens toward you.

Right of Disposal A right to transfer all or some of a person's ownership interest in real property.

Right of Enjoyment A right to enjoy the benefits of land ownership without outside interference.

Right of Use Right of land ownership to make it productive. Part of the bundle of rights.

Right of Way An easement giving the holder the right to cross another person's land.

Right to Regulate Laws Laws enacted by governments dealing with the police power they reserve for themselves.

Riparian Rights The water rights of a landowner whose property is adjacent to or crossed by a river.

Rod A land measurement equaling 16.5 feet.

Rough-Ins Any type of interior work to a house or building that is not part of the finish work.

Running with the Land Binding or benefiting the successive owners of a piece of property, rather than terminating when a particular owner transfers his or her interest. Usually refers to easements or restrictive covenants.

Rural The country or beyond the suburban area.

R-Value The measure of the efficiency of insulation in a structure. R-values measure thermal resistance, which indicates whether or not the inside temperature is flowing to the outside. The higher the R value, the better the insulating properties.

S

Sale Price The price that property actually sells for.

Sales Comparison Approach An appraisal method that indicates the value of real property by comparing the property being appraised with other comparable properties. Data are collected and adjustments are made for differences. Also called **Market Approach** or **Sales Comparison Method**.

Salvage Value The value of a property's useful components that can be removed before demolition.

Sample A smaller random selection of data from the population.

Scarcity A physical characteristic of real property that says there is a limited supply of real estate; the perceived supply of a good or service relative to the demand for the item.

Scatter Diagram Graphs used to study the relationship between two variables.

Scope of Work The type and extent of research and analyses in an appraisal or appraisal review assignment. (USPAP 2014-2015 Edition, p. U-4)

Second Mortgage A mortgage that is in second position in lien priority. When the first mortgage is paid off, the second mortgage will move into its position unless the second mortgage is subordinated.

Secondary Data Data that is compiled by other parties and used by the appraiser.

Secondary Mortgage Market The market where loan originators bundle and sell loans to obtain a new (replenished) source of funds for additional lending.

Section Part of a township, one-mile by one-mile square, used for the government survey system; one section equals 640 acres, 36 sections equal one township.

Security Instrument An instrument that gives the creditor the right to have the collateral sold to satisfy the debt if the debtor fails to pay according to the terms of the agreement.

Segmentation A process that involves identifying and categorizing the various sub-markets that exist within a larger market, focusing on participants on the demand side of the market.

Seller Financing When a seller extends credit to a buyer to finance the purchase of the property; this can happen instead of or in addition to the buyer obtaining a loan from a third party, such as an institutional lender.

Seller's Market A situation in the real estate market where sellers can choose from a large number of buyers looking for property in an area.

Septic System A type of private sewage disposal system used in areas that do not have public sewers.

Service Companies The companies in an area that serve the needs of the base companies, base industries, and their employees.

Servient Tenant The owner of a servient tenement is someone whose property is burdened by an easement.

Servient Tenement A property that is burdened by an easement.

Setback Requirements Provisions in a zoning ordinance that do not allow structures to be built within a certain distance of property lines.

Severalty Ownership by a single individual or entity (such as a corporation), as opposed to co-ownership.

Short-lived Item A component of the property that is expected to be replaced during the life of a property.

Side Yard The area between a building and one side boundary of the lot on which it is located.

Signature Personalized evidence indicating authentication of the work performed by the appraiser and the acceptance of the responsibility for content, analyses, and the conclusions in the report. (USPAP 2014-2015 Edition, p. U-4)

Simple Regression Analysis A mathematical/statistical tool used to exam the relationships between two variables using a linear or straight line equation to estimate an outcome based on the mathematical model.

Single-Use Property A property that is specifically designed and/or built for the user, or one with a unique use that would likely not fit other users.

Sinking Fund An account in which money is deposited and allowed to accumulate to cover a future expense.

Sinking Fund Factor Amount set aside on a periodic basis so that, when compounded at a given interest rate for a defined term, it will accumulate to a specified future sum.

Site A parcel of land with enhancements that make it ready for a building or structure.

Site Value The value of land with enhancements that make it ready for a building or structure.

Situs A term used to describe the place where something exists, an area of preference, or preference by people for a certain location.

Six Functions of $1 Financial functions that use compound interest to demonstrate the time value of money (TVM) under various scenarios. The six functions of a dollar are: Future value of $1; Future value of $1 per period, Sinking fund factors, Present value of $1, Present value of $1 per period, and Amortization. These functions are related and apply to various analysis techniques used by appraisers and investors for value analysis.

Social Forces One of the broad forces of value, which entails the composition, preferences, attitudes, and habits of people.

Soft Costs Costs in a project that are variable (costs other than labor or materials) Also called **Indirect Costs**.

Solar panels Cells which use the sun's light to either heat water or generate electricity.

Spanish Colonial Revival Architecture Characterized by a combination of detail from several eras of Spanish and Mexican architecture, the style is marked by the use of smooth plaster and stucco wall and chimney finishes, low-pitched clay tile, shed, or flat roofs, and terra cotta or cast concrete ornaments.

Special Assessment A tax levied only against properties that benefit from a public improvement (e.g., a sewer or street light), to cover the cost of the improvement; this creates a **special assessment lien**, an involuntary lien.

Special-Purpose Property A property that has limited and specific uses, such as a church. Also called **Special-Use Property**.

Specific Data Information that is relevant to the subject property itself. Two types of specific data are **subject property data** and **comparative purpose data**.

Spot Zoning An illegal rezoning that favors or restricts one landowner without justification.

Square Foot Method A method for determining the cost of a building, relying on **cost manuals.** Sometimes called the **Cost Manuals Method.**

Stability The second stage a neighborhood goes through in its life cycle, when the area is built up to the point where there is little, if any, vacant property. Also called **Equilibrium**.

Standard Deviation Statistical measure that calculates the variation from the mean. Describes the dispersion of a population or sample in a data set.

Standing Seam A type of roof, usually made from metal.

Standing Stock Completed construction projects (e.g., houses).

State Implementation Plan (SIP) A study required by Federal Environmental Protection Agency to help states meet national air quality standards.

Statistic Numerical value derived from a sample of the population that represents the data in some meaningful way.

Statistical Inference Process of drawing conclusions in relation to a population on use of a random sample.

Statistics A type of mathematics applied to the collection, organization, and analysis of data.

Statute A law enacted by a state legislature or the U.S. Congress.

Statute of Frauds A law that requires certain types of contracts to be in writing and signed to be enforceable.

Steering Channeling prospective buyers or tenants to particular neighborhoods based on race, religion, national origin, or ancestry.

Stigmatized Property A property made undesirable to most people by a past event, often a crime or environmental hazard.

Subdivision 1. A piece of land divided into two or more parcels. 2. A residential development.

Subdivision Analysis Method A method of valuing land that could be developed, by taking the total projected market value of the finished project and subtracting all costs of development and entrepreneurial profit and incentive.

Subdivision Covenants and Restrictions Assist the appraiser with determining legal compliance issues regarding the subject property and are also important in the highest and best use analysis.

Subdivision Regulations State and local laws that must be complied with before land can be subdivided.

Subdivision Plat Maps Are filed in public records and best illustrate the characteristics of a platted lot described by lot and block description.

Subject Property Property for which a value opinion is sought.

Subject Property Data Specific data that includes information on the subject property site and improvements.

Sublease When a tenant transfers only part of his or her right of possession or other interest in leased property to another for part of the remaining lease term (as opposed to an assignment, where the tenant gives up possession for the remainder of the lease term).

Sub-Markets A subset of the larger real estate market.

Substitution A principle that says an informed buyer will not pay more for a property, or a feature in a property, than a comparable substitute.

Substructure The area of a structure that is below grade.

Suburban An area that is outside a city, yet is connected either by proximity or economic factors.

Suggested List Price A value that would be low enough to attract buyers, yet high enough to leave room for negotiations.

Superadequacy A feature of an improvement that is more than is necessary for the operation of the improvement.

Superstructure The area of a structure that is above grade.

Supply and Demand A principle of economics that says, for all products, goods and services, when supply exceeds demand, prices will fall and when demand exceeds supply, prices will rise.

Support, Lateral The support that land receives from the land adjacent to it.

Support, Subjacent The support that the surface of land receives from the land beneath it.

Support Rights Right to have one's land supported by land adjacent to and beneath it.

Surplus Productivity A principal that states that land value is based on the net income it produces or can command once various agents of production have been satisfied.

Surplus Site Land or site that is not needed for the highest and best use of the subject and does not have potential for sell-off or an autonomous highest and best use.

Survey The process of locating and measuring the boundaries of a property, and identifying the improvements, encroachments, and easements associated with that land.

Sustainability Using today's resources wisely so as to not deplete them for future generations.

T

Taking When the government acquires private property for public use by appropriation, it is called a taking. The term is also used in inverse condemnation lawsuits, when a government action has made private property useless.

Tangible Property Items that can be held or touched (usually personal property).

Tax, Property An annual tax levied on the value of real property.

Taxation The process of a government levying a charge on people or things.

Tear-down Properties When properties are worth less than the underlying land, and thus, people are willing to incur the costs of tearing down the present structure to use the land.

Tenancy, Joint A form of co-ownership in which the co-owners have equal undivided interests and the right of survivorship. Joint tenancy must have the four unities present.

Tenancy, Periodic A leasehold estate that continues for successive periods of equal length (such as week-to-week or month-to-month) until terminated by proper notice from either party.

Tenancy at Sufference Possession of property by a holdover tenant.

Tenancy at Will A leasehold estate with no specified termination date or specified period of time.

Tenancy in Common A form of co-ownership in which two or more persons each have an undivided interest in the entire property (unity of possession), but no right of survivorship.

Tenant Someone in lawful possession of real property, especially someone who has leased property from the owner.

Terms of Sale Incentives (other than financing) or things of value included in the sale price to induce the buyer to buy, but not part of the real property. Terms of sale are sometime also known as "conditions of sale" or "sale concessions."

Time Value of Money (TVM) The financial principle that infers that due to its ability to earn interest, a dollar today is more valuable than a dollar received in the future.

Timeshares Grant the right to use (or possess) a property for a specified period of time (the right may or may not be accompanied with an ownership interest in the property).

Title Actual lawful ownership of real property. Title is not a document. Title is a *concept*.

Topography The physical characteristics of the surface of a parcel of land.

Township Square divisions of land, 6 miles by 6 miles, in the government survey system. One township contains 36 sections.

Township Lines East-west lines that run parallel to base lines at six mile intervals in the government survey system.

Township Section A square portion of a township that contains 640 acres and measures 1 mile by 1 mile.

Trade Fixtures Equipment installed for use in a business that can be removed before the lease expires or the property is conveyed. Trade fixtures are considered personal property.

Transferability The ability to freely buy, sell, encumber, or dispose of property in any way the owner sees fit.

Transition A complete change of land use.

Trespass An unlawful physical invasion of property owned by another.

Triple Net Lease A lease that requires the lessee to pay all expenses, including taxes, maintenance, and insurance.

Truth-in-Lending Act (TIL) Federal law requiring lenders to disclose consumer credit costs to promote informed use of credit.

Trusses Assembled wood pieces, formed from several smaller pieces of wood, in a triangular shape that form the basis of support for a roof.

Tuckpointing The process of replacing old, broken, or missing mortar joints in brick or block with new mortar material.

Tudorbethan Style Also called **Mock Tudor** in the twentieth century, first appeared as an architectural style in England in the mid- to late-nineteenth century based on the characteristics of the earlier Tudor style.

Type and Definition of Value Purpose of the appraisal.

Typical Buyer A buyer acting in his or her own best interest, without undue pressure, influence, or emotional attachment, and who would rationally and readily accept a less expensive substitute, if one is available in the -marketplace.

Typical Purchaser In the context of appraisal, who the person(s) most likely to buy the property would be - appraisers analyze typical purchaser behavior.

U

U-Factor The measure of thermal conductivity in windows. Unlike R-values, where the higher number indicates better insulating properties, in windows, the lower the number, the better insulation the window provides.

Underimprovement When the improvements do not conform to the highest and best use of the site, thus the property does not achieve maximum value.

Undivided Interest Gives each co-owner the right to possession of the whole property, not just a fraction of it. Fractional portion of the ownership, not the physical property.

Uniform Appraisal Dataset (UAD) Defines all fields required for an appraisal submission for specific appraisal forms and standardizes definitions and responses for a key subset of fields to enhance data quality and promote consistency.

Uniform Collateral Data Portal (UCDP) A single portal for the electronic submission of appraisal data files to Freddie Mac and Fannie Mae and facilitates the electronic collection of appraisal report data.

Uniform Residential Appraisal Report (URAR) A standard appraisal report form used by lenders and appraisers because it has been developed and approved by secondary mortgage market participants Fannie Mae and Freddie Mac.

Uniform Standards of Professional Appraisal Practice (USPAP) Professional appraisal standards promulgated by The Appraisal Foundation, and widely recognized throughout the United States as accepted standards of appraisal practice.

Uniqueness A physical characteristic of real property that says that each piece of land, each building, and each house is a different piece of real estate. Also called **Non-homogeneity**.

Unique Property A property that is specialized, over-improved, architecturally different, one of a kind, etc.

Unit-In-Place Method A method for determining the cost of a building that estimates the cost of reproducing it, by determining the unit cost of each of the component parts of the structure and adding them together based on actual need and usage.

Unit of Comparison A component with which a property can be divided for the purpose of comparison such as square foot, living unit, etc.

Unity of Interest When each co-owner has an equal interest (share of ownership) in a property.

Unity of Possession When each co-owner is equally entitled to possession of the entire property, because the ownership interests are undivided.

Unity of Time When each co-owner acquired title at the same time.

Unity of Title When each co-owner acquired title through the same instrument (e.g., deed, will, or court order).

Upgrades Changes to a builder's "standard" product, which are of a higher quality.

Urban Refers to a city.

Urea-Formaldehyde Foam Insulation A type of insulation popular at one point because it could be blown into an existing structure. It is now banned for home use by the EPA due to potential health risks from its toxic fumes.

Useful Life The period of time a structure or a component of the structure can be expected to function for the purpose it was designed for and relates only to physical deterioration.

USPAP Standards Rule 1-2 States that an appraiser is not required to value the whole when the subject of the appraisal is, among other things, a physical segment.

Utilities Essential utility services such as water, sewer, gas, electric, and telephone.

Utility The ability of a good or service to satisfy human wants, needs, or desires.

V

Vacancy A unit or area of a building that is not rented.

Vacancy and Collection Losses Estimate of how much future income may be lost when a building is not full or tenants fail to pay the rent.

Vacancy Rate A percentage rate for all units comprised of the total number of unrented days divided by the total number of rentable days in a year.

Valuation Services Services pertaining to aspects of property value. (corresponding comment is not presented) (USPAP 2014-2015 Edition, p. U-4)

Value The monetary relationship between properties and those who buy, sell, or use those properties. (corresponding comment is not presented) (USPAP 2014-2015 Edition, p. U-4)

Value (Real Estate) A dollar equivalent of real estate under specific conditions. There may be many types of value, such as:

1. Market
2. Investment
3. Book
4. Insurance
5. Liquidation
6. Salvage
7. Value-in-use
8. Assessed
9. Mortgage
10. Going Concern

Value, Assessed The value placed on property by a taxing authority for the purposes of taxation. With real estate, this value is usually a fraction of true value.

Value, Asset The value of property based on specific investment criteria.

Value, Book The value of property as capital, based on accounting methods.

Value in Use The value of property to the owner, or other specified party, as it is presently being utilized, or for a specific use, without necessarily considering highest and best use or present market value.

Value, Insurance The amount that property can be insured for, usually only representing the replacement costs of the structure and disregarding any value for the land.

Value, Investment The value of a property to a particular investor based on that investor's specific investment expectation and criteria.

Value, Liquidation The value a property could get if sold under duress or in a must-sell situation with less than typical market exposure.

Value, Loan The amount of money a lender is willing to loan to someone to finance a particular piece of property.

Value, Market Generally, the most probable price that a property should bring in a competitive and open market. There could be many definitions. The appraiser must always identify the definition of market value and cite its source in the report

Value, Salvage Value of a property's useful components that can be removed before demolition.

Value in Use The value of property to the owner as it is presently being utilized, without considering highest and best use or present market value (e.g., the value that property actually contributes to the owner's business).

Variable Expenses Operating expenses necessary to the property, but dependent on the property's occupancy level.

Variable Interest Rate A rate of interest that changes with economic conditions or other indicators.

Variance A permit obtained from the local zoning authority allowing the holder to use property or build a structure in a way that violates the zoning ordinance.

Variance, Area A variance that permits a property owner to bend the rules regarding building size, height limits, setbacks, side yards, parking, etc.

Variance, Use A variance that permits a property owner to use land in a way that's not allowed in that zone—such as commercial use in a residential zone.

Vaulted Ceiling A type of ceiling that rises as it follows the roof line, extending to the roof peak. Also called a **Cathedral Ceiling**.

Veteran's Administration (VA) The government agency that guarantees mortgage loans for eligible veterans.

Victorian Architecture Refers to numerous architectural styles during, for the most part, the Victorian era.

VIM A formula used to derive the appropriate multiplier from the transaction data: V (sale price) / I (gross monthly rent) = M (multiplier).

VOC materials – which are *Volatile Organic Compounds*

W

Waste Destruction, damage, or material alteration of property by someone in possession who holds less than a fee estate, such as a life tenant or lessee.

Water Rights The right to use water in or from a river, stream, or lake.

Weighted Average A statistical method that gives more importance to certain results.

Weighted Mean Datum points assigned a percentage of the total to compensate for data that may not be truly representative of the sample or population.

Wraparound Mortgage An existing loan on a property is retained while the lender gives the buyer another, larger loan.

Workfile Documentation necessary to support the appraiser's analyses, opinions, and conclusions. (USPAP 2014-2015 Edition, p. U-4)

Y

Yield The total amount of money that can be made from an investment.

Yield Capitalization An income approach to appraisal, with the overall rate of return, including discounted cash flow, considered.

Z

Zoning Government regulation of the uses of property within specified areas.

Zoning, Down When tighter restrictions are placed on land usage in a given area. The primary way this is done is by changing zoning laws with regard to building density or setback requirement to allow fewer buildings.

Zoning, Exclusionary A zoning law that effectively prevents certain groups (e.g., minorities, people with lower income) from living in a community.

Zoning, Pass-Through When zoning laws are set up in a hierarchical fashion, such that all uses above the current zoning are permitted.

Zoning, Spot An illegal rezone that favors (or restricts) a particular property owner (or a small group of owners) without justification.

Zoning Laws Local ordinances dividing a city, county, etc., into zones, specifying different types of land use in different areas. This is a type of government restriction via police power.

Zero Net Energy A building which uses zero energy from outside sources, and in many cases, emits zero net carbons.

Index